Break-even Analyses

Break-even Analyses

Basic Model, Variants, Extensions

Marcell Schweitzer
Eberhard-Karls-University of Tübingen

Ernst Trossmann
University of Hohenheim, Stuttgart

Gerald H. Lawson
Southern Methodist University, Dallas

JOHN WILEY & SONS

Chichester · New York · Brisbane · Toronto · Singapore

BREAK-EVEN ANALYSES Basic Model, Variants, Extensions
English Language edition copyright ©1992 by John Wiley & Sons Ltd
Original German edition published under the title of BREAK-EVEN-ANALYSEN
Grundmodell, Varianten, Erweiterungen.
Copyright ©1986 by C. E. Poeschel Verlag, Stuttgart

Library of Congress Cataloging-in-Publication Data:

Schweitzer, Marcell.
   [Break-even analyses.   English]
   Break-even analyses : basic model, variants, extensions / Marcell
Schweitzer, Ernst Trossmann, Gerald H. Lawson.
      p.   cm.
   Translation of : Break-even-Analysen : Grundmodell, Varianten,
Erweiterungen.
   Includes bibliographical references and indexes.
   ISBN 0-471-93065-2
   1. Break-even analyses. I. Trossmann, Ernst. II. Lawson, G. H.
(Gerald Hartley) III. Title.
HD47.25.S3913   1992
658.15'54—dc20   91–609
                                                          CIP

British Library Cataloguing in Publication Data:

A catalogue record for this book is
available from the British Library.

   ISBN 0-471-93065-2

Typeset in 10/12 pt Times by
Dobbie Typesetting Limited, Tavistock, Devon
Printed and bound in Great Britain by
Courier International Ltd, East Kilbride

Contents

Preface

The rapid political changes and consequential economic developments in eastern Europe, which were symbolised by the fall of the Berlin Wall in November, 1989, have caused a renaissance of interest in German business administration (*Betriebswirtschaftslehre*) in many European countries. It can now reasonably be speculated that German managerial methods and managerial style will strongly influence the new generations of managers, and therefore the organisation of economic activity, in the former European communist regimes following, and indeed during, their transition to market economies. There are thus important tactical reasons for greater Anglo-American interest in German perspectives on specific areas of analysis for business decision-making and control.

The origins of German business administration can be traced back to the end of the nineteenth century and, in many respects, it has evolved quite independently of Anglo-American developments in that subject. This is especially true of such areas of cost and managerial accounting as cost management, standard costing and cost and production theory. The German dimension of these subject-areas and its influences on break-even analysis in a German context are an important feature of this book.

In the German-speaking world the basic idea of break-even analysis as an instrument of business planning is anything but new. Nevertheless, compared with other planning techniques, and in stark contrast to its popularity in the USA, it has, until comparatively recently, for many years been conspicuous by its virtual absence from the German scene. Whereas, reflecting longstanding tradition, the omission of a comprehensive treatment of break-even analysis from American textbooks and lecture courses on management accounting would be almost unthinkable, renewed interest in the technique in the German-language countries is, as just implied, a fairly recent event. It is therefore not surprising that most of the post-war literature on break-even analysis has its origins on the North American continent. Whilst notable individual German language contributions have regularly appeared hitherto, the significant increase in their frequency is also a recent phenomenon.

Starting with the original basic model, this book comprehensively, and synoptically, examines the familiar individual variants of break-even analysis, including a cash flow specification, as well as a number of the authors' own extensions of the break-even technique. The authors' own developments reinforce a comprehensive evaluation of the widely dispersed literature on break-even analysis, mainly of US origin, which is intended to avail the reader of approaches that are either little known or relatively inaccessible.

The conditions governing the application of the authors' extensions are tailored to those which obtain in practice whilst the extensions themselves relate to particular production functions. Thus, single and multi-dimensional break-even approaches to single-stage multiproduct manufacture are analysed at different levels of complexity. They are also extended to a multi-stage production function. On the one hand, these approaches are intended as a total analysis embodying an (adequate) specification of its intermediate constituent stages and, on the other, as the computation of product stage-related break-even information. One particular extension demonstrates how specific influences on production inputs and production costs can be taken into account in break-even analyses founded on production-theoretic principles. Further focal points are different forms of dynamic, non-linear and stochastic break-even analysis together with the formulation of a multi-goal concept of break-even analysis.

A paramount aim of this book is to demonstrate practical applications of the approaches which are examined in detail in its individual chapters. To this end, actual examples of the application of the break-even technique are included in the text. In some cases this involves slight modifications, or simplifications, of the managerial problems for which background information and the necessary quantitative data were made available by the firms in question. These cases are concerned with the production of: glass components for television sets, limestone, polyurethane foam material, pig-meat products, Christmas trees, textile products from towelling material and spun glass products, etc. A number of firms have been very supportive in the construction of these examples in not only helping us to obtain sector, firm or production-specific information but, above all, in making data available. Our debt to all participating firms is gratefully acknowledged.

The intensely practical orientation of this book makes it a suitable reference manual for business planners and decision-makers for the analysis and resolution of a range of break-even ("threshold") problems. As a comprehensive integrated overview of break-even analysis, it can also be recommended to final year undergraduate and graduate students of accounting, finance, operational research and business administration.

In producing this book we encountered numerous tasks for which we required considerable support. We sincerely thank all of those who have contributed to its completion with their ready help, endurance and conscientiousness. We also gratefully acknowledge generous financial support from the Esmée Fairbairn Charitable Trust, without which the publication of this text in the English language would not have been possible.

This book has also been translated into Japanese, by Professor Miyoshi Morimoto and into Chinese, by Mr Fajie Wei, for which we are very grateful. These translations show, also, how important break-even analyses are for industrial management.

Marcell Schweitzer
Ernst Trossmann
Gerald H. Lawson

May, 1991

Symbols and Abbreviations

a, a_0, a_1, a_2	regression parameters
a_i, a_{ij}	production coefficient
$A(x, t)$	(in 4.V) payments as a function of sales volume x and time t
b	capacity limit of a factor input
b_j	capacity limit of a factor input j
B	(in 3.II) contribution block
c	constant
c_i	additional unit costs incurred at the production centre for good i
C_j	(in 4.IX) sales receipts (cash collected from customers) in year j
CE_j	(in 4.IX) capital expenditure at end-year j
d	unit contribution
$\hat{d}$	contribution margin ratio, contribution : turnover ratio
d_i	unit contribution of product i
D	total contribution
e	Euler's number, $e = 2.71828 \ldots$
$\tilde{e}$	slope coefficient of sales revenue line
$\exp(x)$	$= e^x$, exponential function at point x
E	total sales revenue
E^f	(in 4.V) fixed sales revenue
$E(\ldots)$	(in 3.VI and 4.VII) expected value
$E(x, t)$	(in 4.V) receipts as a function of sales volume x and time t
$f_{ij}(\ldots)$	general transformation function
$\tilde{f}_{ij}(\ldots)$	input function
$f_{ij}^{(1)}(\ldots)$	components of the general transformation function that are independent of the level of production
$f_{ij}^{(2)}(\ldots)$	components of the general transformation function that are a function of the level of production
F	probability of an erroneous decision
$g(\xi)$	(in 4.IV.2) break-even point function
g_{ij}	total requirements of good i for the production of good j
g_j	(in 4.IX) inflation in year j
g_j'	(in 4.IX) rate of change in unit capital expenditure in nominal terms in year j
g_j''	(in 4.IX) rate of change in total capital expenditure in nominal terms in year j
G	profit
$h(\ldots), H(\ldots)$	cost function

H_j	(in 4.IX) liquidity change in year j
i, j	indices for goods 1, 2, . . ., n
I_j	(in 4.IX) book value of inventory at end-year j
IV_j	(in 4.IX) inventory volume at end-year j
J_j	(in 4.IX) replacement investment in year j
k	unit cost
k	as index: product group
k^f	average fixed costs per unit
$k^{v, a}$	(in 4.V) variable payments per unit
k_i^v	variable costs for product i
K	total costs
K'	marginal costs
K^a	costs which result in cash payments
K^f	fixed costs
K^v	total variable costs
$K^{f, a}$	fixed costs which give rise to payments
	(in 4.V) fixed production payments made once a year
$K^{v, a}$	constituent part of total variable cost which gives rise to payments
$K_0^{f, a}$	(in 4.V) initial expenditure on a long-term production project
K_i^f	fixed cost of product i
l_j	(in 4.IX) dividends paid to shareholders in year j
$\ln x$	natural logarithm of x
m_j	(in 4.IX) equity capital raised (or repaid) in year j
M	(in 4.VIII) set of break-even points
n	number of types of good
N_j	(in 4.IX) medium/long term debt raised (or repaid) in year j
p	(in 4.V) interest rate, cost of capital
p{. . .}	probability density for unit sales revenue, selling price
p_j	(in 4.IX) selling price in year j
p_j^f	(in 4.IX) rate of change in fixed costs in year j
p_j^v	(in 4.IX) rate of change in unit variable cost in year j
q	unit sales revenue, selling price
q_i	price of good i (in 4.III also: transfer price)
Q_j	(in 4.IX) growth investment in year j
r	profitability
r_i	production quantity (total requirements, total inputs) of product i
r_{ij}	total input of good i in the production of good j
$r_i^{(1)}$	requirements of good i that are independent of the level of output
$r_i^{(2)}$	output-related requirements of good i
R	solution region
$\tilde{R}$	risk-chance relation at a break-even point
$\hat{R}$	risk level at a break-even point
$R(x, s)$	(in 4.V) cumulative net cash flows to point in time s for a sales volume of x per unit of time
s_j	(in 4.IX) interest paid in year j
sp_j	(in 4.IX) rate of change in selling prices in year j
S	margin of safety

S_T	cumulative compounded net cash flows at a terminal date
t	time-index or time-parameter
t	(in 4.IV.2) temperature in °C
t	(in 4.VII) deviation level
t_k, t_s	random variable denoting the quality of input k or s
T_j	(in 4.IX) corporation tax paid in year j
TCF_j	(in 4.IX) target cash flow in year j
TRC_j	(in 4.IX) trade creditors (payables) at end-year j
TRD_j	(in 4.IX) trade debtors (receivables) at end-year j
U	uncertainty costs at a break-even point
U_j	(in 4.IX) real rate of increase in capital expenditure in year j
UC_j	(in 4.IX) unit inventory book value at end-year j
v_j	(in 4.IX) rate of change in sales volume in year j
V	loss
w_j	(in 4.IX) short term debt raised (or repaid) in year j
W_j	(in 4.IX) historic cost depreciation charged to year j
x	level of production or output
x	(in the case of regression analysis in 4.IV.2) independent variable, regressor
$\bar{x}$	critical output, cross-over point
x_0	break-even point
$x^{\exp}$	expected sales volume
$x^{\max}$	production capacity limit
x_i	output of product i that is sold in the market
$\bar{x}_i$	break-even point for product i
$\tilde{x}_i$	(in the case of regression calculations in 4.IV.2) ith observed value of variable x
x_{it}	(in 4.V) output of product i in period t
x_j	(in 4.IX) sales volume
$\hat{x}_1, \hat{x}_2$	coordinates of the corner points of a break-even hyperplane
X	(in 4.V) total volume of production over a particular number of periods
X_j	(in 4.IX) written down book values of assets displaced in year j
y	(in the case of regression calculations in 4.IV.2) dependent variable
$\bar{y}_i$	(in the case of regression calculations in 4.IV.2) ith observed value of variable y
Y_j	(in 4.IX) proceeds in year j of assets displaced
z	(in 4.V) compound interest factor
$\hat{z}_i$	(in 4.II) input quantity of restricted capacity at the break-even point of product i
Z_j	(in 4.IX) operating payments in year j
$\mathcal{A}$	direct requirements matrix, matrix of production coefficients
$\hat{e}_j$	vector of input determinants for the production of good j
$\mathcal{E}$	unit matrix
$\mathcal{G}$	total requirements matrix
$\varkappa$	vector of production quantities

x	vector of output volumes
α	regression parameter
$\alpha_{k,i}$	indicator variable for product k and interval i (in 4.V)
β	regression parameter
γ	(in 4.IX) outstanding payables (trade creditors) expressed as a proportion of previous year's accrued revenue expenditure
γ_i	contribution of product i per bottleneck unit
δ_j	intensity of the production of product j
$\zeta(x_0)$	(in 4.VII.3) transformation of the break-even point x_0 into supplementary variable to facilitate the use of an approximation formula for the probability distribution
λ_i	weighting parameters for product i
μ	mean value
μ_d	(in 4.VII) mean value of the random variable d
μ_K	(in 4.VII) mean value of fixed costs K^f
ξ	(in 4.IV.1, generally) example of an additional cost determinant which is not variable with respect to the volume of production (in 4.IV.2) absolute atmospheric humidity in g/m^3
ξ^r	(in 4.IV.2) relative atmospheric humidity
$\xi^{max}(t)$	saturation humidity: maximum absolute atmospheric humidity at temperature t
ξ_i	(in 4.IV.2) ith observed value of absolute atmospheric humidity
ρ	(in 4.V) logarithmic interest rate in continuous compounding
$\hat{\rho}$	(in 4.VII) correlation coefficient
ρ_{ij}	input of good i per work unit in the manufacture of product j
$\bar{\rho}_{ij}$	observed value of actual input per work unit ρ_{ij}
σ	standard deviation
σ^2	variance
σ_x^2	(in 4.VII) variance of a random variable x
σ/μ	coefficient of variation
$\varphi(z)$	density of the standard normal distribution at point z
Φ	(in 4.IX) outstanding receivables (trade debtors) expressed as a proportion of previous year's sales
$\Phi(z)$	integral from φ to point z, value of the distribution function of a standard normally distributed random variable z
$\Phi_j(r_j)$	value of the function for the number of work units required at production centre j for production quantity r_j
$\psi(y)$	density function of a logarithmic normally distributed random variable
$\Psi(x_0)$	(in 4.VII) distribution function of random variable x_0
$\Omega(z)$	function of the values listed in Appendix II, Table A.2 which is derived from the normal distribution as follows:

$$\Omega(z) = \varphi(z) - z(1 - \Phi(z)).$$

Chapter 1

Problem Definition for
Break-even Analysis

Economic transactions, especially decisions concerning the allocation of scarce resources, are usually perceived to have both positive and negative effects. Individuals who think in economic terms are primarily interested in transactions in which the positive and negative consequences can in some way be influenced. In some cases the outcome may be fully determined by the decision-maker whereas in others it may only be partially or indirectly controllable if at all. Frequently situations arise in which negative consequences are present on a constant, relatively large scale whilst the positive consequences consist of many small individual contributions or vice versa. The question then of interest is: how many small positive individual contributions are needed to equalise the large negative effect; or, how many small negative individual portions can be accepted before the bonus of a positive basic contribution is consumed?

Numerous examples of the situations contemplated here are to be found in daily life. For example, in buying pretzels a private individual may have the choice between two bakers: one in close proximity who offers pretzels of average quality; and, another who is further afield but who has particularly tasty pretzels. If it is a question of buying only a few pretzels (positive consequences on a small scale) the longer journey to the more distant baker (fixed negative consequence on a comparatively larger scale) would not be worth the trouble. However, in the case of a larger purchase quantity, because the respective small positive individual contributions are additive, the negative consequence of the journey to the superior baker is matched with an adequate positive equivalent.

A similar consideration confronts a motorist who, with an eye on his fuel-gauge, checks whether the detour to a filling station which sells cheap gasoline is justified by a sufficiently large tank capacity. Similarly, a professional football club weighs up whether the transfer fee for a player who is for sale will be equalised by a corresponding increase in goal-scoring opportunities and more chances of victory.

The foregoing questions also arise within a firm in comparisons of a product's equipment and other fixed costs with its sales revenue. Thus, in the simplest case, it is necessary to determine the production level, or sales volume, at which particular cost components are covered and beyond which profit will be earned. This latter example illustrates the conventional conception of the problem described in this book. The other examples indicate that methods for treating this problem are in no way restricted to applications of cost, sales revenue and output analysis. On the contrary, in many areas of business management questions arise which can be interpreted as applications of this same basic problem.

By way of illustration, two further examples are mentioned which, in contrast to the previously mentioned cases, are characterised by a juxtaposition of relatively large positive consequences with a multiplicity of small additive negative effects. The first example relates to the purchaser of a home, who may have the opportunity to buy a house cheaply in a vicinity that is away from the centre of the locality, places of work and shopping centres. He has to estimate, for example, how many journeys from this potential residential area, causing negative consequences in the form of additional costs in terms of time and money, will countervail the positive effect of the cheaper house. The second example is concerned with a typical case of a long-term financial transaction. An insurer receives a particular sum of money (positive consequence of a fixed magnitude) as consideration for a fixed monthly pension (negative consequences) for life from an agreed date. Here the question is: how many pension payments can the insurer make whilst still earning a surplus, i.e. from what date, allowing for compound interest, will the original sum of money be consumed.

All of the examples given above are concerned with the calculation of profit or utility thresholds, the *break-even points*. The exact ascertainment of such points, the requisite data preparation and further related analysis are the tasks of *break-even analysis*. In that break-even analyses can be employed in many managerial decision-making problems and facilitate adequate decision preparation, such methods can justifiably be regarded as instruments of business management. Nowadays they are frequently included in the methodology of the controlling function.

The following chapters start with a presentation of the traditional basic model of break-even analysis. Following an analysis of the (restrictive) conditions in which the model can be applied, variants and extensions are examined in turn.

Chapter 2

Basic Model of Break-even Analysis

I. CHARACTERISATION OF THE BASIC MODEL OF BREAK-EVEN ANALYSIS

1. The Concept of Break-even Analysis

Break-even analysis is always a question of comparing the positive and negative effects of actions which can be varied in scope. In the traditional basic model of break-even analysis, a firm's sales revenue constitute the positive effects whilst the negative effects are the total costs associated therewith. Both depend, among other things, upon the level of output which, in the basic model, is regarded as the sole determinant of total costs and sales revenue. An essential prerequisite for this particular application of break-even analysis is the division of total costs into two components. The one component comprises costs which are fixed with respect to the level of output, that is, costs which, independent of the level of output and variations therein, remain at the same level. The other component is represented by such costs as vary in direct proportion to the level of output.

At low production levels total costs generally exceed sales revenue because of the fixed cost component. In this event losses are sustained. However, the relationship between sales revenue and total costs improves as the level of output increases. In the absence of countervailing factors, there are therefore output levels at which sales revenue exceeds total costs and at which profits are achieved. Of particular interest in this situation is the knowledge of the output levels at which a loss changes to a profit. Threshold points of this nature, at which no profit is earned and no loss is sustained, are called *profit-thresholds* or *break-even points*. All models and calculations which help determine such break-even points, which investigate the dependence of break-even points upon their determinants and which arithmetically analyse measures for the attainment of the exceeding of break-even points, or for the maintaining of such situations, can be subsumed under the notion of *break-even analysis*.

Numerous designations for characterising the break-even problem are suggested and applied. Instead of the term "break-even point", which has become more naturalised than any other, the following are commonly encountered in the German literature: contribution condition, contribution point, profit threshold, critical point, utility threshold, profitability threshold, dead point, and full cost contribution point.

2. Historical Development of Break-even Analysis

Historically speaking, the category of questions relating to break-even analysis numbers among the oldest topics of managerial thought. In Germany *Johann Friedrich Schär* (1846–1924) and *Karl Bücher* (1847–1930) can be cited as scholars who were preoccupied at a very early stage with this problem-area. About 1910 *Schär* (1911 [Handels-betriebslehre] p. 134 et seq.) developed a formula for calculating the "dead point" and illustrated its use with a numerical example. At about the same time, *Bücher* (1910 [Massenproduktion] p. 429 et seq.) started researches on the profitability of installing different production procedures for the same product by reference to production volume. Using the example of book manufacture, he calculated the "utility thresholds" for the change from manual to mechanical copying and for the change from mechanical copying to book printing (1910 [Massenproduktion] p. 437 et seq.). His deliberations led to his "law of mass production" which, formulated generally under three heads of arrangement using today's terminology, can be summarised as follows (cp. Bücher, 1910 [Massenproduktion] p. 441 et seq.):

(1) From a cost standpoint, a production procedure employing a high level of technology is less advantageous in producing small numbers of units than is a lower level of production technology. Only when the level of output exceeds a particular minimum number of units is a more highly mechanised procedure more cost advantageous. The break-even point of the procedure in question is higher, the greater are fixed costs as a proportion of total costs.

(2) Beyond the break-even point, unit costs are further reduced by an increasing level of output.

(3) The reduction in unit costs caused by further increases in the level of output is degressive and eventually reaches a limit beyond which a further increase in output volume does not offer further appreciable cost advantages. "The utility peak of mass production" with the procedure in question "lies directly below this utility limit." (1910 [Massenproduktion] p. 442).

This synopsis shows that the substance of Bücher's law of mass production simultaneously contemplates, and meshes together, two different break-even effects which are better analysed separately (cp. Kosiol, 1973 [Betriebsgrösse] p. 1088 et seq.):

(a) the break-even analysis for the change from one procedure to another (cp. point (1) in the above synopsis)

(b) the break-even analysis within the same procedure, here conveyed as the calculation of a "utility limit" (cp. points (2) and (3) in the above synopsis)

The (relative) savings which can be attained by changes in procedure are described as *production procedure cost economies* (cp. Lücke, 1962 [Massenproduktion] p. 338); and, because considerations of this nature are pre-eminent when variations in a firm's scale are contemplated, reference is also made to *cost economies of scale* (cp. Kosiol, 1973 [Betriebsgrösse] p. 1081 et seq.).

The unit cost savings that can be realised by an increase in the level of output, using the same facilities, are described as *output-related or activity level-related cost economies* (cp. Kosiol, 1973 [Betriebsgrösse] p. 1089 et seq.).

For some considerable time, the work of Bücher and Schär constituted the sole contributions to break-even analysis in the German-speaking world. A few publications, some of which made original contributions to the subject (e.g. Jenny, 1922 [Charakteristik] and Hildebrandt, 1925 [Rentabilitätsverhältnisse]) first appeared in 1920. However, many of them merely reproduced earlier knowledge (see in this regard Haidacher, 1969 [Break-even-Punkt] p. 207 et seq.). In the following decades, the treatment of break-even analysis in German business administration continued to be of an isolated, somewhat sporadic, character. Only in recent years has break-even analysis received greater attention in textbooks, in journals and in reports on applications.

Compared with this meagre treatment in the German-speaking world, break-even analysis has at all times received much greater attention in the Anglo-American literature. As early as 1904, a detailed arithmetic and graphical treatment of a break-even problem could be found under the catchword "Oncost" in the six-volume reference book Encyclopaedia of Accounting (cp. Mann, 1904 [Oncost] p. 216 et seq.). In the Anglo-American world, *Charles Edward Knoeppel* (1881–1936) and *Walter Rautenstrauch* (1880–1951), who also presented appropriate diagrams, are cited first and foremost as authors of break-even analysis. A very much earlier conceptual approach to the same problem area is, however, exemplified by a publication by *Dionysius Lardner* (1850, [Railway Economy]) (cp. herewith Haidacher, 1969 [Break-even-Punkt] p. 176). Nevertheless, the presentation of the Knoeppel profit-graph (cp. Knoeppel, 1933 [Engineering]) is one of the first comprehensive English-language treatments of the break-even idea. It also covers the calculation of different critical points which he designates as "danger point", "unhealthy point" etc. The word construction "break-even-chart" is ascribed to Rautenstrauch who used it to designate his graphical presentation of profit threshold analyses. The lesser-known author Williams (1922 [Technique] p. 50 et seq.) first used the descriptions *"break-even"* and *"break-point"* in 1922 for the critical points which were previously unknown, or circumscribed, in the English-language literature (cp. Haidacher, 1969 [Break-even Punkt] pp. 182, 185). The first book (1922 [Profits]) which was mainly devoted to break-even considerations stemmed from Rautenstrauch. It appeared in 1930, when, evidently stimulated by the world economic crisis, a complete series of English-language publications on the break-even problem area was produced. Alongside *Rautenstrauch, Knoeppel* can be regarded as one of the most important authors on this theme at that time. In the years that followed, interest in the break-even theme subsided. Only since the Second World War, can a persistent stream of English-language publications on break-even analyses be observed.

Like those in the German language, the most recent English-language publications are mainly concerned with break-even analysis under conditions of risk and uncertainty, i.e. with the development of a stochastic version of break-even analysis.

3. The Break-even Chart as a Graphical Presentation of the Break-even Relationship

The determination of the break-even point in the basic model can be lucidly presented in the form of a graph. Among other things, it is described as a *break-even chart, break-even diagram* or *profit graph*.

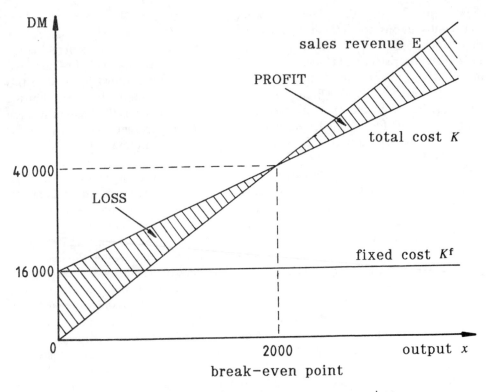

Figure 1 Break-even chart as a cost-revenue comparison

Figure 1 shows a break-even chart of this nature. In the simple case presented it is assumed that the total costs (K) and sales revenue (E) of the product in question depend upon the level of activity (x). Here by activity is meant the number of units produced and sold. In the graph, the activity level is measured on the abscissa whereas units of value are marked on the ordinate. Cost and sales revenue functions are depicted in such a system of coordinates. The following data are used for illustrative purposes:

Costs are split into a fixed component amounting to DM 16 000 which is independent of the level of output and variable costs of DM 12 per unit. This results in the linear cost curve. Unit sales revenue amounts to DM 20 and yields a linear sales revenue curve. The break-even point (the profit threshold) is given by the intersection of the two linear functions. It is reached at a sales revenue of: 2000 · DM 20 = DM 40 000. At this level of output (and sales), costs also amount to DM 40 000, namely [DM 16 000 + 2000 · DM 12]. At all output levels below 2000 units losses are sustained. In the extreme case of business closure ($x=0$), losses sustained are exactly equal to the magnitude of fixed costs. When production is undertaken, losses are continuously reduced as the break-even point is approached. At that stage, losses change into profits and, in the case in question, increase thereafter. If the relationships are linear, profits increase linearly up to the limit of capacity.

In break-even diagrams of the kind illustrated in Fig. 1, total costs are compared with total sales revenue. Such graphs are also called cost-sales revenue diagrams, cost-turnover diagrams or cost-volume-(analysis) charts or cost-volume-profit-(analysis) charts.

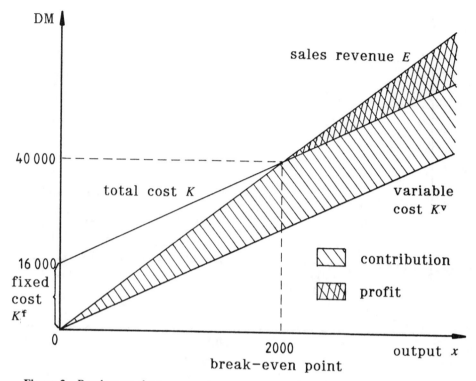

Figure 2 Break-even chart as a cost-revenue comparison showing total contribution

If, additionally, the curve of variable costs K^v is plotted on this chart, the increase in total contribution can be illustrated as the difference between sales revenue and variable costs. In the example, the variable costs are a linear function of output and amount to DM 12 per unit. The equation for the variable cost curve is therefore: $K^v(x) = 12x$ (cp. Fig. 2).

The Fig. 3 presentation relates only to total contribution D. Here total sales revenue and total costs are not depicted explicitly; on the contrary, the basic idea of comparing the constant amount of fixed costs as a contribution block with the continuously changing total contribution becomes particularly clear. Unit contribution is given by unit sales revenue minus unit variable cost. In the present example, there is a (constant) unit contribution of (DM 20 – DM 12) = DM 8. The total contribution is calculated by multiplying the latter by the level of output: $D(x) = 8x$. If the total contribution curve is plotted on the break-even diagram, the break-even point is given by the intersection of this curve with the fixed cost line K^f (cp. Fig. 3).

The representations so far presented are concerned with total cost, total sales revenue, total contribution and their related level of output. A second possible form of graphical break-even analysis is a presentation based on unit values. However, this presentational variant is less commonly used. Figure 4 is the unit form equivalent of Figs 1 and 2.

In Fig. 4 unit sales revenue q is compared with unit cost k. The break-even point lies at the intersection of the curves of these two magnitudes. In the example, unit sales revenue is a constant DM 20 and the unit sales revenue curve is therefore parallel to the output axis. The same applies to unit variable costs which are plotted as a straight

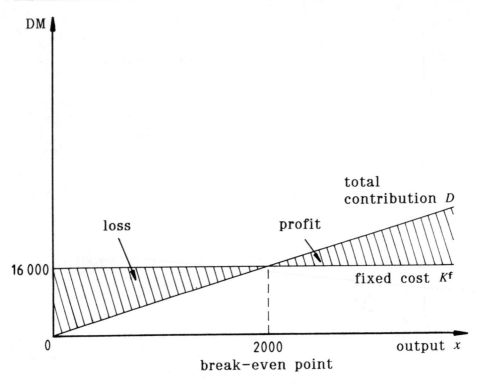

Figure 3 Break-even chart as a comparison of fixed cost and total contribution

line $k^v(x) = 12$. When depicted graphically fixed cost per unit always takes the form of a rectangular hyperbola. At an output level x, the amount of fixed costs, K^f, attributed to a unit of output averages $k^f = K^f/x$. As fixed costs amount to DM 16 000 in the present example, the unit fixed cost function is:

$$k^f(x) = \frac{16\,000}{x}.$$

To ascertain the full cost per unit, k, unit variable cost must be added to the latter:

$$k(x) = \frac{16\,000}{x} + 12.$$

In the graphical representation this involves an upward parallel shift in the unit fixed cost curve by 12 units. At the break-even point $x = 2000$, unit sales revenue, q, is equal to unit full cost k:

$$k = \frac{16\,000}{2000} + 12 = 20.$$

In Fig. 4, the unit contribution d can be read off as the vertical distance between the (horizontal) unit sales revenue and unit·variable cost functions. The rectangle demarcated

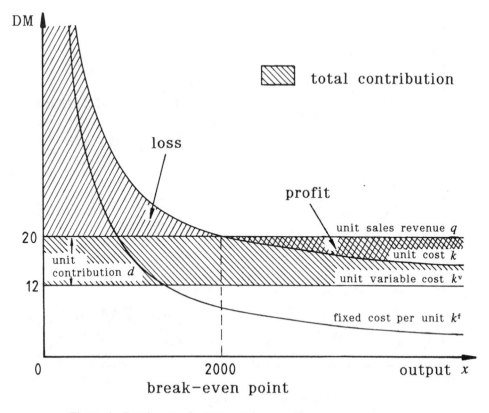

Figure 4 Break-even chart as a unit cost-unit revenue comparison

by these two horizontals, the ordinate and the vertical for any output x specifies the total contribution at that output level. Beyond the break-even point, the magnitude of the profits which arise can also be depicted by a surface (cp. the hatched area in Fig. 4).

Finally, Fig. 5 shows the analogue of Fig. 3. In this case, unit contribution and unit fixed costs are represented by the horizontal $d = 8$ and the hyperbola $k^f = 16\,000/x$ respectively. Total contribution margin and profit are, as in Fig. 4, represented as surfaces.

Of the individual versions of the break-even chart, the Figs 1 and 3 representations, which show total magnitudes, are of particular importance. To be sure the unit cost and revenue versions elucidate the relationships in the same way but the computation of fixed costs per unit can easily give the impression that cost allocation is intended. However, this is definitely not the purpose of break-even analysis which is always contribution margin-oriented.

4. Break-even Computational Technique

(a) Cost Analysis for Break-even Computations

A precondition for the implementation of break-even calculations, of the basic form so far characterised, is a division of total costs into fixed and variable components.

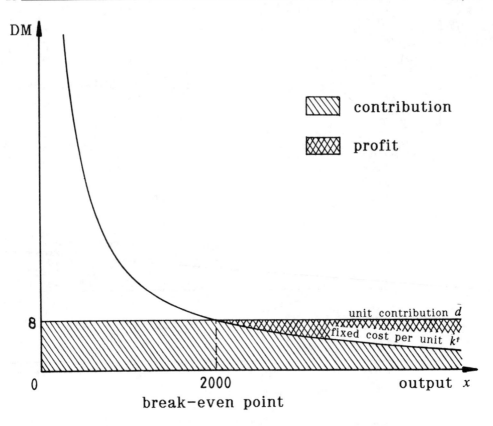

Figure 5 Break-even chart as a comparison of unit contribution and fixed costs per unit

In the simplest case which is considered next, this means that the variable costs vary in some way with activity, i.e. with the level of output x in the present context, whilst fixed costs, which are independent of the level of output, always take on the same constant magnitude. In the basic break-even analysis model, it is assumed that variable costs are a linear function of output. Non-linear cost functions can, as a rule, only be gained from special empirical observations. Moreover, as yet, there are scarcely any cost decomposition procedures for dealing with them. Frequently a division of total costs into fixed and linear-variable components is regarded as adequate. Decreasing or increasing or semi-variable costs must, using an approximation, be divided into fixed and proportional variable components.

A number of available methods facilitates cost decomposition of this nature, which is not only of fundamental importance to break-even analyses but also to all systems of direct costing. They can be characterised with three attributes:

(1) Differentiation of cost decomposition.
(2) Time reference of cost decomposition.
(3) Method of substantiating cost decomposition.

The attribute *differentiation* is concerned with the question of the extent to which, in decomposing costs, types of cost should be distinguished. If the cost analysis is not differentiated, a firm's total costs (or those of a business segment or cost centre for which costs are to be analysed) are regarded as a single magnitude and are divided into fixed and proportional variable components without distinguishing between individual cost types. If applied individually to each type of cost, or to different groupings of cost types, this division into fixed and variable costs is described as analytical cost decomposition (cp. Kilger, 1981 [Plankostenrechnung] p. 358). As a rule it can be assumed that cost decomposition will be the more reliable, accurate and useful, the greater its degree of differentiation. If a production process is stringently subdivided down to the smallest constituent process, the origin of costs can frequently be based upon production-theoretic findings. The constituent cost functions that are to be specified can thus be based on production-theoretic transformation functions which frequently can also be validated by reference to technical-physical relationships (cp. herewith Schweitzer and Küpper, 1974 [Produktionstheorie] p. 165 et seq.).

Time reference refers to the basis of the data for cost decomposition. This may be a question of actual cost data or of costs used for planning purposes. Actual costs are historic values. A cost decomposition based on the latter data may, as an ex-post computation, therefore be intended as a means of determining the fixed and variable components of the total costs which were incurred. As an historically-oriented basis, actual costs are frequently drawn on in the budgeting of future costs and the fixed/variable dichotomy can facilitate a more accurate ex-ante computation. To project the past on to future relationships is, however, only justified if, because of the presence of satisfactorily-validated regularities, it can be ensured that the structure of these relationships does not change over time. In many cases it may therefore be sensible to project costs solely on the basis of historic data that have been adjusted for exceptional influences, or using data which have been forecast by reference to particular projected cost functions.

The nature and magnitude of the projected numbers which are used as the basis of a cost analysis depend upon the purpose of the budget. On the one hand the aim may be a pure forecast of expected costs whilst, on the other, the pre-eminent intention may be to prescribe cost targets in a narrow sense. In the case of a pure cost forecast, costs should be forecast in their expected form and composition using the best validated cost hypothesis. However, cost targets should be based upon attainable, desired cost levels. This form of cost planning is also called standard costing, budgetary costing or norm costing (cp. Schweitzer and Küpper, 1991 [Systeme] p. 238). Cost numbers in cost statements of this type can be used for managerial control purposes. They are the result of particular computations, which facilitate the choice of one of several alternatives by reference to implicitly or explicitly formulated objectives. They therefore embody evaluations and depict the state of affairs a firm is endeavouring to attain, the current situation or that which is expected in the future. Standard costs usually serve as allowed, or target, costs for individual cost centres. They are intended to promote efficient cost behaviour in general or the realisation of particular partial measures, that are expressed in cost terms, and which are embodied in an optimal plan. Cost decompositions that are based on standard costs, therefore, also do not reveal the present cost structure, or that which is expected in the future, but reflect an aspired, frequently optimal, level and composition of cost. Cost decompositions based on such data are of particular importance to break-even analyses. If a particular alternative plan is to be evaluated with break-even analyses, cost decompositions based on budgetary-standard costing data constitute an appropriate first analytical step.

The third feature of the cost decomposition procedure is the *method with which that analysis is substantiated*. Here a distinction can be made between two fundamental approaches: either the proportions of fixed and variable costs are directly determined without recourse to various cost numbers; or, they are derived from an analysis of many cost numbers. The former approach is adopted when fixed and variable cost components (undifferentiated or differentiated according to cost type) are estimated analytically by experts. The promulgation of an aspired cost composition is a further example of this approach. It is characterised by a clear-cut division of costs and requires no special computational technique. If, by contrast, cost decomposition is based upon a multiplicity of cost numbers, from which the required division is to be ascertained, special computational procedures are needed. Various cost numbers and the related levels of activity constitute the starting point. In order to determine the levels of fixed and proportional variable costs therefrom, a simple manual scatter diagram procedure, a regression analysis procedure, or the "mathematical procedure" of cost decomposition can be used (cp. Schweitzer and Küpper, 1991 [Systeme] p. 319 et seq.; Horngren, 1982 [Cost Accounting] p. 290 et seq.).

Using the simple *scatter diagram* procedure, the available total cost values and their related activity levels are plotted in two-dimensional space measuring the latter on the abscissa and the former on the ordinate. The scatter diagram which thus emerges gives a first insight into the form of the dependence of costs upon the chosen determinant (in this case upon the level of output as a measure of activity level). A decomposition of total costs solely into the two basic categories of fixed and proportional variable costs is only justified if the points plotted in the scatter diagram are approximately distributed about a fictitious line. If not, a check should be made to determine whether non-linear cost dependences are present or whether, using other cost determinants, which can be introduced instead of, or in addition to, the independent variables previously used, a more precise representation of cost dependences is possible.

If the scatter points can be approximated with a straight line, such a line can, in the simplest case, be fitted by eye and drawn in by hand (cp. Mellerowicz, 1970 [Kalkulationsverfahren] p. 60; Horngren, 1982 [Cost Accounting] p. 290) as in Fig. 6. The straight line fitted in the scatter diagram results in the desired division into fixed and variable costs: the intercept to the ordinate gives the level of fixed costs whilst unit variable cost is derived from the slope of the line. The manual scatter diagram procedure is simple but very inaccurate. Because the results so derived are in many cases only of limited use, it is frequently advisable to cross-check optical estimates with supplementary calculations. One recommendation, for example, is that the arithmetic means of the abscissa and ordinate values should be fitted to the point which has these two coordinates. The straight line should then be turned on this point until it constitutes the best optical approximation of the scatter points (cp. Nebelung, 1950 [Ermittlung] p. 419; Kilger, 1981 [Plankostenrechnung] p. 353).

Regression analysis procedures are always much *more accurate* than methods based on optical estimates. Regression procedures involve the use of equations in locating the desired cost line by resorting to mathematics. However, it must first be resolved what should count as the "best" straight line approximation of a scatter of points. As the best approximation is regarded as that which is closest to the scatter points, the fixing of the regression line depends upon how the distance of the straight line from the individual points is measured. Among others, the following measures suggest themselves:

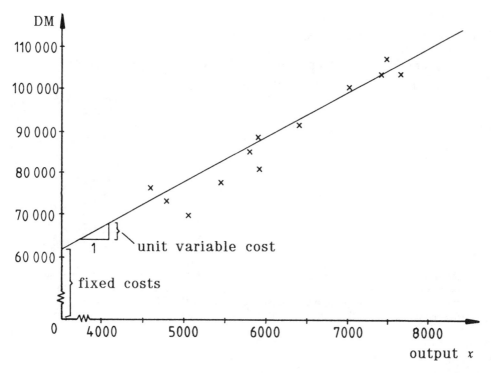

Figure 6 Scatter diagram showing a straight line fitted by eye to costs and their related output levels

—the sum of the absolute horizontal coordinate differences from the individual points to the fitted straight line,
—the sum of the absolute vertical coordinate differences,
—the sum of the absolute horizontal and vertical coordinate differences,
—the square root of the sum of the squared horizontal coordinate differences,
—the square root of the sum of the squared vertical coordinate differences.

Point distances from a regression line measured as vertical coordinate distances can be rationally interpreted in probabilistic-theoretic terms in that a deviation from the line (at the same abscissa value) can be regarded as random value, namely, residual error. For this reason the latter measurement is the most frequently used. The regression line is determined in a manner such that the previously-mentioned square root is minimised. This computational method of determining the regression line is called the "ordinary least squares method". It facilitates the computation of unique regression line parameter values which give the division of costs into fixed and proportional components that is sought. By way of example, the Fig. 6 scatter diagram coordinates are presented in Fig. 7, and these are used to compute the equation for the ordinary least squares regression line as illustrated. The computational formulae used are derived in basic textbooks on statistical and econometric methods (cp. e.g. Schneeweiss, 1978 [Ökonometrie] p. 41 et seq.).
    The equation for the regression line is:

$$K = 16\,000 + 12x. \qquad (2.1)$$

(1) *Given*: 12 observations $(\bar{x}_i, \tilde{K}_i)$ $(i=1, 2, \ldots, 12)$:

Observation	Output $\bar{x}_i$ in units of volume	Cost $\tilde{K}_i$ in DM
1	4 635	77 574
2	4 812	74 835
3	5 045	71 184
4	5 460	78 403
5	5 788	85 907
6	5 880	89 937
7	5 925	82 291
8	6 395	92 651
9	7 036	101 511
10	7 382	104 735
11	7 451	108 712
12	7 631	105 540

(2) *Required*: a regression function $K(x)=K^f+k^v \cdot x$, for which the sum of the squared deviations $\Sigma_{i=1}^{12} [\tilde{K}_i - K(\bar{x}_i)]^2$ is minimised. The characteristic parameters K^f and k^v of this function are uniquely determined according to the following relation (cp. e.g. Schneeweiß, 1978 [Ökonometrie] 44):

$$k^v = \frac{\sum_{i=1}^{12} (\bar{x}_i - \bar{x})(\tilde{K}_i - \bar{K})}{\sum_{i=1}^{12} (\bar{x}_i - \bar{x})^2}; \qquad K^f = \bar{K} - k^v \cdot \bar{x},$$

where $\bar{x}$ and $\bar{K}$ denote the mean values

$$\bar{x} = \frac{1}{12} \sum_{i=1}^{12} \bar{x}_i = \frac{73\,440}{12} = 6\,120; \qquad \bar{K} = \frac{1}{12} \sum_{i=1}^{12} \tilde{K}_i = \frac{1\,073\,280}{12} = 89\,440$$

(3) *Computation*

Observation	$(\bar{x}_i - \bar{x})$	$(\bar{x}_i - \bar{x})^2$	$(\tilde{K}_i - \bar{K})$	$(\bar{x}_i - \bar{x}) \cdot (\tilde{K}_i - \bar{K})$
Column	1	2	3	4
1	− 1 485	2 205 225	− 11 866	17 621 010
2	− 1 308	1 710 864	− 14 605	19 103 340
3	− 1 075	1 155 625	− 18 256	19 625 200
4	− 660	435 600	− 11 037	7 284 420
5	− 332	110 224	− 3 533	1 172 956
6	− 240	57 600	497	− 119 280
7	− 195	38 025	− 7 149	1 394 055
8	275	75 625	3 211	883 025
9	916	839 056	12 071	11 057 036
10	1 262	1 592 644	15 295	19 302 290
11	1 331	1 771 561	19 272	25 651 032
12	1 511	2 283 121	16 100	24 327 100
	0	12 275 170	0	147 302 184

continued

continued

(4) Using the computational table, k^v is given by:

$$k^v = \frac{\text{sum of column 4}}{\text{sum of column 2}} = \frac{147\,302\,184}{12\,275\,170} = 12.000011 \simeq 12$$

$$K^f = \overline{K} - k^v \cdot \overline{x} = 89\,440 - 12 \cdot 6120 = 16\,000$$

(5) *Result*: The regression function is: $K = 16\,000 + 12x$.

(6) Coordination of the regression values with the observation points:

i	$\tilde{x}_i$	Regression value $K(\tilde{x}_i)$
1	4 635	71 620
2	4 812	73 744
3	5 045	76 540
4	5 460	81 520
5	5 788	85 456
6	5 880	86 560
7	5 925	87 100
8	6 395	92 740
9	7 036	100 432
10	7 382	104 584
11	7 451	105 412
12	7 631	107 572

(7) *Graphical presentation*:

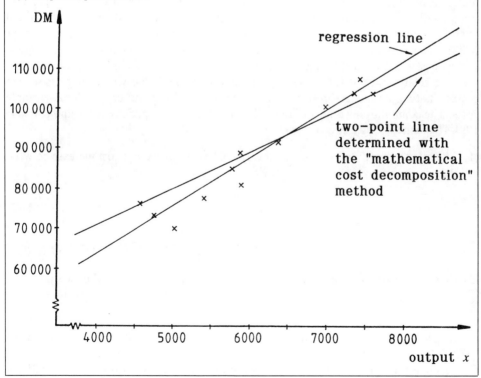

Figure 7 Computation of a cost regression line using the ordinary least squares method

Thus, according to this cost decomposition, fixed costs amount to DM 16 000, whereas unit proportional variable cost is DM 12.

A regression line computation may also be based on other measures of residual error. However, for mathematical reasons it is frequently a more complex calculation. In general the use of different residual errors results in different regression line solutions. Hence, in using such procedures it must be ensured that the chosen residual errors are amenable to a sensible interpretation. If, as in the present example, the ordinary least squares method is applied, this holds true because the minimisation of the sum of the squared vertical distances means that the sum of the deviations of the actual total costs from those given by the regression line (at all output values for which there is an observation) is as low as possible. Squaring deviations has the effect that the smaller deviations are regarded as being relatively insignificant whilst larger deviations have greater weight in the calculation—this can also be regarded as being justified.

The basic idea of regression analysis is always to find an average curve trend which approximates the position of a (greater) number of points without these points themselves having to be on the regression curve. In contrast, the idea of *mathematical cost decomposition* is concerned with finding a curve on which the given points actually lie. The mathematical cost decomposition technique is attributable to Schmalenbach (cp. 1919 [Selbstkostenrechnung] p. 294 et seq.) and is intended for the location of linear functions. A construction of non-linear functions which passes through a number of given points is generally not sensible for managerial purposes because functions of this kind may have a very strongly erratic zigzag trend between those points. On the other hand this method is appropriate for the derivation of linear functions. Thus, depending upon available information, a finitesimal analysis (class analysis) or an infinitesimal analysis (point analysis) can be applied (cp. Schweitzer and Küpper, 1991 [Systeme] p. 321). The class analysis which is normally applied proceeds from two (different) given cost values, K_1, K_2 and the related values of the determinants being investigated (in this case the related output levels) x_1, x_2. If a straight line is drawn through these two points, its two parameters in turn define the levels of fixed and proportional variable costs. The computation comprises the following three steps (cp. Schweitzer and Küpper, 1991 [Systeme] p. 321 et seq.):

(1) The calculation of unit proportional variable cost as an average cost increase between the two points:

$$k^v = \frac{K_2 - K_1}{x_2 - x_1}. \qquad (2.2)$$

If, for example, given the points ($\tilde{x}_1 = 4635$, $\tilde{K}_1 = 77\,574$) and ($\tilde{x}_2 = 7631$, $\tilde{K}_2 = 105\,540$), k^v takes on the value $k^v = 9.334\,4$.

(2) Calculation of the marginal cost K' for total output at one of the two points:

$$K'(x_1) = k^v \cdot x_1. \qquad (2.3)$$

In the example the total marginal cost for the first point amounts to $K'(4635) = 43\,265$.

(3) Calculation of the residual cost R as the difference between total cost K and the computed marginal cost for the total output at the same point:

$$R = K_1 - K'(x_1). \tag{2.4}$$

In the example, residual cost at the first point amounts to: $R = 34\,309$.

In the previously-mentioned finitesimal analysis, the residual cost indicates the level of the intercept of the straight line fitted to the given points and thereby the magnitude of the fixed costs. In the example, the fixed costs and unit proportional variable costs were thus DM 34 309 and DM 9.33 respectively.

An analogous calculation is possible in the case of the *infinitesimal* analysis. It proceeds from a single point, the coordinates and slope of which must be known. The slope coefficient that is given is directly interpreted as the rate of unit variable cost k^v. If the relationships are linear, the level of fixed cost is again given by the residual cost which is computed as above. If, in one infinitesimal analysis, there are several points with the requisite data, a comparison of their slopes and residual costs provides an indication of the extent to which the assumption of a linear cost function is justified. It is only in the case of linear functions that the residual costs are equal at all points of the curve and correspond to the fixed costs. To be sure the same information can usually be obtained more simply and more lucidly by manual computation by drawing a scatter diagram. In the case of non-linear cost behaviour, the residual costs should be regarded solely as formal computational magnitudes.

Frequently the so-called mathematical cost decomposition is also applied if more than two cost values are available. Because, in this situation, preferably two points, a "high" and a "low", which are as far distant as possible, are drawn upon, this method is designated "high-low method" or "high-low points method" in the English-language literature (cp. e.g. Horngren, 1982 [Cost Accounting] p. 292; Matz and Usry, 1980 [Cost Accounting] p. 516 et seq.). It can be assumed that a restriction to two points yields significantly less accurate results than does the use of all available data. In the example computed above, the largest and smallest values in the data set, which was also used in illustrating the ordinary least squares method (cp. Fig. 7) were drawn upon. The resultant linear function

$$K = 34\,309 + 9.33x \tag{2.5}$$

deviates considerably from the ordinary least squares regression line (2.1) (cp. Fig. 7)

$$K = 16\,000 + 12x.$$

Only in exceptional cases does the mathematical cost decomposition method produce a straight line which approximates all available points in a usable manner. Hence, given more than merely two values, it is always advisable to carry out a regression calculation. In a manual calculation, mathematical cost decomposition can, at best, only give a preliminary indication of the orders of magnitude of the fixed and variable cost components which are sought.

If the decomposition is effected with a computational procedure in accordance with the second kind of substantiation, that is, on the basis of an analysis of a multiplicity of cost values, then, notwithstanding the broad data basis, questionable results may still arise. For example, a negative value for fixed costs is computationally possible.

Alternatively, the computation may produce a result whereby, as a function of output, instead of rising proportionality, the regression line actually falls. If, in such cases, the computed result does not conform to reality and, further, if data and computational errors have been eliminated, a scrutiny of the available data is necessary to determine whether they are concentrated in a relatively small observation interval. In the latter event, the points accumulate in a small region of the scatter diagram. Whether, in such a situation, one works by eye, with a regression analysis, or with the mathematical two-point decomposition, the location of the equilibrium line will always be determined by random influences because the available cluster of points can be roughly interpreted as a single point. Even a slight deviation of a point from the centre of a cluster of observations with a small circumference will have a significant effect on the position of regression lines. If it is then not possible to take new cost values as a computational basis, a change to an a priori determination of cost proportions is, in certain circumstances, advantageous because, conceptually, the determinant can also be varied to an extent which would not be appropriate in practice. If this also does not yield usable results, it is advisable to examine whether the cost determinant that has been modelled is suitable. Frequently more precise cost predications can be gained by changing to other, or alternatively-measured, cost determinants which are additionally, or complementarily, introduced.

The individual features of the three cost decomposition characteristics, namely, differentiation, time-reference and nature of substantiation, allow adequate procedures of cost decomposition to be combined for any practical application.

"*Multistage analytical cost forecasting*" (cp. primarily Kilger, 1981 [Plankosten-rechnung] p. 359) which is sometimes categorised under this heading can be characterised as an analytical method of cost decomposition that is based upon a number of cost values. Because this form of cost decomposition requires the calculation of costs for different activity levels, it is also suitable for the treatment of cost functions comprising partially non-linear functions. Whether, in such cases, a separation solely into the two components of fixed and variable is indeed to be recommended, is questionable (cp. Kilger, 1981 [Plankostenrechnung] p. 359). An overview of the classification of cost decomposition procedures is presented in Fig. 8.

(b) Computational Formulae for the Break-even Point

After applying a cost decomposition procedure, total costs K are partitioned into a fixed constituent K^f and a variable constituent K^v. The notions of fixed and variable relate to the behaviour of the corresponding cost constituents with respect to variations in the level of activity x, which is here interpreted as the output volume of the firm's products. Total costs therefore have the following structural form:

$$K(x) = K^f + K^v(x). \tag{2.6}$$

To calculate break-even points, sales revenue E, expressed as a function $E(x)$ of output x is required in addition to costs. The levels of output x_0 at which sales revenue and costs are equal are break-even points. They are given by equating sales revenue and total costs:

$$E(x_0) \overset{!}{=} K(x_0) \quad \text{or} \quad E(x_0) \overset{!}{=} K^f + K^v(x_0). \tag{2.7}$$

Procedures of cost decomposition						
Feature	Type					
(1) Differentiation	Non-differentiated (global, summary)			Analytical		
(2) Time reference	With the use of actual costs	With costs used for planning purposes				
		For forecasting purposes		For decision-making purposes		
(3) Method of substantiating	Deter-mination	Derivation from a multiplicity of cost values				
				Using the mathematical method		
		In a scatter diagram by eye	With regression analysis	By fin-itesimal analysis (=two-point method)	By infin-itesimal analysis	

Figure 8 Classification of the procedures of cost decomposition

If this equation is solved for x_0, the break-even points are obtained in explicit form. The total contribution $D(x)$ is computed as an intermediate step. It can be expressed as the difference between sales revenue and variable costs:

$$D(x) := E(x) - K^v(x). \qquad (2.8)$$

At the break-even point the total contribution is equal to the fixed costs:

$$D(x_0) \overset{!}{=} K^f. \qquad (2.9)$$

If the functions are of the same form as those in the above example, an explicit computation of break-even points is always possible. In this case there is an exact break-even point. The equations for this example are:

$$E(x) = 20x$$
$$K^f = 16\,000$$
$$K^v(x) = 12x$$
$$K(x) = K^f + K^v(x) = 16\,000 + 12x$$
$$D(x) = E(x) - K^v(x) = 20x - 12x = 8x.$$

The break-even point is therefore an output of 2000 units:

$$D(x_0) = K^f$$
$$8x_0 = 16\,000$$
$$x_0 = 2000.$$

In the basic model it is generally assumed that the sales revenue function is linear:

$$E(x) = q \cdot x. \tag{2.10}$$

Thus, total sales revenue is calculated by multiplying unit selling price q by output x. Furthermore, if variable costs are expressed as a linear function

$$K^v(x) = k^v \cdot x \tag{2.11}$$

with k^v as unit variable cost, the contribution can in general be written:

$$D(x) = E(x) - K^v(x) = q \cdot x - k^v \cdot x$$
$$\text{or } D(x) = (q - k^v) \cdot x = d \cdot x \tag{2.12}$$

where d denotes the unit contribution $(q - k^v)$. The condition (2.9) for the contribution now gives:

$$d \cdot x_0 \overset{!}{=} K^f. \tag{2.13}$$

If, in the case of linear cost and sales revenue functions, the unit contribution d is positive, the break-even point can therefore be computed by dividing the fixed cost K^f by the unit contribution d:

$$x_0 = \frac{K^f}{d} \quad \text{or} \quad x_0 = \frac{K^f}{q - k^v}. \tag{2.14}$$

For the example the calculation is:

$$x_0 = \frac{K^f}{d} = \frac{16\,000}{8} = 2000 \text{ units.}$$

II. CONDITIONS FOR APPLYING THE BASIC MODEL OF BREAK-EVEN ANALYSIS

Undertaken in accordance with the basic model, break-even analyses are based upon a series of simplifying assumptions. This is pre-eminently a question of assumptions about the structure of the flow of goods within the firm in question, about cost and output components, about the quantity and quality of information entering the break-even analyses, about relevant feasible objectives and about the time dimension of the model's predictions. These assumptions should be regarded as the conditions under which the basic model of break-even analysis can be applied. A careful examination is necessary to determine whether these conditions, which are frequently taken as given, are actually satisfied. They are characterised individually below.

1. Assumptions about the Structure of the Flow of Goods in the Firm in Question

In the basic model of break-even analysis, only a single independent variable x is employed. As a rule it gives effect to activity, or to the activity level, although these are frequently not unambiguously defined. Being more precise, x is defined as the level of output or, in some circumstances, also as the number of labour hours (of a production centre, of a machine, of a whole department or of the entire business). In all cases it is assumed that all influences which are significant from the standpoint of break-even analysis, above all costs, sales revenue and thus contribution margins, are attributable to one variable alone. Such an assumption can only hold if the firm in question satisfies particular conditions in relation to its production. It is therefore advisable to investigate the types of production to which the basic model of break-even analysis can be applied.

Production types can be depicted by reference to a number of attributes which relate to the features of factor inputs, features of the production process itself and to features of the production programme. In this sense a distinction is made between types of factor input, process types and production programme types (cp. Küpper, 1979 [Produktionstypen] col. 1638). In investigating the production type assumed in the basic model of break-even analysis, the structure of the flow of goods within the firm is of paramount importance. The following attributes define the structure of the flow of goods in detail:

—the number of end-products as an attribute of the programme type,
—the convergence or divergence of goods flow; and,
—the number of work stages as characteristics of the production process.

A *single or multiproduct firm* can be distinguished in accordance with the first-mentioned attribute. Whether a manufacturing process is defined as convergent or divergent, depends upon the numbers of input goods and end-products involved (cp. Kosiol, 1972 [Aktionszentrum] p. 168; Riebel, 1963 [Erzeugungsverfahren] p. 55 et seq.). Four cases can be distinguished accordingly (cp. Fig. 9).

In the case of an *even process*, only one input good and one end-product are involved. Such processes are typically conversion, finishing or similar processes. *Convergent processes* convert several input goods into a single end-product and are therefore also described as synthesising processes. Assembly lines on which indiviudal parts and grouped components are systematically assembled into a single end-product are prime examples of convergent production. The counterpart to convergent processes is represented by *divergent processes*. In this case the goods stream on the output side divides itself into a number of constituents. Thus, divergent processes are also called analytical processes. More precisely, two forms can be distinguished. In the multi(end-)product case, reference is made, to be exact, to *process-determined divergence*. It is the counterpart to *programme-determined divergence* which is present when the same type of end-product

Number of end-products / Number of input goods	One	Two or more
One	Even process	Divergent process
Two or more	Convergent process	Regrouping process

Figure 9   Production processes defined by reference to the number of input and output goods

has several different applications inside the same business (possibly even within the same production process). The goods stream thus divides because the products of the production centre in question are transferred to various recipient centres (cp. Küpper, 1980 [Interdependenzen] p. 109). If, in a production process, convergence and divergence are present simultaneously, reference is made to *regrouping manufacture*. The third mentioned attribute, the number of work stages, finally leads to the distinction between *single-stage* and *multistage production processes.*

Contemplating the attributes of the three previously-discussed types in deciding upon the conditions that need to be satisfied if total production is to be measured with a single variable, it initially appears that, in the absence of significant restrictions, this may only be possible in the case of *single-stage, single-product even production*. In this case the level of output of the (single) end-product can be represented with the variable x. In that the production process is even, usually only a single input good enters production. Given the production volume, the input quantity is uniquely determinable. Furthermore, because of the single-stage character of the manufacturing process, there are no intermediate inventories and the level of output is certain.

The scope for applying break-even analysis would be extremely restrictive were it to be admissible only in the case of single-stage, single-product, even manufacture. However, subject to the satisfaction of particular conditions, the attribution of cost behaviour to a single determinant, as required in the basic model, can also be achieved in the case of a more general production type. Continuing with the case of single-product manufacture; it is generally true of single-stage convergent production that the level of output can, without causing complications, be used as a single variable for the purposes of break-even analyses because output constitutes a usable reference magnitude for the (now different) input goods. To be sure, unambiguous predictions are not possible if the different input goods for the manufacturing process in question are substitutable for each other. In that, in the case of single-stage, single-product manufacture, divergence is by definition absent, it can thus be said that the basic model is validly applicable to *single-stage, single-product manufacture provided the factor inputs are not mutually substitutable*, i.e., are in a fixed ratio.

Turning to *multistage, single-product manufacture*; it may first be noted that, in relation to the convergence or divergence types, there are only small differences compared with the case of single-stage manufacture. In the first manufacturing stage, one or more input goods may be involved which, again, must be in a fixed ratio. In that, in the case of single-product manufacture:

(i) divergence may never be present in the final manufacturing stage; and,
(ii) additional end-products may not emerge in (earlier) manufacturing stages,

a divergent manufacturing process is only possible in an earlier manufacturing stage if, because of convergent processes in later manufacturing stages, intermediate products are again brought together as a single product (cp. Fig. 10). If there are no intermediate inventories at any of the production stages, then, as in single-stage, single-product manufacture, the basic break-even model remains applicable, provided the input goods are in a fixed ratio.

The situation becomes more complicated if inventories are built up and reduced between the individual stages. In such a case the production process can no longer be considered in total but only in terms of its individual manufacturing stages. If, in this situation, the intention is accurate computations, a single determinant of costs, sales revenue and contribution margins is insufficient. Either the inventory changes must be taken explicitly into account; or, a separate break-even analysis must be undertaken for each manufacturing stage. Consequently, an unmodified version of the basic model is inapplicable in both cases. Moreover, if the scope for applying break-even analysis is restricted to an individual production centre, and relates only to the intermediate product manufactured there, the analysis has limited predictive content.

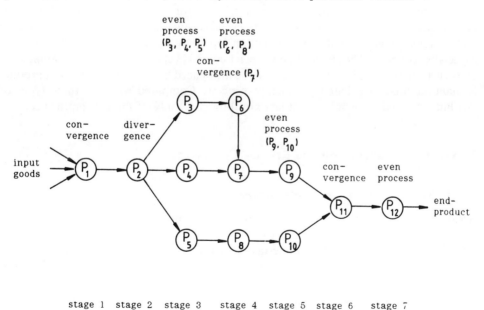

Figure 10 Example of single-product manufacture with convergent and divergent processes in the early manufacturing stages

Finally, in *multiproduct firms*, the basic model of break-even analysis, as a single, comprehensive model, is not applicable. In such situations, costs and sales revenue cannot be sensibly related to a single variable. Nevertheless, in a special case an application is possible, namely, when the different products have independent cost and sales revenue structures so that a separate analysis is possible for each. In this case, several break-even analyses are undertaken in parallel and independently of each other; and the multiproduct firm is treated as a multiplicity of single-product firms. This is only possible under very restrictive conditions. On the one hand, the production processes must be suitably separable. It is not therefore possible to have, for example, production centres in which, in a divergent process, intermediate products are manufactured for use in two or more end-products. On the other hand it must also be possible to attribute the determinants of the break-even analyses adequately to the individual products. In the case of fixed costs at least, the precondition of causal attributability is generally not fulfilled. Also, further determinants of break-even analyses are frequently not adequately imputable to products. As presented in its basic form, the break-even approach can only be applied in these circumstances if each of the different products can be treated like an individual product. This would be conceivable if the output levels of the different products are in a ratio that is held constant. Such a relation approximately obtains in the case of joint production with a fixed ratio of output. Several products can be handled like an individual product if their cost and sales revenue relationships are such that each product has the same unit contribution. These preconditions are, however, only seldom fulfilled. Consequently, in most cases of multiproduct manufacture, the basic model of break-even analysis is not directly applicable. Nevertheless, different extensions of break-even analysis can also be applied in the multiproduct case (cp. on this: Chapter 4).

The number of products, the type of convergence or divergence and the number of work stages are the most important type-attributes for judging the applicability of the basic model or individual variants of break-even investigations. In addition, in individual applications, other attributes of production type play a role (cp. for an enumeration especially Küpper, 1979 [Produktionstypen] col. 1643 et seq.). Thus, for example, the construction of a break-even analysis can be influenced by the fact that a given product is manufactured in a batch production process. Compared with the three types of attributes treated in detail, the others are, however, only of minor significance.

2. Assumptions about Cost and Revenue Components

(a) Activity as a Single Cost Determinant

Break-even analysis should be categorised with systems of direct costing. It requires a decomposition of total costs into their fixed and variable components. This partitioning into fixed and variable costs is undertaken by reference to variations in a single cost determinant. The cost determinant in question is designated *activity* or *activity level*. In concrete terms, activity can, as a rule, be interpreted as the level of output, i.e. as the quantity of manufactured products. In the case of the procedure described, it is assumed that the level of all cost components can be unambiguously ascribed to activity as a sole cost determinant x. Consequently, other cost determinants which could have a complementary effect are thereby neglected.

The conception of a cost function with only a single independent variable, i.e. a single cost determinant is still maintainable if, instead of the level of output, another cost determinant is used. Thus, for example, (manufacturing) labour input hours frequently suggests itself as the choice of independent variable as is perhaps usual in the (American) system of standard costing (cp. e.g. Horngren, 1982 [Cost Accounting] p. 166 et seq.). However, if a switch is made to cost functions with two or more independent variables, the traditional approach to break-even analysis proves to be inadequate. The use of *multidimensional cost functions* thus appears to be very efficient in many cases. Even in the simplest case, in which the output level is regarded as the sole material cost determinant, a switch to a multidimensional cost function is an obvious possibility. It is always a possibility in the case of multiproduct manufacture with end-products in a variable output ratio. The level of output can then be measured for each individual product and can enter the cost function as an individual cost determinant.

In addition to the level of output which, as a rule, is a major determinant of costs, a whole series of further determinants can also play a role and enter the cost function as independent variables (cp. Lassmann, 1981 [Einflussgrössenrechnung] p. 427 et seq.). Proceeding from the individual constituent aspects of cost computation, these determinants can be categorised in three groups. Costs can be defined as an economic assessment of the inputs that are required for production (cp. Schweitzer and Küpper, 1991 [Systeme] p. 28). In the specification (or computation) of costs the following two constituent steps can be distinguished:

(1) the specification or computation of the physical input of goods used for production and
(2) the economic assessment of that input.

In considering cost determinants in a particular context, a distinction can first be made between the determinants of physical consumption and the determinants of the valuation of that consumption. As regards the determinants of the physical consumption, the nature of the good consumed can be used as a further attribute. The consumption of real goods can be contrasted with the consumption of nominal goods. Real goods comprise immovable and movable assets as well as labour input, information and ownership titles. Nominal goods are money and monetary claims.

Information on the *consumption of physical factor inputs* will be available if the production process in question has been the subject of production-theoretic analyses. The most satisfactory situation is one in which production-theoretic analyses of this nature facilitate the formulation of a production function. A production function reproduces general laws or regularities about input–output relationships. For the application which is of interest here, the predictions should be constructed in a manner whereby, for each desired output, the related input is derived from a set of precisely specified determinants. The related level of costs can then be determined from the input which is generally subdivided into a number of different goods. In addition to the output components which are also classified by individual types, the quantitative consumption of production goods specified in the production-theoretic relationships may be a function of, among others, the following determinants:

—the type and quality of input goods,
—the substitution possibilities in the case of some input goods,

—the choice of production procedure,

—process-related sequential decisions such as machine-loading and work allocation,

—intermediate and end-product batch sizes,

—the intensity of activity at individual production centres in the process, i.e. the quantities of the intermediate or end-products per unit of time,

—the state of individual productive units and, consequently, tooling and maintenance expenditure,

—the capacities of individual productive units,

—the requisite product qualities,

—the level of wastage,

—external influences on the production process such as temperature, pressure, humidity, earth tremors, etc.

In the context of production-theoretic analysis it is necessary to ascertain which determinants have an appreciable effect upon the production process in question. The number of determinants, the collective features of which facilitate a satisfactory degree of accuracy in the forecasting of the level of costs, can frequently be kept clearly in view. These determinants almost always comprise the individual types of input good, intermediate good and end-product. There are, in addition, other determinants whose features are specific to the production process in question such as intensity or similar factors. A prerequisite for the recording, formulation and application of the relationship between the consumption of goods and a determinant, that does not represent a quantity of goods, is an operational definition of that determinant and a precise measurement prescription. Precisely the discovery of a suitable means of measuring a determinant, that is initially very difficult to capture, can frequently be regarded as the most important step in the analysis of a production-theoretic relationship.

The *consumption of nominal inputs*, i.e. the financing requirement of the production process, can also be determined by resorting to a special analysis. However, the general state of knowledge that is relevant to a financing requirements analysis of this kind is not as well developed as the physical input–output analysis of real goods. In that a large part of the financing requirement is ascribable to the input of real goods—as, for example, in the case of capital deployed in inventories of input material, semi- and finished products—all production-theoretic determinants are simultaneously determinants of the financial requirement. In addition there is, most importantly, the duration of capital employed as a determinant of the financing requirement. The extent to which the duration of capital employed can be imputed to other determinants requires an analysis in itself. Possible examples of determinants to which the duration of capital employed can be ascribed are: determinants of the production process in general, determinants of the process organisation as well as such determinants of the working capital cycle as the agreed credit periods, the firm's own payments behaviour and the payments behaviour of its customers.

The third aspect of cost concerns *economic assessment*. This is a question of valuing the specified, or forecast, physical consumption of real and nominal goods with suitable (cost) prices thereby making such consumption additive. As indicated below, there are two types of rationale for this kind of valuation (cp. Schweitzer and Küpper, 1974 [Produktionstheorie] p. 160). A distinction is made between the pagatorical cost concept and the individual purpose-related cost concept. In applying the *pagatorical cost concept*, physical consumption is valued with prices relating to either past or future expenditures. This is therefore a question of realised or forecast market prices. Whilst the pagatorical cost concept thus facilitates an objective valuation because that valuation is based on empirically observable data, a valuation in accordance with the *purpose-related cost concept* is dependent upon the specific individual situation in which that concept is applied. The prices used in such a situation are chosen in a manner such that decisions based thereon will best facilitate the attainment of a predetermined objective. This means that in order to determine (cost) prices in applying the purpose-related cost concept, it is necessary to formulate objective functions and, in each case, the decision situation must be exactly defined. In applying the purpose-related cost concept, (cost) prices can only be exactly determined by resorting to mathematical decision-models. The use of approximations therefore frequently proves to be satisfactory.

Which of the two cost concepts should be used in a break-even analysis depends upon the computational purpose for which the analysis is undertaken. As a rule, break-even analysis is concerned with supportive computations which are drawn on in a concrete decision situation. In such a case, the use of costs determined by reference to the purpose-related cost concept is therefore frequently justified. Furthermore, as in the case of all decision-oriented approaches, the principle of relevant costs applies (cp. e.g. Horngren, 1982 [Cost Accounting] p. 363 et seq.). It states that, in evaluating individual alternatives in a decision-making situation, it is necessary and sufficient to take into account such costs as differ, or can at least differ, with respect to the individual alternatives. In particular this means that costs which are the same for each available alternative, i.e. which are independent of, and uninfluenced by, the decision in question, can be omitted from decision-making computations. Break-even analyses are invariably concerned with a future state of affairs. Consequently, all cost magnitudes must be assessed by reference to forecast values. This applies equally to both physical consumption and cost evaluation. In particular it means that historical values, e.g. historic acquisition costs etc., are largely irrelevant to break-even analyses. At best they have a particular informational value, as a basis for forecasting future cost levels, up to the time-horizon of the evaluation (cp. Horngren, 1982 [Cost Accounting] p. 365).

(b) Linearity of the Cost Function

The cost function used in the traditional form of break-even analysis is of a particularly simple structure. This refers not only to the fact that a sole cost determinant, activity, is taken into account, but also to the form of the cost dependence that is assumed. As in the case of (direct) costing systems based on variable costs, it is assumed that the cost dependence can be sufficiently accurately described by reference to two cost categories only. The one category comprises fixed costs which are wholly independent of the attributes of the cost determinant and always remain at the same level. The second category is represented by variable costs, which are assumed to be (largely) proportional to (i.e. vary linearly with) the cost determinant, or which with negligible error, can be assumed to be a linear function of that determinant. This assumption implies that unit variable costs are independent of the features of the cost determinant, in particular, for example, of the level of output. Non-linear cost-behaviour or a stepped fixed cost function are therefore ruled out.

The simple nature of the cost dependence described can only be regarded as a first, most facile attempt at a quantitatively precise specification of an existing, or presumed, dependence. In using the level of output as the determinant of costs, simple cases are readily apparent which cannot be adequately represented with a linear cost function. This applies of course, to a much greater extent, if other cost influences are taken into account. For example, variations in the intensity of a production process frequently reveal a typical U-shaped input consumption function. The dependence of input goods consumption per unit of work as an exactly defined basic unit of the production process which, in turn, is dependent upon the intensity of that process, is captured in a so-called input function (Verbrauchsfunktion). Its development is traceable to Gutenberg (cp. Gutenberg, 1983 [Produktion] p. 314 et seq.). An example of a typical input function is shown in Fig. 11. Non-linearity, as in the input function presented, transfers itself via a production function to the cost function for which, in such a case, the assumption of linear behaviour would not be justified.

The concept of input functions was introduced by Gutenberg as an essential part of his "production function type B". It can be regarded as the model of an entire series of similar production-theoretic relations representing the quantities of input goods as a function of determinants other than the level of output. The greater the extent to which such determinants are allowed for (or must be allowed for) in cost functions, the more inaccurately will a linear cost structure depict the case in point.

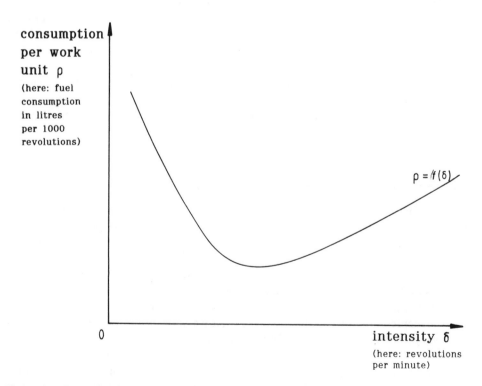

Figure 11 Example of an input function indicating an engine's standard fuel consumption as a function of the number of revolutions

(c) Linearity of the Sales Revenue Function

In the basic model of break-even analysis, total costs are juxtaposed with sales revenue, i.e. output measured in economic terms. As the antonym of costs, "economic output" can generally be defined as an economic valuation of goods that are generated by production (cp. Schweitzer and Küpper, 1991 [Systeme] p. 47). In that, as described in the first section, the basic model of break-even analysis deals with the analysis of profit thresholds in the single-product firm, sales revenue is taken as the relevant economic magnitude in the present sense. In general, instead of sales revenue, a series of other valuation magnitudes are conceivable output performance criteria.

Taking sales revenue as the counterpart of costs, the same can be said of the behaviour of the revenue function as can be said of the behaviour of costs. In the basic model, a univariable, linear sales revenue function is assumed, i.e. a constant selling price per unit. This price is independent of sales volume, i.e. is independent of both the amount that is offered for sale and the quantity that is actually sold. The total sales revenue of the planning period is given by the product of unit sales revenue and the level of output. Thus, as in the case of the cost function, a single determinant alone is allowed for, namely, the level of output, i.e. only a linear functional relationship is permitted. However, in the case of the sales revenue structure also, analogous determinants can be mentioned which influence total sales revenue or cause changes in unit sales revenue. Reference need only to be made to the possibility of quantity discounts, to different sales channels with different packaging, transport or sales commission costs and price differentiations for other different reasons. In addition to such influences as relate to individual end-product types, other influences on sales revenue result from the joint sale of several types of product. Relevant examples are: special conditions granted to particular customers in relation to total order volumes or revenue variations for selling the entire product range. Furthermore, in the case of the simple sales revenue function of the basic break-even model, it is implicitly assumed that precisely the level of output will actually be sold, i.e. there are no inventory adjustments.

Finally, it may also be mentioned that, in imperfectly competitive end-product markets, a firm's price-output function may be negatively inclined. If so, its total revenue function increases at a decreasing rate.

The above reasons lead to the conclusion that in general a more complex sales revenue structure must be assumed than that which appears in the basic model.

3. Assumptions about the Amount and Quality of Information

Break-even analyses of all types are based on a series of data. Different information may be available about the data employed. Each of the individual parameters entering the computation may be characterised by one of the three following informational states:

(1) The parameter is uniquely definable in that it takes on exactly one certain value. The case of the uniquely-valued expectation is a situation characterised by *deterministic information*.
(2) The parameter can take on any one of a number of possible values each of which has a probability of occurrence. This situation is characterised by *stochastic information*. If the probabilities are objectively known, and objectively derivable, or if they can be derived inter-subjectively ex post, e.g. using statistical methods—

reference is made to a risk situation in the narrow sense of the expression. Of course "objective probabilities" of this kind are frequently not available. More usually the known probabilities constitute a numerical picture of the personal estimates of one or several assessors involved. Because these probabilities are merely subjective, the available information is less reliable than in the former case. This is described as a risk situation in the broader sense of the expression.

(3) The parameter has an extremely ambiguous expectation. All that is known is a group of values which contain the parameter that is sought. This group of values embraces at least two, but as a rule a large number of possible outcome values the probabilities of which are unknown. Such a situation is described as the case of *uncertainty*.

Of the three above-mentioned information states, a risk situation with subjective probabilities is perhaps the closest to reality. The case of absolute uncertainty appears to be as exceptional as the deterministic information case. Most managerial models, especially those in the cost accounting area, are nevertheless aligned with the latter situation. In the basic model of break-even analysis it is also assumed that uniquely-valued, certain expectations can be formed about all the requisite data. The sales revenue and cost functions are therefore deterministically formulated. Such an approach is expedient either when the data used are really characterised with a high degree of certainty; or, when it is possible to undertake several parallel computations using adjusted data. Such parallel computations facilitate inferences about the region in which the desired results of the analysis lie, and their degree of reliability, in the sense of sensitivity analysis.

If the information relating to one or more model parameters in a break-even analysis is characterised by risk, a corresponding stochastic approach is more appropriate. Using such a model, the available probabilities can be explicitly built into the computation. On the other hand, hardly any models are to be found in the management and administrative sciences which deal with situations characterised by wholly uncertain information. The predictive power of any analysis that is based on this type of information is in any event dubious.

It can generally be assumed that, in the application of break-even analysis, the required parameters are not all known with complete certainty. This is especially true of magnitudes which are predictions of events that will occur far into the future. This may apply to selling prices or to particular costs. The information will thus be incomplete with respect both to amount and quality. In break-even analyses it may therefore be expedient to supplement deterministic computations with sensitivity analysis or even to switch to stochastic approaches.

4. Assumptions about a Firm's Objectives

The basic model of break-even analysis is intended to indicate the level of output at which neither a profit is earned nor a loss is sustained. This information is of specific interest to firms which ascribe a significant role to the *profit objective* in the context of their goal-systems.

However, in addition to the profit objective, a series of other types of objective also crops up in goal-systems which show some respect for reality. Moreover, in some organisations the profit objective is only of little or, indeed, no significance. This is true, first and foremost, of some of the enterprises in the public sector as well as of enterprises which are pre-eminently of a social character. Information on crucial magnitudes, which is gained in relation to the profit objective in the context of break-even analysis, can, in some circumstances, therefore also be useful in the pursuit of other objectives.

In general, conceptions of objectives can be specified, inter alia in terms of the following components (cp. Wild, 1982 [Planung] p. 58; Heinen, 1971 [Zielsystem] p. 59 et seq.) which thus simultaneously facilitate a partitioning of those objectives:

(1) content of the objective,
(2) aspired dimensions of the objective (decision criterion),
(3) time-dimension to which the objective relates.

Apropos of the *content of the objective*, three categories, namely, formal (economic), production-related and social responsibility objectives can be distinguished (cp. Schweitzer, 1990 [Gegenstand] p. 42). The *social responsibility* content of an objective always concerns a firm's employees or people who are otherwise interested in the firm as individuals or groups. In contrast, the *production-related* content of an objective refers to the production-related tasks of the firm, i.e. to production. The number, quantity, partitioning, type and quality of products, and productive assets, are prime examples. Whilst social responsibility and production-related objectives are, as a rule, measured directly or indirectly with real quantity magnitudes, *formal* objectives are derived from such real magnitudes via a monetary valuation or similar transformation. They are therefore called economic objectives. In addition to profit, pre-eminent examples are: turnover, cost and economic output, i.e. market value of output, the levels of receipts and payments, liquidity levels, and the present value of future (or expected) cash flows.

The aspired *dimensions of the objective* indicate when the attainment of that objective can be presumed. They are also designated decision criterion (cp. Kosiol, 1972 [Aktionszentrum] 212 et seq.; Schweitzer, 1990 [Gegenstand] p. 47 et seq.). Possible ways of specifying the dimensions of the objectives are (cp. Schweitzer, 1990 [Gegenstand] p. 48):

(1) maximisation or minimisation,
(2) satisficing,
(3) attainment of a predetermined point.

In the case of *maximisation or minimisation*, a target result is aimed at which is as large as, or as small as, possible. In contrast, *satisficing* requires the setting, as an objective, of upper or lower limits which represent minimum aspired performance levels. Illustrating the use of the upper limit; if the result is below the predetermined target level, it meets the satisficing criterion. A further downward deviation from the predetermined target level is also acceptable. An example of a satisficing objective with an upper limit is a target cost level, for a particular area of activity, which may on no account exceed a given amount. Equivalent considerations apply to satisficing by reference to a lower limit. Consequently, in the case of a satisficing objective, deviations in one of the directions are always (gladly) accepted (cp. also the *aspiration criterion*: e.g. Dinkelbach, 1975 [Programmierung] col. 3244). On the other hand, the attainment of a predetermined point is a question of minimising deviations in both directions. The intention is therefore to minimise the deviation from an exact predetermined point.

The *time-dimension* relating to the promulgated objective formulation completes its conception by prescribing the point in time at which the objective should be attained or the time-scale to which the objective relates.

The goal conception underlying the basic model of break-even analysis can be concretely described by reference to characteristics of objectives as follows: profit constitutes the content of the objective. In the individual case the aspired profit level is undisclosed. However, it is advisable to have information indicating when a zero profit will be exceeded. This can be sensible in relation to different aspired profit levels. The time-scale is determined by the data context. Thus, in particular, the level of fixed costs is valid for a particular time-interval, perhaps for a year.

Remaining with the profit objective; a modified category of questions is conceivable if the aspired *dimensions of the objective* are changed, i.e. if other decision criteria are adopted. Thus, information indicating the output level, above which a predetermined level of profit will be attained, can be useful. Such information is primarily of importance if the profit objective is neither to maximise nor to minimise, but the attainment of either a fixed profit level or some satisficing minimum profit level.

In switching to *objectives with a different content*, the type of content for which break-even considerations are at all possible and sensible must first be ascertained. Proceeding from the principle which underlies the basic model, it is seen that the magnitude of the objective is defined as the difference between two countervailing (gross) magnitudes: sales revenue (positive component) and costs (negative component). Thus, the basic situation becomes a juxtaposition of a fixed influence in one direction, namely predetermined fixed costs, with continuously accumulating contributions (in this case: unit contributions) that have a countervailing effect. This construct can only be transferred to objectives which are computed as the difference between two gross magnitudes. This feature is to be found in all three types of objectives. However, in certain circumstances, a modified computational approach is necessary to achieve an adequate break-even analysis for non-profit objectives. Frequently questions which arise in the pursuit of another formal objective permit solutions which are closely related to those stemming from the basic approach. If a satisfactory liquidity situation is to be attained, the (critical) level of output at which a zero liquidity balance can be expected, or at which some desired minimum liquidity level is attained, is clearly of interest. In such a case it is possible to work with data material that is constructed in the same manner as that which is used to answer the traditional category of questions in break-even analysis.

Quite a different informational base is, however, necessary if a change is made to objectives having a production-related or social responsibility content. A typical break-even question arising in the pursuit of a production-related objective might be, e.g. "What must the existing order level be if the utilisation level of a machine of a given capacity is to reach at least 80%?". In this example, the production-related objective is definable as the difference between the present and required performance of a machine measured in hours, and this difference, the machine down-time, is not to exceed an upper limit. To compute a corresponding break-even point it would be necessary to have information on the relationship subsisting between the level of output and requisite hours of the machine in question (cp. Fig. 12).

Analogous considerations apply to the following social responsibility question. A firm strives to create a specific internal business climate by reference to a satisficing

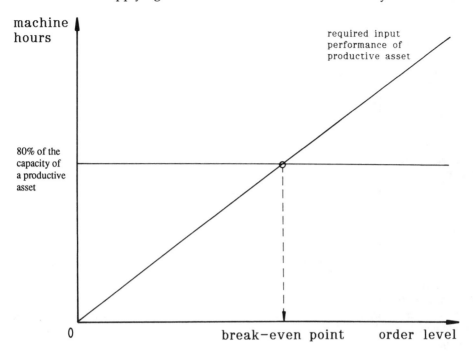

Figure 12   Break-even analysis relating to the production-related objective "minimum loading of a productive asset equal to 80% of its capacity"

criterion. The consequence of an intended reorganisation is a particular deterioration in that climate. It is however known that, with rest breaks, a gradual improvement in the internal business climate can be attained. The question to be answered in this case is: what is the break-even amount of additional rest-time at which the given deterioration in the internal business climate is exactly equalised by the cumulative positive effects? (cp. Fig. 13).

Frequently, break-even analyses are also extremely relevant if an equalisation of magnitudes in different categories of objectives is to be estimated. Thus, it might be questioned whether the expenditure (formal objective) on a new, improved productive asset is compensated by, among other things, a corresponding improvement in product quality (production-related objective). In these cases there is, in addition to the difficulty which in any case frequently arises in the measuring of production-related and social elements, the further problem of weighting objective function attainment levels that are expressed in terms of money and indices respectively.

Although extensions of break-even analyses to objectives of differing content can, in certain circumstances, lead to measurement difficulties, they are nevertheless advisable if the content of such objectives is of importance.

5. Assumptions about the Time-dimension of the Model's Predictions

All data and functions entering the basic model of break-even analysis are valid only for the planning period that is the subject of the analysis. Furthermore, the periodic

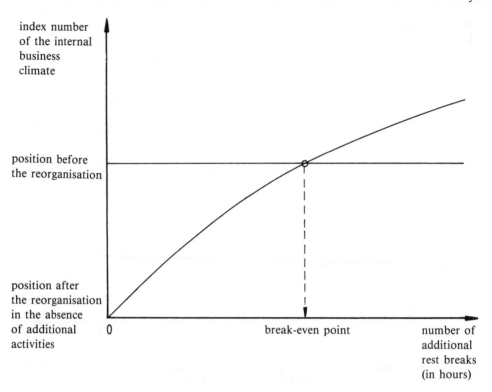

Figure 13   Break-even analysis for the social responsibility objective "holding the internal business climate constant"

magnitudes that are captured are treated as constants and are assumed to be independent of the magnitudes of other periods. In particular, prices, capacities, cost composition and product types do not change within the period in question. Further periods are not analysed. In sum, the basic model is therefore strictly a *static* construct. In all cases in which the previously-mentioned assumptions are not fulfilled, the standard form results of break-even analysis are invalid.

Frequently, cost levels and their composition, unit selling prices and total sales revenue, in short, the break-even budget and contribution margins, change with the effluxion of time. Moreover, in the case of longer-term analyses, the sub-periods in which individual costs, sales revenue or other relevant magnitudes actually occur are of importance. If, for example, the points in time at which the positive and negative break-even components occur are far apart, time-bridging questions arise. In the case of a computation expressed in monetary terms, this at least requires that interest costs should be taken into account. If serial changes in the model's magnitudes, or timing-differences in the occurrence of break-even components are to be allowed for in a break-even computation, a switch to a multiperiod or dynamic model which can capture such dynamic elements is necessary.

The characteristic of *dynamic models* is a linkage of variables with different time-dimensions in a relationship appearing in the model. At least one such relationship must be present if reference is to be made to a dynamic model (cp. Frisch, 1935/36

[Notion] p. 100). Furthermore, within the dynamic model category, a distinction can be made, as required, between stationary and evolutionary models. In the case of stationary models, the relationships subsisting between variables of different time-dimensions are the same over time whereas, in evolutionary models, these relationships also change (cp. e.g. Pressmar, 1974 [Losgrössenanalyse] p. 729 et seq.). Thus, stationary-dynamic models become relevant to break-even analysis if cost rates, prices, quantities or other magnitudes are subject to seasonal variations, and such seasonality repeats itself periodically, for example, annually. However, most dynamic break-even questions are concerned with the tracking and analysis of evolutionary developments. As a rule more substantial model extensions are necessary for this purpose.

6. Summary of the Conditions in which the Basic Model of Break-even Analysis can be Applied

All of the conditions, under which the basic model of break-even analysis can be applied, can be classified in the five categories which were discussed in this chapter. Repeated comprehensive references to these conditions are to be found in the literature (cp. e.g. Horngren, 1982 [Cost Accounting] p. 50 et seq.; Kern, 1974 [Break-even-Analysis] p. 993; Poensgen, 1981 [Break-even-Analysis] p. 308; Raun, 1964 [Limitations] p. 929; Schweitzer and Trossmann, 1980 [Break-even-Analyse]; Tucker, 1980 [Break-even System] p. 68 et seq.; Tucker, 1973 [Einführung] p. 108). They are summarised in the following five groupings:

(1) The structure of the goods flow can be traced to the case of even, single-stage, *single-product manufacture*. Convergence is only possible if the input relations are constant. Divergence is only possible if output and sales conditions (also those of sales revenue) are constant. Multistage production cannot be represented.
(2) The components of break-even analysis comprise costs (negative components) and sales revenue (positive components).

   —Both magnitudes are traceable to a *single determinant* which is the same for both.
   —This determinant is *activity* (i.e. the level of output). Such other possible influences as production-technical magnitudes, procurement and selling prices and inventory volume changes are thereby ignored. Their influence is assumed to be constant, negligible or already indirectly captured (via activity).
   —Costs can be divided into *fixed* (activity independent) and *variable components*.
   —Sales revenue is *fully variable*.
   —Variable costs and sales revenue are *proportional* to their common determinant. Consequently, costs and sales revenue are linear functions.

(3) All of the data and functions which appear in the model are assumed to be certain. *Uniquely-valued expectations* are therefore used.
(4) The *pursuit of profit* constitutes the paramount objective in a firm's goal-system. Profit threshold analysis therefore commends itself.
(5) All of the model's data and functions are of a *static* character. Changes within any period under consideration, or multiperiod developments, are not taken into account. Traditional break-even analysis can nevertheless be readily aligned with a (multiperiod) wealth-maximisation objective.

Chapter 3

Variants of Break-even Analysis

I. SURVEY OF VARIANTS OF BREAK-EVEN ANALYSIS

Numerous variants of break-even analysis are conceivable. They can roughly be divided into two categories. The one is concerned with particular variants of the basic model which deviate only slightly from it. Their distinctive feature lies in a *variation* of the usual break-even questions, either in the application of the analysis to a problem which deviates moderately from the general case handled by the basic model; or, by the addition of particular supplementary questions (cp. also Haidacher, 1969 [Break-even-Punkt] p. 105 et seq.). The purpose of these variants of the model is the gaining of information from the same basic approach in addition to the actual computation of the break-even point.

Forms of break-even analysis which require a greater modification of the break-even model can be classified in the second category. These *extensions* of break-even analysis are dealt with in Chapter 4.

The present chapter is concerned with *variants* of the basic model of break-even analysis. In this first category a distinction can therefore be made between the following variants of the basic model:

—Special *forms of the objective function* are allowed for in the break-even model. This includes the prescribing of a *minimum level of profit* or particular forms of *sub-categorised contribution budgets*. Other approaches in this category are those using *receipts and payments* instead of costs and sales revenue but which otherwise retain an unmodified basic model. Taking account of taxes, the use of *time* as a reference magnitude and a *profitability*, rather than an absolute profit-orientation, are further starting points for this type of variation.
—An analysis is made of the manner in which a break-even point is shifted by *changes in its determinants*. Possible subjects for analysis are changes in the contribution block, especially in fixed costs, changes in the unit contribution as well as simultaneous changes in both magnitudes.
—An investigation is undertaken of the way in which the break-even model can be applied to *replacement investment projects*. This application represents a variation of the basic model because the standard break-even analysis problem can be interpreted as the appraisal of a new investment.
—A difference between output and sales volumes is introduced into the break-even

model with a view to analysing the effect of *inventory volume changes* on break-even points.

Allowing for *sales risk* in the break-even model is also categorised as a variant of break-even analysis. This is not however a question of an alternative break-even model, but purely a matter of a supplement. Thus, the level of risk is ascertained in a special computation which, in principle, can be accommodated in any type of break-even analysis. The computation is intended to indicate the degree to which the break-even analysis is characterised by risk if sales information is uncertain. This adjunct to the basic model of break-even analysis is also dealt with in the present chapter.

II. ALLOWING FOR SPECIAL FEATURES OF OBJECTIVES

1. Prescribing a Minimum Level of Profit

Given a profit-making objective, the level of output beyond which a prescribed profit minimum is attained, and exceeded, can be of interest (cp. Chmielewicz, 1973 [Erfolgsrechnung] p. 215). This is especially the case if, in the light of experience, the break-even output is always exceeded and, as a predetermined objective, a positive satisficing-profit is set at a level G^*. Thus, in addition to the fixed cost block K^f, the *minimum profit level G^** also has to be covered and this results in a minimum required contribution D^* equal to $K^f + G^*$. The break-even point x_0^* can be ascertained from the relation

$$x_0^* = \frac{D^*}{d} = \frac{(K^f + G^*)}{d}. \tag{3.1}$$

Adopting a minimum profit level of $G^* = $ DM 4000 with the same cost and sales revenue relationships as in the previous example, the break-even point is computed as $x_0^* = 2500$ units:

$$x_0^* = \frac{(16\,000 + 4000)}{8} = 2500 \text{ units.}$$

In terms of the break-even graph this is a parallel shifting of the linear cost function by an amount G^* (cp. Fig. 14). If a profit minimum amounting to DM 4000 is to be earned, an output of 2500 units is necessary.

2. Computation of Further Break-even Points

When a minimum profit level is allowed for, a second specific point is designated in addition to the actual break-even point. At this second point, the cumulative contribution is exactly equal to a prescribed level. Analogously, an entire series of further break-even points can be ascertained if the fixed cost block is decomposed and different profit applications are planned (cp. Kern, 1974 [Break-even-Analysis] p. 995; Meredith, 1969 [Decisions] p. 55). This involves an implicitly-assumed ranking which is intended to allocate the contribution margins to cost components or to different profit

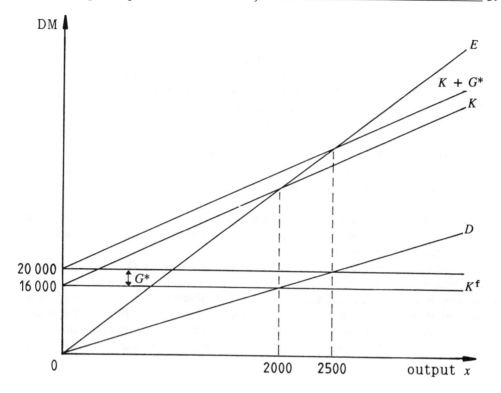

Figure 14 Break-even analysis allowing for a minimum profit level equal to G^*

appropriations. Thus, assume that, in the previous example, the following decomposition of fixed costs of DM 16 000 applies:

		DM
(1)	fixed personnel costs	6000
(2)	fixed interest and depreciation charges	2000
(3)	fixed costs of fixed assets	3000
(4)	further fixed costs	5000

In covering costs, the achieved total contribution margin is to be applied in the order represented by this sequence. To the extent that the total contribution exceeds the fixed cost block, the following profit-appropriation plan applies:

		DM
(5)	distribution of a preference dividend	6000
(6)	distribution of the usual dividend	5000
(7)	employee profit-participation	4000
(8)	self-financing (measured on an accruals basis)	remainder

In this example there are seven contribution points. They can be ascertained arithmetically by dividing the sum of the accumulated fixed costs and required profit levels by the unit contribution $d = $ DM 8:

$$x_1 = \text{DM} \quad 6\,000 : \text{DM 8 per unit} = \quad 750 \text{ units}$$
$$x_2 = \text{DM} \quad 8\,000 : \text{DM 8 per unit} = 1\,000 \text{ units}$$
$$x_3 = \text{DM} \quad 11\,000 : \text{DM 8 per unit} = 1\,375 \text{ units}$$
$$x_4 = \text{DM} \quad 16\,000 : \text{DM 8 per unit} = 2\,000 \text{ units (BEP)}$$
$$x_5 = \text{DM} \quad 22\,000 : \text{DM 8 per unit} = 2\,750 \text{ units}$$
$$x_6 = \text{DM} \quad 27\,000 : \text{DM 8 per unit} = 3\,375 \text{ units (UP}_1)$$
$$x_7 = \text{DM} \quad 31\,000 : \text{DM 8 per unit} = 3\,875 \text{ units (UP}_2)$$

In the break-even chart, the successive contribution points can be presented as intersections of the sales revenue line with the respective individual contribution block lines (cp. Fig. 15). These lines result from a parallel shifting of the (linear) variable cost curve.

Figure 16 illustrates a second type of presentation. In this case the contribution points are given by the intersections of the contribution margin line with the horizontals of the individual contribution blocks.

The contribution points so ascertained have no special names. Only the output level which fully satisfies the contemplated profit participations of shareholders and/or employees is given special emphasis. Such a contribution point is described as an *Unhealthy-Point* (cp. e.g. Kern, 1974 [Break-even-Analysis] p. 995). In the present example there are two unhealthy points (cp. Figs 15 and 16). The first unhealthy point (UP$_1$) indicates that the planned dividend can be fully met whereas UP$_2$, the second,

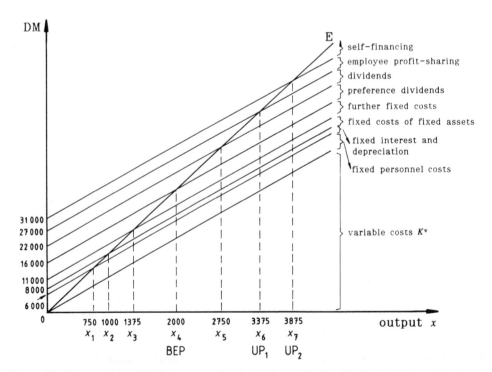

Figure 15 Presentation of different contribution points with the aid of the sales revenue curve and curves of the total contribution block

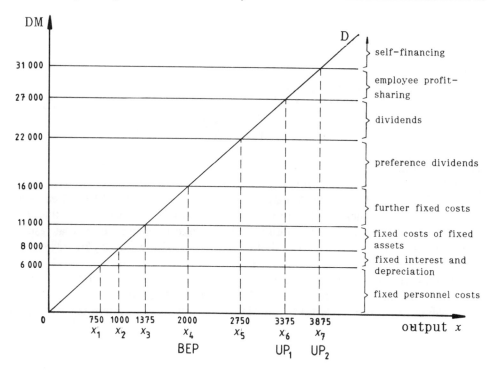

Figure 16 Presentation of different contribution points with the aid of the contribution margin curve

signals that both the latter and the intended level of employee profit-participation can be accommodated in full.

3. Special Computation of Cash Flow Break-even Points

In contemplating objectives which, from a data-structure standpoint, are similar to a profit-making objective, and also of similar importance in many other respects, single-period cash flow objectives appear to be the obvious starting points in modifying the basic break-even model. At first sight, the model's static approach seems to be readily transferable to the single-period cash flow problem. In the latter case sales revenue is frequently equated with sales receipts. However, the cost side is usually categorised in detail and shows the corresponding resultant cash payments so that the categorised costs/payments are presented as negative components. In principle this is an application of the previously-described partitioning into different contribution budgets by reference to cash flow considerations. Costs can thus be divided into those which have a cash flow effect and those which do not. If, in the present example, the components of fixed and variable costs which result in periodic cash payments amount to $K^{f, a} = DM\ 11\ 000$ (out of DM 16 000) and $k^{v, a} = DM\ 9$ (out of DM 12) per unit respectively, the following calculation emerges:

Costs which result in cash payments:
$$K^a(x) = K^{f, a} + k^{v, a}(x)$$
$$= 11\ 000 + 9x$$

Relevant contribution margin:
$$D(x) = 20x - 9x = 11x.$$

Contribution point:
$$K^{f,\,a} \overset{!}{=} D(x)$$
$$11\,000 \overset{!}{=} 11 \cdot x$$
$$x_0^a = \frac{K^{f,\,a}}{d} = \frac{DM\ 11\,000}{DM\ 11/\text{unit}} = 1000\ \text{units.}$$

The contribution point, at which payments are exactly covered, is 1000 units. It is generally described as *"cash point"*, *"liquidity point"*, or *"out-of-pocket point"* (cp. e.g. Gardner, 1955 [Profit Management] p. 53; Kleinebeckel, 1976 [Break-even-Analysen] p. 55 and Tucker, 1980 [Break-Even System] p. 15). In determining this point, it is assumed that available contributions are first used in meeting costs that result in cash payments. The cash flow threshold is the start of the *"cash-flow-region"*. A graphical presentation is shown in Fig. 17.

This approach can be extended in a number of ways so that, for example, payments which are not simultaneously costs can also be taken into account. This type of cash flow analysis can also be undertaken quite independently of cost analysis considerations.

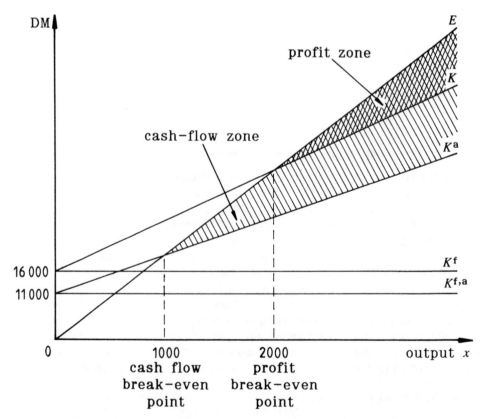

Figure 17 Graphical presentation of a cash flow break-even point

Furthermore, a differentiation of sales revenue showing that which results in periodic receipts and that which does not is frequently expedient.

Finally it should also be emphasised that a priori and empirical analyses of the single and multiperiod relationships between conventionally-measured "accruals" accounting variables and cash flow variables have important implications for both single-period and multiperiod break-even analysis. This proposition is the subject of Section IX in Chapter 4.

4. Time-related Contribution Budgets

As a rule, break-even analyses are formulated with the level of output x as the independent variable. The corresponding contribution points are then output levels. If a relationship between time and production is defined such that the level of output is a unique function of time, break-even analysis can also be constructed with time as the independent variable:

$$x = f(t). \tag{3.2}$$

The contribution points are then *points in time*. They indicate the target dates at which, for example, cash flow or profit thresholds are reached.

In this variant of break-even analysis, a single determinant of both the positive and negative components, is again employed. However, time appears instead of activity— the more usual determinant. It is thus assumed that there is a fixed relationship between

—the behaviour of sales revenue and time
—the behaviour of costs and time.

In the simplest case these relationships are, in turn, assumed to be linear. That is to say, constant levels of sales revenue and costs are assumed to arise per unit of time (e.g. daily, weekly, monthly). Additionally, and independently of the time variable, a particular level of non-recurrent fixed costs is incurred, which must also be accounted for, but which remains unchanged in the period in question. This characterisation makes it clear that this is not a question of sales revenue that varies with the level of activity; or, of costs which are respectively fixed or variable in relation to activity. Rather it is a matter of classifying computational components as time-variable sales revenue, costs which are fixed with respect to time and costs which are variable with respect to time.

A situation in which sales revenue and costs can be traced exclusively to the time-variable must be regarded as a special case. In the case of continuous production, especially mass-production based on the flow principle, it is perhaps conceivable that the same product quantity, the sale of which is certain, is produced in every time-interval. If selling prices, sales levels, the cost structure and cost levels are stationary, constant sales revenue and cost growth can, as described, be projected for every time-interval. In such a situation, time-related *break-even (time) points* can be ascertained in a manner that is analogous to the determination of the cash points described above.

By way of illustration reference is made to the case of a supplier (to a motor vehicle manufacturer) who has the opportunity to conclude a long-term agreement to supply a particular component. Under the terms of the agreement, 1200 units of the relevant components are to be supplied weekly for a 42 working-week year. Unit sales revenue amounts to DM 2.20 and is fully realised in cash. In order to undertake the production, fixed (set-up) costs, in particular for tools, equipment and installations amounting to DM 36 000 need to be incurred of which DM 25 000 will result in actual payments. The manufacturing process involves unit (proportional) variable costs of DM 1.60 of which DM 1.40 will result in payments. In the situation described, the supplier firm can assume that sales revenue, costs, sales receipts and payments relating to this order are ultimately time-dependent. The question of interest to the firm is the minimum time-period for which the supply agreement with the motor vehicle manufacturer should be concluded so that

—the fixed costs initially incurred will at least be covered by the cumulative contribution,
—the original payments in respect of capital expenditure will at least be covered by the cumulative net cash (in)flow.

Two break-even time-points need to be computed in answering this question: first, a cost break-even point and, second, a cash flow break-even time-point.
    The computations are given below.

Cost contribution point *(break-even point)*		*Cash flow break-even point* *(cash point)*	
	DM/unit		DM/unit
Unit sales revenue:	$q = 2.20$	Unit sales receipts:	2.20
Unit variable cost:	$k^v = 1.60$	Unit operating payments:	1.40
Unit contribution:	$d = 0.60$	Unit operating cash flow:	0.80
Weekly contribution margin:		Weekly operating cash flow:	
1200 units/week · DM 0.60/unit		1200 units/week · DM 0.80/unit	
= DM 720/week		= DM 960/week	
Contribution budget:	DM 36 000	Contribution budget:	DM 25 000
Break-even time point:		Cash flow time point:	
$\dfrac{\text{DM } 36\,000}{\text{DM } 720/\text{week}} = 50 \text{ weeks}$		$\dfrac{\text{DM } 25\,000}{\text{DM } 960/\text{week}} = 26.04 \text{ weeks}$	

Both calculations thus follow the same principle that is indicated by formula (2.14) (cp. p. 20). The relationship is presented graphically in Fig. 18.
    With t as a time-parameter for the working-weeks, the sales revenue function is:

$$\tilde{E}(t) = 2.20 \cdot 1200 \cdot t = 2640 \cdot t.$$

It also constitutes the sales receipts function in this case.
    The cost function is:

$$\tilde{K}(t) = 36\,000 + 1.60 \cdot 1200 \cdot t$$
$$= 36\,000 + 1920 \cdot t.$$

The payments function is represented by the relationship:

$$\tilde{A}(t) = 25\,000 + 1.40 \cdot 1200 \cdot t$$
$$= 25\,000 + 1680 \cdot t.$$

The time-points which are sought are indicated by the intersection points of the corresponding curves in Fig. 18. The cash point is approximately 8 months from the start

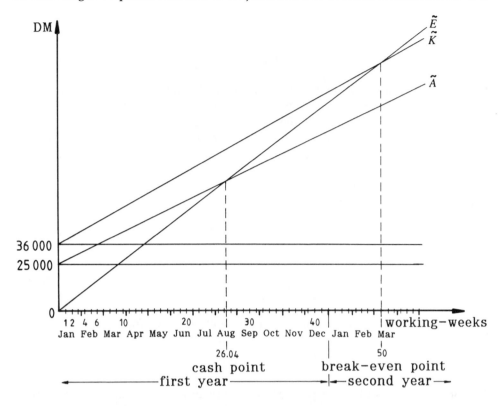

Figure 18 Time-related contribution point analysis

and the actual break-even point is in the first quarter of the second year. In the problem described, these two points provide some orientation for the negotiation of a minimum supply period.

Corresponding to the sub-classification of costs into cash flow and non-cash flow components, a further partitioning is possible which, as in Figs 15 and 16 can primarily be related to further contribution blocks.

5. Allowing for Simple Tax Effects

The individual components of break-even computations are changed in varying degrees by taxation. A series of taxes can be added to either fixed or variable costs. They do not therefore alter the structure of the break-even computation. For example, the following taxes are added to variable costs: customs duties together with most transfer duties and such consumption taxes as those on beer, spirits, coffee, mineral oil, salt and tobacco. To fixed costs can be added, among others, motor vehicle tax, property tax and business wealth tax (cp. Dorn, 1977 [Besteuerung] p. 132). The addition of individual types to the cost categories distinguished here can, depending upon the decision situation in question, have varying effects (on this point cp. also Wagner and Heyd, 1981 [Steuern] p. 922 et seq.).

However, in addition to taxes that are contained in costs, taxes which are a function of profit also have to be paid. These include the business profit tax and corporation income tax as well as other forms of income tax. Allowing for these taxes in break-even computations requires special considerations. In the break-even approaches discussed hitherto, such tax effects have not been taken into account, i.e. only pre-tax profit was considered. In computing the profit threshold this is of no consequence. However, the distinction between pre-tax and post-tax profit is of significance if the intention is to determine break-even points at which some *minimum level of profit* is attained. In this event *post-tax profit* is frequently the appropriate arithmetic basis. As a first step in giving effect to such tax considerations a proportional profit tax at the rate s ($0 \leqslant s < 1$) can be charged (cp. Chmielewicz, 1974 [Gewinnschwellenanalyse] p. 50; Morse and Posey, 1979/80 [Income Taxes] p. 21).

If a post-tax profit amounting to G^* is to be attained, a higher pre-tax profit of $\tilde{G}$ is required which is given by

$$\tilde{G} - s \cdot \tilde{G} = G^* \tag{3.3}$$

whence

$$\tilde{G} = \frac{1}{1-s} G^*.$$

The contribution block for the break-even computation therefore amounts to:

$$K^f + \tilde{G} = K^f + \frac{1}{1-s} G^*. \tag{3.4}$$

The corresponding break-even point x_0^* for the required minimum post-tax profit is given by:

$$D(x_0^*) = K^f + \frac{1}{1-s} G^*. \tag{3.5}$$

Assuming linear relationships then with $D(x) = d \cdot x$:

$$x_0^* = \frac{K^f + \dfrac{1}{1-s} G^*}{d}. \tag{3.6}$$

Using the data of the standard example discussed previously, assume a minimum post-tax target profit level of $G^* = $ DM 4000 and a tax rate of 56%, i.e. $s = 0.56$. The contribution block is thus:

$$K^f + \frac{1}{1-s} G^* = 16\,000 + \frac{1}{1-0.56} \cdot 4000$$

$$= 16\,000 + \frac{4000}{0.44} = \text{DM } 25\,091.$$

With a unit contribution of $d = $ DM 8, the break-even point, x_0^*, for the minimum profit level is given by:

$$x_0^* = \frac{25\,091}{8} \approx 3136 \text{ units.}$$

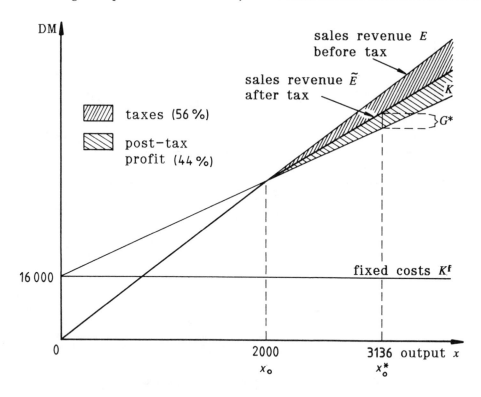

Figure 19 Sales revenue–cost diagram allowing for profit taxes

It should be noted that in the graphical presentation of tax considerations, pre-tax profit is divided in the ratio $s : (1 - s)$, in the example, $0.56 : 0.44$, between taxes and post-tax profit. Both magnitudes increase linearly beyond the profit threshold. In the diagram this is clearly indicated by a corresponding division of the profit scissors (cp. Fig. 19). Thus, two sales revenue curves necessarily emerge: the (previous) pre-tax sales revenue curve E and the post-tax sales revenue curve $\tilde{E}$. The latter is synonymous with the former up to the profit threshold, has a kink at that point, and therefore is flatter. The second part of the post-tax sales revenue curve is linear and has a slope which is ascertained as follows:

Pre-tax sales revenue per unit of output: DM 20.00
less 56% tax on profit per unit of output
       of DM $8 = 0.56 \cdot$ DM 8   = DM   4.48

Post-tax sales revenue per unit of output: DM 15.52

The post-tax contribution margin curve $\tilde{D}$ has a corresponding kink (cp. Fig. 20). Prior to the profit threshold the unit contribution amounts to DM 8 but thereafter is only DM $8 \cdot 0.44 =$ DM 3.52. Figure 20 shows how taxation shifts the break-even point to the right in the case of a DM 4000 profit-minimum.

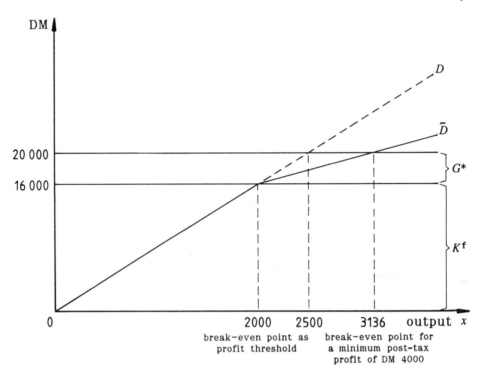

Figure 20 Contribution margin–contribution block diagram allowing for profit taxes

6. Prescribing a Profitability Objective

In addition to an absolute level of profit, relative profit, or *profitability*, often appears in managerial goal conceptions. The consequence for break-even analysis is that (critical) output levels are sought at which the prescribed minimum profitability level is attained. The profitability threshold, i.e. the point at which profitability is zero, is naturally synonymous with the profit threshold. Hence, modified break-even considerations only arise if the attainment of non-zero profitability levels is to be analysed. Also of significance is the question of the basic value to which profit should be related. Thus the frequently contemplated variants of the return on capital do not require the construction of a special form of break-even analysis. In that the capital base (denominator) of the profitability calculation generally does not appear in any of the components of the computation, the required minimum level of profitability can, without difficulty, be converted into an absolute level of profit thereby facilitating the use of the usual break-even approach. The same applies to such other profitability measures as profit per labour hour, profit per machine hour, profit per square foot of sales area etc.

Returning simply to the basic model is not, however, possible if profit is related to a criterion which also appears in the components of the break-even computation. This applies in particular to the return on sales which is illustrated with the following break-even analysis (cp. Chmielewicz, 1974 [Gewinnschwellenanalyse] p. 51; Chmielewicz, 1973 [Erfolgsrechnung] p. 212 et seq.). Return on sales is defined as the ratio of profit to turnover. Profit is given by the difference between total contribution and the fixed cost block. Turnover corresponds to sales revenue. Hence,

$$r = \frac{D(x) - K^f}{E(x)}.$$ (3.7)

Assuming a required return on sales of r^*, the level of output at which that return is attained is ascertained by solving equation (3.7) for x. Given the linear relationships:

$$D = d \cdot x$$
$$E = q \cdot x$$

the computation of the related break-even point x^R is:

$$r^* \cdot q \cdot x^R \overset{!}{=} d \cdot x^R - K^f$$ (3.8)

or

$$(d - r^* \cdot q) \cdot x^R \overset{!}{=} K^f.$$

If $r^* \cdot q < d$, equation (3.8) has a positive solution. The break-even point x^R is then given by the formula

$$x^R = \frac{K^f}{d - r^* \cdot q}.$$ (3.9)

The magnitude of the return on sales which, given the data relationships, is unattainable, can also be inferred from equation (3.8). Only if the required profitability (return on sales) is smaller than the quotient of the unit contribution and unit selling price:

$$r^* < \frac{d}{q},$$ (3.10)

does formula (3.9) have a positive denominator. This constraint will of course only play a role in the case of extreme numerical relationships. In the basic example discussed hitherto, sensible solutions for the break-even point are obtained provided the required return on sales is less than $d/q = 8/20 = 40\%$. For a required return on sales of $r^* = 20\%$, the break-even point x^R derived from (3.9) is:

$$x^R = \frac{\text{DM } 16\,000}{\text{DM } (8 - 0.2 \cdot 20)/\text{unit}} = \frac{16\,000}{8 - 4} \text{ units}$$

$$= 4000 \text{ units}.$$

Figure 21 is a graphical presentation in which the contribution block, comprising fixed costs and a linearly increasing minimum profit, is juxtaposed with total contribution.

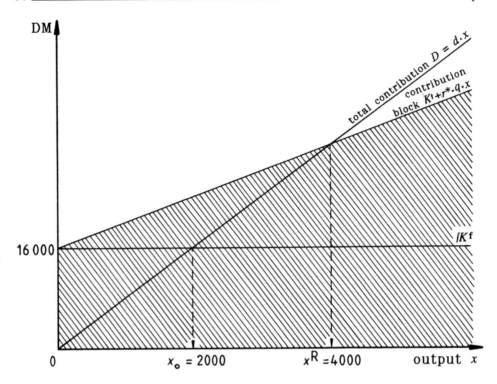

Figure 21 Total contribution–contribution block diagram for a required level of profitability

III. ALLOWING FOR CHANGES IN THE MAGNITUDES OF DETERMINANTS

Determining how contribution points change if the magnitudes of the determinants are varied is an important aspect of break-even analysis (cp. Schweitzer and Küpper, 1991 [Systeme] p. 360; Tucker, 1980 [Break-Even System] p. 48 et seq.; Tucker, 1973 [Einführung] p. 93 et seq.; Kleinebeckel, 1976 [Planung] p. 120 et seq.). Changes in unit sales revenue q, fixed costs K^f, variable costs $K^v(x)$ or required profit and profitability minima can all be treated as variations in the contribution block and contribution margin.

1. Variation in the Contribution Block

The critical levels of output that are computed in break-even analysis can generally be defined as points at which cumulative contributions are exactly equal to a predetermined contribution block B. This contribution block can exactly correspond to fixed costs or may only comprise particular types of costs, or payments, or the sum of cost or payments components or profit levels.

The effect of a change in this contribution block is indicated by Fig. 22.

The total contribution $D(x) = d \cdot x$ is assumed to be unchanged. If the contribution block increases from B_1 to B_2, the break-even point rises from x_1 to x_2.

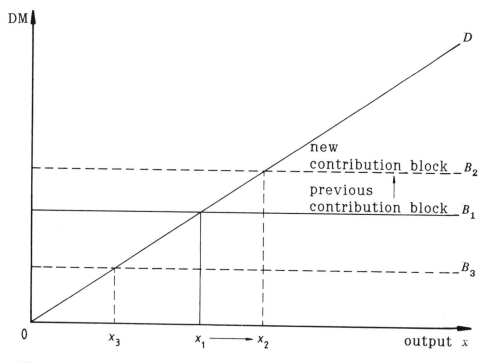

Figure 22 The effect of a change in the contribution block on the break-even point

The change $\Delta x = x_2 - x_1$ is given by:

$$\Delta x = x_2 - x_1 = \frac{B_2 - B_1}{d}.$$ (3.11)

A reduction in the contribution block to B_3 has corresponding effects.

2. Variation in the Unit Contribution

The second component of the break-even model, variations in which result in shifts in contribution points, is the contribution margin function. It is here assumed to be linear. An increase in unit contribution from d_1 to d_2 is depicted graphically as a positive rotating in a mathematical sense (i.e. to the left) of the (linear) contribution margin function $D(x) = d \cdot x$ (cp. Fig. 23). The break-even point thereby falls from x_1 to x_2. The change Δx is given by:

$$\Delta x = x_2 - x_1 = \frac{B}{d_2} - \frac{B}{d_1} = -\frac{B \cdot (d_2 - d_1)}{d_1 \cdot d_2} = -\frac{B \cdot \Delta d}{d_1 \cdot d_2}.$$ (3.12)

The unit contribution increases, for example, if unit sales revenue increases, or unit variable costs decline, or if there is a reduction in a proportional rate of profit tax and vice versa.

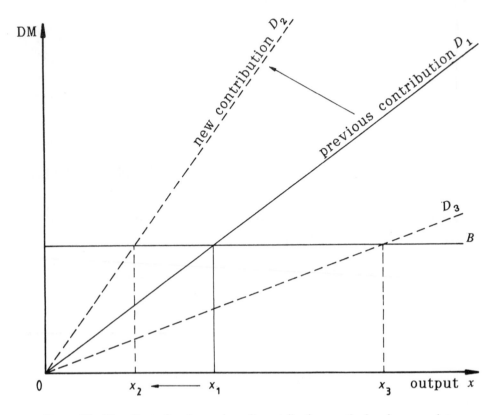

Figure 23 The effect of a change in unit contribution on the break-even point

Variations in unit contribution by successive small amounts are depicted graphically by a family of (linear) contribution margin curves which is known as the *contribution margin cobweb* (cp. Kleinebeckel, 1976 [Break-even-Analysen] p. 58). Its analysis is particularly relevant from a pricing policy standpoint. An alternative presentation for the same application uses a hyperbolic function to indicate all combinations of unit variable costs and selling prices giving the same contribution margin (cp. Kelvie and Sinclair, 1968 [New Technique] p. 37).

3. Compensating Cost Changes

Variations in the two determinants of break-even points, namely, contribution block and contribution margin, should also be examined in conjunction with each other. Here a larger number of applications is conceivable. However, the same considerations apply to all. They are illustrated below with the example of a cost change which results from a reinforcing of advertising measures (cp. Tucker, 1973 [Einführung] p. 205 et seq.; Tucker, 1980 [Break-Even System] p. 123 et seq.; Brown, 1975 [Advertising Costs] p. 44).

The initial contribution block is assumed to amount to $B_1 = $ DM 20 000. It comprises fixed costs and a minimum required profit level. The additional advertising costs amount to DM 5000 and the new contribution block B_2 therefore takes on a value of

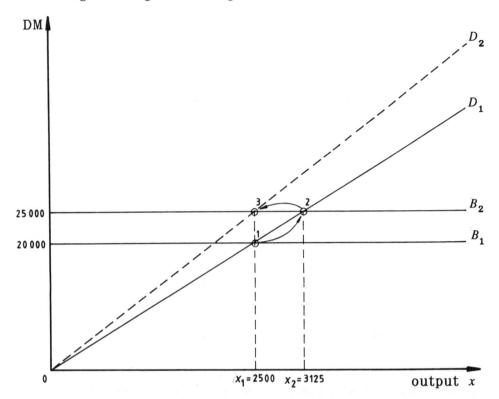

Figure 24 Compensating an increase in the contribution block with an increase in the unit contribution

DM 25 000. With a unit contribution of DM 8, the critical output thus rises from 2500 units to 3125 units (cp. Fig. 24). This means that the advertising measure must bring about an increase in sales volume of at least 625 units.

An increase in advertising costs can, however, also be subject to the constraint that the break-even point (or other contribution points) are to remain unchanged. This may perhaps prove to be expedient from a capacity standpoint. The amount by which the unit contribution must be raised must then be questioned, i.e. it is necessary to ascertain the market price increase that exactly compensates for the increased costs at the existing contribution point. In the example, a block of DM 25 000 is to be exactly covered at an output of 2500 units. This results in a required unit contribution of DM 10. With a unit variable cost of DM 12, the selling price must therefore be increased from DM 20 to DM 22.

The following calculation can generally be made:

Contribution point hitherto:

$$x_1 = \frac{B_1}{d_1}$$

new contribution point:

$$x_2 = \frac{B_2}{d_2}.$$

As the two contribution points are to be equal:

$$\frac{B_1}{d_1} \overset{!}{=} \frac{B_2}{d_2}.$$

Consequently, the new unit contribution d_2 is given by

$$d_2 = \frac{B_2}{B_1} d_1$$

and the change amounts to:

$$\Delta d = d_2 - d_1 = \frac{B_2 - B_1}{B_1} \cdot d_1 = \frac{\Delta B}{B_1} d_1. \tag{3.13}$$

In the example the price change is computed as:

$$\Delta d = \frac{5000}{20\,000} \cdot \text{DM } 8/\text{unit} = \text{DM } 2/\text{unit}.$$

4. Changes in the Relationship between Contribution Block and Unit Contribution

The analysis of variations in the break-even point is of particular importance from a managerial decision-making standpoint. Break-even analyses can be resorted to in decisions on, among other things, product innovations or in make or buy decisions (cp. Tucker, 1973 [Einführung] p. 264 et seq.). In such cases it is always a question of comparing alternatives which have differing contribution block–contribution margin relationships. In the general case, one alternative is characterised by a relatively low contribution block and a relatively low contribution margin, whilst a second alternative has a relatively high contribution block and also a relatively high contribution margin. In this situation, the profitability of choosing the one or the other alternative depends upon the level of output. That is to say, at low levels of output one of the alternatives is superior whereas, at high output levels, the other alternative may be preferable. Thus, the break-even question which arises in this case concerns the level of output at which the alternatives are equally attractive, i.e. at which a switch from one alternative to the other makes economic sense. Such break-even points are also called *critical outputs* or *crossover points* (cp. e.g. Tucker, 1980 [Break-Even System] p. 188).

In numerous managerial decisions a comparison of alternatives can be reduced to the calculation of critical output levels. The main applications are make or buy decisions and decisions on the choice of manufacturing process. However, the same approach can also be used, for example, to evaluate alternative price strategies (cp. Gibson, 1972 [Strategies] p. 10; Meredith, 1969 [Decisions] p. 109 et seq.); or, to investigate the effects of wage increases on the contribution block and contribution margins (cp. Kleinebeckel, 1983 [Break-even-Analyse] p. 52 et seq.).

The relationship characterised above can be illustrated by reference to a typical comparison of manufacturing procedures. A choice is to be made between two alternative fixed assets. Lower fixed costs are associated with Procedure 1 which, however, requires

Table 1

	Procedure 1	Procedure 2
Fixed costs	DM 16 000	DM 36 000
Unit variable costs	DM 12	DM 5
Unit sales revenue	DM 20	DM 20
Unit contribution	DM 8	DM 15

higher unit variable costs. The use of Procedure 2, which is more highly automated, requires higher fixed costs and lower unit variable costs. The data of the example are enumerated in Table 1.

If the break-even points are computed for both procedures, it turns out that Procedure 1 already reaches the profit region at $x_0^{(1)} = 2000$ units whereas Procedure 2 first becomes profitable at $x_0^{(2)} = 2400$ units. Given a required minimum profit of $G^* = \text{DM } 9600$, then, in this example, the ranking of contribution points is reversed:

$$x^{*(1)} = \frac{\text{DM } (16\,000 + 9600)}{\text{DM } 8/\text{unit}} = 3200 \text{ units}$$

$$x^{*(2)} = \frac{\text{DM } (36\,000 + 9600)}{\text{DM } 15/\text{unit}} = 3040 \text{ units.}$$

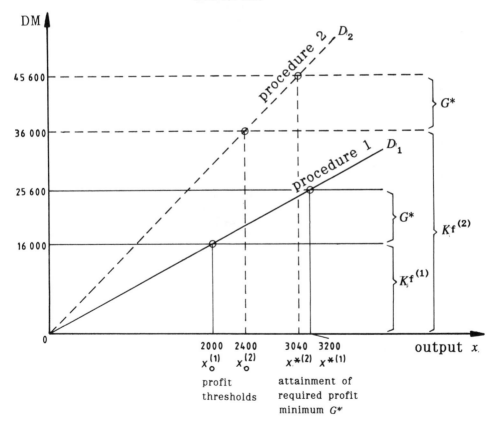

Figure 25 Break-even analysis for comparing different procedures

The break-even diagram in Fig. 25 shows the reversal of the rankings of the break-even points in graphical form. The fact that the ranking of the contribution points, at which the minimum required profit G^* is attained, conflicts with the rankings of the profit thresholds, indicates the existence of an output level at which the costs of the two alternatives are equal. This critical output $\tilde{x}$ is derived arithmetically by equating the costs of the two procedures:

$$\text{costs of Procedure } 1 \overset{!}{=} \text{costs of Procedure } 2$$
$$16\,000 + 12x \overset{!}{=} 36\,000 + 5x.$$

The critical output is therefore given by:

$$\tilde{x} \approx 2857 \text{ units.} \tag{3.14}$$

Up to the critical output total costs are lower in the case of Procedure 1. Above the critical output the advantage of the lower variable costs becomes decisive and Procedure 2 becomes more economic. The behaviour of the respective cost functions and the critical output $\tilde{x}$ are shown in Fig. 26. The choice between the two procedures will, assuming the profit motive, depend upon the forecast sales volume.

The following further designations are, among others, used in addition to the more familiar 'critical output' to describe the point at which the costs of alternative procedures are equal (cp. Haidacher, 1969 [Break-even-Punkt] p. 103 et seq. and the literature cited there): crossover point, degression threshold, marginal unit number, critical unit number,

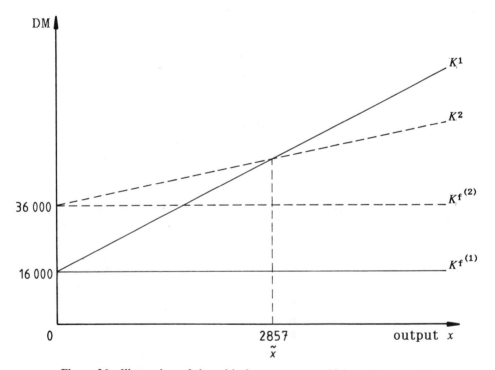

Figure 26   Illustration of the critical output $\tilde{x}$, at which costs are equal

critical activity number, critical performance intensity, machine breakpoint, utility threshold (of business size), utility limit (of business size). In the literature, fundamental considerations concerning the substitution of variable costs with fixed costs in the case of increasing output are frequently tied to a succession of alternative procedure comparisons of the form characterised in the foregoing paragraphs. Thus, the following (plausible) assumptions, for which a multiplicity of examples can be found, are usually made (cp. Lücke, 1962 [Massenproduktion] p. 340 et seq.):

—For each product there are various production procedures which differ from each other primarily because they have different fixed-variable cost ratios.
—Increasing fixed costs are associated with a lowering of unit variable costs.
—As a rule the procedure with the higher fixed cost burden is the more "modern" type, i.e. a more highly mechanised or automated procedure which, because of lower personnel and material requirements, effects savings in variable costs (often in spite of higher individual costs in the case of energy and other inputs).
—The cost changes resulting from the sequential switching from one procedure to that with the next highest fixed costs are such that the critical outputs for these switches also portray a strongly increasing trend (cp. Fig. 27).

It follows from the foregoing assumptions that, with increasing output, successive changes in productive procedure by reference to unit costs are (economically)

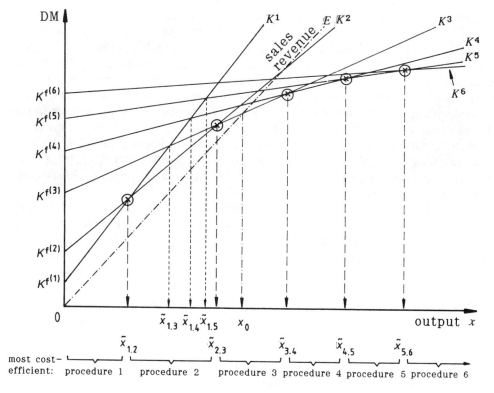

Figure 27 Critical outputs for successive changes in procedures

advantageous. A general law relating to the substitution of fixed costs for variable costs can be derived by assuming:

(i) that product demand continuously increases over time and that there are consequential increases in production and sales volumes; and,

(ii) that firms' production decisions really are based on unit cost criteria and that they therefore switch to new production procedures in accordance with critical output levels or at least approximately in accordance therewith.

A consideration, in conjunction with the foregoing assumptions, of procedure-determined (plant scale) cost reduction (cp. Bücher's law of mass-production in Chapter 2.I.2) leads to the conclusion that, among other things, a general increase in fixed costs, the substitution of human labour with machines and increasing automation can be substantiated on both technical and economic grounds (on this cp. Lücke, 1962 [Massenproduktion] p. 340 et seq.).

Independently of such far-reaching interpretations, the critical output computations for production procedure switches, and their presentation in diagrams as in Fig. 22, show that, in the case of linear cost curves, output regions can be indicated for which individual procedures are the most cost efficient. These regions are demarcated by the computed critical outputs. However, it cannot be concluded that, with sequentially-increasing production, Procedure 1 should first be installed and that, on reaching the critical level of output $\bar{x}_{1,2}$, a change to Procedure 2 followed by corresponding switches to procedures 3, 4, 5 and 6 are economically expedient. Rather should the computation of critical outputs be regarded as a preliminary analysis for investigating which, of two or more procedures, is the most cost-efficient alternative in relation to the expected volumes of production and sales. Implicit in such a preliminary analysis is the assumption that initially no procedure has been installed. However, the computation of an output level beyond which (in relation to particular costs) it is expedient to switch from a previously installed procedure to a new procedure is an entirely different matter. A break-even analysis for this decision situation must juxtapose, as a negative component, the additional costs resulting from the decision with a positive component in the form of the unit variable cost savings. The break-even point which is ascertained in this way is synonymous, only under special conditions, with the critical output computed above. A method of analysing a replacement investment of the type described on a break-even basis is described in Section IV below.

In interpreting critical values that are computed as described above, and illustrated graphically in Figs 26 and 27, it must also be noted that such values are break-even points for use in a comparison of individual procedures. Consequently, they are computable independently of the sales revenue situation and do not therefore facilitate predictions as to whether a break-even point in the sense of a profit threshold will actually be attained or not. It is therefore conceivable that critical outputs lie below the break-even point denoted by zero profit. The sales revenue curve in Fig. 27 (the broken chain), which results in a break-even point x_0, lies between critical points $\bar{x}_{2,3}$ and $\bar{x}_{3,4}$. Hence, Procedure 1 and Procedure 2 are both unprofitable. Only by using Procedure 3 does it become possible, because of its lower variable costs, to produce at a profit, i.e. when the output x_0 is exceeded. Thus for Procedures 1 and 2 there are no profit thresholds at all. In the case of Procedure 3 the profit threshold is at output x_0 whereas the break-even levels of output of the other productive procedures take on somewhat higher values.

IV. APPLICATION TO REPLACEMENT INVESTMENTS

A replacement investment decision is concerned with the question of whether the replacement of an existing operation is economically expedient. A variant of the break-even approach provides an appropriate arithmetic analysis of this question. This analysis is illustrated here by reference to a typical example of a replacement investment whereby an entire production procedure is treated as an investment proposal. The proposal therefore includes not only productive assets but, most importantly, the engaging of the requisite, suitably qualified personnel, raw materials and other input factors. The present installation, Procedure 1, gives rise to, i.e. causes, annual fixed costs of DM 16 000 and variable costs of DM 12/unit. The question to be resolved is whether Procedure 1 should be replaced by Procedure 2 to which fixed costs of DM 36 000 and variable costs of DM 5/unit are ascribable. Using break-even analysis, the aim is to determine the annual level of production above which the replacement of Procedure 1 with Procedure 2 is economically worthwhile. From the computation of the critical output of 2857 units (cp. (3.14)), no more can be inferred than that, for a forecast output level not exceeding 2857 units, Procedure 1 is preferable and that Procedure 2 is superior thereafter. However, this computation does not take account of the costs of switching from Procedure 1 to Procedure 2. The latter costs include, first and foremost, all costs incurred in connection with the disinvestment of the present operation and its liquidation, together with the costs of installing the replacement and its introduction. As a rule, change-over costs comprise one-off costs that can only be adequately allowed for by resorting to a differentiated multiperiod approach in which such costs can be juxtaposed with the positive and negative components arising in other periods. However, break-even analysis basically uses static values which, in the present context, must therefore be interpreted as periodic averages applying to the project's entire service life.

To determine whether and, if so, to what extent, components of the change-over costs are already included in the fixed costs specified for the procedures, the principle adopted in determining the fixed costs for Procedures 1 and 2 should first be elucidated. In this regard, interest costs and depreciation charges are of particular significance because, precisely in their case, the actual individual periodic payments relating thereto vary considerably. Hence, the computed averages for these two items play an important role. Interest costs and depreciation charges are magnitudes allocated to periods on an accruals basis and, as average values, intend an even allocation of acquisition outlays, which are usually undertaken at the beginning of an asset's service life, and of the actual interest payments on the capital still deployed in the project in the individual periods. In determining such an even distribution, a value trend is to be assumed for the investment in question. In the absence of more accurate information a linear value trend is usually assumed. If the acquisition cost of Procedure 1 is DM 50 000, and its disposal value is assumed to be DM 10 000 at the end of its normal service life of ten years then, adopting the linearity assumption, the initial value of DM 50 000 at the beginning of year 1 will decline linearly to DM 10 000 at the end of the tenth year (cp. Fig. 28).

Thus, the annual depreciation charges are computed from the relation:

$$\text{Annual depreciation charge} = \frac{\text{acquisition cost} - \text{disposal value at the end of the asset's useful service life}}{\text{useful service life in years}} \qquad (3.15)$$

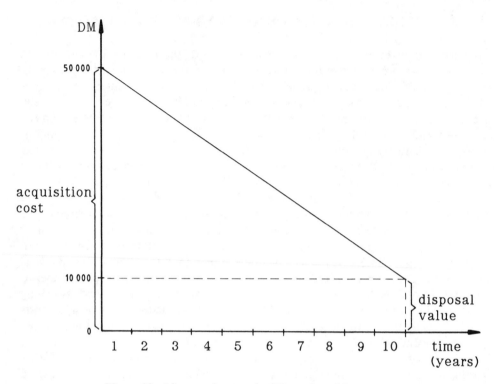

Figure 28 Linear value trend of Procedure 1 investment

Annual average notional interest is computed by reference to average capital employed:

$$\begin{matrix} \text{Annual} \\ \text{interest} = \\ \text{costs} \end{matrix} \frac{\begin{matrix} \text{acquisition cost} + \\ \text{disposal value at the end of the asset's useful service life} \end{matrix}}{2}$$

$$\cdot \frac{\text{notional interest rate}}{100} \tag{3.16}$$

The following values apply to Procedure 1 (a 10% notional interest rate is assumed):

Annual depreciation charges   (DM 50 000 − DM 10 000)/10 = DM 4000
Annual interest costs   [(DM 50 000 + DM 10 000)/2] · 10% = DM 3000
Other periodic fixed costs (maintenance, repairs, insurance,
     cost of space, fixed personnel costs, etc.)   DM 9000

_____

Annual fixed costs for Procedure 1   DM 16 000

The following values are assumed for Procedure 2:

Acquisition cost   DM 150 000
Useful service life   12 years
Disposal value at the end of the procedure's useful service life   DM 30 000

The related fixed costs of Procedure 2 may be classified as follows:

Annual depreciation charges	DM 10 000
Annual interest costs	DM 9 000
Other fixed costs	DM 17 000
Fixed costs for Procedure 2:	DM 36 000

The basis of the calculation of the fixed costs of the two procedures is the assumption that both will be deployed for their entire useful service lives. This assumption does not hold if, before the end of its ten-year useful service life, Procedure 1 is replaced by Procedure 2. In the latter event it would be necessary to check the accuracy of the assumption, about the *value trend* within the useful service life, against the circumstances as at the replacement date. On the other hand, in calculating the fixed costs of Procedure 2, it must be determined whether changes in the acquisition costs are included in the computation. The latter also include payments for delivery, machinery construction and installation, and other general set-up costs for Procedure 2. These magnitudes are perhaps calculated on the assumption of a completely new installation and must therefore be re-examined if Procedure 1 is to be replaced by Procedure 2. In certain circumstances, modification costs are incurred in respect of building alteration and reorganisation whilst other acquisition cost components may be saved.

The examination of the levels of fixed costs for Procedures 1 and 2 is related here to the consideration of the economic expediency of introducing the replacement investment in question. The implementation date of the replacement investment is significant because the appraisal of Procedure 1 can only be sensibly related to the (remaining) future years of its total useful service life. This not only means that it is necessary to check whether, in the light of the actual information, the values of the individual cost components are still realistic; most importantly it also means that the averages for determining the cost magnitudes must be restricted to the residual useful service life of Procedure 1. Values realised in past periods are irrelevant to the decision analysis of the replacement investment. The extent to which they deviate from previously-derived forecast values is perhaps of interest. Such deviations have, at most, an indirect influence, namely, to the extent that they result in the application of a corrective to forecast cost values for the residual useful service life discussed here.

The development of forecast and actual costs for Procedure 1 is recorded in Fig. 29. Columns (3), (4) and (5) contain values which were forecast before the start of the investment. Average annual fixed costs of DM 16 000 and average (linear) unit variable costs of DM 12 were calculated from these numbers. After the first six years the costs which actually arose are known and are shown in columns (6) and (7). Column (6) which records "other fixed costs" shows an actual six-year average which exceeds that which was originally forecast whereas the actual values of the procedure's variable costs are somewhat lower than their predicted values. In this example these deviations result in corresponding adjustments to the originally-forecast values for years 7 to 10 (inclusive).

Compared with the original forecasts, other fixed costs (cp. column (9)) and unit variable costs (cp. column (10)) are increased by 10% and reduced by DM 1.35 respectively.

Finally, the possible asset disposal value of Procedure 1 is also of significance. If the asset is displaced at the end of year 6, proceeds of DM 14 000 can be reckoned with.

Year	Forecast values at the start of the project					Values actually realised		Values forecast at the current planning date (end of year 6)		
	Depreciation	Interest	Disposal value	Other fixed costs (maintenance, repairs, insurance etc.)	Unit variable cost	Other fixed costs	Unit variable cost	Disposal value	Other fixed costs	Unit variable cost
	(1)	(2)	(3)	(4)	(5)	(6)	(7)	(8)	(9)	(10)
1				5 000.00	11.00	4 000.00	9.50			
2				8 000.00	11.00	8 500.00	9.70			
3				8 000.00	11.50	10 000.00	9.90			
4				8 000.00	11.50	9 500.00	10.60			
5				12 000.00	12.00	13 000.00	10.80			
6				9 000.00	12.00	10 000.00	10.80	14 000.00*		
(sub-total)	→	→	10 000.00*	(50 000.00)	(69.00)	(55 000.00)	(61.30)	8 000.00*		
7				9 000.00	12.50				9 900.00	11.15
8				10 000.00	12.50				11 000.00	11.15
9				10 000.00	13.00				11 000.00	11.65
10				11 000.00	13.00				12 100.00	11.65
Average	4 000.00	3 000.00		9 000.00	12.00				11 000.00	11.40

Annual fixed costs: DM 16 000.00

*At the end of the year

Figure 29 Development of costs for Procedure 1 whilst in service

This forecast value is perhaps supported by a firm offer from a potential purchaser or may at least be relatively well corroborated by market enquiries. The proceeds of the displaced asset at end-year 6 can be compared with the written down book value of the original investment. The latter is given by the original acquisition cost less the cumulative depreciation charges up to end-year 6:

Acquisition cost:	DM 50 000
− 6 · 4000	DM 24 000
Written down book value:	DM 26 000

The deviation between the possible disposal value from the written down book value can be variously interpreted. First, the disposal value may have been generally over-estimated. This would mean a lowering of the value trend line in Fig. 28 and require a reduction in the forecast disposal value at the end of the useful service life. Second, for the same terminal disposal value the form of the written down book value function can differ from that shown in Fig. 28, e.g. could be concave. A third possible explanation is that there is a difference between the external market's estimate of the "value" of the investment project and that of the firm itself. It is usually said that the market is not prepared to offer the full equivalent for the remaining capital employed as consideration for a cession of the project. In the present case the deviation at the end of year 6 amounts to DM 12 000. This is taken as a reason for reducing the forecast disposal value at end-year 10 from DM 10 000 to DM 8000.

The new forecast values in columns (8), (9) and (10) in Fig. 29 constitute the computational basis of the costs for the comparison of Procedure 1 with 2. Both the originally forecast values and those realised in the first six years are of no consequence to the cost computation. The (linear) unit variable costs for the remaining useful service life of four years (7 to 10 (inclusive)) can, as the average of the values in column (10) of Fig. 29, be estimated at DM 11.40. Similarly, the other fixed costs given in column (9) for the remaining four years of useful service life have an average value of DM 11 000. Depreciation charges and interest costs are based on the capital still deployed in the project. This latter value is, to a significant extent, of a hypothetical nature and can be variously estimated. The only fairly objective, verifiable approach lies in adopting the current disposal value as capital deployed (cp. Blohm and Lüder, 1983 [Investition] p. 151). Thus, at the beginning of the seventh year of useful service life, capital employed can be estimated at DM 14 000. The latter value declines to DM 8000 by the end of the tenth year. From these values the following depreciation charges and interest costs for the years 7 to 10 (inclusive) are obtained:

Annual depreciation charges	(DM 14 000 − DM 8000)/4 = DM 1500
Annual interest costs	[(DM 14 000 + DM 8000)/2] · 10% = DM 1100

It should be noted that in the case of the replacement investment, depreciation charges and interest costs should be based not only on the additional net investment outlays that are required, but on the total invested capital (cp. Blohm and Lüder, 1983 [Investition] p. 152 et seq.) because the residual resources that have hitherto been invested in the old asset continue to be deployed in the future. It is assumed that the acquisition cost of Procedure 2 on the change-over from Procedure 1 corresponds to the amount (given above) required for a new investment in Procedure 2 (DM 150 000). The following figures therefore emerge:

Expenditure on the change-over from Procedure 1 to Procedure 2 (acquisition cost of assets of Procedure 2, modifications to foundations, installation costs of new additional fixtures and fittings, adaptation of preceding and succeeding assets in the production life, retraining of personnel etc.):   DM 150 000
less proceeds realised from the sale of assets of Procedure 1 (net of removal and transport costs)   DM   14 000

Additional net investment outlays to be financed   DM 136 000
plus amount of investment which remains deployed (hitherto in the old asset, now in the new project)   DM   14 000

Total amount of investment   DM 150 000

The additional annual fixed costs which arise on the implementation of the replacement investment can now be computed as:

Annual depreciation charges
   Procedure 2   DM 10 000
   Procedure 1   DM   1 500

Additional depreciation charges resulting from the
   replacement investment   DM   8 500

Annual interest costs
   Procedure 2   DM 9 000
   Procedure 1   DM 1 100

Additional fixed costs resulting from the replacement investment   DM   7 900

Other periodic fixed costs
   Procedure 2   DM 17 000
   Procedure 1   DM 11 000

Additional other fixed costs resulting from the replacement
investment   DM   6 000

Total additional fixed costs resulting from the replacement
investment   DM   22 400

Following the implementation of the replacement investment, the annual fixed cost burden increases by (computed) additional fixed costs amounting to DM 22 400 compared with those which would arise on the retention of (existing) Procedure 1. The break-even analysis can be related to this amount. The constant unit variable cost savings which are juxtaposed with the additional fixed cost burden amount to (cp. Fig. 29, column (10)): DM $(11.40 - 5) = $ DM 6.40. Hence, the investment facilitating the change of procedure is advantageous if at least

$$x_0 = \frac{\text{DM } 22\,400.00}{\text{DM } 6.40/\text{unit}} = 3500 \text{ units}$$

are produced (and sold) annually. Figure 30 shows the graphical presentation.

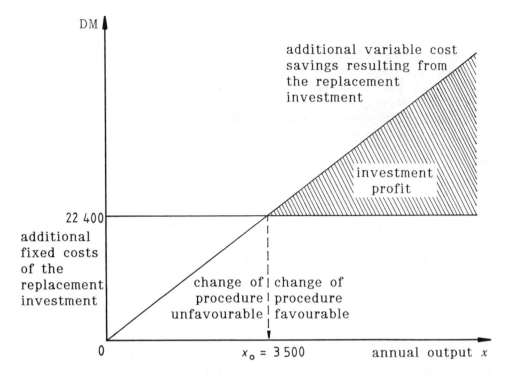

Figure 30 Profitability of a replacement investment (switch from Procedure 1 to Procedure 2)

The application of the method of break-even analysis that is presented above, to a replacement investment shows that in determining the additional fixed costs of the replacement investment it is generally not correct to take the difference between the independently (for a new investment) computed fixed costs of the two procedures (in this case DM 36 000 – DM 16 000 = DM 20 000). Similarly, it is not correct to take the corresponding difference between the constant unit variable costs (in this case DM 12 – DM 5 = DM 7). Instead the values which apply at the time of the decision should be used. In an exceptional case these will at best correspond only by chance with the latter cost differences. This is because in the present problem the decision is not a choice between Procedure 1 and Procedure 2. It is a choice, between the retention of Procedure 1 or a change-over from Procedure 1 to Procedure 2, at a point in time at which the former procedure has already been in service for a number of years. This means, firstly, that all cost magnitudes for Procedure 1 can only be related to its possible remaining service life and; secondly, that they must be up-dated by reference to the additional information which has arisen in the meanwhile. In particular, the disposal value which is actually realisable does not correspond to the written-down book value of the original asset. Additionally, the expenditure for the change-over from Procedure 1 to Procedure 2 differs from the independently-ascertained acquisition and installation expenditures for Procedure 2 so that a special computation is required for that reason too. The break-even point so determined provides some guidance for decision-making purposes on the question of whether the periodically-recurrent fixed cost supplement is "worthwhile", i.e. whether there is a commensurate saving in the constant unit variable costs. It must be questioned whether each year (or at least for an average of several years), a production volume can be achieved which exceeds the break-even output of 3500 units that is computed in the example. Only if this condition can be satisfied should a replacement investment be implemented. As regards the conception of the break-even analysis that is described above, it should be noted that this is a variant of the basic model and is therefore of a static type. Particularly in the case of a judgement about a typical multiperiod problem, like an investment decision, a static approach naturally proves to be especially problematic. It is subject to a number of restrictions all of which are ultimately ascribable to the non-recognition of the timing differences of costs (cp. Blohm and Lüder, 1983 [Investition] p. 153 et seq.). Thus, a multiperiod break-even analysis of problems of this nature is frequently more advisable (cp. 4.V).

V. INCLUSION OF INVENTORIES

Break-even analysis usually proceeds from the assumption that *output* and *sales volume levels* are equal. If this is not the case, inventory changes must be taken into account and the minimum production and sales volumes also fall apart. The computation of the break-even point depends on how the production costs of the inventory changes are ascertained. Moreover, the question that is to be answered with the aid of break-even analysis also plays a role. If the question is (say), "*At what level of output is neither a loss sustained nor profit achieved?*" the nature of the calculation remains unchanged. Should the question relate to *sales volume*, a distinction has to be made depending upon whether the inventory changes are valued on a full cost or partial cost basis. If, adopting the latter basis, they are valued at variable cost, the inventory changes have no effect on the structure of the break-even analysis because the contribution block remains unchanged. Only if constituents of the contribution block, allocated fixed costs or the profit mark-up, also enter the valuation of the inventory changes, is it necessary to modify the computation (cp. Chmielewicz, 1974 [Gewinnschwellenanalyse] p. 50). In the case of an inventory reduction, the sales volume relates to a larger contribution block. In the stocking up of a depot the contribution block is reduced by the amounts that are allocated to the inventory increase. Consider an inventory change of L units (in the case of an inventory addition, L is positive) and assume that the unit fixed cost overhead rate (and possibly profit etc.) applicable to that change amounts to k^f. The new contribution block $\tilde{B}$ is therefore given by:

$$\tilde{B} = B - L \cdot k^f. \tag{3.17}$$

If inventories are increased $(L > 0)$, the break-even point is lower because the contribution block is also lower. To determine the fixed costs overhead rate k^f which is charged to each unit of output, total production volume must, among other things, be known. In the simplest case of a full-cost computation of this nature, the fixed cost overhead rate of k^f per unit is determined by dividing total fixed costs by the production volume M:

$$k^f := \frac{K^f}{M}. \tag{3.18}$$

If, in the basic example, it is assumed that in a particular period a total output of 4000 units is produced, the fixed cost overhead rate per unit amounts to:

$$k^f = \frac{\text{DM } 16\,000}{4000 \text{ units}} = \text{DM } 4.00/\text{unit.}$$

If the production volume is expected to exceed the sales volume in the period in question there is a resultant inventory increase. In this example it is assumed to amount to $L = 500$ units. Hence, the contribution block is reduced by

$$L \cdot k^f = 500 \cdot \text{DM } 4 = \text{DM } 2000.$$

The break-even point is now no longer $x_0 = 2000$ units but is equal to:

$$\tilde{x}_0 = \frac{\tilde{B}}{d} = \frac{(16\,000 - 2000)}{8} = \frac{14\,000}{8} = 1750 \text{ units.}$$

This means that already at the 1751st unit of sales, profit will be attained. The lowering of the profit threshold lies in the fact that, because of the fixed cost allocation, profit of DM 2000 has already been "credited". However, because the corresponding 500 production units have merely increased the inventories, this profit is not yet realised. Thus, the crux of the matter is the allocated profit that is traceable to the full-cost principle. Correspondingly, an allocated loss would, in accordance with (3.17), be taken into account in a later period when the inventories are reduced. In that event the consequences would be a higher break-even point. These considerations indicate that the charging of fixed cost overhead rates to different volumes, in this case in the valuation of inventory changes, is subject to the same weaknesses as the entire full cost accounting system (cp. Schweitzer and Küpper, 1991 [Systeme] p. 296 et seq.).

VI. ALLOWING FOR SALES RISK

1. Components of Sales Risk

Break-even analysis is a planning instrument and, consequently, is an aid to the preparation of information about future processes. Break-even information is especially important for decisions on whether or not the manufacture of a given product ought to be undertaken. Using the results of break-even analysis, a decision can be related to magnitudes which, in the main, are readily definable. For instance, break-even analyses are undertaken, and expected sales volumes are forecast, in the planning of product innovations. Simply stated the decision then is: produce only if the forecast sales volume exceeds the break-even point. This approach is problematical in that it is based on deterministic forecasts of future sales volumes. Thus, the considerable risks which characterise such sales volume forecasts, and therefore the decision based thereon, are not taken into account.

The production decision risk lies in the possibility that an ex-post evaluation by reference to the sales volume actually achieved will indicate that an alternative decision would have been more profitable. In this event the forecast volume deviates from the actual sales volume (or that which would actually have been possible) to such a considerable extent that the forecast volume has led to an erroneous decision. Accordingly, this risk can be more concretely described as *sales risk*. This risk lies in the possibility of one of the two following outcomes, both of which prove to be unfavourable in product innovation decisions (cp. Bierman, Bonini and Hausman, 1981 [Analysis] p. 144; Coenenberg, 1967 [Absatzrisiko] p. 345 et seq.):

(1) The expected sales volume x^{exp} *exceeds* the break-even point x_0 and the product is therefore produced. But in the event it is only possible to sell volume x which is below the break-even point. The resultant loss V_1 amounting to the unrecovered fixed costs is given by:

$$V_1(x) = K^f - d \cdot x = d \cdot (x_0 - x). \qquad (3.19)$$

(2) The expected sales volume x^{exp} lies *below* the break-even point x_0 and production is not undertaken. It transpires later that a volume x, which exceeds the break-even output level, could have been sold. A profit equal to

$$V_2(x) = d \cdot (x - x_0) \qquad (3.20)$$

is therefore forgone.

Corresponding to the two unfavourable outcomes, there are two favourable outcomes which constitute an ex-post justification of the decision that was taken.

Proceeding from the assumption that a probability distribution can be specified for the multivalued sales volume expectation, from which an expected value can also be computed, the sales risk can be partitioned into three components (cp. Bierman, Bonini and Hausman, 1981 [Analysis] p. 147; Coenenberg, 1967 [Absatzrisiko] p. 347). The sales risk is correspondingly higher,

—the higher the unit contribution (because the possible losses increase accordingly);
—the nearer is the expected sales volume to the break-even point (because the scope for favourable sales volumes is correspondingly smaller);
—the greater is the dispersion of the probability distribution (because the greater is the probability that the actual sales volume deviates significantly from the forecast quantity).

Correspondingly the sales chances, i.e. the profit possibilities of a production decision, are higher,

—the higher the unit contribution (because the possible profits increase accordingly);
—the greater the deviation between the expected sales volume and the break-even point (because the scope for favourable sales volumes is all the greater);
—the smaller is the dispersion of the probability distribution (because the greater is the probability that the actual sales volume is in close proximity to the forecast sales volume).

A comparison indicates that, as components of sales risks and sales chances, the gap between expected sales volume and break-even point and the dispersion of the probability distribution are countervailing influences. On the other hand, the unit contribution intensifies both the sales risk and sales chances. Yet this points to the fact that in a risk evaluation the contribution margin does not influence an evaluation that is based on a *comparison* of quantified risks and quantified chances.

A satisfactory and correct inclusion of sales risk in break-even analyses requires a fundamental qualitative appraisal of individual risk components and, most importantly, also of the reliability and quality of the available information for forecasting sales volumes. This general analysis of risk can be supported with criteria that are comparatively easy to compute. Using such criteria an attempt is made to quantify sales risk. Five risk measures are primarily recommended (cp. also Coenenberg, 1967 [Absatzrisiko] p. 347 et seq.):

—the margin of safety,
—the probability of an erroneous decision,
—the risk-chance relation,
—the expected uncertainty costs,
—the risk level criterion.

2. The Margin of Safety as a Break-even Risk Measure

The computation of a *margin of safety* S is the simplest attempt to capture sales risk arithmetically (cp., e.g. Tucker, 1980 [Break-Even System] p. 44; 1973 [Einführung] p. 87 et seq.). It indicates the extent to which the expected sales volume $x^{\exp}$ can change before the break-even point x_0 is attained.

$$S = \frac{x^{\exp} - x_0}{x^{\exp}}. \tag{3.21}$$

It can be inferred from the definitional equation that the margin of safety is primarily intended for a situation in which the expected sales volume $x^{\exp}$ *exceeds* the break-even point x_0. In that event the coefficient is positive. In the case of sales forecasts which lie *below* the break-even point it takes on a negative value but is amenable to the same interpretation. The margin of safety is only a rough measure for capturing sales risk. As an individual value its predictive power is small. In comparing different applications (of the margin of safety), production orders can however be ranked by reference to an increasing margin: the greater the margin of safety the greater the extent to which forecasts can fluctuate without influencing the quality of the decision taken, i.e. the lower is the sales risk. Margins of safety for different cases can be compared without difficulty because, defined in accordance with (3.21), the margin of safety is a relative magnitude.

Nevertheless the weakness of this measure lies in the fact that it makes use neither of a valuation—attainable or contribution margins foregone do not enter the calculation—nor information on the probability of sales outcomes. Precisely the latter characteristic makes the margin of safety a dubious and, in some circumstances, dangerous instrument (cp. also Coenenberg, 1969 [Entscheidungskriterien] p. 177 et seq.). Of the possible sales volumes, the margin of safety only takes account of those between x_0 and $x^{\exp}$. Moreover, the possible sales volumes that are included are unweighted, i.e. all volumes are taken (at least implicitly) to be equiprobable.

3. The Probability of an Erroneous Decision as a Break-even Risk Measure

In using the *probability of an erroneous decision*, the intention is to find a quantitative expression for the risk of taking an inadequate decision. Assuming that a decision to produce will be taken, this is a question of the probability that the sales volume is below the break-even point. This is called the *probability of a loss* (cp. Coenenberg, 1967 [Absatzrisiko] p. 348). The probability of an erroneous decision for this case can therefore be specifically defined as:

probability of an erroneous decision F (if production is undertaken)
$\quad\quad$:= probability of sales volumes occurring which lie
$\quad\quad\quad\quad$ below the break-even point x_0: $p\{x < x_0\}$. $\hfill$ (3.22)

On the other hand, a decision not to produce becomes an erroneous decision if, after the event, it turns out that a profitable sales level could have been attained. The probability of the latter can be specified as:

probability of an erroneous decision F (if production is not undertaken)
$\quad\quad$:= probability of sales volumes occurring which are
$\quad\quad\quad\quad$ above the break-even point x_0: $p\{x > x_0\}$. $\hfill$ (3.23)

The definition for this second case indicates that it is a question of the *probability of earning a profit*.

The matters so far considered can be illustrated with an example. The break-even point for a product, with fixed costs and unit contribution of DM 16 000 and DM 8 respectively, is 2000 units. In addition, production capacity is now assumed to be 6000 units.

Depending upon the information relating to future sales volumes, there are various ways of proceeding. For a decision based on imperfect information it is, as a basis for further considerations, most convenient to assume a complete probability distribution for the region of possible sales volumes. Here, for illustrative purposes, it is assumed that the sales volume is normally distributed with a mean of 2500 and standard deviation of 750 units. This actually means that a specific probability is assigned to each positive (and each negative) sales volume even though such probabilities decline rapidly with increasing deviations from the mean value of 2500 units. Thus, meaningless sales volumes are also depicted in the model. In particular, negative numbers and values exceeding the production maximum of 6000 units are included. But it should also be acknowledged that the specifying of a continuous standard distribution function anyway represents an approximation which, among other things, is chosen in order to exploit the computational advantages of this type of function. Moreover, in order to be able to work correctly within the model, the probability function must be truncated to the left and right. The missing values which make up the total probability to one must then be distributed proportionately in order to have a probability function which conforms to the rules. The results are likely to be little affected because of the insignificance of the correction but the computational advantages are gained from the choice of a normal distribution. To the extent that this is justifiable, i.e., if the parts of the probability function that are to be cut off constitute no more than an insignificant probability, this additional error can be readily accepted in most cases in addition to the approximation error which is present anyway.

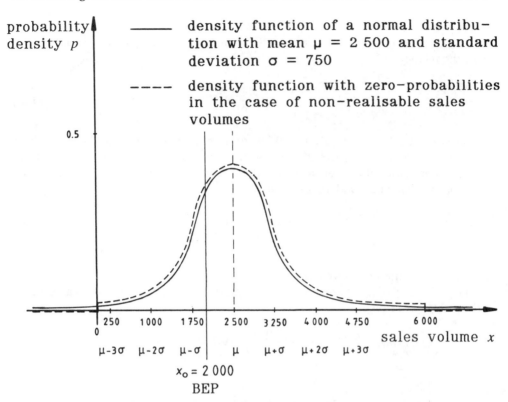

probability
density p

——— density function of a normal distribution with mean μ = 2 500 and standard
deviation σ = 750

‒ ‒ ‒ ‒ density function with zero-probabilities
in the case of non-realisable sales
volumes

Figure 31 Approximation of the probability distribution for the sales volume with a truncated
and a complete normal distribution density function

Figure 31 shows the density function for the normal distribution given in the example. To the left of the zero quantity, and to the right of the sales volume of 6000 units, the probability of the event must actually be zero. It can be seen that in approximating the sales probabilities with the normal distribution given above (cp. the continuous curve in Fig. 31), the probabilities in these regions are indeed not equal to zero but they only deviate from zero to an insignificant extent. If the integral under the normal distribution density function is calculated between the (limiting meaningful) values of sales volumes of 0 and 6000, the result is 0.999 569 4 instead of the required value of 1 for an exact computation. This means that, in this example, it is necessary to multiply all probability densities in the region of interest with the factor 1.000 43 in order to work correctly (dashed curve in Fig. 31). It is obvious that this changes the absolute numbers only to a negligible extent. In the interests of a simpler computation this deviation can therefore be accepted especially since the truncated normal distribution is an approximation anyway.

If, following these preliminary considerations, a normal distribution with a mean value $\mu = 2500$ and a standard deviation $\sigma = 750$ is now assumed, the probability of an erroneous decision can be simply ascertained:

The break-even level is 2000 units. The density of the standard normal distribution (mean value = 0, standard deviation = 1) is denoted with $\varphi(z)$ at point x and its integral to the value z is represented by $\Phi(z)$, i.e. $\Phi(z)$ gives the probability that the variable in question takes on a value which is smaller than or, at most, equal to x. In accordance with the relation

$$z = \frac{x - \mu}{\sigma},$$

(3.24)

in this case namely, $z = (x - 2500)/750$, every normal distribution can be traced back to the standard normal distribution for which functional values of interest are to be found in numerical tables (for the values that are relevant here see the tabular extracts in Appendix II). The standardised value

$$z = \frac{2000 - 2500}{750} = -\frac{2}{3}$$

corresponds to the break-even point $x = 2000$.

The probability of an erroneous decision if production is undertaken is, in accordance with (3.22), given by:

$$F_{\substack{\text{undertaking} \\ \text{production}}} = p\{x < 2000\} = \int_{-\infty}^{-2/3} \varphi(x)\, dx$$

$$= \Phi\left(-\frac{2}{3}\right)$$

$$= 0.2525$$

$$= 25.25\%.$$

Correspondingly, the probability of an erroneous decision if production is not undertaken is given by (3.23):

$$F_{\substack{\text{not undertaking} \\ \text{production}}} = p\{x > 2000\} = \int_{-2/3}^{\infty} \varphi(x)\, dx$$

$$= 1 - \int_{-\infty}^{-2/3} \varphi(x)\, dx = 1 - \Phi\left(-\frac{2}{3}\right)$$

$$= 1 - 0.252\,5 = 0.747\,5 = 74.75\%.$$

For the computation of the numerical values, the table of cumulative probability values in Appendix II was used.

In questioning the predictive power of the computed probabilities of an erroneous decision, it can first be noted that, in the present example, the risk in not undertaking production is almost three times as great as that of undertaking production. This means that in undertaking production a much smaller probability of an erroneous decision must be reckoned with. It is also obvious from both the definition and the computation that the probabilities of the two possible decisions add up to 100%. Consequently, in accordance with this risk measure, the situation appears to be the more uncertain the closer the two values are to each other. In the limit, the two probabilities of an erroneous decision are each 50%. Here the risk is at its highest and the decision is then at its most difficult. If it is assumed that the decision taken is that which has the lower probability of being erroneous, then the risk level of the chosen alternative is always no more than 50%. It can now be questioned to what extent the probability of an erroneous decision adequately captures the individual components of sales risk (cp. Section VI.1) in a practical sense. Assuming a normal distribution, the risk indicator of the probability of an erroneous decision is larger (and therefore closer to 50%) the greater is the standard deviation and the closer is the proximity of the break-even point to the mean value of the distribution. These components of sales risk are captured in this way. In contrast, the level of the contribution margin is not captured in this risk measure and it does not influence the probability of an erroneous decision.

It should be pointed out that the same form of computation and interpretation of the probability of an erroneous decision apply to other, especially discrete, distribution functions (see the following example). Particularly noteworthy is the case in which probabilities facilitating a quantitative evaluation of the individual sales possibilities can in no way be assumed. If a risk measure is nevertheless to be computed, it is necessary to work with assumptions. The simplest approach is to assume equal probabilities in the relevant region. In the example, all sales volumes between 0 and 6000 would be ascribed a probability of 1/6000:

$$p(x) = \begin{cases} \dfrac{1}{6000} & \text{for } 0 < x \leqslant 6000 \\ 0 & \text{otherwise.} \end{cases} \tag{3.25}$$

Thus the probabilities of an erroneous decision can be computed as above. The probabilities of an erroneous decision are given by:

$$F_{\substack{\text{undertaking} \\ \text{production}}} = p\{x < 2000\} = \int_0^{2000} \frac{1}{6000}\, dx$$

$$= \frac{2000}{6000} = \frac{1}{3} \tag{3.26}$$

$$F_{\substack{\text{not undertaking} \\ \text{production}}} = p\{x > 2000\} = \int_{2000}^{6000} \frac{1}{6000}\, dx$$

$$= \frac{6000 - 2000}{6000} = \frac{2}{3}.$$

Also, on the assumption of equal probabilities the risk of an erroneous decision in not undertaking production ($F = 2/3$) is significantly higher than the risk of an erroneous decision in undertaking production. In assuming equal probabilities, the upper limit of the analysis (here 6000 units) is of greater significance than in the case of distributions which, like the normal distribution, flatten out at the extremes. It is therefore strongly emphasised that, instead of the capacity limit, a maximum demand quantity or another more suitable value can be used. Subject to the qualification of greater uncertainty because of less precise starting information, the probability of an erroneous decision if equal probabilities are assumed, can be interpreted in the same way as the corresponding probability for other types of distribution.

4. The Risk-chance Relation as a Break-even Measure

The fact that a risk measure of the kind hitherto presented does not allow for the risk components of the contribution margin level, induced Kolbe (1967 [Theorie] p. 55 et seq.) to propose a generalised risk measure which he calls *risk-chance relation*. He considers only the case of a weak information base, which initially does not include a probability distribution, and therefore assumes equal probabilities. Additionally he starts, albeit using different designations, with the probabilities of an erroneous decision. Assuming equal probabilities, this risk measure can also be construed as a range relationship on the sales volume axis. Figure 32 indicates that, in the illustrative case, undertaking production refers to the relation of the range 0 to 2000 to the range 0 to 6000. This consideration induced Kolbe (1967 [Theorie] p. 59 et seq.) to propose an extension to the (additional) inclusion of the contribution margin components in

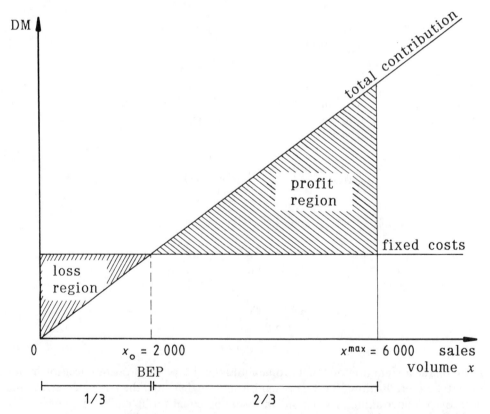

Figure 32 Presentation of the probability of an erroneous decision (equal probabilities assumption) together with the profit and loss regions for the computation of the risk-chance relation

the risk measure. This extension constitutes a comparison of the *areas* representing the loss region and the combined loss and profit regions as presented in Fig. 32 (cp. Kolbe, 1967 [Theorie] p. 66), as a replacement for the comparison of the range relationships:

Risk-chance relation:

$$\tilde{R}_{\substack{\text{undertaking}\\\text{production}}} := \frac{\text{loss region}}{\text{loss region} + \text{profit region}} \tag{3.27}$$

Analogous to the risk-chance relation if production is undertaken is the corresponding relation for the rejection of production:

Risk-chance relation:

$$\tilde{R}_{\substack{\text{not undertaking}\\\text{production}}} := \frac{\text{region of profit forgone}}{\text{loss region} + \text{profit region}} \tag{3.28}$$

The rationale of the risk-chance relation is that the loss or profit regions represent the multiplication of the previous ranges on the sales volume axis with corresponding values.

Generally this calculation can be greatly simplified by using the following computation of the loss and profit regions:

$$\text{Loss region} = \int_0^{x_0} (K^f - d \cdot x)\, dx = \left(K^f - \frac{d}{2} \cdot x_0\right) \cdot x_0 = \frac{K^f}{2} \cdot x_0$$

$$\tag{3.29}$$

$$\text{Profit region} = \int_{x_0}^{x^{\max}} (d \cdot x - K^f)\, dx = \left(\frac{d}{2} \cdot x^{\max} - K^f\right) \cdot x^{\max} + \frac{K^f}{2} \cdot x_0$$

The risk-chance relation if production is undertaken then reduces to:

$$\tilde{R}_{\substack{\text{undertaking}\\\text{production}}} = \frac{\dfrac{K^f \cdot x_0}{2}}{\left(\dfrac{d}{2} \cdot x^{\max} - K^f\right) \cdot x^{\max} + \dfrac{K^f}{2} \cdot x_0 + \dfrac{K^f}{2} \cdot x_0}$$

$$= \frac{1}{\left(\dfrac{x^{\max}}{x_0} - 2\right) \cdot \dfrac{x^{\max}}{x_0} + 2}$$

$$= \frac{1}{\left(\dfrac{x^{\max}}{x_0} - 1\right)^2 + 1}. \tag{3.30}$$

The analogous computation when production is rejected is:

$$\tilde{R}_{\substack{\text{not undertaking} \\ \text{production}}} = \frac{1}{1 + \dfrac{1}{\left(\dfrac{x^{\max}}{x_0} - 1\right)^2}} . \qquad (3.31)$$

In the example considered hitherto, the following values emerge:

$$\text{Loss region} = (16\,000 - 8000) \cdot 2000 = 16 \text{ mill.}$$
$$\text{Profit region} = (24\,000 - 16\,000) \cdot 6000 + 16 \text{ mill.} = 64 \text{ mill.}$$

Risk-chance relation if production is undertaken:

$$\tilde{R}_{\text{undertaking production}} = \frac{16 \text{ mill.}}{16 \text{ mill.} + 64 \text{ mill.}} = 20\%$$

or using (3.30)

$$\tilde{R}_{\text{not undertaking production}} = \frac{1}{(3-1)^2 + 1} = \frac{1}{5} = 20\%$$

According to Kolbe (cp. 1967 [Theorie] p. 66), the risk measure so obtained—he also calls it a "risk level"—comprehensively expresses managerial risk. Nevertheless the usefulness of the risk-chance relation is extremely dubious. Coenenberg (cp. 1967 [Absatzrisiko] p. 352) raises the objection that its definition is based on the assumption of equiprobable realisable sales volumes. This shortcoming seriously restricts the scope for applying this risk measure. It is thus not clear how the profit and loss areas are to be weighted if additional (unequal) probabilities for the sales volumes are to be taken into account.

However, even if (possible) sales volumes with equal probabilities can be justifiably assumed, the risk-chance relation has little predictive power. The applicability of the calculation is subject to the restriction that the maximum demand does not exceed the maximum production level (and therefore the maximum sales volume). Whilst, as suggested above, e.g. in the computation of an erroneous decision, the probability of a demand exceeding both the production and sales volumes level can also be included without difficulty (thereby correctly reducing the probability of an erroneous decision in undertaking production), this is not possible in the case of the risk-chance relation. In that, in the latter case, the profit region is dealt with explicitly, the highest sales volume that can be allowed for is the capacity limit. Even if a greater demand is considered possible, the risk-chance relation is not reduced by it although the sales risks undoubtedly become smaller.

Furthermore the transformation (3.30) shows that, in the computation of the risk-chance relation, no value standards of any kind are finally taken into account. The magnitude of the risk-chance relation is determined exclusively by the ratio of the maximum level of production to the break-even point ($x^{\max} : x_0$). Hence, the risk-chance relation is a direct unique function of the "probability of an erroneous decision", that was described above given the assumption of equal probabilities. The predictive power of the previously normalised magnitude $x^{\max}/x_0$ does not, however, increase because it is subject to a transformation as in (3.30). In sum, the risk-chance relation can therefore be regarded as a heuristic conception of a risk index which, from the standpoint of predictive power, does not go beyond the simple probability of an erroneous decision in the equal probabilities case. It has no logical basis and, moreover, its scope for application is restricted to a few cases. It therefore hardly facilitates an adequate interpretation.

5. Expected Uncertainty Costs as a Break-even Risk Measure

The components of sales risk are fully and convincingly captured by *expected uncertainty costs*. The basic idea underlying this approach is the capturing of sales risk with a cost magnitude. This at least ensures that the individual components are not only weighted with their probabilities of occurrence but also with their values. The conception of uncertainty costs rests on the computation of losses or forgone profits which are the consequence of an erroneous decision. A decision to produce results in a loss if the quantity demanded x is below the break-even point x_0. The loss is equal to $V_1(x)$ (cp. (3.19)). It can be interpreted as a numerical expression of *uncertainty*. Simultaneously it indicates the value that can be ascribed to information about the actual sales volume. The money amount $V_1(x)$ is at stake; for the procurement of perfect information about the product sales possibilities, no more than DM $V_1(x)$ should have been paid. It is different if the actual sales volume x exceeds (as expected) the break-even point x_0. In that case no loss arises; also the value of the corresponding information would be nil—the decision would not turn out differently. Thus, in the case of sales volumes x, which exceed the break-even point x_0, the *uncertainty costs* are to be assessed at zero. In the case of a decision to undertake production, the resultant uncertainty cost function is given by:

$$U_{\substack{\text{undertaking} \\ \text{production}}}(x) = \begin{cases} V_1(x) = d \cdot (x_0 - x) & \text{for } x < x_0 \\ 0 & \text{otherwise.} \end{cases} \tag{3.32}$$

Because the actual sales volume is not known, the possible uncertainty costs for all conceivable sales volumes must be summarised in a single measure. To this end it is helpful if, for each possible realisable volume x, a probability density $\pi(x)$ can be given. If so, the following expected value $E(U)$ can be computed in the case in question (cp. Coenenberg, 1967 [Absatzrisiko] p. 349):

$$E(U_{\substack{\text{undertaking} \\ \text{production}}}) = \int_0^\infty U_{\substack{\text{undertaking} \\ \text{production}}}(x) \cdot \pi(x)\, dx$$

$$= \int_0^{x_0} V_1(x) \cdot \pi(x)\, dx. \tag{3.33}$$

In the latter expression, the uncertainty costs $U(x)$ of possible sales volumes are weighted with their probabilities and summed. The expected value so obtained is a measure of the sales risk of the product in question in the case of a decision to undertake production.

Corresponding calculations can be made for a decision not to produce (cp. (3.20)):

$$U_{\substack{\text{not undertaking} \\ \text{production}}}(x) = \begin{cases} V_2(x) = d \cdot (x - x_0) & \text{for } x > x_0 \\ 0 & \text{otherwise} \end{cases} \tag{3.34}$$

$$E(U_{\substack{\text{not undertaking} \\ \text{production}}}) = \int_0^\infty U_{\substack{\text{not undertaking} \\ \text{production}}}(x) \cdot \pi(x)\, dx$$

$$= \int_{x_0}^\infty V_2(x) \cdot \pi(x)\, dx. \tag{3.35}$$

In both cases the value of the expected uncertainty costs expresses the sales risk quantitatively. This is also of special interest if, when innovation decisions are contemplated, different products need to be compared. Furthermore, in the context of break-even analysis, the expected value of uncertainty costs indicates the maximum amount that can be expended in gaining additional information about future sales volumes. Complete information about the future sales volume has (at most) a value equal to the maximum loss that would be sustained in the absence of that knowledge, i.e. in the event of a decision based on existing information (cp. Bierman, Bonini and Hausman, 1981 [Analysis] p. 144). This magnitude is given by the expected value of uncertainty costs. Hence, the expected value given by formula (3.33) should be chosen if, without further information, production would be undertaken, whereas formula (3.35) should be used if, in the absence of additional information, production would not be undertaken.

Assume that a normal distribution with density function $\varphi_{\mu, \sigma}$ is adopted as the probability information for sales volumes and that, for the reasons already outlined above, the region of possible sales volumes is again extended from $-\infty$ to the left and $+\infty$ to the right. Hence, making use of formula (3.32) or (3.34), the expected uncertainty costs can be derived from formulae (3.33) and (3.35):

Expected value of uncertainty costs

—if production is undertaken:

$$E(U_{\substack{\text{undertaking} \\ \text{production}}}) = \int_{-\infty}^{x_0} d \cdot (x_0 - x) \cdot \varphi_{\mu, \sigma}(x) \, dx \tag{3.36}$$

—if production is not undertaken:

$$E(U_{\substack{\text{not undertaking} \\ \text{production}}}) = \int_{x_0}^{\infty} d \cdot (x - x_0) \cdot \varphi_{\mu, \sigma}(x) \, dx. \tag{3.37}$$

In the earlier example the mean and standard deviation amount to $\mu = 2500$ and $\sigma = 750$ respectively. The expected value of the uncertainty costs if production is undertaken can, using the transformation in Appendix I, therefore be computed in accordance with formula (A.5) (cp. also Bierman, Bonini and Hausman, 1981 [Analysis] p. 147 et seq.):

$$d = 8; \qquad x_0 = 2000;$$

$$z_0 = \frac{x_0 - \mu}{\sigma} = \frac{2000 - 2500}{750} = -\frac{2}{3}$$

$$E(U_{\substack{\text{undertaking} \\ \text{production}}}) = d \cdot \sigma \cdot \Omega(-z_0) \tag{3.38}$$

$$= 8 \cdot 750 \cdot \Omega(2/3).$$

The value $\Omega(2/3)$ in Table A.3 of Appendix II is 0.1511. Using the latter value,

$$E(U_{\substack{\text{undertaking} \\ \text{production}}}) = 8 \cdot 750 \cdot 0.1511 = 906.60$$

is the computed value of the expected value of the uncertainty costs if production is undertaken. Analogously, using formulae (3.37), (A.7) and (A.6), $E(U_{\text{not undertaking production}})$ is given by:

$$
\begin{aligned}
E(U_{\substack{\text{not undertaking} \\ \text{production}}}) &= d \cdot \sigma \cdot \Omega(z_0) \\
&= 8 \cdot 750 \cdot \Omega(-2/3) \\
&= 8 \cdot 750 \cdot [\,\Omega(2/3) + 2/3\,] \\
&= 8 \cdot 750 \cdot [\,0.1511 + 0.6667\,] \\
&= 4\,906.60.
\end{aligned} \tag{3.39}
$$

The values can be interpreted as follows: if a decision to produce is taken, then, should the sales volume be less than the break-even level, an average loss of DM 906.60 is to be expected. If it is decided not to produce, average profit amounting to DM 4 906.60 is forgone in a situation in which a sales volume exceeding the break-even point would have been possible.

If the expected value orientation on which this computation is based is adopted for decision-making purposes, the computed uncertainty costs facilitate a further proposition: if production is decided upon, no more than DM 906.60 can justifiably be paid for complete information. Moreover, in that in the event of a loss, costs of only DM 906.60 are expected, then, in accordance with this conception, no more than this amount should be paid for information on whether the loss will materialise or not.

Coenenberg (cp. 1969 [Entscheidungskriterien] p. 175 et seq.) shows that a strict expected uncertainty cost orientation presumes a particular *risk-preference relation* on the part of the decision-maker. This elucidates the fact that the expected uncertainty costs cannot be drawn upon directly as a decision magnitude and only capture risk in a particular numerical manner. If it is intended to evaluate and rank existing production alternatives with each other with the aid of a magnitude which includes risk, a prior transformation into utility criteria using a Bernoulli utility function is more advisable. In the latter event, magnitude-dependent risk-preferences can be suitably portrayed (on this issue cp. Coenenberg, 1969 [Entscheidungskriterien] p. 178 et seq., p. 186 et seq.).

6. The Ratio of Expected Costs and Expected Profits as a Break-even Risk Measure

Logically pursuing a notion based upon a computation of uncertainty costs leads to a consideration of expected advantages. In deciding upon production this means that, in addition to expected losses in the unfavourable case, the expected profits in the favourable case are also computed. If they are defined analogously to the uncertainty costs, it can be seen that they correspond exactly to the costs specified in (3.37). The losses of DM 906.60 which are expected in the unfavourable case thus compare with the profits of DM 4 906.60 which are expected in the favourable case.

Hence, in supplementing the previous risk measures, the concept of uncertainty costs can also be employed as a relative risk measure. The expected uncertainty costs can thus be related to the expected profits of the favourable case and thereby express the relationship between the loss expectation and profit expectation as a *risk level* $\hat{R}$:

Risk level if production is undertaken:

—for the example: $\hat{R} = $ DM 906.60/DM 4 906.60 $= 18.5\%$

—in general:

$$\hat{R} = \frac{\text{expected uncertainty costs in the unfavourable case}}{\text{expected profits in the favourable case}} \tag{3.40}$$

Assuming normally-distributed sales volumes, and using computational formula (A.5) as well as (A.7) with (A.6), this definition can be transformed as follows:

$$\hat{R}_{\substack{\text{undertaking} \\ \text{production}}} = \frac{d \cdot \sigma \cdot \Omega(-z_0)}{d \cdot \sigma \cdot \Omega(z_0)} = \frac{d \cdot \sigma \cdot \Omega(-z_0)}{d \cdot \sigma \cdot [\Omega(-z_0) - z_0]}$$

$$= \frac{1}{1 + \dfrac{(-z_0)}{\Omega(-z_0)}} \tag{3.41}$$

If it is decided not to produce the analogous definition is:

Risk level if production is not undertaken:

$$\hat{R} = \frac{\text{expected uncertainty costs in the unfavourable case (i.e. profit forgone)}}{\text{expected profits in the favourable case (i.e. obviated losses)}} \tag{3.42}$$

A transformation as in (3.41) gives:

$$\hat{R}_{\substack{\text{not undertaking} \\ \text{production}}} = \frac{1}{1 + \dfrac{z_0}{\Omega(z_0)}} \tag{3.43}$$

The latter measure expresses the sales risk by reference to all of the above-mentioned (p. 74 et seq.) components; in particular the sales volume probabilities of occurrence act as weights in the calculation. The transformation (3.41) shows that ultimately the risk level $\hat{R}$ is independent of the absolute level of the contribution margin. Whilst, as always, the unit contribution d naturally enters the computation of the break-even point x_0, it is, on the other hand, directly taken into account only in the absolute uncertainty costs. By contrast the standard deviation is explicitly required for transforming the standardised value z_0 in (3.41) and it therefore exercises a direct influence on the risk level.

The definition and formulae for the risk level make it clear that this is a question of a comparison of *partial expected values* for the favourable and unfavourable situations. Hence the predictive power of the risk level criterion goes beyond the probability of an erroneous decision to the extent that it not only captures the risk of a decision as a probability of occurrence but, in addition, also takes account of the (relative) level of disadvantages which arise in a situation that is characterised by risk.

In the case of a normal distribution, both risk measures can be computed, in accordance with (3.24), from the standardised values z_0 of the break-even point. The formulae show that, compared with the probability of an erroneous decision, the risk level criterion does not rank the alternatives in a different order. It does, however, change the ranking intervals between successively ranked alternatives. This is of special significance in situations in which not only the most advantageous alternative from a given group is sought but in which propositions about the "similarity" of risk are to be made. Products which show significantly disparate risks judged by reference to the risk level criterion may, in some circumstances, be shown to be of almost equal risk when evaluated by reference to the probability of an erroneous decision and vice versa.

Compared with the concept of uncertainty costs it can be stated that the risk level criterion expresses the partial loss expectation in relative terms. The advantage of a relative measure over an absolute measure is that the expected disadvantages (the uncertainty costs) can be viewed in relation to the corresponding advantages (the profit chances). However, if a decision is to be well-based, both the absolute and relative magnitudes of uncertainty costs are of interest (see in this regard the example presented in Fig. 33). It should be noted that formula (3.37) is only usable as the computational basis of the expected profits in (3.40) because, in the simple relationship presented here, profits forgone are taken to be the uncertainty costs that are incurred when production is not undertaken. The conception so characterised can also be readily applied if the uncertainty costs are otherwise defined. Under certain circumstances there is then a loss of the symmetry between (3.36) and (3.37).

7. Comparison of the Individual Risk Measures

To conclude the treatment of sales risk in the basic break-even model, the individual risk measures are (in three examples) again juxtaposed. In the first example, this is a question of comparing three alternative products, A, B and C, one of which is to be chosen for production. One of the products is that which has served as the example hitherto. It is now designated product A and it is juxtaposed with a product B, the future sales volume of which can also be represented in the form of a normal distribution. All relevant data are listed in Fig. 33 and all risk measures hitherto examined are computed for the three alternative products.

The product of the expected sales volume (i.e. expected value of the normal distribution in question) and unit contribution less fixed costs, gives DM 4000 for A and B and DM 4900 for product C. Hence, the expected profits are positive in all three cases and indicate that production should be undertaken.

The decision, corresponding to this favourable forecast, which results in the choice of *the product that is to be manufactured* is now examined. If the decision is based on profit expectations, product C would be the best alternative with the other two products being ranked equally. Because of the non-deterministic character of the information, it is however advisable also to draw on risk measures in making the decision. A comparison of the magnitudes for the individual alternatives that are shown in Fig. 33 indicates that, the decision that would be taken depends upon the risk measure that is applied. It is not however only the preferred "best" alternative, and therefore the ranking of alternatives, which changes with respect to the individual risk measures. In a pairwise comparison it also turns out that, in the case of risk measures which give

Production alternatives	Product A	Product B	Product C	
Data:				
fixed costs K^f	DM 16 000.00	DM 24 750.00	DM 26 600.00	
unit variable cost k^v	DM 12.00	DM 7.75	DM 9.00	
unit sales revenue q	DM 20.00	DM 14.00	DM 16.00	
production capacity limit x^{max}	6000 units	11 000 units	10 000 units	Evaluation of alter-
assumed probability distribution of sales p	Normal distribution	Normal distribution	Normal distribution	natives by reference
mean value μ	2500 units	4600 units	4 500 units	to the
standard deviation σ	750 units	875 units	1 000 units	respective
Computations:				risk
unit contribution d	DM 8.00	DM 6.25	DM 7.00	measures
break-even output x_0	2000 units	3960 units	3800 units	($\geqslant$: denotes
expected value of total profit	DM 4 000.00	DM 4 000.00	DM 4 900.00	preferred)
Risk measures if it is decided to produce:				
margin of safety S given by (3.21) ($x^{exp}: = E(x) = \mu$)	20.0%	13.9%	15.6%	$A \geqslant C \geqslant B$
Probability of an erroneous decision F given by (3.22)	25.3%	23.2%	24.2%	$B \geqslant C \geqslant A$
[ditto assuming equal probabilities]	[33.3%]	[36.0%]	[38.0%]	$[A \geqslant B \geqslant C]$
[Risk-chance relation $\tilde{R}$ given by (3.30) (equal probabilities distribution necessarily assumed)]	[20.0%]	[24.0%]	[27.3%]	$[A \geqslant B \geqslant C]$
Expected value of uncertainty costs U given by (3.38)	DM 906.60	DM 740.78	DM 1 000.30	$B \geqslant A \geqslant C$
risk level $\hat{R}$ given by (3.41)	18.5%	15.6%	17.0%	$B \geqslant C \geqslant A$

Figure 33 Evaluation of the production of three alternative products with different risk measures assuming a continuous probability distribution for sales volume

consistent rankings, the relative evaluation intervals are completely different. This emphasises that the individual measurements capture different aspects of business sales risk or that they are heuristic magnitudes with limited predictive power. Of special interest in Fig. 33 is the comparison of alternatives A and C which exhibit different profit expectations. This is not taken into account in the simpler risk measures. Because of the small interval between the expected sales volume and break-even point, product C is actually ascribed a higher risk by the margin of safety whilst the "probability of an erroneous decision" for C is smaller than that of A. It is however important that alternative C indeed exhibits higher uncertainty costs but a lower "risk level' than alternative A. Here it is seen that, notwithstanding its higher uncertainty costs, the profit-loss relationship of alternative C is more favourable than that of alternative A. If then the absolute level of uncertainty costs of approximately DM 1000 appears tolerable to the decision-maker, he will, in comparing A and C, judge alternative C to be more favourable because its uncertainty costs are matched by relatively greater profit expectations ($17\% < 18.5\%$) than in the case of alternative A. It may be objected that the higher profit chances of C are already evident from the total profit expectation. Here DM 4900 in the case of C are matched by only DM 4000 in the case of A. However, the case of product B reveals the difference in the ranking by the total expected value of profits and the ranking in accordance with (examined in an appropriate relation) partial-expected values of profits and losses. Judged by reference to "risk level", product B is ranked as the most advantageous. It has a "risk level" of 15.6%, compared with 18.5% in the case of A, whilst both products each have a total profit expectation of DM 4000.

If the total profit expectation is the same for two alternatives, the uncertainty costs and the "risk level" concepts essentially lead, in other respects, to the same evaluation of alternatives. This is made clear in the following transformation. The profit expectation G can be written:

$$G = \mu \cdot d - K^f = \mu \cdot d - x_0 \cdot d = (\mu - x_0) \cdot d \qquad (3.44)$$

Using (3.24) the standard deviation σ can be presented as

$$\sigma = \frac{\mu - x_0}{-z_0}.$$

Substituting the latter into the formula (3.38) for the expected uncertainty costs yields:

$$E(U) = d \cdot \sigma \cdot \Omega(-z_0) = d \cdot \left(\frac{\mu - x_0}{-z_0} \right) \cdot \Omega(-z_0) \qquad (3.45)$$

$$= d \cdot (\mu - x_0) \cdot \frac{\Omega(-z_0)}{-z_0} = G \cdot \frac{\Omega(-z_0)}{-z_0}.$$

Consequently, using the risk level formula (3.41), the expected uncertainty costs are, after the following simple transformation, ascertainable from the total profit expectation and risk level:

$$E(U) = G \cdot \frac{1}{\frac{1}{\hat{R}} - 1}. \qquad (3.46)$$

This relationship clearly shows that two alternative products with the same profit expectation G are ranked the same way with both the expected uncertainty costs criterion and the risk level criterion. Figure 33 indicates that, in accordance with the uncertainty costs criterion, and also in accordance with the risk level criterion, alternative B is preferable to alternative A. Overall it can be concluded that the absolute level of the expected uncertainty costs is especially significant if the alternatives that are to be evaluated have different total profit expectations. It is then advisable to determine

Appraisal of a decision in favour of production	Production A"					

Data:
  fixed costs K^f
  unit variable costs k^v
  unit sales revenue q
  production capacity
  limit x^{max}
  assumed probability
  distribution:
	DM 16 000.00
	DM 12.00
	DM 20.00
	
	6000 units					

possible sales volumes x	1000	2000	3000	4000	5000	6000
probability $p(x)$	20.0%	37.5%	25.0%	10.0%	5.0%	2.5%

Computations:
  unit contribution d
  break-even output x_0
  mean value $\bar{x}$
  (expected sales volume)
  expected value
  of total profit
	DM 8.00
	2000 units
	$\bar{x} = 200 + 750 + 750 + 400 + 250 + 150$
	$= 2500$ units
	
	DM 4 000.00					

Risk measures if it is decided to produce
  margin of safety S given
  by (3.21) $(x^{exp} = \bar{x})$
  probability of an
  erroneous decision F
  given by (3.22)
  [ditto assuming
  equal probabilities]
  [risk-chance relation
  $\bar{R}$ given by (3.30) (equal
  probabilities distribution
  necessarily assumed)]
  expected value of
  uncertainty costs U
  given by (3.33)
 	
  expected value of
  profits
 	
  risk level $\hat{R}$ given
  by (3.41)
	20%
	
	$F = p\{x < 2000\} = \displaystyle\sum_{x < 2000} p(x) = p(1000) = 20\%$
	
	[33.3%]
	
	[20%]
	
	$E(U) = \displaystyle\sum_{x < 2000} d \cdot (2000 - x) \cdot p(x)$
	$= 8 \cdot (2000 - 1000) \cdot 20\% = 8 \cdot 200 = \text{DM } 1600$
	
	$E(G) = \displaystyle\sum_{x \geq 2000} d \cdot (x - 2000) \cdot p(x)$
	$= 8 \cdot (1000 \cdot 25\% + 2000 \cdot 10\%$
	$+ 3000 \cdot 5\% + 4000 \cdot 2.5\%)$
	$= 8 \cdot 700 = \text{DM } 5600$
	
	$\hat{R} = \dfrac{1600}{5600} = \dfrac{200}{700} = 28.6\%$					

Figure 34 Evaluation of the production of a product with different risk measures assuming a discrete probability distribution for sales volume

Production alternatives considered for rejection	Product A′	Product B′	
Data:			
fixed costs K^f	DM 16 000.00	DM 24 750.00	
unit variable cost k^v	DM 12.00	DM 7.75	
unit sales revenue q	DM 20.00	DM 14.00	
production capacity limit x^{max}	6000 units	11 000 units	
assumed probability distribution of sales p	Normal distribution	Normal distribution	
mean value μ	1250 units	3000 units	
standard deviation σ	750 units	875 units	
Computations:			Product alternative to be eliminated on the basis of the risk measure in question
unit contribution d	DM 8.00	DM 6.25	
break-even output x_0	2000 units	3960 units	
expected value of total profit	DM − 6 000.00	DM − 6 000.00	
Risk measures in the event of a decision to reject production:			
margin of safety S given by (3.21) ($x^{exp} := E(x) = \mu$)	− 60.0%	− 32.0%	A
probability of an erroneous decision F given by (3.23)	15.9%	13.6%	B
[ditto assuming equal probabilities]	[66.7%]	[64.0%]	[B]
[risk-chance relation $\bar{R}$ given by (3.31) (equal probabilities distribution necessarily assumed)]	[80.0%]	[76.0%]	[B]
expected value of uncertainty costs U given by (3.39)	DM 499.92	DM 377.41	B
risk level $\hat{R}$ given by (3.43)	7.7%	5.9%	B

Figure 35 Evaluation of a decision to forgo the production of a product using different risk measures and assuming a continuous probability distribution for sales volume

whether the expected uncertainty costs do not exceed a prescribed upper limit. On the other hand, using the "risk level" criterion, a meaningful ranking of alternatives can also be constructed for different profit expectations.

The second example (presented in Fig. 34) shows the application of the foregoing considerations to a situation characterised by *discrete probabilities*. In this case it is assumed that only particular sales volumes are conceivable—it may be a question of standardised end-product units or the known requirements of particular large customers who may, or may not, constitute the entire demand for the product. These sales volumes have known discrete probabilities which add up to 100%. The computation of the individual risk measures, which are presented in Fig. 34, shows that the discrete probabilistic approach does not basically differ from that of the continuous probability distribution.

An example of an evaluation of a *decision not to undertake production* is presented in Fig. 35. The starting point in this case is a requirement to eliminate one of two products (A' and B') that have been produced hitherto. According to the available (stochastic) sales forecasts, losses are expected in the case of both products, i.e., the expected total contribution falls short of the product fixed costs in both cases. This deficit, the expected loss, amounts in both cases to DM 6000. For particular reasons it is not possible to eliminate both product A' and product B'. The two products are perhaps complementary to a third, which is produced in any event, but mutually substitutable. Figure 35 shows how the individual risk measures are to be computed and interpreted in the case of a product abandonment decision. The dubious character of those risk measures which make no reference to the probability distribution is particularly prominent. Thus, the risk-chance relation adjudges the rejection of production to be of a higher risk in the case of both products (80% and 76% respectively) than the undertaking of production although the profit expectation takes on a negative value ab initio. The differences in the evaluation of the alternatives (80% to 76%) can, on the other hand, be regarded as being insignificant in this situation. In contrast, the margin of safety indicates a large evaluation difference between the two alternatives (-60% : -30%) and clearly adjudges alternative A to be the candidate for elimination. However, the probability of an erroneous decision, uncertainty costs and "risk level" criteria give a more reliable picture. At times alternative B is identified, by a narrow but clear margin, as the product to be eliminated. At the same time this margin is estimated somewhat higher by the risk level and uncertainty cost criteria (7.7% : 5.9% and DM 500 : DM 377, i.e. approximately 130 : 100 in both cases) than by the probability of an erroneous decision criterion (15.9% : 13.6%, i.e. approximately 117 : 100).

Chapter 4

Extensions of Break-even Analysis

I. SURVEY OF EXTENSIONS OF BREAK-EVEN ANALYSIS

The previous chapter dealt with modifications of break-even analysis that vary only slightly from the basic model or supplement it with additional considerations. They were described as variants of break-even analysis. These variants should be distinguished from forms of break-even analysis which, in particular respects, require a different conceptual foundation for the model. They are called *extensions* of break-even analysis and are intended to broaden the scope of break-even analysis by lifting some of the restrictions on its application. The break-even models that are necessary for this purpose retain the principle of the break-even approach but are indeed adapted to a more general category of questions.

The nature of the extensions to break-even analysis can be characterised by reference to the restrictions on the application of the basic model which those extensions surmount. A distinction can be made between the following extensions:

—The assumptions of the basic model about the structure of the goods flow within the firm are lifted. This is a step-wise process. Break-even models for *single-stage, multiproduct manufacture* are introduced as a first step. These are used as the foundation for presenting break-even approaches in the case of *multistage multiproduct manufacture*.

—The assumptions of the basic model concerning the recognition of merely a single determinant in the cost and output functions are lifted. In this regard a break-even model is proposed which is based on realistic, *multidimensional production functions*.

—The assumption concerning the static character of the basic model is removed. In *multiperiod break-even analysis models*, the serial changes in, and serial relationships subsisting between production, cost and sales revenue can be adequately recognised.

—The linear cost and sales revenue functions of the basic model are removed. The break-even analysis becomes *non-linear*.

—The assumption that all information required for the break-even analyses is known deterministically is removed. Models for *stochastic break-even analysis* are formulated. In contrast to the simple recognition of sales risk in an appended computation of risk measures in the case of the basic (deterministic) model, the determinants of break-even points in stochastic break-even analyses are considered stochastically. Hence, probabilistic propositions concerning the attainment, or the position, of break-even points need to be formulated.

—The assumption of the alignment of the basic model with a single objective of cost recovery or profit attainment is removed. Break-even approaches for the simultaneous *recognition of several objectives* are advanced.

Extensions of break-even analysis require, at least in part, the comprehensive changes to the traditional approach of break-even analysis to which the present chapter is devoted.

II. BREAK-EVEN ANALYSIS FOR SINGLE-STAGE MULTIPRODUCT MANUFACTURE

1. Adaption of the Multiproduct Case to the Single-product Model

(a) Basic Possibilities for the Single Variable Treatment of the Multiproduct Case

One of the most stringent restrictions on the application of the basic break-even model is the assumption of single-stage, single-product manufacture. Whilst multistage production processes can of course be interpreted, in a correspondingly rough and ready undetailed analysis, as a single-stage process, this type of reduction in problem complexity by reference to end-products is, as a rule, not possible. Two cases can indeed be cited in which a slightly modified basic model can also be used for multiproduct analysis.

(1) The production processes can be clearly separated and may therefore be considered as single-product processes running in parallel.
(2) The different products can be related to a unidimensional measure with which they can be jointly measured.

In both cases a univariable break-even analysis, the interpretation of which differs from that of the basic model, is feasible.

(b) Partitioning Multiproduct Analysis into a Manifold
 Univariable Break-even Computation

In previously discussing the conditions in which the basic break-even model can be applied, it was noted that separate single-product analyses are possible if all of the determinants of the break-even analysis can be clearly separated. Thus, first and foremost, fixed costs and, if necessary, further components of the contribution block, must be unambiguously attributable to the individual products. There can be no product interdependence which affects the individual components of the break-even computation. It is obvious, at least in relation to fixed costs, that these preconditions are not satisfied in most cases. Even if the different products do not pass through the same processes, the services provided by individual (service) cost centres, from which components of the fixed block originate, are in the end not unambiguously allocatable to the individual product types (cp. also Scherrer, 1983 [Kostenrechnung] p. 293). The same applies to those constituents of fixed costs which result from the provision of administrative and managerial services.

In this situation one expedient, among others, is, adopting other criteria, arbitrarily to allocate to products those constituents of the fixed cost block that cannot be imputed to products in accordance with the *causality principle* or *identity principle* (cp. Schweitzer and Küpper, 1991 [Systeme] p. 137 et seq.; Riebel, 1982 [Einzelkostenrechnung] p. 75 et seq.). Such criteria are intended to facilitate independent break-even computations and are as follows (cp. Schweitzer and Küpper, 1991 [Systeme] p. 140 et seq.):

—the proportionality principle,
—the average principle,
—the corresponding output principle,
—the capacity to bear principle.

In applying the *proportionality principle*, a reference magnitude is sought that can be used as a proportional allocation basis. Conceivable quantity bases are, for example, metering measures and measures of time, space and weight, whilst various cost magnitudes, or prices, are possible value bases. The measures sought should vary approximately in proportion to the costs that are to be allocated. This requirement must of course remain unsatisfied in the allocation of fixed costs. However, cost allocation in accordance with the *average principle* is possible. Adopting this basis, costs are allocated to production in a manner such that each unit, or chosen allocation basis, is burdened with the same amount of cost. But in this case, and in contrast to the assumption underlying the proportionality principle, no proportional relationship between costs and reference magnitudes is assumed. The *corresponding output principle* which was originated by Helmut Koch (cp. Koch, 1966 [Kostenrechnung] p. 102) requires a cost allocation in accordance with the relationship subsisting between output magnitudes. Output constituents which contribute a greater share to total output are allocated a correspondingly larger amount of cost. For cost allocation purposes it is therefore necessary to construct a key magnitude in which, above all, the quantity and value of orders are embodied, i.e. the sales volume and turnover magnitudes of each product type. In applying the *capacity to bear principle*, costs are ultimately allocated to products in accordance with their cost absorption capacities. Product gross profits or contribution margins are used as measures of absorption capacity. Products with higher contribution margins are allocated a higher share of fixed costs than are products with smaller contribution margins.

The application of the capacity to bear principle is illustrated here with an example. The relation of unit contributions is used as the basis for allocating fixed costs (cp. Schweitzer and Küpper, 1991 [Systeme] p. 363 et seq.). The firm in question manufactures two products, A and B, which are characterised by the values given in Table 2.

Table 2

	Product A	Product B
Selling price	$q_1 = $ DM 19.50	$q_2 = $ DM 29.50
Unit variable costs	$k_1^v = $ DM 13.00	$k_2^v = $ DM 27.00
Unit contribution	$d_1 = $ DM 6.50	$d_2 = $ DM 2.50
Directly attributable fixed costs	$K_1^f = $ DM 9000	$K_2^f = $ DM 20 000
Capacity limit for manufacture and sales	$x_1^{max} = 4000$ units	$x_2^{max} = 20 000$ units

Table 3

	Product A	Product B
Directly attributable fixed costs	DM 9 000	DM 20 000
Allocated fixed costs	DM 26 000	DM 10 000
Total fixed costs	DM 35 000	DM 30 000
Unit contribution	DM 6.5	DM 2.5
Break-even point	5385 units	12 000 units

Fixed costs total DM 65 000. Allowing for the fixed costs that are directly attributable to A and B, the remaining fixed costs of DM 36 000 would be allocated in accordance with their unit contributions as follows:

Product A: $6.50/(6.50+2.50) \cdot$ DM 36 000 $=$ DM 26 000
Product B: $2.50/(6.50+2.50) \cdot$ DM 36 000 $=$ DM 10 000.

Using the latter cost allocations, separate break-even analyses can be undertaken. They give the results shown in Table 3.

In the two product case, the following formulae for computing break-even points when fixed costs are allocated in accordance with unit contribution ratios (cp. Schweitzer and Küpper, 1991 [Systeme] p. 363) are generally valid:

Break-even point for product A:

$$\bar{x}_1 = \frac{K_1^f + \dfrac{d_1}{d_1+d_2} \cdot (K^f - K_1^f - K_2^f)}{d_1} \tag{4.1}$$

Break-even point for product B:

$$\bar{x}_2 = \frac{K_2^f + \dfrac{d_2}{d_1+d_2} \cdot (K^f - K_1^f - K_2^f)}{d_2}. \tag{4.2}$$

In the n-product case, the break-even point for the ith product is computed from the formula:

$$\bar{x}_i = \frac{K_i^f + \dfrac{d_i}{\sum d_i}\left(K^f - \sum_{i=1}^{n} K_i^f\right)}{d_i} \tag{4.3}$$

In interpreting the computed values in the present example it is advisable to examine the capacity restrictions on the production of both products. If, namely, the decision to continue production is based upon the results of the computation presented above, the manufacture of product A should be suspended. This product is subject to a capacity limit of 4000 units whilst its break-even point is only attained at an output of 5385 units. Evaluated on this basis, product A is apparently unprofitable. On the other hand, product B is profitable above an output of 12 000 units. Consequently, it is expected to be profitable below its capacity limit of 20 000 units. If the firm in question actually implements these decisions, that is, commences the production of product B on its own, it finds itself in the following cost situation:

Total fixed costs	DM 65 000
Obviated fixed cost directly attributable to A	DM 9 000
Remaining fixed costs	DM 56 000

The break-even point of B with respect to the remaining amount of fixed costs is 22 400 units and therefore exceeds its capacity limit. This indicates that, in the case of the decision in question, an overall loss is sustained. If, by contrast, exactly the maximum quantity of A, namely 4000 units is produced, the resultant new computation for product B is:

Total fixed costs	DM 65 000
Recovered from the production of 4000 units of product A: 4000 units at DM 6.50/unit =	DM 26 000
To be recovered from product B	DM 39 000

In this situation the break-even point of B is 15 600 units so that it is now possible actually to attain a profit within the capacity limits. The relationships are illustrated in Fig. 36.

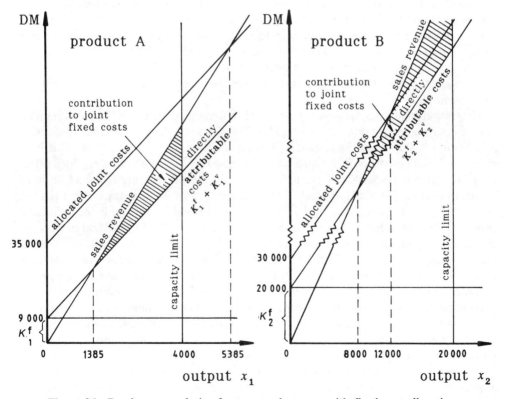

Figure 36 Break-even analysis of a two-product case with fixed cost allocation

The previous example illustrates the ambiguity of an arbitrary allocation of fixed costs to individual products which does not reflect causality. It makes no difference which allocation principle is applied. If fixed costs are not directly attributable to products, the corresponding fixed cost block must be analysed as one sum total. It has to be recovered in total from the contributions of the entire product line with no preconceived notions about the requisite amounts of their individual contributions. All predetermined allocation bases must be arbitrary and can cause erroneous decisions. In the previous case only a simultaneous break-even analysis is adequate. In that both joint and product-specific fixed costs arise, a two-stage approach is expedient (cp. Section III).

(c) Reference Back to the Single-product Case using a Unidimensional Measurement of Multiproduct Output

The unidimensional measurement of a number of different products requires the construction of a special index number because simple addition is precluded by the disparate product attributes. Dean (1952 [Break-Even Analysis] p. 237 et seq.) has exhaustively analysed this problem. He basically distinguishes between output indices and input indices which, in turn, can be further classified by reference to the structural weighting of the individual goods magnitudes included in the index. Figure 37 provides a survey which distinguishes basic index number types.

The definition of an *output index* is obviously needed for the measurement of output. It embodies the sum of the weighted outputs of the individual goods. Most frequently selling prices are used as weights so that *turnover* becomes the output index. This case can be further categorised by reference to the prices that are used for the weighting process. Relevant considerations are forecast prices that are actually expected and standardised prices which have been normalised in a particular way. In the case of a weighting with prices, the resultant index number can be interpreted as a value magnitude (here turnover).

The output index can, however, be defined in a manner such that the index number can be interpreted as a quantity magnitude. The simplest example of such a definition is the simple addition of the respective outputs of the individual products. This is of course only possible when it is a question of principally the same products which differ only in negligible respects. An example of such an output measure is the addition of tonnages of different kinds of steel. The unidimensional output index is then: tons of steel (of any given type). In the latter case there is an equal weighting. If the individual product types are indeed closely related with respect to production method or product characteristics, but have outputs which are not directly additive, it can be checked whether product additivity can be effected by resorting to equivalence figures. As in the case of the *equivalence calculation* itself, the applications usually comprise such types of manufacture as beer production, wire drawing, rolled sheet metal manufacture, brick-making, spinning and weaving. In these cases the equivalence numbers are constructed on the basis of technical relationships. Weights, volumes, lengths, relationships subsisting between machine and production times, the quantity relationships subsisting between particular raw material inputs etc. are typical equivalence numbers of this kind.

In addition to a quantity weighting, a value weighting can also be considered in defining a quantity index for output. In that event, the equivalence numbers are not based on technically-oriented relationships but upon cost magnitudes. Most usual are a weighting

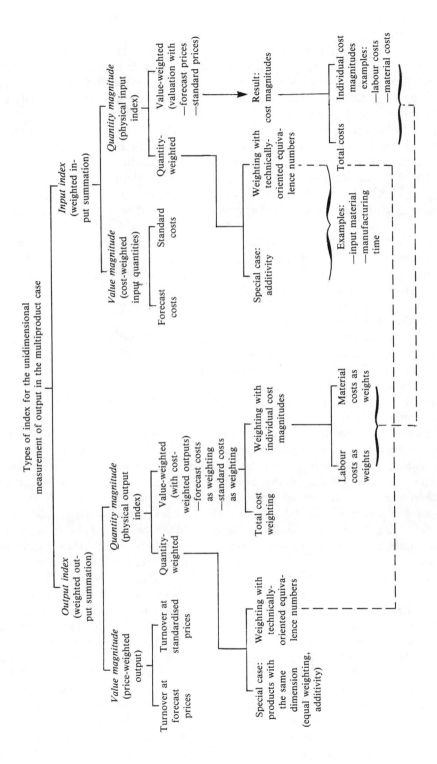

Figure 37 Survey of index types for the unidimensional measurement of output in the multiproduct case

with labour cost per quantity unit of product type and a weighting with material costs per quantity unit.

The second type of production index is the *input index*. An input index is especially advisable if similar factor inputs enter each of the products in question. The different end-products are frequently very numerous and hardly amenable to a unified measure whilst, by comparison, the number of factor inputs is small. On the other hand, it may be that input quantities permit a connection with the corresponding output types. An input index is suitable for such (roughly) divergent processes. It can be expressed as a value magnitude, in which case it reflects product-related total costs; or also as a quantity magnitude. As weights, quantities or values again become relevant possibilities (cp. Fig. 37). An example of a quantity-weighted input quantity index is the total manufacturing time for a particular output programme whereby all manufacturing times are normalised by reference to a basic qualification. That is to say, the times of more highly valued manufacturing work are weighted, prior to addition, with a factor which is greater than one. This factor is however determined by reference to a technically-oriented basis, e.g. on the basis of labour values. An example of a value-weighted input quantity index is the sum of manufacturing times whereby all times are likewise normalised by reference to a basic qualification. Higher grade work has a weight exceeding one here also but the weighting factors are, however, determined by reference to the different labour costs.

It should be noted, as indicated by the overview presented in Fig. 37, that, in some cases the same index can be obtained in two types of interpretation. Taking as an example an output index in which output quantities are weighted with the costs of appropriate inputs, e.g. the wage costs in respect of the work contained in the output; the result is formally the same as in the case of an input index which directly measures the total labour input using wage costs as weights.

The most frequently encountered types of output index are *turnover* and, in the case of the manufacture of a product group, *quantities standardised* with equivalence numbers. Input indices which frequently occur are material or manufactured quantities (*throughputs*) and manufacturing times (for examples cp. Kilger, 1981 [Plankostenrechnung] p. 328 et seq.). In addition to individual manufacturing times, the principal time-dimension is *machine hours* (cp. Tucker, 1980 [Break-Even System] pp. 27, 38, 137 and 1973 [Einführung] pp. 64, 227). There are hardly any reports of applications of a total production index comprising a conceivable combination of different constituent indices. The cost factors of individual types of input are, as a rule, used as an index if they are largely proportional to other factor inputs. Thus, Dean (1952 [Break-Even-Analysis] p. 240) reports that, in the manufacture of ovens, the direct wage costs which constituted no more than a small component of manufacturing costs, were nevertheless closely related to most of the other cost components. In that case the standard individual wage costs were a suitable input index. In general the ease with which they can be specified and interpreted are advantages of input indices. By contrast, the danger of inaccuracies in the measuring of production is greater. On the one hand the relationships between input and output can frequently not be assumed to be simply proportional whilst, on the other hand, problems often emerge in aligning the "correct" inputs with the output that is analysed because different production processes overlap; and, different product manufacturing times complicate the input–output relationship. If cost or other value components enter the index definition, the use of standardised magnitudes is frequently advisable because the ultimate intention is to gain a quantitative picture of production to facilitate a juxtaposition of costs and revenues only in the break-even computation.

The application of production indices is only correct as long as the relationships assumed in the index structure are valid (cp. Poensgen, 1981 [Break-Even-Analysis] p. 308; Weinwurm, 1970 [Break-Even Analysis] p. 306). This is explained hereafter by reference to three typical examples. As a (single) reference magnitude for break-even analysis, a quantity-based input index, a quantity-based output index and turnover as a value-based output index are respectively drawn upon in these cases.

(d) Break-even Analysis in the Joint Production Case as an Example of the Application of a Quantity-based Input Index

In the following example, an *input index* based on input material is used because the process in question is characterised by divergent relationships which, technically speaking, are stationary. Such a case of joint production is exemplified by the butchery business. Thus, assume that a butcher purchases half-pigs in the 30–60 kg class for further processing. The purchase price is DM 5.40/kg. He cuts up the half-pigs so procured into a multiplicity of different types of meat, some of which he uses in sausage making. The following costs can be directly attributed to the joint processing of a half-pig:

50 kg of pig-meat at DM 5.40/kg	DM 270
Further material inputs (primarily seasoning and ingredients for sausage production)	DM 70
Directly attributable wages	DM 60
Directly attributable overhead costs (energy, packing etc)	DM 50
Variable costs of cutting up a 50 kg half-pig	DM 450

The above costs can be attributed to the total pig-meat preparation process. However, as in every joint process, they are not attributable to the individual joint products. On the other hand, the sales revenue of the individual joint products are known. In that the quantity relationships subsisting between the joint products in this example are largely predetermined, it is also useful to relate the sales revenue to the dimension "kilogram of half-pig processed". To this end, the joint products must be listed in conjunction with the weight and price data which can be expected on average. Table 4 shows a computation for five different products instead of the 50–60 product types which actually emerge. It is assumed that the half-pig to be cut up weighs 50 kg.

If, therefore, a half-pig is considered in total, sales revenue averaging DM 1749.10/50 kg = DM 34.98/kg can be reckoned with. In this way the output-related sales revenue is traced back to the pig-meat input as an input index. Using this input magnitude as the main variable, a break-even analysis can be undertaken. With variable costs of DM 450/50 kg = DM 9/kg, a contribution margin of DM (34.98–9) = DM 25.98, which relates to a kilogram of pig-meat input, can be calculated. The following periodic fixed costs are to be covered:

Fixed personnel costs (mainly sales personnel)	DM 6 400
Space costs (rent)	DM 2 000
Energy costs (refrigeration and lighting, etc.)	DM 480
Other costs (packing, administration etc.)	DM 360
Periodic fixed costs	DM 9 240

Table 4

	Volume consumed (kg)	Sales volume (kg)	Selling price per kg (DM)	Sales revenue (DM)
First category meat (filet, loin)	7.840	7	67.50	472.50
Second category meat (chops, neck and shoulder pieces)	18.360	17	44.60	758.20
Third category meat (belly pieces, small parts, minced meat)	14.000	14	28.70	401.80
Used for sausage-making	5.600	7	15.80	110.60
Remainder, bones, waste	4.200	3	2.00	6.00
	50.000	—	—	1 749.10

The following break-even point can therefore be computed:

$$\frac{\text{DM } 9240}{\text{DM } 25.98/\text{kg}} = 356 \text{ kg.} \tag{4.4}$$

This break-even point needs to be interpreted with the aid of the product index employed. It states that profit is attained if the average sales composition is in accordance with Table 4; and, if the volume of pig-meat products sold corresponds to a meat-input of 356 kg.

This interpretation is subject to two qualifications. First, all computations always relate to a half-pig and not to an individual kilogram. Were all half-pigs to weigh exactly 50 kg, it could be said that the butcher would enter the profit region were he to process and sell eight half-pigs. In that a complete half-pig is processed all at once, the cost function constitutes a stepped function (cp. Fig. 38). Secondly, the computations based on the chosen input index are only correct if the quantity relations that are used in constructing the average sales revenue also actually transpire. Thus, another break-even point emerges if, for example, perhaps first all of the cheaper and then, later, the more expensive products are sold (cp. Fig. 38).

The two modes of linearisation just described do not of course restrict the scope for applying the chosen index magnitude to the same degree as the assumption of a known, stationary production and revenue structure.

(e) Example of Break-even Analysis with a Quantity-output Index as a Reference Magnitude

The following example of the unidimensional measurement of a multidimensional output programme is taken from the textile industry. In the production of underclothes, e.g. T-shirts, a constant assortment can also be assumed. It is not determined by production technicalities but results from market demand. Thus, a textile producer may know that in selling 100 T-shirts to the retail trade, the quantities sold are always distributed in approximately the same way between sizes 3, 4, 5, 6 and 7.

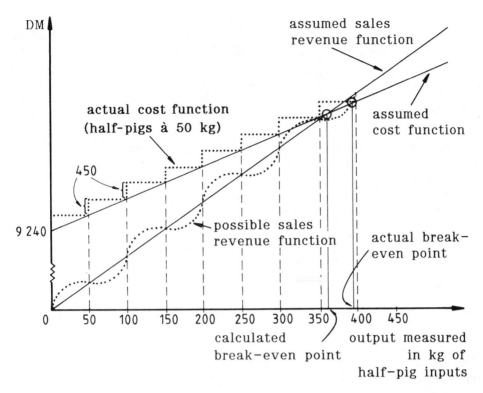

Figure 38 Unidimensional break-even analysis in the multiproduct case with an input index as the reference magnitude

Size	3	4	5	6	7	Σ
Quantity	13	25	35	18	9	100

If it is intended to analyse the cost–profit situation appertaining to a particular T-shirt model, this distribution can thus be assumed.

The production equipment of a new T-shirt variant which is produced in sizes 3 to 7 (inclusive) is assumed to cause fixed set-up costs of DM 35 000. The question is therefore: what minimum level of production needs to be sold in order to cover costs? The cost and sales revenue data given in Table 5 are assumed to apply:

Table 5

Size		3	4	5	6	7
Selling price	(DM)	5.50	6.00	6.00	6.50	7.00
Variable	(DM)	2.70	2.90	3.20	3.45	3.65
Unit contribution (DM)		2.80	3.10	2.80	3.05	3.35

In the context described, it is advisable to use an output index, for measuring the activity level, which reflects the quantity relations subsisting between the individual T-shirt sizes. Here product packets are defined in accordance with the usual composition of sales. To facilitate a simpler interpretation, a product packet is defined in a manner such that the basic size class 5 is represented with exactly one unit. A product package comprises the following quantities of the individual size-classes:

Size	3	4	5	6	7
Quantities	0.371	0.714	1	0.514	0.257

This is therefore a question of a quantity-weighted quantity index of output. The costs and sales revenue attributed to a product package are derived from the following computation.

Sales revenue per product package:

$$\text{DM } 5.50 \cdot 0.371 + \text{DM } 6.00 \cdot 0.714 + \text{DM } 6.00 \cdot 1$$
$$+ \text{DM } 6.50 \cdot 0.514 + \text{DM } 7.00 \cdot 0.257 = \text{DM } 17.46$$

Costs per product package:

$$\text{DM } 2.70 \cdot 0.371 + \text{DM } 2.90 \cdot 0.714 + \text{DM } 3.20 \cdot 1$$
$$+ \text{DM } 3.45 \cdot 0.514 + \text{DM } 3.65 \cdot 0.257 = \text{DM } 8.98$$

The contribution margin per product package is therefore DM 8.48 and, consequently, the break-even point x_0 for T-shirt production is given by:

$$x_0 = \frac{\text{DM } 35\,000}{\text{DM } 8.48/\text{pp}} = 4127 \text{ pp.}$$

Beyond the 4128th product package, the T-shirt production enters the profit region. Because size 5 is normalised to a quantity of 1, it is enough to relate the sales numbers to size 5. The break-even proposition can therefore also be simplified: as soon as 4128 units of size 5 of the T-shirt in question have been sold, then, going by previous experience, specific quantities of the other sizes have also been disposed of so that, overall, production has reached the profit region.

The difficulty in arriving at a solution to the multiproduct break-even analysis described above lies in the assumed quantity relation. In the case of a new product, precise research is therefore necessary to determine whether the product that is planned can be based upon a previously-observed size distribution. A special forecast is required to estimate the expected size distribution. The product type could match the demand for individual sizes in either a particularly strong or particularly weak manner.

(f) Example of Break-even Analysis with Turnover as a Reference Magnitude

The third example of a unidimensional break-even analysis is concerned with the production of glass tubes for monochrome television sets. In the case in point, these tubes are produced in six different sizes and qualities. Neither the ratio of the individual product outputs is technically determined as in joint production, nor are there particular sales-size relationships as in the case of underclothing manufacture. The sales of the

Table 6

	Type of tube					
	A	B	C	D	E	F
Unit selling price DM (q_i)	27.00	43.00	21.00	35.00	16.50	24.50
Unit variable costs DM (k_i^v)	24.80	27.30	17.55	28.75	15.10	21.20
Forecast sales volume in units (x_i^{max})	300 000	75 000	200 000	25 000	150 000	400 000

individual product types are largely independent of each other. An individual expected sales volume for each product type for the forthcoming year can of course be given. These volumes together with the cost and revenue data for the six tube types, A to F, are presented in Table 6.

A simple addition of the tube volumes is not possible because of the disparate nature of the individual types. A volume-weighted output index cannot be contemplated because appropriate equivalence numbers are absent. The measurement of activity with an input index is inadvisable in the present example because of significant differences in manufacturing procedures as well as in cost and revenue structures. In order, therefore, to measure output, the value magnitude *turnover* is taken as an index. The break-even question is then: at what level of turnover is the profit region entered? This is a question of a break-even analysis in which costs, sales revenue and contribution margins on the one hand are juxtaposed with sales revenue, i.e. with turnover, on the other. This type of break-even analysis is therefore also called cost-volume-analysis or cost-volume-profit-analysis (cp. Horngren, 1982 [Cost Accounting] p. 43 et seq.). In a related graph, turnover is the independent variable.

In the American textbooks and American reports on applications, a univariable break-even analysis, based on turnover as the single reference magnitude for all positive and negative components, is treated as the most important break-even model. The following version is the one which is most frequently used (cp., for example, Wright, 1962 [Costs] pp. 16–33; Kilger, 1981 [Plankostenrechnung] p. 710 et seq.; Haberstock, 1982 [Grundzüge] p. 156 et seq.). Payments are employed instead of costs and the ascertainment of *cash points* is therefore the objective of the break-even analysis (cp. Chapter 3.II.3). Moreover, the analysis is, as a rule, supplemented with a "margin of safety" computation (cp. Chapter 3.VI.2). In this context the latter criterion indicates the percentage by which the turnover can decline before the break-even turnover is reached (cp. Kilger, 1981 [Plankostenrechnung] p. 710):

$$\text{margin of safety} = \frac{\text{forecast turnover} - \text{break-even turnover}}{\text{forecast turnover}} \tag{4.5}$$

The total analysis is expressed in terms of the relationship between turnover and payments, or net cash flow, and the principal magnitude is the relationship of net cash flows (as opposed to contribution margins) to turnover. It is called *profit–volume-ratio* ("*P/V-ratio*") or, more precisely, *contribution margin ratio* ("*C/M-ratio*", cp. e.g. Matz and Usry, 1980 [Cost Accounting] pp. 692, 700; Moore and Talbott, 1978 [Application] p. 32; Tucker, 1980 [Break-Even System] p. 16; Tucker, 1973

[Einführung] p. 40; Wright, 1962 [Costs] p. 16). An attempt is made to forecast this ratio for individual products, and for product groups, as well as for an entire firm. Here the pre-eminent aim is the ascertainment of a linear relationship. In concretely identifying P/V functions, the previously described methods for determining linear cost functions are used. Prominent among these is the ordinary least squares method. Wright (1962[Costs] p. 16) draws attention to the fact that this version of break-even analysis with the related break-even chart is, in many ways, regarded as one of the most important contributions to management science.

In the example of television (tube) production considered here, the intention is to analyse the cost–turnover, sales revenue–turnover and contribution margin–turnover relationships. The P/V or C/M ratio then corresponds to the *contribution margin ratio*, i.e. the ratio of a product's unit contribution to its selling price. The following fixed costs are to be covered collectively by all tube types:

Depreciation charges and interest costs for the glass melting vat and other equipment	DM 900 000
Basic energy charge for the melting vat	DM 300 000
Maintenance costs of manufacturing equipment	DM 500 000
Costs of line management	DM 1 200 000
Further fixed costs of producing monochrome television tubes	DM 100 000
Total fixed costs to be covered	DM 3 000 000

Forecast sales volumes are used as a basis for determining total turnover. The computations are set out in Table 7.

The computation indicates that a total turnover of approximately DM 28.7 mill. and a total contribution of DM 4.2 mill. are forecast. In the case of the forecast sales volumes for the television tubes in question it can be assumed overall that a turnover of DM 1 embodies a contribution margin of DM 0.146 95. The average contribution margin

Table 7

	Type of tube						
	A	B	C	D	E	F	Σ
Forecast turnover $(q_i \cdot x_i)$ in thousands of DM	8 100	3 225	4 200	875	2 475	9 800	28 675
Unit contribution (d_i) in DM	2.20	15.70	3.45	6.25	1.40	3.30	—
Forecast total contribution $(d_i \cdot x_i)$ in DM	600 000	1 177 500	690 000	156 250	210 000	1 320 000	4 213 750
Contribution margin ratio $\left(\hat{d}_i = \dfrac{d_i}{q_i} = \dfrac{d_i \cdot x_i^{max}}{q_i \cdot x_i^{max}} \right)$ = contribution margin as % of turnover	8.15	36.51	16.43	17.86	8.48	13.47	14.69

ratio is in general computed from the formula given below. The symbols used hitherto are supplemented with an index i which denotes product type and the summations are across all product types ($i = 1, 2, \ldots, n$). The forecast sales volumes of product i is designated x_i^{max}.

Average contribution margin ratio $\hat{d} = \dfrac{\text{total turnover of forecast quantities} - \text{total variable costs of forecast quantities}}{\text{total turnover of forecast quantities}}$

$$= \frac{\sum q_i \cdot x_i - \sum k_i^v \cdot x_i}{\sum q_j \cdot x_j} \tag{4.6}$$

or,

$$\hat{d} = \frac{\sum d_i \cdot x_i^{max}}{\sum q_j \cdot x_j^{max}} \qquad \text{with } d_i = q_i - k_i^v. \tag{4.7}$$

Using the product-related contribution margin ratios $\hat{d}_i$, the average contribution margin ratio $\hat{d}$ can be computed as follows:

$$\hat{d} = \frac{\sum d_i \cdot x_i^{max}}{\sum q_j \cdot x_j^{max}} = \frac{\sum \dfrac{d_i}{q_i} \cdot q_i \cdot x_i^{max}}{\sum q_j \cdot x_j^{max}} = \sum \hat{d}_i \cdot \frac{q_i \cdot x_i^{max}}{\sum q_j \cdot x_j^{max}}. \tag{4.8}$$

In (4.8) the product contribution margin ratios are weighted with their turnover/total turnover proportions. Using the average contribution margin ratio $\hat{d}$, the break-even turnover for covering fixed costs can be expressed as a lump sum, namely,

$$x_0 = \frac{K^f}{\hat{d}}. \tag{4.9}$$

In the case of the production of television tubes, the break-even point x_0 for covering the fixed costs of DM 3 mill. is given by:

$$x_0 = \frac{\text{DM } 3\,000\,000}{14.694\,856\%} = \text{DM } 20\,415\,307.$$

This result merely gives a first insight into the break-even situation in the present case. The profit threshold is only reached at a turnover of DM 20.4 mill. if, for this part of the forecast annual total turnover, the contribution margin ratio of 14.695% is actually obtained. This will be the case if the sales volumes of the television tubes A to F reflect their forecast ratios, i.e. are in the ratios 300 : 75 : 200 : 25 : 150 : 400. This would mean that the development of the sales volumes of all six types of tubes in the course of the year conforms to the forecast. However, this cannot be generally assumed. For example, at the start of the year it may turn out that whilst the demand for tube A is very large, the demand for tube B is quite small. In that event, the average contribution margin ratio achieved at the beginning of the year is lower than the expected 14.695% and the break-even point would be at a correspondingly higher level.

In order to give break-even analysis predictive power, notwithstanding the inherent uncertainty, *Anderson* (1975 [Expanded Breakeven Analysis] p. 31 et seq.) suggests the following procedure.

Rank the products by reference to their contribution margin ratios. In the present example this results in the ranking

$$B—D—C—F—E—A$$

whereby products B and A have the highest and lowest sales revenue-related contribution margins respectively. Two extreme situations can now be recognised. On the one hand, turnover may develop in a manner such that the products with the higher contribution margin ratios are first sold at their respective forecast levels whilst, on the other, the situation may be reversed. Anderson describes these two possibilities as *optimistic* and *pessimistic* outcomes (cp. Anderson, 1975 [Expanded Breakeven Analysis] p. 32). A break-even analysis of the two cases results in optimistic, early break-even and pessimistic, late break-even points respectively.

Table 8 Break-even analysis in the optimistic case

Ranking of products	Contribution margin ratio (%)	Total contribution per product	Cumulative total contribution	Turnover per product (thousands of DM)	Cumulative turnover (thousands of DM)
B	36.51	1 177 500	1 177 500	3 225	3 225
D	17.86	156 250	1 333 750	875	4 100
C	16.43	690 000	2 023 750	4 200	8 300
F	13.47	1 320 000	3 343 750 ←	9 800	18 100
E	8.48	210 000	3 553 750	2 475	20 575
A	8.15	660 000	4 213 750	8 100	28 675

The break-even point is reached with the sale of product F of which, to cover costs

$$\frac{DM\ (3\,000\,000 - 2\,023\,750)}{13.469\,388\%} = \frac{DM\ 976\,250}{13.469\,388\%} = DM\ 7\,247\,917$$

must be sold.

Thus, in addition to the turnover of DM 8 300 000 that has already been attained, further turnover of DM 7 247 917 from tube F must be achieved. Hence, in the optimistic case the required total turnover amounts to DM 15 547 917.

In the pessimistic case (cp. Table 9) the break-even point is reached with the sale of product D of which, to cover costs

$$\frac{DM\ (3\,000\,000 - 2\,880\,000)}{17.857\,143\%} = \frac{DM\ 120\,000}{17.857\,143\%} = DM\ 672\,000$$

must also be sold.

The latter computation therefore shows that, in the pessimistic case, the required total turnover amounts to DM 25 247 000.

It can be inferred from the analysis of the two extreme situations that, in the present example, the break-even point (which would initially be computed at DM 20.4 mill.) can, if the forecast data actually materialise, vary between DM 15.5 mill. and DM 25.2 mill. This range of variation can be presented graphically by plotting contribution margin curves, for the turnover sequences for the optimistic and pessimistic cases, in a contribution

Table 9 Break-even analysis in the pessimistic case

Ranking of products	Contribution margin ratio (%)	Total contribution per product	Cumulative total contribution	Turnover per product (thousands of DM)	Cumulative turnover (thousands of DM)
A	8.15	660 000	660 000	8 100	8 100
E	8.48	210 000	870 000	2 475	10 575
F	13.47	1 320 000	2 190 000	9 800	20 375
C	16.43	690 000	2 880 000	4 200	24 575
D	17.86	156 250	3 036 250 ←	875	25 450
B	36.51	1 177 500	4 213 750	3 225	28 675

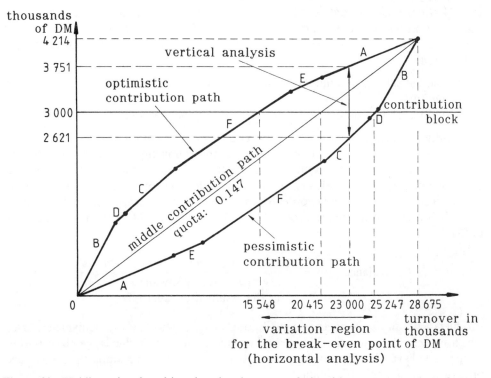

Figure 39 Unidimensional multiproduct break-even analysis with turnover as the reference magnitude

margin–contribution block diagram. Anderson calls these curves optimistic and pessimistic paths (cp. Anderson, 1975 [Expanded Breakeven Analysis] p. 32). The optimistic contribution path is depicted by an upwardly-arched curve which joins the zero point and the forecast total contribution. A break-even chart which is based upon the optimum sequence of product sales is therefore described as a "hip roof" P/V chart (cp. e.g. Wright, 1962 [Costs] p. 27).

Figure 39 illustrates the relationships in the example of the television tube production. This graph clearly indicates that the break-even analysis so presented illustrates one of the numerous variants of the analysis, each of which can be undertaken in the present situation.

Thus the break-even level in relation to a higher or lower contribution block (e.g. to allow for a profit minimum, cp. 3.II) can be examined. Here also there is a complete interval of possible break-even points. Analyses of this kind are designated *horizontal* by Anderson (1975 [Expanded Breakeven Analysis] p. 32). Correspondingly a *vertical analysis* can be used to explore the contribution level that is achieved at a particular level of turnover. There is an interval here too which, in Fig. 39, is illustrated at a turnover of DM 23 000 000. It shows that, at this turnover level, the total contribution can vary between DM 2 621 250 and DM 3 751 343.

The latter method can also be conjoined with a special *deviation analysis* (cp. Klipper, 1977/78 [Breakeven Analysis] p. 51 et seq.; and Tucker, 1973 [Einführung] p. 231 who describes a different procedure). For this analysis it is assumed that the sales programme specified by the forecast sales volumes of the individual products is the planned product mix. Hence the middle contribution margin path in Fig. 39 represents the curve of the planned contribution margin. Consequently, if, at a particular turnover level, the actual contribution deviates from the planned contribution, there can be two causes of such a deviation:

(1) the actual sales programme deviates from that which was planned (*product mix deviation*)
(2) actual variable costs deviate from planned variable costs (*cost deviation*).

To facilitate a simple separation of these two types of deviation Klipper (cp. 1977/78 [Breakeven Analysis] p. 52 et seq.) proposes the following procedure whereby: an analytical "*equivalence selling price*" is ascertained for each product in addition to its actual selling price. This equivalence price is intended to express the price at which the product would need to be sold in order to realise precisely the average contribution margin ratio. It is ascertained from the formula (cp. Klipper, 1977/78 [Breakeven Analysis] p. 52):

$$\text{Equivalence price} = \frac{\text{actual contribution margin in DM}}{\substack{\text{average contribution margin} \\ \text{at the assumed product mix}}} = \frac{d_i}{\bar{d}} \tag{4.10}$$

Products with an above-average contribution margin ratio have an equivalence price which exceeds their actual selling price, products with a below-average contribution margin ratio have a lower equivalence price. In the television tube example the equivalence prices shown in Table 10 obtain.

The manner in which, using these equivalence prices, the product-mix deviation and the cost deviation are ascertained can be illustrated with the following example. For a particular period the sales of television tubes amount to DM 23 000 000 giving a total

Table 10

Type of tube	A (DM)	B (DM)	C (DM)	D (DM)	E (DM)	F (DM)
Actual price	27.00	43.00	21.00	35.00	16.50	24.50
Contribution per unit ($\div 14.694856$ %)	2.20	15.70	3.45	6.25	1.40	3.30
Equivalence price	14.97	106.84	23.48	42.53	9.53	22.46

Table 11

Type of tube	Realised sales volume	Turnover at actual prices (DM)	Turnover at equivalence prices (DM)
A	160 000	4 320 000	2 395 200
B	74 000	3 182 000	7 906 160
C	195 000	4 095 000	4 578 600
D	23 000	805 000	978 190
E	84 000	1 386 000	800 520
F	376 000	9 212 000	8 444 960
	Total:	23 000 000	25 103 630

contribution of DM 3 400 000. However, with an average contribution margin ratio of 14.695%, a contribution of DM 23 000 000 (14.694 856%) = DM 3 379 817 should have been achieved on the latter turnover. The total deviation between the planned and actual contribution margin amounts to:

$$\text{planned contribution} - \text{actual contribution} = \text{DM } 3\,379\,817 - \text{DM } 3\,400\,000 = \text{DM } -20\,183 \tag{4.11}$$

The deviation turns out to be negative because the planned contribution was exceeded. To analyse the deviation, it is necessary to determine the composition of the achieved turnover of DM 23 000 000. Using the equivalence prices it is then necessary to ascertain an equivalence turnover total for the individual product volumes given in Table 11.

Computed in terms of equivalence prices, the resultant turnover is thus about 10% higher than if expressed at actual prices. This shows that the product mix was more favourable than was planned. Products with higher contributions figure more prominently in the actual product mix than was planned and those with lower contributions figure less prominently. This explains part of the contribution margin deviation. Expressing turnover in terms of equivalence prices a contribution of DM 25 103 630 (14.694 856%) = DM 3 688 942 should have been achieved. This amount is described as the *equivalence contribution margin*. It can be used in computing the *product mix deviation*:

$$\text{product mix deviation:} = \text{planned contribution} - \text{equivalence contribution}$$
$$= \text{DM } 3\,379\,817 - \text{DM } 3\,688\,942 \tag{4.12}$$
$$= \text{DM } -309\,125.$$

The remainder of the total deviation constitutes a *cost deviation*. It takes on the following value:

$$\text{cost deviation:} = \text{equivalence contribution} - \text{actual contribution}$$
$$= \text{DM } 3\,688\,942 - \text{DM } 3\,400\,000 \tag{4.13}$$
$$= \text{DM } 288\,942.$$

The product mix deviation is negative because the composition of the sales volume is more favourable than planned. The positive cost deviation indicates that the cost situation is less favourable than planned. However, because of the favourable composition of sales volume, the significant increase in costs is not obvious.

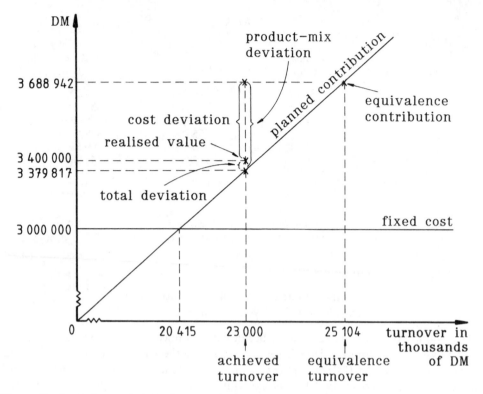

Figure 40 Deviation analysis in the case of multiproduct, unidimensional break-even analysis

This information can only be conveyed by partitioning the deviation in the manner described. The product mix and cost deviations add up to the total deviation.

$$
\begin{aligned}
\text{total deviation} &= \text{product mix deviation} + \text{cost deviation}\\
\text{DM} - 20\,183 &= \text{DM} - 309\,125 \qquad + \text{DM } 288\,942
\end{aligned}
\tag{4.14}
$$

These deviations can also be illustrated in a break-even diagram as in Fig. 40 (cp. Klipper, 1977/78 [Breakeven Analysis] p. 53).

The method of multiproduct break-even analysis illustrated with the example of television tube production uses turnover as the index of production and can therefore remain as a unidimensional approach. The showing of break-even point variation regions, as in the horizontal analysis in Fig. 39, or the ascertainment of a product-mix deviation as in Fig. 40, should not, however, conceal the reality that sales volume forecasts for each product type constitute an essential element of the approach.

First and foremost the computation of the average contribution margin ratio is based on the forecast sales volume numbers in addition to the middle contribution margin path. The specified product volumes are used to forecast the composition of sales volume. They are also used, in ascertaining the optimistic and pessimistic contribution margin paths, to determine the turning points of the curves. The forecast sales volumes are thus used as *weights* in the dimensional reduction. In that, in contrast to the cases illustrated by the two other examples, these sales volume numbers are not systematically related, their use as weights is extremely problematical. An inaccurate forecast in the case of a single product càn make the entire analysis questionable. The crucial element of the approach is the forecast of the total sales volumes which are stringently adhered to in the subsequent analysis. This has the seemingly paradoxical consequence that those products which, at the start of the analysis period, are sold at a rate which is well in excess of the average are, for the remainder of that period, to be assessed with below-average volumes so that the forecast total volume will not be exceeded. The opposite applies to products which, at the beginning of the period in question, are sold at below-average rates. It is thus assumed that the originally forecast sales volumes can be accorded greater reliability than can the sales volumes which are actually realised during the period of the analysis. This assumption is only justified in some cases. A further objection concerns the fact that frequently the maximum sales volumes of different products are mutually dependent because of *common restrictions*. This situation cannot be handled by the present approach. It is in fact a structural characteristic of the approach that the individual product volumes are specified as constants independently of further determinants.

2. Multidimensional Break-even Analysis in the Case of Multiproduct Manufacture

(a) Break-even Analysis in the Multiproduct Case without Capacity Restrictions

The examples of the analyses described in the previous section indicate that, in the multiproduct case, it is possible to work with univariable break-even analysis only in exceptional cases. The cases which permit the problem to be reduced to one of single-product manufacture are very restricted in scope. In general a simultaneous analysis of alternative combinations of the volumes of the different types of goods cannot be avoided.

In the case of the multiproduct firm, break-even analysis is intended to indicate the critical output levels at which the total contribution is exactly equal to the prescribed contribution block. By way of illustration the two-product situation is first assumed. The firm's total fixed costs are chosen as the contribution block. The sales revenue and cost functions are assumed to be linear. The total contribution depends upon the output levels (x_1, x_2) of the two products:

$$D(x_1, x_2) = D_1(x_1) + D_2(x_2)$$

$$\text{more precisely: } D(x_1, x_2) = d_1 \cdot x_1 + d_2 \cdot x_2. \tag{4.15}$$

All output combinations (x_1, x_2) with

$$D(x_1, x_2) = K^f \tag{4.16}$$

constitute a break-even point. The set of break-even points lies on a *straight line* (cp. Schweitzer and Küpper, 1991 [Systeme] p. 362; Kaplan, 1982 [Management Accounting] p. 141 et seq.). It is the graphical representation of the equation

$$d_1 \cdot x_1 + d_2 \cdot x_2 = K^f. \tag{4.17}$$

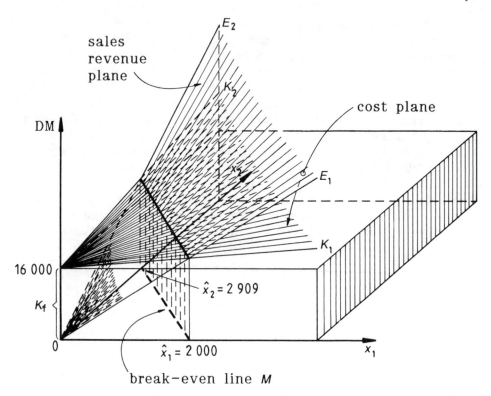

Figure 41 Break-even analysis for two products in a sales revenue-cost diagram

Assuming fixed costs of DM 16 000, unit sales revenue of DM 20 and DM 50 for products 1 and 2 respectively, and variable costs of DM 12 and DM 44.50 for products 1 and 2 respectively then, with contribution margins of $d_1 =$ DM 8 and $d_2 =$ DM 5.50, the resultant equation is:

$$8 \cdot x_1 + 5.5 \cdot x_2 = 16\,000. \tag{4.17}$$

All non-negative pairs which conform to this equation are *break-even points*. They form the set

$$M = \{(x_1,\, x_2) \in \mathbb{R}^2_+ \mid 8x_1 + 5.5x_2 = 16\,000\}. \tag{4.18}$$

This relationship can be presented graphically in a sales revenue-cost diagram (cp. Fig. 41) and also in a contribution margin diagram (cp. Fig. 42).

This set "*M*" forms the *break-even line*. The two end-points of this line are characterised by the disappearance of one of the two variables. They are $(\hat{x}_1,\, 0) =$ (2000, 0) and $(0,\, \hat{x}_2) = (0,\, 2909)$. The respective positive numbers $\hat{x}_1$ and $\hat{x}_2$ are the quotients given by the fixed costs and the individual contribution margins:

$$\hat{x}_1 = \frac{K^{\mathrm{f}}}{d_1} = \frac{16\,000}{8} = 2000 \text{ units}$$

$$\hat{x}_2 = \frac{K^{\mathrm{f}}}{d_2} = \frac{16\,000}{5.5} = 2909 \text{ units}. \tag{4.19}$$

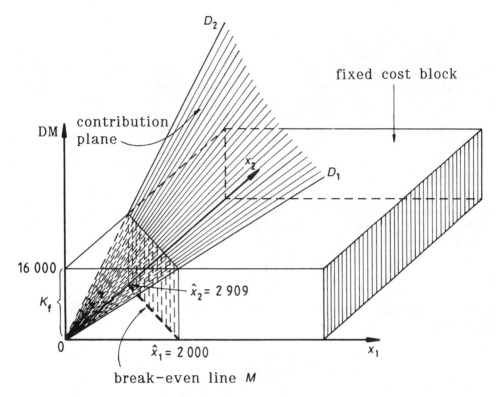

Figure 42 Break-even analysis for two products in a contribution margin diagram

The break-even line can be described as the set of all points on the connecting line between these two corner points. Intermediate points are designated with convex linear combinations of the corner point coordinates. If λ is a parameter which only takes on values between 0 and 1, all intermediate points have coordinates of the form:

$$\lambda \cdot (\hat{x}_1, 0) + (1 - \lambda) \cdot (0, \hat{x}_2)$$
$$= \lambda \cdot (2000, 0) + (1 - \lambda) \cdot (0, 2909) \qquad (4.20)$$
$$= (2000 \cdot \lambda, \; 2909 - 2909 \cdot \lambda).$$

Consequently, the break-even line can be represented with the set

$$M = \{(2000 \cdot \lambda, \; 2909 - 2909 \cdot \lambda) \,|\, \lambda \in [0, 1]\}. \qquad (4.21)$$

For example, for $\lambda = 0.5$, the resultant product quantity combination is $x_1 = 1000$, $x_2 = 1455$; and, for $\lambda = 0.2$, $x_1 = 400$, $x_2 = 2327$.

The same procedure can be extended to the n product case. In the case of linear relationships, the *break-even set M* is also derived by equating the total contribution with the contribution block B:

$$d_1 \cdot x_1 + d_2 \cdot x_2 + \cdots + d_n \cdot x_n = B \qquad (4.22)$$

$$\sum_{i=1}^{n} d_i \cdot x_i = B.$$

Thus, all break-even points form a linear combination of product quantities which are weighted with their unit contribution d_i. Instead of being a single *point* in the case of one product, or a *line* in the case of two products, the break-even points in the n-dimensional case lie on the non-negative part of a *hyperplane*. It can be designated *break-even hyperplane* and when there are more than three products ($n > 3$) can no longer be represented graphically. The break-even hyperplane is however fully specified by the set

$$M = \{(x_1, x_2, \ldots, x_n) \in \mathbb{R}^n_+ \mid \sum_{i=1}^{n} d_i \cdot x_i = B\}. \tag{4.23}$$

A computation of separate *break-even corner points* for each indiviudal product improves the insights provided by the break-even hyperplane. The corner point $\hat{x}_i$ for the ith product is computed on the assumption that the production quantities of the other goods $j(j = 1, 2, \ldots, n, j \neq i)$ are zero. If so, the contribution block B is juxtaposed solely with the contribution margin of the ith product. An isolated break-even point $\hat{x}_i$ is computed from:

$$\hat{x}_i = \frac{B}{d_i} \qquad \text{for } i = 1, 2, \ldots, n. \tag{4.24}$$

Hence, n non-negative corner points of the break-even hyperplane are known. They have the following coordinates:

isolated corner point of the 1st product: $(\hat{x}_1, 0, 0, \ldots 0)$
isolated corner point of the 2nd product: $(0, \hat{x}_2, 0, \ldots, 0)$
$\vdots \qquad \vdots \qquad \vdots \qquad \vdots$

isolated corner point of the ith product: $(0, \ldots, 0, \hat{x}_i, 0 \ldots 0)$
$\vdots \qquad \vdots \qquad \vdots \qquad \vdots \qquad \qquad \uparrow$
$\qquad \qquad \qquad \qquad \qquad \qquad i$th component
isolated corner point of the nth product: $(0, 0, \ldots, 0, \hat{x}_n)$.

All convex linear combinations of these n break-even corner points are also break-even points. Conversely, in that each break-even point can be represented as a convex linear combination of precisely these corner points, then, if the latter are known, the break-even hyperplane is easy to characterise. Each break-even point can be represented as the following kind of sum:

$$\lambda_1 \cdot (\hat{x}_1, 0, 0, \ldots, 0) + \lambda_2 \cdot (0, \hat{x}_2, 0, \ldots, 0) + \lambda_3 \cdot (0, 0, \hat{x}_3, 0, \ldots, 0)$$
$$+ \cdots + \lambda_i \cdot (0, \ldots, 0, \hat{x}_i, 0, \ldots, 0) + \cdots + \lambda_n \cdot (0, 0, \ldots, 0, \hat{x}_n) \tag{4.25}$$
$$= (\lambda_1 \hat{x}_1, \lambda_2 \hat{x}_2, \lambda_3 \hat{x}_3, \ldots, \lambda_n \hat{x}_n) \text{ with } \lambda_i \geqslant 0 \text{ and } \sum_{i=1}^{n} \lambda_i = 1.$$

The break-even set is therefore determined from the equation

$$M = \{(\lambda_1 \hat{x}_1, \lambda_2 \hat{x}_2, \ldots, \lambda_n \hat{x}_n) \mid \lambda_i \geqslant 0 \quad \text{for } i = 1, 2, \ldots, n \quad \text{and} \quad \sum_{i=1}^{n} \lambda_i = 1\}. \tag{4.26}$$

The computation of the break-even hyperplane in the case of television tube manufacture, that was dealt with in the previous section, can be illustrated numerically. There

Table 12

Product i	1	2	3	4	5	6
Type of tube	A	B	C	D	E	F
Unit contribution (d_i) in DM	2.20	15.70	3.45	6.25	1.40	3.30
Break-even corner point $\left(x_i = \dfrac{\text{DM } 3\,000\,000}{\text{DM } d_i/\text{unit}}\right)$	1 363 636	191 083	869 565	480 000	2 142 857	909 091

are $n = 6$ products and the fixed cost contribution block amounts to DM 3 000 000. The isolated break-even corner points which need to be computed take on the values given in Table 12.

The break-even hyperplane is therefore described by the following set of points:

$$M = \{(1\,363\,636 \cdot \lambda_1, \ 191\,083 \cdot \lambda_2, \ 869\,565 \cdot \lambda_3, \ 480\,000 \cdot \lambda_4,$$
$$2\,142\,857 \cdot \lambda_5, \ 909\,091 \cdot \lambda_6) | \lambda_1, \lambda_2, \ldots, \lambda_6 \geqslant 0; \tag{4.27}$$
$$\lambda_1 + \lambda_2 + \cdots + \lambda_6 = 1\}.$$

Each corner point is an element of this break-even hyperplane and can thus be characterised by the fact that $\lambda_i = 1$ for exactly one i whilst, for the other five parameters, $\lambda_j = 0 (j \neq i)$.

Some further examples of break-even points in the television tube case are listed in Fig. 43. In break-even point example 1, the parameters $\lambda_1, \lambda_2, \ldots, \lambda_6$ have the same value. The mid-point of the break-even region is characterised by this constellation. In break-even point example 2, the parameter values are computed from the forecast sales volumes that were specified in the previous section. As a weighting parameter λ_i for product i, its share of the forecast total contribution for the forecast sales values was chosen. In break-even point example 2, λ_i is given by:

$$\lambda_i = \frac{d_i x_i^{\max}}{\sum d_j x_j^{\max}} \qquad \text{for } i = 1, 2, \ldots, 6. \tag{4.28}$$

The construction of this point makes it clear that it represents precisely the product mix that is implicitly assumed in the unidimensional analysis of the same case in Figs 39 and 40. The multidimensional break-even analysis presented here reveals that this is merely one of a multitude of possible break-even points which have the same total sales volume. The break-even point in example 3, in any case, also has a total sales volume of DM 20 415 307 for the same contribution. Further points with the same attributes are readily computable. Finally, example 4 specifies a further break-even point with a sales volume value of DM 23 000 000 (cp. also Fig. 40).

(b) Break-even Analysis in the Multiproduct Case with
Isolated Capacity Restrictions

In the case of a univariable, single-product break-even analysis it is hardly necessary to give special consideration to capacity restrictions. After determining the break-even

Break-even point example	Types of tubes	Chosen parameters	Quantity (units)	Turnover (DM)	Contri- bution (DM)
1	A	$\lambda_1 = 0.166\,667$	227 273	6 136 371	500 001
	B	$\lambda_2 = 0.166\,667$	31 847	1 369 421	499 998
	C	$\lambda_3 = 0.166\,667$	144 928	3 043 488	500 002
	D	$\lambda_4 = 0.166\,667$	80 000	2 800 000	500 000
	E	$\lambda_5 = 0.166\,666$	357 143	5 892 860	500 000
	F	$\lambda_6 = 0.166\,666$	151 515	3 712 118	500 000
	Total	1.000 000	—	22 954 258	3 000 001
2	A	$\lambda_1 = 0.156\,6297$	213 586	5 766 822	469 889
	B	$\lambda_2 = 0.279\,4429$	53 397	2 296 071	838 333
	C	$\lambda_3 = 0.163\,7496$	142 391	2 990 211	491 249
	D	$\lambda_4 = 0.037\,0810$	17 799	622 965	111 244
	E	$\lambda_5 = 0.049\,8367$	106 793	1 762 085	149 510
	F	$\lambda_6 = 0.313\,2601$	284 782	6 977 159	939 781
	Total	1.000 000	—	20 415 313	3 000 006
3	A	$\lambda_1 = 0.105\,420$	143 755	3 881 385	316 261
	B	$\lambda_2 = 0.210\,646$	40 251	1 730 793	631 941
	C	$\lambda_3 = 0.213\,750$	185 870	3 903 270	641 252
	D	$\lambda_4 = 0.017\,096$	8 206	287 210	51 288
	E	$\lambda_5 = 0.039\,830$	85 350	1 408 275	119 490
	F	$\lambda_6 = 0.413\,258$	375 689	9 204 381	1 239 774
	Total	1.000 000	—	20 415 314	3 000 006
4	A	$\lambda_1 = 0.216\,310$	294 968	7 964 136	648 930
	B	$\lambda_2 = 0.169\,697$	32 426	1 394 318	509 088
	C	$\lambda_3 = 0.139\,370$	121 191	2 545 011	418 109
	D	$\lambda_4 = 0.047\,079$	22 598	790 930	141 238
	E	$\lambda_5 = 0.059\,844$	128 237	2 115 911	179 532
	F	$\lambda_6 = 0.367\,700$	334 273	8 189 689	1 103 101
	Total	1.000 000	—	22 999 995	2 999 998

Figure 43 Selected points from the break-even hyperplane in the television tube case

point it can, if necessary, be ascertained whether that point lies above or below the capacity limit. This presents no difficulty because both the capacity limit and the break-even point can be expressed in the same dimension. The situation is not as simple in multiproduct manufacture which is subject to *capacity restrictions*. In such a case, possible break-even points are always characterised by a combination of non-negative output levels of all of the products involved. Hence, a restriction on the output of one product influences the required output levels of the other products. In order to cover the joint contribution block, a contribution forgone in the case of one product must be evened out with higher contributions, i.e. higher output levels, from the other products. An additional mutual dependence of product outputs arises if the capacity limits for each product cannot be determined in isolation but only for some or all products jointly. This holds true if different products go through the same work stations.

The capacity available at such a station can, in these circumstances, only be used sequentially in manufacturing the products in question. In sum, the following cases of capacity restrictions can be distinguished:

—each product is subject to a *capacity restriction*; these capacity limits can, however, be independently specified in *isolation*;
—there is a *joint bottleneck* for several products; the capacity restriction can only be allowed for simultaneously;
—there are *two or more joint bottlenecks*; a simultaneous approach subject to two or more restrictions is therefore required.

Isolated capacity restrictions are examined in this section. They require only a slight modification to the multidimensional multiproduct analysis presented previously. The corner points of the break-even region are first determined. No further considerations are necessary if the capacity limit of a product i exceeds its (determined in isolation) break-even quantity $\hat{x}_i$. In the reverse situation x_i^{max} is less than $\hat{x}_i$ where x_i^{max} denotes the capacity limit for product i. In this event, the isolated break-even point is not an admissible point in the break-even region because the related output level is in no way capable of being produced. This also means that the corner point of the break-even region at which the output of product i is maximised, also contains in every case *non-zero* outputs of further products. With its contribution margin, product i alone cannot cover the contribution block. An exact specification of the latter corner point is however difficult. Apart from the output of the ith product itself, which lies at the capacity limit x_i^{max}, it is not possible to specify in a non-arbitrary manner which further products should be drawn upon in order to cover the contribution block. Given an *admissible* corner point for each product, the break-even set would, as above, be completely captured. The ambiguity outlined leads to the following approach: the (computed as described but nevertheless inadmissible) corner points are resorted to in the usual way in determining the break-even output. This is subject to the qualification that the maximum values of their weights λ_i in the coordinate computation of the break-even points must be such that the capacity limit is not exceeded. The maximum weights λ_i^{max} are ascertained as follows:

From $x_i \leqslant x_i^{max}$ and $x_i = \lambda_i \cdot \hat{x}_i$ it follows that:

$$\lambda_i \hat{x}_i \leqslant x_i^{max} \qquad \text{or} \qquad \lambda_i \leqslant \frac{x_i^{max}}{\hat{x}_i} \tag{4.29}$$

and therefore: $\lambda_i^{max} := \dfrac{x_i^{max}}{\hat{x}_i}$.

Only when λ_i^{max} is less than one does this actually constitute a restriction on the choice of weight λ_i. The break-even set M in the case of isolated product capacity restrictions is in general given by

$$M = \{(\lambda_1 \hat{x}_1, \lambda_2 \hat{x}_2, \ldots, \lambda_n \hat{x}_n) \,|\, 0 \leqslant \lambda_i \leqslant \lambda_i^{max} \quad \text{for } i = 1, 2, \ldots, n \quad \text{and} \quad \sum_{i=1}^{n} \lambda_i = 1\}.$$

$$\tag{4.30}$$

Table 13

No. i	Type of tube	Capacity limit (x_i^{max})	:	Isolated break-even maximum $(\hat{x}_i)$	=	Maximum value of the weighting parameter (λ_i^{max})
1	A	300 000	:	1 363 636	=	0.2200
2	B	75 000	:	191 083	=	0.3925
3	C	200 000	:	869 565	=	0.2300
4	D	25 000	:	480 000	=	0.0521
5	E	150 000	:	2 142 857	=	0.0700
6	F	400 000	:	909 091	=	0.4400

If, in the present context, it is assumed that specifying the production levels x_i^{max} in the glass television tube example is a question of capacity limits, the maximum values λ_i^{max} of the weighting parameters are given in Table 13.

In that all maximum values λ_i^{max} are less than one, allowing for the specified capacity restrictions implies a reduction in the break-even region on each product axis. Hence, no product can of itself cover the contribution block. The break-even set M of feasible points is given by:

$$M = \{(1\,363\,636 \cdot \lambda_1, \ 191\,083 \cdot \lambda_2, \ 896\,565 \cdot \lambda_3, \ 480\,000 \cdot \lambda_4,$$
$$2\,142\,857 \cdot \lambda_5, \ 909\,091 \cdot \lambda_6) \,|\, 0 \leqslant \lambda_1 \leqslant 0.2200;$$
$$0 \leqslant \lambda_2 \leqslant 0.3925; \ 0 \leqslant \lambda_3 \leqslant 0.2300; \ 0 \leqslant \lambda_4 \leqslant 0.0521; \qquad (4.31)$$
$$0 \leqslant \lambda_5 \leqslant 0.0700; \ 0 \leqslant \lambda_6 \leqslant 0.4400;$$
$$\lambda_1 + \lambda_2 + \lambda_3 + \lambda_4 + \lambda_5 + \lambda_6 = 1\}.$$

(c) Break-even Analysis in the Multiproduct Case with a Joint Bottleneck

In the break-even analysis presented thus far, joint production bottlenecks have not been accommodated within the analysis. However, if two or more products go through the same manufacturing stages, isolated capacity limits for individual products are frequently not determinable. It is more generally the case that a work station's existing capacity restricts the possible output of all products simultaneously. It is not necessary to capture each of the existing individual capacities comprising the production process in question in attempting a break-even analysis of such situations. It is in fact enough to include those capacities in the analysis which, going by experience or forecasts, represent potential bottlenecks. The simplest case of this is one in which only a *single bottleneck* needs to be taken into account.

In general, multiproduct break-even analysis subject to a single capacity bottleneck can be defined as the following problem: determine the non-negative production outputs x_i of the n products $i = 1, 2, \ldots, n$, at which the sum of their individual contributions covers a prescribed contribution block B:

$$\sum_{i=1}^{n} d_i x_i \overset{!}{=} B \qquad (x_i \geqslant 0 \ \text{for} \ i = 1, 2, \ldots, n). \qquad (4.32)$$

It is, however, necessary to satisfy the bottleneck capacity constraint. The existing capacity is denoted by b and the capacity utilised by a unit of product i is represented by the production coefficient a_i. The constraint to be satisfied is therefore:

$$\sum_{i=1}^{n} a_i x_i \leqslant b. \qquad (4.33)$$

(4.32) and (4.33) precisely formulate the break-even analysis problem in the single bottleneck case. The set M of attainable break-even points is in general given by:

$$M=\{(x_1, x_2, \ldots, x_n)\in \mathbb{R}_+^n \mid \sum d_i x_i = B; \sum a_i x_i \leqslant b\} \qquad (4.34)$$

Figure 44 indicates how, in the two-product case, part of the break-even set, here the break-even line, is rendered inadmissible by the addition of the capacity constraint. The remaining, admissible part of the break-even set is captured by (4.34). Of course the latter reproduces the required break-even hyerplane only to a limited extent from an operational standpoint. To facilitate the transfer of the solution procedure applied above to the case now analysed, a transformation is advisable. In order to obviate computations in two different dimensions, in (4.32) in output levels and in (4.33) in capacity units, both conditions are formulated in capacity units, i.e. in bottleneck units. This is possible because only one bottleneck is present. The following transformation therefore applies to (4.32):

$$\sum_{i=1}^{n} d_i x_i = \sum_{i=1}^{n} \frac{d_i}{a_i} \cdot a_i x_i \stackrel{!}{=} B$$

$$\sum_{i=1}^{n} \gamma_i \cdot z_i \stackrel{!}{=} B \qquad (z_i \geqslant 0 \text{ for } i=1, 2, \ldots, n). \qquad (4.35)$$

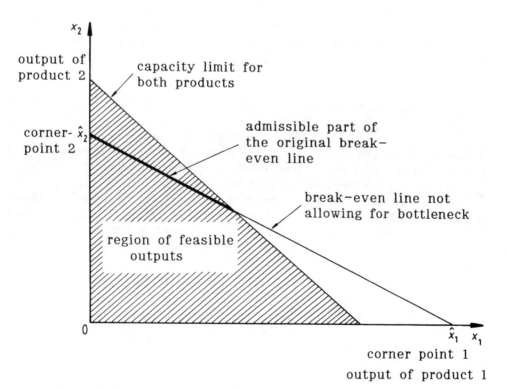

Figure 44 Reduction in the break-even set caused by a joint capacity limit

The bottleneck units that are substituted for product i now appear as a variable z_i. An important parameter in the present context is $\gamma_i := d_i/a_i$, *the contribution margin per bottleneck unit*. This parameter also enters further production decision models which have been developed for this situation (cp., for example, Schweitzer and Küpper, 1991 [Systeme] p. 366). The constraint (4.33) now runs:

$$\sum_{i=1}^{n} z_i \leqslant b. \tag{4.36}$$

Isolated break-even points can now be computed as outlined above. The exclusive manufacture of product i (zero output levels for all other products) results in a break-even point $\hat{z}_i$, expressed in bottleneck units, given by:

$$\hat{z}_i := \frac{B}{a_i}. \tag{4.37}$$

The computed value of $\hat{z}_i$ indicates the number of units of bottleneck capacity that are required for the manufacture of product i in equalising the contribution block B. Such a value calculated in isolation is not necessarily feasible. If perhaps $\hat{z}_i > b$, i.e. the break-even input quantity $\hat{z}_i$ for product i exceeds capacity b, then, in each case, a positive output level for product i must be combined with a sufficiently large output of a product j, the break-even input quantity $\hat{z}_j$ of which is below the capacity limit. In general the set of break-even corner points can again be expressed as a convex linear combination of the computed break-even corner points subject, additionally, to a capacity constraint:

$$M = \{(x_1, x_2, \ldots, x_n) \mid x_i = \frac{\lambda_i \hat{z}_i}{a_i},\ 0 \leqslant \lambda_i \leqslant 1;\ \sum_{i=1}^{n} \lambda_i = 1;\ \sum_{i=1}^{n} \lambda_i \hat{z}_i \leqslant b\}. \tag{4.38}$$

The capacity constraint restricts the choice of parameters $\lambda_1, \lambda_2, \ldots, \lambda_n$, in the manner specified so that, in the case of some of the parameters i, the variation interval of λ_i does not extend from 0 to 1 but has a smaller value.

Each of the factor inputs constitutes possible bottlenecks in industrial firms. In addition to actual material inputs used in manufacture, the relevant bottleneck can also be caused by such constituents of manufacturing capacity as labour time, machine hours or the capacity of manufacturing assets, available amounts of capital, restrictions on sales channels etc.

This procedure can be illustrated with an example. It is concerned with the manufacture of chalk sandstones which are supplied in four different forms. Their production is mainly undertaken on a highly mechanised production line and includes mixing, pressing and various hardening processes. The 2000 annual hours of running time which constitute the capacity of this production line also represent the bottleneck in the production process in question. The scales of all other capacities such as procurement, and others like the post-hardening processes and warehousing, are sufficient by comparison with that of the bottleneck capacity. The contribution block comprises the total fixed costs of the production process in point. They are:

	DM
Fixed space costs	1 625 000
Fixed personnel costs	2 069 875
Fixed costs of assets	
—depreciation, interest	281 250
—maintenance	543 750
Costs of moulds	172 000
Fixed costs of transport	147 500
Other fixed costs	160 625
Total of annual fixed costs	5 000 000

The data given in Table 14 are available for the four types of chalk-stone.

The utilisation of the bottleneck capacity is modelled from the relevant production coefficients. They specify the input time of the production line for every 10 000 units of each individual type of chalk-stone. Using this information, the unit contributions d_i, the contribution margins per bottleneck unit γ_i and the isolated break-even input quantities of the corner points $\hat{z}_i$ can be computed. One running hour of the production line is chosen as the bottleneck unit. The results obtained are shown in Table 15.

The input quantities for the isolated break-even corner points specify the number of hours the productive assets must run, in always producing the same product, in order to cover costs. In that there is fixed annual capacity of 2000 hours, it turns out that the exclusive production of chalk sandstone type 2, or of chalk sandstone type 4, would not result in the attainment of the profit threshold. In general the break-even points of the running times of the asset are distributed between the products in accordance with a convex linear combination of the computed corner point input quantities. The running hours of the production line which are allocated to the individual chalk-stone types, and the resultant outputs are determined as given in Table 16.

Table 14

	Type of stone (i)			
	A 1	B 2	C 3	D 4
Unit selling price (DM q_i)	0.8695	1.1200	1.8550	2.6000
Unit variable costs (DM k_i^v)	0.5028	0.6238	0.8423	1.4897
Production coefficient (asset input in hours per 10 000 units) (a_i)	1.4235	2.4866	2.8945	4.7635

Table 15

	Type of stone (i)			
	A 1	B 2	C 3	D 4
Unit contribution (DM d_i)	0.3667	0.4962	1.0127	1.1103
Contribution per running hour of the production line (DM γ_i)	2 576.05	1 995.50	3 498.70	2 330.85
Ranking	2	4	1	3
Input hours of the isolated break-even corner points (h $\hat{z}_i$)	1 940.96	2 505.64	1 429.10	2 145.14

Table 16

Type of stone (i)	Inputted asset running hours ($\hat{z}_i \cdot \lambda_i$)	:	Production coefficient ($\alpha_i \cdot 10\,000$)	=	Resultant output ($\hat{x}_i \cdot \lambda_i$)
A1	$1\,940.96 \cdot \lambda_1$	:	1.4235	=	$13\,635\,125 \cdot \lambda_1$
B2	$2\,505.64 \cdot \lambda_2$	:	2.4866	=	$10\,076\,570 \cdot \lambda_2$
C3	$1\,429.10 \cdot \lambda_3$	:	2.8945	=	$4\,937\,295 \cdot \lambda_3$
D4	$2\,145.14 \cdot \lambda_4$	:	4.7635	=	$4\,503\,285 \cdot \lambda_4$

The constraints for the choice of admissible parameters are:

$$\lambda_1 + \lambda_2 + \lambda_3 + \lambda_4 = 1, \quad 0 \leqslant \lambda_1, \lambda_2, \lambda_3, \lambda_4 \leqslant 1$$

$$1\,940.96 \cdot \lambda_1 + 2\,505.64 \cdot \lambda_2 + 1\,429.10 \cdot \lambda_3 + 2\,145.14 \cdot \lambda_4 \leqslant 2000. \tag{4.39}$$

Further restrictions on the choice of parameters can be derived from the capacity restriction. It is known that the isolated break-even corner point input time of chalk sandstone type B is 2 505.64 hours. In order actually to arrive at a realisable running time, the parameter λ_2 may take on a maximum value of:

$$\lambda_2 = \frac{2000}{2505.64} = 0.7982.$$

Then of course the break-even condition cannot be satisfied. Thus, in order to cover costs when manufacturing product B, part of the manufacturing capacity must be reserved for a product which provides a higher bottleneck-related contribution margin. The most desirable product in this sense is C. Hence to determine the highest output of product B at which the attainment of a break-even level is possible, the bottleneck capacity must be divided between products B and C. If so, $\lambda_1 = 0$, $\lambda_4 = 0$, $\lambda_3 = 1 - \lambda_2$. The value of the parameter λ_2 satisfies the equation:

$$2505.64 \cdot \lambda_2 + 1429.10 \cdot (1 - \lambda_2) = 2000$$

whence,

$$\lambda_2 = 0.5303.$$

Using the available data, the calculated corner output of product 2, which enters the production programme represented by the break-even hyperplane can therefore take on a maximum parameter value of 0.5303. In the case of product D, $\lambda_4 \leqslant 0.7973$ is ascertained in the same way. The entire set of attainable break-even points can be specified as follows:

$$\begin{aligned} M = \{ & (x_1 = 13\,635\,125 \cdot \lambda_1, \; x_2 = 10\,076\,570 \cdot \lambda_2, \\ & x_3 = 4\,937\,295 \cdot \lambda_3, \; x_4 = 4\,503\,285 \cdot \lambda_4) \mid \\ & 0 \leqslant \lambda_1 \leqslant 1; \; 0 \leqslant \lambda_2 \leqslant 0.5303; \; 0 \leqslant \lambda_3 \leqslant 1; \\ & 0 \leqslant \lambda_4 \leqslant 0.7973; \; 1940.96 \cdot \lambda_1 + 2505.64 \cdot \lambda_2 \\ & + 1429.10 \cdot \lambda_3 + 2145.14 \cdot \lambda_4 \leqslant 2000 \}. \end{aligned} \tag{4.40}$$

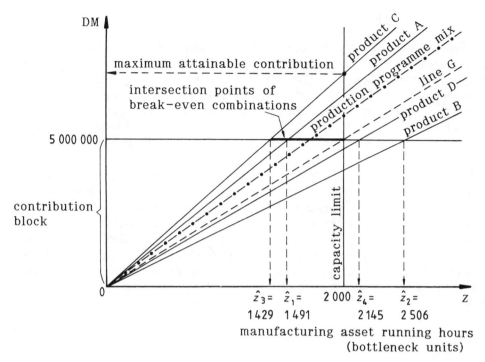

Figure 45 Contribution margin–contribution block diagram (contribution cobweb) for multiproduct analysis with a joint bottleneck

Figure 45 illustrates a graphical representation of the latter bottleneck analysis. The contribution lines of the four types of chalk sandstone are included in a system of coordinates in which the bottleneck unit is used as a reference magnitude. These contribution lines can be described as a *contribution cobweb* (cp. Kleinebeckel, 1983 [Break-even-Analyse] p. 43). It is seen that, in the case of isolated production, only products A and C have a break-even corner point with an attainable (manufacturing) asset input time. The precise form of product-mix that is specified by (4.40) gives a contribution line which lies between the contribution line of product C and the line G.

The emphasised (thick) part of the contribution block line in Fig. 45 denotes possible intersection points of contribution lines of product mixes which are members of the break-even set. A two-dimensional representation of the four-product case can of course only be regarded as an incomplete additional aid. A complete representation of the relationships of a four-product analysis is not possible in two or three-dimensional graphs.

(d) Simultaneous Break-even Analysis in the Multiproduct Case with Two or more Joint Capacity Restrictions

If two or more products are manufactured in a firm, every conceivable combination of outputs is not usually attainable. More usually there are restrictions which stem from the procurement, manufacturing, sales and finance functions (cp. Schweitzer and Küpper, 1991 [Systeme] p. 362 et seq.). Aside from the special case of a single restriction that has just been discussed, a break-even analysis for the multiproduct case must embody a comprehensive mathematical model. In the majority of applications a linear procedure proves to be adequate. The use of *linear programming models* in dealing with break-even questions has been widely proposed. The basic idea is traceable to Charnes, Cooper and Ijiri (cp. 1963 [Break-even Budgeting] p. 16 et seq.; cp. also Ijiri, 1965 [Goals] p. 38 et seq.; Jaedicke, 1961 [Analysis] p. 9 et seq.; Kaplan, 1982 [Management Accounting] p. 145 et seq.; Schweitzer and Trossmann, 1980 [Break-even-Analyse] p. 30 et seq.). However, such approaches are frequently not used to find a solution to the actual break-even problem but for the maximisation of the total contribution subject to constraints. Here the previously-defined more general problem is retained, namely, to find the points at which a specified contribution block is covered.

The core of a linear approach to multiproduct analysis with two or more restrictions is the capturing of the capacity constraints with a system of linear inequalities. Thus, a capacity restriction is specified with two kinds of parameters: on the one hand with capacity b_i; and, on the other, with the production coefficients a_{ij} for $j = 1, 2, \ldots, n$. The two parameters are measured in the same dimension. A production coefficient a_{ij} indicates how many units of restricted capacity type i are necessary for the production of a unit of output of product j. Assuming m restrictions and n products, and again using x_j to denote the output of product j ($j = 1, 2, \ldots, n$), then, in general, existing capacity restrictions can be represented with the following system of linear inequalities:

$$\sum_{j=1}^{n} a_{ij} x_j \leqslant b_i \qquad \text{for } i = 1, 2, \ldots, m \tag{4.41}$$

or, written in detail:

$$
\begin{aligned}
a_{11}x_1 + a_{12}x_2 + a_{13}x_3 + \cdots + a_{1, n-1}x_{n-1} + a_{1n}x_n &\leqslant b_1 \\
a_{21}x_1 + a_{22}x_2 + a_{23}x_3 + \cdots + a_{2, n-1}x_{n-1} + a_{2n}x_n &\leqslant b_2 \\
\vdots \qquad \vdots \qquad \vdots \qquad \cdots \qquad \vdots \qquad \vdots \\
a_{i1}x_1 + a_{i2}x_2 + a_{i3}x_3 + \cdots + a_{i, n-1}x_{n-1} + a_{in}x_n &\leqslant b_i \\
\vdots \qquad \vdots \qquad \vdots \qquad \cdots \qquad \vdots \qquad \vdots \\
a_{m1}x_1 + a_{m2}x_2 + a_{m3}x_3 + \cdots + a_{m, n-1}x_{n-1} + a_{mn}x_n &\leqslant b_m.
\end{aligned}
\tag{4.42}
$$

The set of outputs which simultaneously satisfies all of these inequalities defines a *solution region R*. All *attainable* combinations of the n products lie in this region. Only for these attainable outputs is a break-even analysis sensible. Break-even analysis is therefore a question of determining output programmes $(x_1, x_2, \ldots, x_n)$ with contribution margins which exactly equalise the predicted contribution block B:

$$d_1 x_1 + d_2 x_2 + \cdots + d_n x_n = \text{B}. \tag{4.43}$$

They form a break-even plane M. Outputs are now sought which both lie on the break-even plane M and are feasible, i.e. are located in the solution region R. They correspond to the sub-set $R \cap M$. If, as in the present context, restrictions are formulated linearly, such questions can be resolved by resorting to the solution procedures to which systems of linear inequalities are amenable (cp. Tschernikow, 1971 [Ungleichungen] p. 106 et seq.). In practical applications it is usually advisable to change the structure of the problem to that of the formal structure of a general linear programming problem in order, thereby, to facilitate the use of software that is available for the simplex method. Using the latter, linear planning problems can be solved in standard fashion.

The linear procedure for computing the break-even hyperplane for two products is illustrated in the example which follows. The break-even hyperplane of the two-product case is a line in which case a graphical presentation is also still possible.

The production of the two products is restricted by three types of capacity overall. Both products make use of a productive asset (I) which has a total available capacity of 54 000 hours in the planning period. The production of a unit of product 1 requires an input of 6 hours from this asset whereas the corresponding production coefficient for a unit of product 2 is 27 hours. Consequently the resultant capacity requirement is described by the following inequality:

$$\text{(I)} \qquad 6x_1 + 27x_2 \leqslant 54\,000.$$

Additionally two further resources are used which, in the planning period, are only available in limited supply. The inequalities resulting therefrom are:

$$\text{(II)} \qquad 6x_1 + 7x_2 \leqslant 16\,800$$
$$\text{(III)} \qquad 20x_1 + 6x_2 \leqslant 36\,000.$$

These inequalities result in the solution region R which is presented in Fig. 46. The outputs sought are those for which the contribution margin

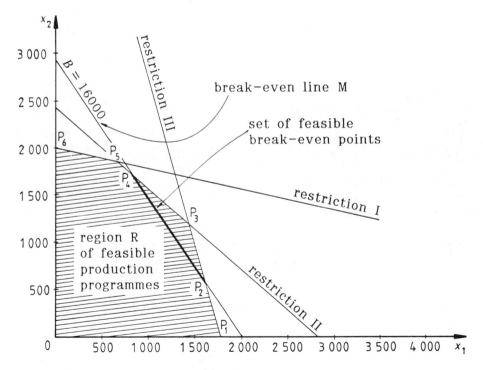

Figure 46 Solution region R (hatched area) of feasible output combinations. The break-even line (set M) intersects the solution region

$$D = 8x_1 + 5.5x_2$$

exactly covers a given contribution block B. There are thus two conceivable cases:

(1) Such contribution points are to be found in the solution region. This is the case, for example, if the contribution margins are to cover a fixed cost block of DM 16 000. To determine the set $R \cap M$ of all break-even points, procedures for solving systems of linear inequalities can be used.

(2) There are no contribution points of the required kind in the solution region. This applies, for example, to a contribution block of DM 25 000. All attainable combinations of outputs produce a contribution of less than DM 25 000. The system of linear inequalities has no solution. However, information on outputs which come closest to achieving the specified contribution level can of course constitute important information. In this case a linear optimisation model, for ascertaining the points at which the deviation of the contribution block line (its points form the set M) from the solution region is minimised, can be devised.

In cases in which there are many restrictions and such different magnitudes as fixed costs, minimum retained profit and minimum distributions to shareholders constitute the contribution block, it frequently cannot be perceived at the outset whether attainable contribution points actually exist. In that event, a linear optimisation model can be formulated for determining an alternative combination of outputs that deviates minimally from the break-even line (cp. Charnes, Cooper and Ijiri, 1963 [Break-even Budgeting] p. 21 et seq.). If, in the example, B = DM 16 000 is to be recovered, the structure of the model is:

Minimise

$$Z = x_6 + x_7$$

$$
\begin{aligned}
\text{subject to} \quad 6x_1 + 27x_2 + x_3 &= 54\,000 \\
6x_1 + 7x_2 + x_4 &= 16\,800 \\
20x_1 + 6x_2 + x_5 &= 36\,000 \\
8x_1 + 5.5x_2 + x_6 - x_7 &= 16\,000
\end{aligned}
\tag{4.44}
$$

and $x_1, \ldots, x_7 \geqslant 0$,

whereby x_3 to x_7 are slack variables.

The variables x_6 and x_7 specify the deviations above and below the contribution line which are to be minimised. These deviations are here assumed to be of equal weight in both directions. The objective is therefore to minimise the sum of x_6 and x_7. Only one of the two variables x_6 and x_7 differs from zero in an admissible solution because a solution point on the given line cannot simultaneously deviate above and below it. However, the formulation of an actual constraint to meet the requirement that at least one of the two variables x_6 and x_7 disappears can be waived. The structure of the linear model described, especially the objective function, guarantees, in an optimal solution, that at most one of the two variables x_6 and x_7 takes on a value that is not equal to zero.

1. Tableau point P_0			$c_1 = 0$	$c_2 = 0$	$c_3 = 0$	$c_4 = 0$	$c_5 = 0$	$c_6 = -1$	$c_7 = -1$
c_{basis}	Basis	Solution	x_1	x_2	x_3	x_4	x_5	x_6	x_7
$c_3 = 0$	x_3	54 000	6	27	1	0	0	0	0
$c_4 = 0$	x_4	16 800	6	7	0	1	0	0	0
$c_5 = 0$	x_5	36 000	(20)	6	0	0	1	0	0	⇐
$c_6 = -1$	x_6	16 000	8	5.5	0	0	0	1	−1
	Z_j	−16 000	−8	−5.5	0	0	0	−1	1
	$Z_j - c_j$		−8	−5.5	0	0	0	0	2

⇑

Figure 47 Starting tableau for the solution of the simultaneous multiproduct formulation using the simplex procedure (contribution block B = DM 16 000)

If there are attainable outputs at which the contributions reach the aspired level, the minimisation result is zero. This means that deviations neither appear below ($x_6 = 0$) nor above ($x_7 = 0$) the break-even line. On the other hand, if the level of the contribution block is so high that no feasible output combination is sufficient, the objective function takes on a positive value in the results given by the linear optimisation approach.

If the linear planning model formulated in (4.44) is solved by resorting to the *simplex method* (cp., e.g. Müller-Merbach, 1973 [Operations Research] p. 88 et seq.), it turns out that the first case obtains. The first tableau of the iteration is presented in Fig. 47. The start of the computation is denoted by P_0.

After two iterations a solution is found that gives an objective function value of zero and which indicates a minimum. This relates to point P_2. The corresponding final tableau is presented in Fig. 48. It gives the coordinate values (1645, 516) for P_2.

An examination of the rows of the dual values (last line of Fig. 48) reveals a peculiarity. It is not only the basis variables x_1, x_2, x_3, x_4 that have a dual value of zero, so too does the non-basis variable x_5. This indicates that the solution to the problem is ambiguous. In addition to P_2 there must be at least one further solution with the same objective function value ($x_6 + x_7 = 0$). In fact x_4 can be swapped with x_5. The result of such a swap is shown in Fig. 49. The value of the objective function is the same whilst the coordinates of the solution point are (852, 1670). This is point P_4.

The tableau in Fig. 49 also indicates the ambiguity that is present: the dual value of x_4 is zero although x_4 is a non-basis variable. A further swap would, however, lead back to P_2. Hence, all solutions are known.

The solution to the linear optimisation model that was formulated indicates that point P_2 and point P_4 likewise facilitate the attainment of a zero minimum value for the objective function. Hence, all points which lie on the line connecting P_2 and P_4 are also solutions to the optimisation model. P_2 and P_4 have the respective coordinates (1645, 516) and (852, 1670). The set of feasible break-even points that is sought is therefore given by:

$$R \cap M = \{(x_1, x_2) \mid x_1 = \lambda \cdot 1645 + (1 - \lambda) \cdot 852;$$
$$x_2 = \lambda \cdot 516 + (1 - \lambda) \cdot 1670; \ 0 \leqslant \lambda \leqslant 1\} \tag{4.45}$$

3. Tableau point P_2			$c_1=0$	$c_2=0$	$c_3=0$	$c_4=0$	$c_5=0$	$c_6=-1$	$c_7=-1$
c_{basis}	Basis	Solution*	x_1	x_2	x_3	x_4	x_5	x_6	x_7
$c_3=0$	x_3	30 194	0	0	1	0	$\frac{183}{62}$	$-\frac{252}{31}$	$\frac{252}{31}$
$c_4=0$	x_4	3 316	0	0	0	1	$\left(\frac{23}{62}\right)$	$-\frac{52}{31}$	$\frac{52}{31}$ ⇐
$c_1=0$	x_1	1 645	1	0	0	0	$\frac{11}{124}$	$-\frac{3}{31}$	$\frac{3}{31}$
$c_2=0$	x_2	516	0	1	0	0	$-\frac{4}{31}$	$\frac{10}{31}$	$-\frac{10}{31}$
	Z_j	0	0	0	0	0	0	0	0
	Z_j-c_j	0	0	0	0	0	0	1	1

*Rounded.   ⇑

Figure 48 Final tableau for the solution of simultaneous multiproduct formulation using the simplex procedure (contribution block B = DM 16 000)

4. Tableau point P_4			$c_1=0$	$c_2=0$	$c_3=0$	$c_4=0$	$c_5=0$	$c_6=-1$	$c_7=-1$
c_{basis}	Basis	Solution*	x_1	x_2	x_3	x_4	x_5	x_6	x_7
$c_3=0$	x_3	3 809	0	0	1	$-\frac{183}{23}$	0	$\frac{120}{23}$	$-\frac{120}{23}$
$c_5=0$	x_5	8 939	0	0	0	$\left(\frac{62}{23}\right)$	1	$-\frac{104}{23}$	$\frac{104}{23}$ ⇐
$c_1=0$	x_1	852	1	0	0	$-\frac{11}{46}$	0	$\frac{7}{23}$	$-\frac{7}{23}$
$c_2=0$	x_2	1 670	0	1	0	$\frac{8}{23}$	0	$-\frac{6}{23}$	$\frac{6}{23}$
	Z_j	0	0	0	0	0	0	0	0
	Z_j-c_j	0	0	0	0	0	0	1	1

*Rounded.   ⇑

Figure 49 Tableau of the second solution to the simultaneous multiproduct formulation using the simplex procedure (contribution block B = DM 16 000)

3. Tableau point P_3			$c_1 = 0$	$c_2 = 0$	$c_3 = 0$	$c_4 = 0$	$c_5 = 0$	$c_6 = -1$	$c_7 = -1$
c_{basis}	Basis	Solution*	x_1	x_2	x_3	x_4	x_5	x_6	x_7
$c_3 = 0$	x_3	14 123	0	0	1	$-\dfrac{63}{13}$	$\dfrac{15}{13}$	0	0
$c_2 = 0$	x_2	1 154	0	1	0	$\dfrac{5}{26}$	$-\dfrac{3}{52}$	0	0
$c_1 = 0$	x_1	1 454	1	0	0	$-\dfrac{3}{52}$	$\dfrac{7}{104}$	0	0
$c_6 = -1$	x_6	7 023	0	0	0	$-\dfrac{31}{52}$	$-\dfrac{23}{104}$	1	-1
	Z_j	$-7\,023$	0	0	0	$\dfrac{31}{52}$	$\dfrac{23}{104}$	-1	1
	$Z_j - c_j$		0	0	0	$\dfrac{31}{52}$	$\dfrac{23}{104}$	0	2

*Rounded.

Figure 50 Final tableau for the solution of the simultaneous multiproduct formulation with a contribution block of DM 25 000

In Fig. 46 the set of feasible break-even points is represented with a thick line. An infinitely large number of feasible break-even points will therefore cover a contribution block of DM 16 000. This is an example of the first of the two possibilities given above.

The problem of finding a solution is somewhat different in the case of a contribution block B = DM 25 000. Using the same approach the application of the simplex procedure results in the final tableau shown in Fig. 50.

As is shown by the row of the dual values, the extreme value of the function to be minimised is arrived at. It is unambiguous. The point that is found has the coordinates (1454, 1154) and at that location the objective function does not take on a value of zero. The slack variable x_6 has a value of 7023. This shows that, given the existing cost–sales revenue relationships and the capacity limits, a contribution block of DM 25 000 cannot be covered.

As shown by the solution value of the variable x_6, the maximum attainable contribution still remains DM 7023 below DM 25 000. In the best case, DM (25 000 – 7023) = DM 17 977 can thus be achieved. The solution arrived at using the simultaneous linear procedure consequently produces a contribution which, given the restrictions, falls short of the aspired contribution level but most nearly approaches it. The graphical presentation (cp. Fig. 51) also makes it clear that the computed output combination, namely P_3, is that in the feasible production region which is nearest to the contribution block line.

In the procedure presented, the deviations below (x_6) and above (x_7) the break-even line can also be valued with different weightings. This changes the solution in any event in the second case if none of the feasible points are also break-even points.

Because of its generality the simultaneous linear break-even analysis model has a broad area of application. It can also be used to formulate all of the extensions of break-even

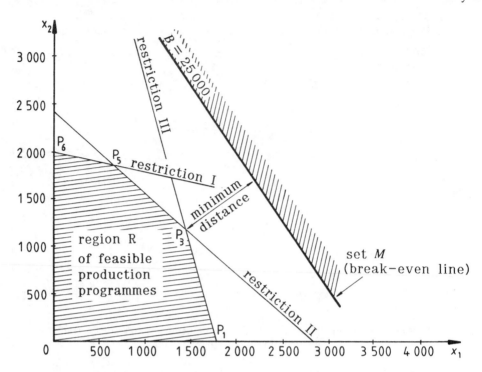

Figure 51 Solution region in the illustrative example. The break-even line for a contribution block of DM 25 000 contains no feasible points

analysis, that were brought up in the single-product case, in an analogous multiproduct manner. Only the graphical presentation is rendered more difficult or impossible.

If the multidimensional analysis proves to be too differentiated, related products can be subsumed in *product groups*. Frequently a dimensional reduction of the problem is possible, with no loss either of accuracy or of breadth of information, if suitable production indices are used for some product types instead of output units. If, namely, the same index can be used simultaneously for two or more products, such product types can be jointly measured on the same scale. In contrast to the use of production indices in the case of the univariable multiproduct analysis, the use of the index can, however, be restricted here to those product types for which the chosen index actually represents an adequate measuring rod. It is suggested, for example, that such products as are processed in the same work stations should be measured in terms of the manufacturing hours of those stations instead of in input units (cp. Weinwurm, 1970 [Break-even Analysis] p. 306). All products which pass through the chosen work stations can then be analysed in one dimension. Instead of the number of different product types, the (frequently smaller) number of different work stations then determines, in the most favourable case, the number of determinants and thus the dimension of the break-even analysis. The break-even analysis then yields break-even points expressed in the form of minimum (or maximum) numbers of manufacturing hours in the different work stations. Their allocation to products within a work station consequently remains equally as open as, for example, the choice of a particular break-even point on a break-even hyperplane.

III. BREAK-EVEN ANALYSIS IN THE CASE OF MULTISTAGE MULTIPRODUCT MANUFACTURE

1. Break-even Problems in the Case of Multistage Manufacture

Break-even analyses are based on a comparison of positive and negative components. Negative components are frequently the costs which are juxtaposed with positive components in the form of sales revenue. Expressed more generally, break-even analyses are concerned with a comparison of a contribution block with contribution margins. Only if the two components are known is a break-even analysis possible. This condition is satisfied in the case of single-stage production. In the case of multistage computations it is, by contrast, generally only possible to specify cost and revenue components in the final production stage. Whilst the costs of the intermediate production stages are known, this is usually not true of sales revenue and contributions. Nevertheless, information on the points beyond which particular fixed costs of individual production stages are covered would be of interest. A definitive resolution of this question is only possible if the contribution realised after the final production stage can be appropriately allocated to the prior production stages. In some cases such an allocation can be achieved by resorting to the market and transfer prices of individual intermediate products (see Section 3 below). The contributions of the individual production stages which constitute the unit contribution of an end-product can then be ascertained.

If selling prices cannot be specified for the prior production stages such an allocation is not possible. If not, the total achieved contribution can only be imputed in a specified order of priorities to the computational blocks of the individual production stages. The simplest case in point is that of *multistage single-product manufacture*. An example is given in Fig. 52 in which break-even points for the sequential recovery of the fixed cost blocks of the individual production stages are ascertained.

The break-even analysis becomes more complicated if the goods flow exhibits any kind of *convergence or divergence*. Thus, in the case of a divergent goods flow structure, at least part of the fixed costs of the divergent stage cannot be separately imputed to the succeeding stages. In fact these fixed costs are attributable to the intermediate product in question independently of its subsequent use. In the case of divergence, a more exact distinction between programme-determined and process-determined divergence can be made (cp. Küpper, 1980 [Interdependenzen] p. 109). A feature of programme-determined divergence is that the same intermediate product is transferred to different (subsequent) centres in the production process where, for example, it then enters the manufacturing processes of different end-products. In the case of process-determined divergence, however, different end-products emerge in the same constituent process either in a fixed ratio of output or in an output ratio which is variable only within narrow limits. The various forms of multistage contribution costing frequently reflect the basic notion of an approximate *programme-determined divergent goods flow*. A method of break-even analysis conforming to the latter situation is presented in sub-section 2 below. *Process-determined divergence* is a question of joint production. As described in the example of pig-meat processing in Section II.1.d, a quantity-based input index can frequently be used in this situation for the purposes of break-even analysis. The application of this procedure, at the production centres at which there is a process-determined goods flow, simplifies the analysis of the multistage structure. It then becomes a problem with a simpler (convergent or divergent) structure.

1st produc-tion stage	2nd produc-tion stage	3rd produc-tion stage	4th produc-tion stage	5th produc-tion stage

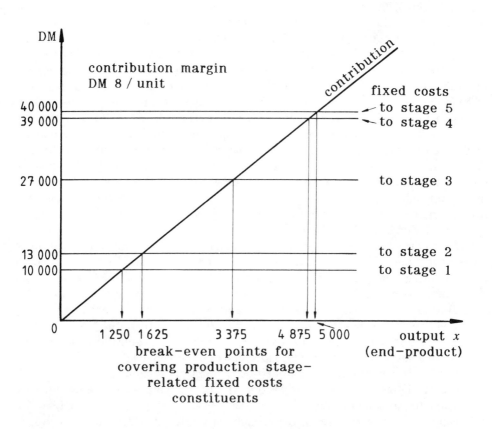

input good →○→→○→→○→→○→→○→ end-product

fixed costs	10 000	3000	14 000	12 000	1000

total DM 40 000

end-product unit variable costs	2.00	3.00	1.00	4.00	7.00

total DM 17.00

selling price: DM 25.00

contribution margin DM 8 / unit

contribution

fixed costs

40 000 — to stage 5
39 000 — to stage 4

27 000 — to stage 3

13 000 — to stage 2
10 000 — to stage 1

0   1 250 1 625   3 375   4 875 5 000   output x (end-product)

break-even points for covering production stage-related fixed costs constituents

Figure 52 Break-even analysis in the multistage, single-product case with no stage-related sales revenue information

When the goods flow *structure is convergent*, two or more input or intermediate goods are combined into either a new intermediate product or end-product. In such a case, the costs of the input goods are of course separately available whereas, as a rule, sales revenue and contribution margins are only known for the ultimate end-product. A break-even analysis is therefore based upon this end-product. The convergent structure reveals itself only in the determination of costs whereby appropriate quantities of input goods are added. Given information on the sales revenue and contribution margins of individual intermediate products then, as in the case of programme-determined divergence, additional break-even results can be derived.

In the following pages, multistage break-even analysis is first presented for a divergent production structure which is predominantly programme-determined. It is assumed that problem simplifications which are possible for reasons concerning constituent joint production processes, or in simple convergence cases, have already been made. In the presentation, a distinction is made between the (more frequent) case, in which prices and contribution margins are not available for the intermediate stages of the production process, and that in which (transfer) prices for intermediate products are known. Thereafter, a general approach to the determination of break-even surfaces for multistage production is derived.

2. Multistage Break-even Analysis in the Absence of Prices for Intermediate Products

(a) Analysis of a Two-product Problem

Fundamental to a break-even analysis of multistage production is the procedure in the case of programme-determined divergence. In such a situation sales revenue information is normally absent in the prior production stages but is available for the end-products. Costs which arise before, and in, a divergence centre should be attributed to an intermediate product which, at such a centre, is variously utilised. Costs which arise after a divergence centre should, however, be allocated to one of the various products which are produced in the subsequent centres. This cost allocation is equally valid for both fixed and variable cost components. However, whilst divergence has no consequences for the unit variable costs of each end-product, the ascertaining of the fixed costs of each product results in ambiguities. The example in Fig. 53 makes this clear.

Input goods, which are the same for the two end-products in this example, give rise to fixed costs of DM 36 000. Thereafter, and subsequent to the divergence centre, further fixed costs arise which can however be separately specified for each product. This example is the same as that in Section II.1.b except that the production process is now interpreted as a two-stage procedure. Hence, more precise predictions are possible. The break-even computation can be based on the assumption that product-related, separate fixed costs are first to be recovered from the achieved contribution margins and that components of the joint fixed cost block are recovered thereafter.

In the example, the selling prices of products A and B are DM 19.50 and DM 29.50 respectively. Given the data in Fig. 53, the contribution margin of product A is DM 6.50. The isolated break-even point of product A is a an output $\hat{x}_1 =$ DM 9000/DM 6.50 per unit = 1385 units. In the case of product B, the contribution of DM 2.50 results in an isolated break-even point $\hat{x}_2 = 8000$ units. The computed values specify the respective outputs beyond which the products contribute to the recovery of such fixed

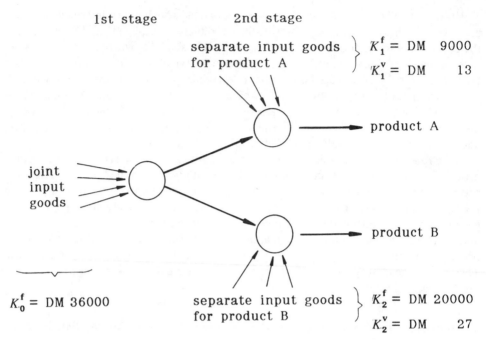

Figure 53 Production structure for an example of two-stage two-product manufacture

costs as can only be attributed jointly to the two products. Fixed costs amounting to DM 36 000 have to be covered jointly. Each unit of product A which is sold in excess of its isolated break-even point of 1385 units contributes DM 6.50 to these joint fixed costs. The corresponding unit contribution from product B in excess of its isolated break-even point of 8000 units is DM 2.50. Analogously to the single-stage case, the break-even outputs are given by the following equation:

$$d_1 \cdot (x_1 - \hat{x}_1) + d_2 \cdot (x_2 - \hat{x}_2) = K_0^f \tag{4.46}$$

or

$$6.50 \cdot (x_1 - 1385) + 2.50 \cdot (x_2 - 8000) = 36\,000.$$

The joint break-even line can be more precisely characterised by computing the break-even corner points, namely:

$$(1) \quad \bar{x}_1 = \frac{36\,000}{6.50} + 1385 = 6923; \quad \bar{x}_2 = 8000$$

$$(2) \quad \bar{x}_1 = 1385; \quad \bar{x}_2 = \frac{36\,000}{2.50} + 8000 = 22\,400.$$

The joint break-even line is therefore precisely captured by the following set:

$$M = \{(x_1, x_2) \mid x_1 = 6923 \cdot \lambda_1; \; x_2 = 22\,400 \cdot \lambda_2; \; \lambda_1, \lambda_2 \geqslant 0; \; \lambda_1 + \lambda_2 = 1\}. \tag{4.47}$$

This result does not allow for the capacity restrictions on the two products. It is only possible to realise such outputs as lie below capacity limits of 4000 units and 20 000 units for products A and B respectively. This imposes an additional restriction on the break-even points. The chosen parameter value λ_1, for product A must not exceed

$$\lambda_1^{max} = \frac{4000}{6923} = 0.57\,778$$

The corresponding maximum parameter value that can be chosen for B is

$$\lambda_2^{max} = \frac{20\,000}{22\,400} = 0.89\,286.$$

The set of feasible break-even points is therefore given by (4.47) subject to the additional constraints $\lambda_1 \leqslant 0.57\,778$ and $\lambda_2 \leqslant 0.89\,286$.

The relationships can still be presented graphically because the example deals with the two-product case. Figure 54 clearly shows that initially two mutually independent unidimensional break-even analyses are carried out. A joint multiproduct analysis for

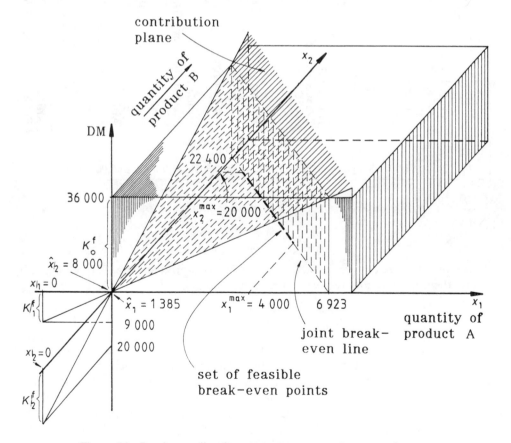

Figure 54   Break-even line for two-stage, two-product manufacture

1st stage	**Firm as a whole** Fixed costs at the level of the firm as a whole DM 500 000.00										
2nd stage	**Product group 1** Product group fixed costs DM 10 000 000.00						**Product group 2** Product group fixed costs DM 3 500 000.00				
3rd stage	Article group 11 Article group fixed costs (DM): 800 000.00			Article group 12 Article group fixed costs (DM): 200 000.00		Article group 13 Article group fixed costs (DM): 2 000 000		Article group 21 Article group fixed costs (DM): 2 500 000.00			Article group 22 Article group fixed costs (DM): 500 000.00	
4th stage	Article 111 Product fixed costs: DM 60 000.00	Article 112 Product fixed costs: DM 120 000.00	Article 113 Product fixed costs: DM 10 000.00	Article 121 Product fixed costs: DM 54 000.00	Article 131 Product fixed costs: DM 80 000.00	Article 132 Product fixed costs: DM 60 000.00	Article 211 Product fixed costs: DM 12 000.00	Article 212 Product fixed costs: DM 75 000.00	Article 213 Product fixed costs: DM 58 000.00	Article 221 Product fixed costs: DM 100 000.00	Article 222 Product fixed costs: DM 100 000.00
Unit contribution (DM):	12.00	18.00	5.00	3.00	2.50	6.00	50.00	30.00	55.00	0.50	1.80

Figure 55 Example of a multistage fixed cost classification

determining the break-even surface which, in the two-product case, is represented by a line, then begins at the respective break-even points.

(b) Analysis of a Multiproduct Problem

The principle underlying the break-even analysis of the two-product case can be applied to any desired number of stages and products. The production structure which actually exists is of course frequently simplified for internal accounting purposes. In cost analysis convergent goods flows raise fewer problems than does the case of a divergent structure. It is therefore also found that applied accounting concepts predominantly accentuate the related cost allocation problems. This is a question of *periodic accounting for cost units* and/or cost centres (*operating reports*) based on variable costs.

A typical cost classification is shown in Fig. 55. It is a computational approach which delineates three stages. In the first stage, services which cannot however be unambiguously allocated, are provided in respect of two product groups. These services, possibly management and administrative services, give rise to fixed costs amounting to DM 500 000. In a second stage, services are provided, e.g. for product group 1, which cannot however be precisely allocated in accordance with the further threefold sub-classification of the three article groups 11, 12 and 13. Finally, in a third stage, the goods stream diverges further, namely, from article groups into individual articles. If the services provided in the individually-depicted stages are designed fictitious "intermediate products" 0, 1, 2, 11, 12, 13, 21 and 22 respectively, the production structure assumed in Fig. 55 can be presented as a network. Figure 56 shows this structure of goods flow. It is clear that, in substance, only the cases of divergence are explicitly analysed.

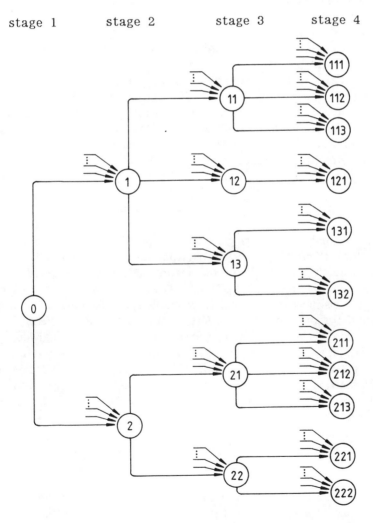

Figure 56 Production structure for the example of multistage fixed cost classification in Fig. 55

In the production process in question, many instances of convergence may also have arisen. These are indicated with arrows in Fig. 56. They do not cause any special cost accounting problems. For this reason no explicit reference is made to instances of convergence in computational tables like Fig. 56. They partially determine the magnitude of the variable costs.

In the interests of clarity, the sub-totals of variable costs are not explicitly included in either Fig. 55 or Fig. 56. Only the product unit contributions are given.

In the present case, isolated individual product break-even points for the recovery of total fixed costs can only be computed if the joint fixed costs of an intermediate production stage are arbitrarily allocated to end-products. For example, it has been suggested that a particular product mix should be assumed so that product group recovery factors can be ascertained (cp. Lägel, 1980 [Nutzschwellen] p. 123). If it is desired to avoid this kind of arbitrary allocation, a differentiated multistage break-even analysis must be undertaken. It is advisable to begin with the lowest sub-classification, i.e. with the end-products. At this level, isolated break-even points can first be calculated. For example, product 111 has an isolated break-even point of 5000 units for covering fixed costs amounting to DM 60 000 which are directly attributable to this product. The next step requires the ascertainment of the break-even surface for an entire article group. To ensure that the computation is clearly arranged, it is advisable to begin with the fixed costs which accumulate as from this stage. Thus, article group 11 shows a contribution block of DM 990 000 comprising joint fixed costs of DM 800 000 and product-related fixed costs of DM 60 000, DM 120 000 and DM 10 000 respectively. The joint contributions of the three products in article group 11 must contribute to the equalisation of cumulative fixed costs amounting to DM 990 000. The equation for determining the break-even points is therefore:

$$12x_1 + \dot{1}8x_2 + 5x_3 = \text{DM } 990\,000.$$

As shown in the analysis of the single-stage multiproduct case, a separate break-even corner point for each product can be derived from this equation. The break-even surface is then demarcated by convex, linear combinations of these corner points. The corner points and parametric presentation of the break-even surface are specified in Fig. 57.

The weighting parameters λ_i express the proportions in which the individual products contribute to the recovery of the fixed costs in question. However, because this block also contains fixed cost constituents which are directly attributable to individual products, the parameter λ_i must take on a particular minimum value if each product is at least to cover its own fixed costs. Thus, product 111's isolated fixed costs of DM 60 000 are included in a contribution block amounting to DM 990 000. To cover its own fixed costs of DM 60 000, product 111's share in the recovery of the fixed cost block of article group 11 must at least amount to

$$\lambda_{111}^{\min} = \frac{\text{DM } 60\,000}{\text{DM } 990\,000} = 0.06061$$

Product 111 contributes, over and above its own fixed costs, to the recovery of the joint fixed costs of article group 11 only if the parameter λ_{111} is greater than this marginal value.

The break-even analysis is continued at the higher stages with the same approach as that adopted at the article group level. Figure 57 shows the individual computational results. At each stage a further form of minimum condition is added to the parameter λ_i. The goods flow of the firm as a whole is analysed at the first stage. At this level there are minimum conditions for the recovery of the product group-related contribution blocks of product groups 1 and 2, minimum conditions for the recovery of the product-related contribution blocks of article groups 11, 12, 13, 21 and 22; and, minimum conditions for the isolated recovery of the product-related fixed costs of the eleven products. The parameter minima thus specify the proportion of total fixed costs that is directly attributable to products, article groups and product groups. They must at least cover this proportion of the total fixed costs. Thus, it can be inferred from Fig. 57 that, of total fixed costs of DM 20.7 mill., approximately 64.6% is directly attributable to product group 1. Of this amount, approximately 4.8% can be directly imputed to article group 11 which contains 0.3% isolated fixed costs attributable to product 111. In the present example, the set of break-even points forms a hyperplane in 12-dimensional space. It can be characterised with its corner points. If it is also intended that at least the isolated costs should be recovered in the prior production stages, the set of break-even points is thereby subject to a constraint in which case only part of the hyperplane represents admissible break-even points.

The multistage break-even analysis described here shows the possible ways of recovering the fixed costs of the various production stages without excluding conceivable alternatives from the analysis as a result of an arbitrary allocation of joint cost constituents to the products in question. This procedure therefore gives a more precise insight into the cost features of a multistage production process than does an allocation of the fixed cost constituents of prior production stages to end-products on the basis of "capacity to bear" or by reference to other principles. The procedure reflecting the multistage break-even computation presented here can be applied in the same way to any desired number of products and production stages. In certain circumstances it is sufficient to undertake the computation for individual, selected production stages e.g. for the first and end-product stages.

3. Multistage Break-even Analysis with known Transfer Prices for Intermediate Products

Hitherto in the multistage analysis it has been assumed that prices could not be specified for the services provided at the intermediate stages of production. In the case of multistage production this is very frequently so. In some cases, however, the *prices* of some, or all, intermediate products are known. This is pre-eminently the case if intermediate products are sold in external markets—in which case the relevant selling prices are known—or when the same types of intermediate product can be bought in external markets at known buying prices. In some circumstances it is necessary appropriately to modify such price information in using it in break-even analyses or for other cost computational purposes (cp. Schweitzer and Küpper, 1991 [Systeme] p. 380). Thus, buying prices must be supplemented with procurement costs and selling prices must be reduced in respect of sales revenue diminutions. In the absence of an external market for an intermediate product, a transfer price is, in some cases, nevertheless ascertainable under certain assumptions (cp. Schweitzer and Küpper, 1991 [Systeme] p. 379).

Article	111	112	113	121	131	132	211	212	213	221	222
4th stage — Contribution block (DM)	60 000	120 000	10 000	54 000	80 000	60 000	12 000	75 000	58 000	100 000	100 000
Isolated break-even point (units)	5 000	6 667	2 000	18 000	32 000	10 000	240	2 500	1 055	200 000	55 556
3rd production stage — Article group Contribution block (DM)	11 · 990 000			12 · 254 000	13 · 2 140 000		21 · 2 645 000			22 · 700 000	
Corner points (units)	82 500	55 000	198 000	84 667	856 000	356 667	52 900	88 167	48 091	1 400 000	388 889

3rd production stage — Break-even surface:

For articles 111, 112, 113 — set of all points $(x_{111}, x_{112}, x_{113})$ satisfying:
$$x_{111} = 82\,500 \cdot \lambda_{111}$$
$$x_{112} = 55\,000 \cdot \lambda_{112}$$
$$x_{113} = 198\,000 \cdot \lambda_{113}$$
where $\lambda_{111} + \lambda_{112} + \lambda_{113} = 1$, $\lambda_i \geq 0$ for $i = 111, 112, 113$

For article 121: $x_{121} = 84\,667 \cdot \lambda_{121}$, where $\lambda_{121} = 1$

For articles 131, 132 — set of all points (x_{131}, x_{132}) satisfying:
$$x_{131} = 856\,000 \cdot \lambda_{131}$$
$$x_{132} = 356\,667 \cdot \lambda_{132}$$
where $\lambda_{131} + \lambda_{132} = 1$, $\lambda_{131}, \lambda_{132} \geq 0$

For articles 211, 212, 213 — set of all points $(x_{211}, x_{212}, x_{213})$ satisfying:
$$x_{211} = 52\,900 \cdot \lambda_{211}$$
$$x_{212} = 88\,167 \cdot \lambda_{212}$$
$$x_{213} = 48\,091 \cdot \lambda_{213}$$
where $\lambda_{211} + \lambda_{212} + \lambda_{213} = 1$, $\lambda_i \geq 0$ for $i = 211, 212, 213$

For articles 221, 222 — set of all points (x_{221}, x_{222}) satisfying:
$$x_{221} = 1\,400\,000 \cdot \lambda_{221}$$
$$x_{222} = 388\,889 \cdot \lambda_{222}$$
where $\lambda_{221} + \lambda_{222} = 1$, $\lambda_{221}, \lambda_{222} \geq 0$

Minimum condition for the isolated recovery of product-related fixed costs	$\lambda_{111} \geq$ 0.06061	$\lambda_{112} \geq$ 0.12121	$\lambda_{113} \geq$ 0.01010	$\lambda_{121} \geq$ 0.21260	$\lambda_{131} \geq$ 0.03738	$\lambda_{132} \geq$ 0.02804	$\lambda_{211} \geq$ 0.00454	$\lambda_{212} \geq$ 0.02836	$\lambda_{213} \geq$ 0.02193	$\lambda_{221} \geq$ 0.14286	$\lambda_{222} \geq$ 0.14286
2nd production stage — Product group contribution block (DM)	1 · 13 384 000						2 · 6 845 000				
Corner points (units)	1 115 333	743 556	2 676 800	4 461 333	5 353 600	2 230 667	136 900	228 167	124 455	13 690 000	3 802 778

2nd production stage — Break-even surface:

Set of all points $(x_{111}, x_{112}, x_{113}, x_{121}, x_{131}, x_{132})$ satisfying:
$$x_{111} = 1\,115\,333 \cdot \lambda_{111}$$
$$x_{112} = 743\,556 \cdot \lambda_{112}$$
$$x_{113} = 2\,676\,800 \cdot \lambda_{113}$$
$$x_{121} = 4\,461\,333 \cdot \lambda_{121}$$
$$x_{131} = 5\,353\,600 \cdot \lambda_{131}$$
$$x_{132} = 2\,230\,667 \cdot \lambda_{132}$$
where $\lambda_{111} + \lambda_{112} + \lambda_{113} + \lambda_{121} + \lambda_{131} + \lambda_{132} = 1$, $\lambda_i \geq 0$ for $i = 111, 112, 113, 121, 131, 132$

Set of all points $(x_{211}, x_{212}, x_{213}, x_{221}, x_{222})$ satisfying:
$$x_{211} = 136\,900 \cdot \lambda_{211}$$
$$x_{212} = 228\,167 \cdot \lambda_{212}$$
$$x_{213} = 124\,455 \cdot \lambda_{213}$$
$$x_{221} = 13\,690\,000 \cdot \lambda_{221}$$
$$x_{222} = 3\,802\,778 \cdot \lambda_{222}$$
where $\lambda_{211} + \lambda_{212} + \lambda_{213} + \lambda_{221} + \lambda_{222} = 1$, $\lambda_i \geq 0$ for $i = 211, 212, 213, 221, 222$

| Minimum condition for the isolated recovery —of article-related contribution blocks | $\lambda_{111} + \lambda_{112} + \lambda_{113} \geq$ 0.07397 | | | $\lambda_{121} \geq$ 0.01898 | $\lambda_{131} + \lambda_{132} \geq$ 0.15989 | | $\lambda_{211} + \lambda_{212} + \lambda_{213} \geq$ 0.38641 | | | $\lambda_{221} + \lambda_{222} \geq$ 0.10226 | |
| —of product-related fixed costs | $\lambda_{111} \geq$ 0.00448 | $\lambda_{112} \geq$ 0.00897 | $\lambda_{113} \geq$ 0.00075 | $\lambda_{121} \geq$ 0.00403 | $\lambda_{131} \geq$ 0.00598 | $\lambda_{132} \geq$ 0.00448 | $\lambda_{211} \geq$ 0.00175 | $\lambda_{212} \geq$ 0.01096 | $\lambda_{213} \geq$ 0.00847 | $\lambda_{221} \geq$ 0.01461 | $\lambda_{222} \geq$ 0.01461 |

1st production stage

Contribution block of the firm as a whole (DM): 20 729 000

Corner points (units): 1 727 417 | 1 151 611 | 4 145 800 | 6 909 667 | 8 291 600 | 3 454 833 | 414 580 | 690 967 | 376 891 | 41 458 000 | 11 516 111

Break-even surface: set of all points $(x_{111}, x_{112}, x_{113}, x_{121}, x_{131}, x_{132}, x_{211}, x_{212}, x_{213}, x_{221}, x_{222})$ satisfying:

$$x_{111} = 1\,727\,417 \cdot \lambda_{111}$$
$$x_{112} = 1\,151\,611 \cdot \lambda_{112}$$
$$x_{113} = 4\,145\,800 \cdot \lambda_{113}$$

$$x_{121} = 6\,909\,667 \cdot \lambda_{121}$$
$$x_{131} = 8\,291\,600 \cdot \lambda_{131}$$
$$x_{132} = 3\,454\,833 \cdot \lambda_{132}$$

$$x_{211} = 414\,580 \cdot \lambda_{211}$$
$$x_{212} = 690\,967 \cdot \lambda_{212}$$
$$x_{213} = 376\,891 \cdot \lambda_{213}$$

$$x_{221} = 41\,458\,000 \cdot \lambda_{221}$$
$$x_{222} = 11\,516\,111 \cdot \lambda_{222}$$

where $\lambda_{111} + \lambda_{112} + \lambda_{113} + \lambda_{121} + \lambda_{131} + \lambda_{132} + \lambda_{211} + \lambda_{212} + \lambda_{213} + \lambda_{221} + \lambda_{222} = 1$
$\lambda_i \geq 0$ for $i = 111, 112, 113, 121, 131, 132, 211, 212, 213, 221, 222$

Minimum condition for the isolated recovery

— of the product group-related contribution blocks:

$$\lambda_{111} + \lambda_{112} + \lambda_{113} + \lambda_{121} + \lambda_{131} + \lambda_{132} \geq 0.64567$$
$$\lambda_{211} + \lambda_{212} + \lambda_{213} + \lambda_{221} + \lambda_{222} \geq 0.33021$$

— of the article-group related contribution blocks:

$$\lambda_{111} + \lambda_{112} + \lambda_{113} \geq 0.04776 \qquad \lambda_{121} \geq 0.01225 \qquad \lambda_{131} + \lambda_{132} \geq 0.10324$$
$$\lambda_{211} + \lambda_{212} + \lambda_{213} \geq 0.12760 \qquad \lambda_{221} + \lambda_{222} \geq 0.03377$$

— of the product-related fixed costs:

$\lambda_{111} \geq$ 0.00289	$\lambda_{112} \geq$ 0.00579	$\lambda_{113} \geq$ 0.00048	$\lambda_{121} \geq$ 0.00261	$\lambda_{131} \geq$ 0.00386	$\lambda_{132} \geq$ 0.00289	$\lambda_{211} \geq$ 0.00058	$\lambda_{212} \geq$ 0.00362	$\lambda_{213} \geq$ 0.00280	$\lambda_{221} \geq$ 0.00482	$\lambda_{222} \geq$ 0.00482

Figure 57 Multistage break-even analysis for the example in Fig. 55

For the purposes of break-even analysis, prices that can actually be realised in the market place are naturally of paramount importance.

By specifying prices, an unambiguous break-even point can be determined. An appropriate classification of variable costs is also a prerequisite. The variable costs of all production stages for the example of multistage production considered hitherto are classified in Fig. 58. The respective (constant) production coefficients are specified on the arrows. It has already been noted that the specification of the goods flow system is abbreviated. Thus, at each production centre, factor input streams which do not cause cost accounting difficulties are ignored. The variable costs which are traceable to such factor inputs are therefore reproduced in Fig. 58 as dashed arrows. For example, the variable costs of product 111 emerge as follows: the production of a unit of intermediate product 1 costs DM 1.75. Four units of the latter, costing DM 7, are required by each unit of intermediate product 11. Additionally, further variable costs amounting to DM 3 are incurred on product 11 making a total of DM 10 per unit. The production coefficient of intermediate product 11 for end-product 111 is 3. Hence, in the case of product 111, unit variable costs of DM 30 initially result from inputs of the previous stage. Further unit variable costs amounting to DM 28 are incurred and total unit variable cost is therefore DM 58. Given a selling price of DM 70, this product yields a unit contribution of DM 12.

Additional variable costs of DM 0 are indicated on several nodes in Fig. 58. This means that in these production centres there are fixed costs only (cp. Fig. 55). A zero production coefficient indicates, in addition, that the services provided by a service centre are not received by other centres as individual units but only in total. Thus centres 0 and 2 obviously do not provide intermediate products in the form of further inputs that can be counted, but they do provide joint managerial and administrative services for entire product or article groups.

The further analysis is explained by reference to product 111. Using the known intermediate product prices, the basic idea is to allocate the total unit contribution of DM 12, which is yielded jointly by all production stages, to the individual stages of the production process. The respective prices of saleable or procurable intermediate products are given in parentheses in Fig. 58 and are indicated by exit arrows. The price of product 1 is DM 2. Allowing for costs of DM 1.75, a unit contribution of DM 0.25 therefore arises. If further calculations are based on this price of DM 2, the variable costs of product 11 amount to DM 11 and a unit contribution of DM 1.50 arises. The costs of the end-product finally add up to DM 65.50 and its unit contribution is only DM 4.50. In this particular divergent production process the total contribution of DM 12 is, making allowance for the production coefficients, apportioned between the four stages as follows:

		DM
1st stage	(product 0)	0.00
2nd stage	(product 1)	$0.25 \cdot 4 \cdot 3 = 3.00$
3rd stage	(product 11)	$1.50 \cdot 3 = 4.50$
4th stage	(product 111)	4.50
Contribution of a branch in the production network		12.00

Using unit contributions computed for intermediate products, isolated break-even

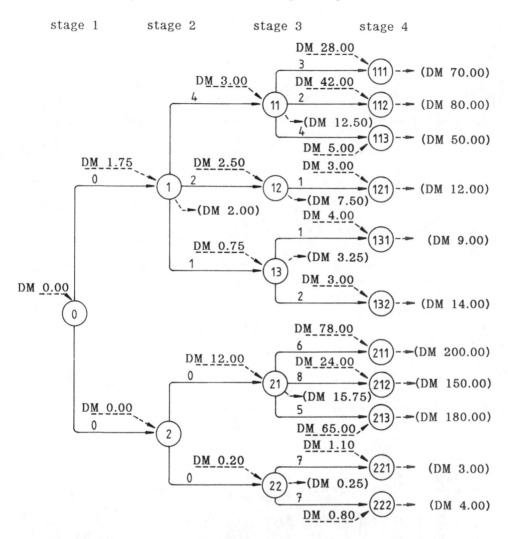

Figure 58 Classified variable costs and prices of intermediate and end-products for the example of multistage production

analyses can be undertaken for all intermediate or end-products for which price information is available. Such an analysis is illustrated by Fig. 59.

Unambiguous break-even points can be computed for all centres other than production centres 0 and 2. They indicate the respective product total outputs above which the recovery of fixed costs is guaranteed. This applies irrespective of the product's use. For example, product 11's costs are recovered at an output of 533 333 units. Whether this quantity is sold externally, or used in further production is irrelevant.

Product 113 represents a special case in which, in the final production stage, a *negative unit contribution* of DM − 5 arises. In total, production branch 1–11–113 yields a contribution of DM (50 − 45) = DM 5. However, this latter contribution results from a joint contribution of DM 10 from stages 2 and 3 (in relation to an end-product unit

4th stage

Article	111	112	113	121	131	132	211	212	213	221	222
Price per output unit (DM)	70.00	80.00	50.00	12.00	9.00	14.00	200.00	150.00	180.00	3.00	4.00
Variable costs: —transfer prices of inputs from the previous stage (DM) / —production coefficient	12.50 / 3	12.50 / 2	12.50 / 4	7.50 / 1	3.25 / 1	3.25 / 2	15.75 / 6	15.75 / 8	15.75 / 5	0.25 / 7	0.25 / 7
• variable costs of inputs from the previous stage (DM)	37.50	25.00	50.00	7.50	3.25	6.50	94.50	126.00	78.75	1.75	1.75
• further variable costs of the production stage in question (DM)	28.00	42.00	5.00	3.00	4.00	3.00	78.00	24.00	65.00	1.10	0.80
Total variable cost (DM)	65.50	67.00	55.00	10.50	7.25	9.50	172.50	150.00	143.75	2.85	2.55
Contribution per output unit (DM)	4.50	13.00	-5.00	1.50	1.75	4.50	27.50	0.00	36.25	0.15	1.45
Fixed cost block of the production stage (DM)	60 000	120 000	10 000	54 000	80 000	60 000	12 000	75 000	58 000	100 000	100 000
Break-even point (in output units)	13 333	9 231	—	36 000	45 714	13 333	436	—	1 600	666 667	68 966

3rd stage

Intermediate product	11	12	13	21	22
Price per output unit (DM)	12.50	7.50	3.25	15.75	0.25
Variable costs: —transfer prices of inputs from the previous stage (DM) / —production coefficient	2.00 / 4	2.00 / 2	2.00 / 1	—	—
• variable costs of inputs from the previous stage (DM)	8.00	4.00	2.00	—	—
• further variable costs of the production stage in question (DM)	3.00	2.50	0.75	12.00	0.20
Total variable cost (DM)	11.00	6.50	2.75	12.00	0.20
Contribution per output unit (DM)	1.50	1.00	0.50	3.75	0.05
Fixed cost block of the production stage (DM)	800 000	200 000	2 000 000	2 500 000	500 000
Break-even point (in output units)	533 333	200 000	4 000 000	666 667	10 000 000

Isolated break-even points of the 3rd production stage: 666 667

Products 21 and 22 must also contribute to the recovery of the fixed costs of the earlier production stages.

		1	2
2nd stage	Intermediate product		
	Price per output unit (DM)	2.00	(No price exists)
	Variable costs (DM) (there are no variable costs of the input costs of the previous stage)	1.75	
	Contribution per output unit (DM)	0.25	(A unit contribution is not determinable) contribution margin function: $\dfrac{3.75x_{21}+0.05x_{22}}{3\,500\,000}$
	Fixed cost block of the production stage (DM)	10 000 000	(Cumulative fixed costs of stages 2 and 3: 6 500 000)
	Break-even point or set of break-even points (in output units)	Isolated break-even point of the 2nd production stage: 40 000 000	$x_{21}=$ 1 733 333 $\cdot \lambda_{21}$ $x_{22}=130\,000\,000 \cdot \lambda_{22}$ with $\lambda_{21}, \lambda_{22} \geqslant 0$, and $\lambda_{21}+\lambda_{22}=1$
		Product 1 must also contribute to the recovery of the fixed costs of earlier production stages.	Isolated recovery of the fixed costs of later production stages: $\lambda_{21} \geqslant 0.384615$ | $\lambda_{22} \geqslant 0.076923$
1st stage	Intermediate product	0	
	Specification per unit Contribution function	Price, variable costs and unit contribution do not exist for product 0. $0.25x_1+3.75x_{21}+0.05x_{22}$	
	Fixed cost block of the production stage (DM)	500 000	
	Break-even set (in output units)	Cumulative fixed costs of stages 1, 2, 3, to be jointly covered from products 1, 21, 22 are: 17 000 000 $x_1 = 68\,000\,000 \cdot \lambda_1;\ x_{21}=4\,533\,333 \cdot \lambda_{21};\ x_{22}=340\,000\,000 \cdot \lambda_{22}$ with $\lambda_1, \lambda_{21}, \lambda_{22} \geqslant 0,\ \lambda_1+\lambda_{21}+\lambda_{22}=1$	
	Minimum conditions for the isolated recovery of fixed costs of later production stages	$\lambda_1 \geqslant 0.093458$	$\lambda_{21}+\lambda_{22} \geqslant 0.382353$ $\lambda_{21} \geqslant 0.147059$ | $\lambda_{22} \geqslant 0.029412$

Figure 59 Multistage break-even analysis when intermediate product prices are known

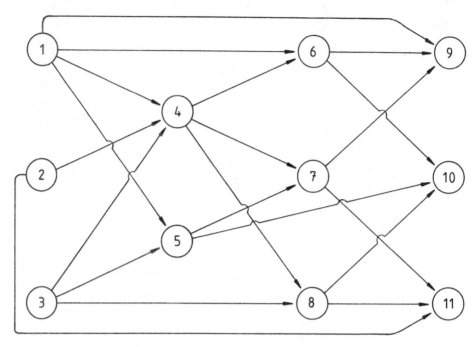

Figure 60   Example of a structure of production

of product 113) of which the final stage absorbs DM 5. A negative contribution signifies that the production of the product in question has an adverse effect on profit-making goals. In this case it is more profitable to sell the intermediate products of prior stages than to carry through the production process to a conclusion.

4. General Approach for the Determination of Break-even Surfaces in the Case of Multistage Manufacture

The multistage break-even analysis procedure hitherto illustrated with examples is now presented in a general summarised form. It is first necessary to capture the goods flow system of production. An example of the latter is illustrated by Fig. 60.

Next, the goods streams are costed at cost rates or prices in order to depict the value structure of the production process. For the purposes of break-even analysis it is advisable to analyse the resultant variable and fixed costs separately. The analysis of variable costs links with a representation of the input, throughput and output flows in the production process. To this end, use is made of the general approach of input–output analysis for the firm (cp. Kloock, 1969 [Input-Output-Modelle] p. 66 et seq.; Schweitzer and Küpper, 1974 [Produktionstheorie] p. 48 et seq.). The production process is partitioned into production centres $i = 1, 2, \ldots, n$. Each of the latter is defined as a centre which produces a specific (unique) intermediate or end-product. For simplicity this product can be symbolised with the same index i. The goods streams which flow between the production centres collectively constitute the input–output relationships of the analysis. The total quantity delivered by production centre i is designated r_i in the equations which follow. Some part of this quantity can be used as an input to further production processes whilst the remainder, which is designated x_i, is sold in the external market place. In order more accurately to define the (re-inputted) input flows, variables r_{ij} are also specified. The goods quantities represented by r_{ij} specify the production which flows from centre i to centre j $(i, j = 1, 2, \ldots, n)$. Thus, in the case of each production centre i, the total production quantity r_i is given by:

$$r_i = r_{i1} + r_{i2} + \ldots + r_{in} + x_i. \tag{4.48}$$

If the entirety of production centres i $(i = 1, 2, \ldots, n)$ is so formulated, (4.48) forms a system of equations of the firm's goods flows. The quantity of goods flowing between two production centres i, j can be more accurately determined in that it can be expressed as a *transformation function* (cp. Kloock, 1969 [Input-Output-Modelle] p. 44; Schweitzer and Küpper, 1974 [Produktionstheorie] p. 47). Here a Leontief transformation function is adopted (cp. Section IV for other versions). It is fully determined by the production coefficient a_{ij} which specifies the relation between the output r_j of a centre and the input drawn from centre i:

$$r_{ij} = a_{ij} \cdot r_j \qquad \text{for } i, j = 1, 2, \ldots, n. \tag{4.49}$$

The substitution of this transformation function into the system of goods flow equations yields:

$$r_i = a_{i1} \cdot r_1 + a_{i2} \cdot r_2 + \cdots + a_{in} \cdot r_n + x_i \qquad \text{for } i = 1, 2, \ldots, n. \tag{4.50}$$

Using matrix notation with $\varkappa = (r_1, r_2, \ldots, r_n)'$; $x = (x_1, x_2, \ldots, x_n)'$ and $\mathscr{A} = (a_{ij})_{i,j}$, the input–output system is:

$$\varkappa = \mathscr{A} \cdot \varkappa + x. \tag{4.51}$$

It can be decomposed as follows:

$$\mathscr{E} \cdot \varkappa - \mathscr{A} \cdot \varkappa = x \qquad \text{or} \qquad (\mathscr{E} - \mathscr{A}) \cdot \varkappa = x$$
$$\varkappa = (\mathscr{E} - \mathscr{A})^{-1} \cdot x. \tag{4.52}$$

This assumes that the matrix $(\mathscr{E} - \mathscr{A})$ is invertible. The resultant matrix $\mathscr{G} := (\mathscr{E} - \mathscr{A})^{-1}$ is called a total requirements matrix and is fundamental to the further analysis. Its components are symbolised with g_{ij} $(i, j = 1, 2, \ldots, n)$. Equation (4.52) now runs

$$\varkappa = \mathscr{G} \cdot x \tag{4.53}$$

Hence the input of good i for the realisation of programme $(x_1, x_2, \ldots, x_n)$ is given by:

$$r_i = \sum_{j=1}^{n} g_{ij} \cdot x_j. \tag{4.54}$$

Using this basic production–theoretic relationship, the variable production costs can be clearly determined. *Additional* unit costs c_i, that are incurred at its production centre, should be specified for each good i which may be the original input good or also intermediate product. The definition of the costs constituting c_i is confined to additional costs because the costs of in-going goods flows are separately allowed for to the extent that they are contained in the initially-defined goods types $i = 1, 2, \ldots, n$. If a *transfer price* q_i is known for product i, that price should be used at the point at which product i re-enters as an input component. This is also the procedure that was adopted in the example in the previous section. The transfer price q_i exceeds the sum of the relevant variable costs by a contribution margin d_i. In attempting to determine transfer prices for intermediate products an (initially unknown) contribution margin d_i is therefore contemplated for each good in addition to costs c_i. The unit contribution d_i is zero if no transfer price is known. The variable costs are therefore computed as follows:

$$K^v = \sum_{i=1}^n (c_i + d_i) \cdot r_i \qquad (4.55)$$

or, using (4.54):

$$K^v = \sum_{i=1}^n (c_i + d_i) \cdot \sum_{j=1}^n g_{ij} \cdot x_j. \qquad (4.56)$$

In the latter equation, the contribution margins $d_i (i = 1, 2, \ldots, n)$ are still unknown. They are ascertained by juxtaposing prices and variable costs. To this end, variable costs in (4.56) are restated as:

$$K^v = \sum_{j=1}^n \underbrace{\sum_{i=1}^n (c_i + d_i) \cdot g_{ij} \cdot x_j}_{k_j^v}. \qquad (4.57)$$

Unit variable costs k_j^v for each product j can be derived from the latter equation. The unit contribution for product j is the difference between price and variable costs:

$$d_j = q_j - k_j^v = q_j - \sum_{i=1}^n (c_i + d_i) \cdot g_{ij} \qquad \text{for } j = 1, 2, \ldots, n. \qquad (4.58)$$

The contribution margin variables appear on both sides of (4.58) and the intention is to solve the n equations representing that system with respect to those variables. Accordingly (4.58) is first transformed with the vectors

$$\begin{aligned} \mathscr{q} &= (q_1, q_2, \ldots, q_n)', \\ \mathscr{c} &= (c_1, c_2, \ldots, c_n)', \\ \mathscr{d} &= (d_1, d_2, \ldots, d_n)' \end{aligned} \qquad (4.59)$$

and expressed as:

$$\begin{aligned} \mathscr{d}' &= \mathscr{q}' - (\mathscr{c}' + \mathscr{d}') \cdot \mathscr{G} \\ &= \mathscr{q}' - \mathscr{c}'\mathscr{G} - \mathscr{d}'\mathscr{G}. \end{aligned} \qquad (4.60)$$

Solving with respect to $\mathscr{d}$:

$$\mathscr{d}' \cdot (\mathscr{E} + \mathscr{G}) = \mathscr{q}' - c' \mathscr{G}$$
$$\mathscr{d}' = (\mathscr{q}' - c' \mathscr{G}) \cdot (\mathscr{E} + \mathscr{G})^{-1}.$$

It is assumed that the matrix $(\mathscr{E} + \mathscr{G})$ is invertible. Using (4.60), the contributions of all production stages can be directly specified. Denoting the elements of the matrix $(\mathscr{E} + \mathscr{G})^{-1}$ with $\tilde{g}_{ij}$, the contribution of good j $(j = 1, 2, \ldots, n)$ is given by:

$$d_j = \sum_{i=1}^{n} \underbrace{(q_i - \sum_{k=1}^{n} c_k \cdot g_{ki})}_{*} \cdot \tilde{g}_{ij}. \tag{4.61}$$

To determine the contribution margin of a good j, the prices of all goods $i = 1, 2, \ldots, n$ are thus formally required. Following the procedure adopted in the previous section, the parentheses designated with an asterisk (*) are set equal to zero in the case of goods i for which there are no transfer prices. Contribution margins are therefore set at zero at centres i at which prices are not known. This conforms with the proposition that contributions can only arise at centres the productive output of which can be realised (internally or externally) at market prices. In general the price q_i of the ith good is known or is given by:

$$q_i = \sum_{k=1}^{n} c_k \cdot g_{ki}. \tag{4.62}$$

Once the contributions of each product are known, they can then be compared in total with the contribution blocks. The following total contributions are generated:

$$\sum_{j=1}^{n} d_j \cdot r_j. \tag{4.63}$$

Equation (4.63) allows for the possibility that contribution margins can be generated at all centres within the production process. For any production centre j for which this is not the case, $d_j = 0$. The contribution block is represented by the fixed costs. They can be classified by reference to the individual centres and contain a component which is not centre related:

$$K^f = K_0^f + \sum_{i=1}^{n} K_i^f.$$

The break-even points $(\hat{r}_1, \hat{r}_2, \ldots, \hat{r}_n)$ then satisfy the equation:

$$\sum_{j=1}^{n} d_j \cdot \hat{r}_j = K^f \tag{4.64}$$

which yields the break-even points of the firm as a whole. If a limited break-even proposition at the level of the individual production stage is desired, both sides of equation (4.64) must be restricted to a particular set of goods type j, which are combined in $\tilde{J}$:

$$\sum_{j \in J} d_j \cdot \hat{r}_j = \sum_{j \in J} K_j^{\mathrm{f}}. \tag{4.65}$$

This general approach comprehensively shows how a break-even analysis can be undertaken in the case of multistage production. The above two examples of cases of non-existent and known prices of intermediate products respectively are special cases of the general procedure outlined here.

5. Computation of Production-stage Related Break-even Information

In addition to an overall assessment of the production process, the problem of assessing the profitability of certain measures taken at a particular production stage, and which result in a particular level of fixed costs, frequently arises in multistage manufacture. The assessment becomes problematical if contributions cannot be ascertained for the production stage in question because of the absence of an external market for the intermediate product. Thus, it might be questioned whether it is "worthwhile" incurring the production costs of injection equipment for moulding door-handles made of synthetic material which are attached to various types of refrigerator, deep-freeze, washing machine and dish-washer. It is hardly appropriate to apportion the contribution margins generated by these end-products to the door-handle. A market price is also absent.

Break-even analyses undertaken in such a case should proceed from the following consideration: break-even analysis is of significance in relation to *decision-making situations*. If no decision is imminent, and the measures to be undertaken are therefore eventually determined by particular pressures, the scope for applications of break-even analysis is restricted. In that event, both positive and negative information are of no consequence. Such a situation is present in the last-mentioned example if there is no alternative to the door-handle and its-method of production. The only question then is: are articles requiring this door-handle to be produced at all (in which case they must, among other things, also bear the fixed costs incurred on the door-handle) or are they to be entirely forgone? In such a situation, a break-even analysis related to the end-product would have greater predictive power. In cases in which a production-stage related break-even analysis is meaningful, a decision-making situation is thus present. The alternative which is to be evaluated is also matched with at least one other available (mutually exclusive) alternative. In a comparison of these alternatives, the initially non-recognisable, positive components of the contemplated action can be computed. The individual steps in a production-stage related break-even analysis are therefore:

(1) The action to be evaluated should be *precisely* defined.
(2) The *available alternatives*, assuming the contemplated action is not taken, should be specified. This might involve, for example, the retention of a previously-realised alternative or the choice of a new alternative.
(3) The action contemplated and the alternative thereto should be compared by reference to *relevant criteria* reflecting a firm's objectives. This may be a question, for example, of production or sales volumes, fixed and variable costs, sales revenue changes etc. In capturing such influences on a firm's objectives, problems can arise if the alternatives differ primarily with respect to objectives which cannot be accurately quantified.

(4) The negative and positive components of the contemplated and mutually exclusive alternative should be juxtaposed in a *break-even computation*.

A few variants of the example of the door-handle production may elucidate the principle underlying this approach.

In *Example 1* the door-handle has already been produced hitherto but in another way. The retention of the manufacturing procedure previously adopted would result in variable costs per door-handle of DM 0.0355. Additional fixed costs would not arise. Switching to a new procedure requires the setting-up of the injection equipment and further equipment and installation costs. The latter fixed costs amount to DM 20 000. However, the unit variable costs of this alternative would only amount to DM 0.02. In the break-even analysis, fixed costs of DM 20 000 must, on the basis of these data, be compared with unit cost savings of DM 0.0155. The break-even point for the switch of procedure is therefore: (DM 20 000/DM 0.0155/unit) = 1 290 323 units. The setting-up of the new injection equipment would be worthwhile for an output of door-handles exceeding the latter number.

In *Example 2*, the door-handle in question has not been manufactured hitherto. If it is now introduced, one of two procedures may be chosen: procedure A with fixed costs of DM 20 000 and unit variable costs of DM 0.02; or, procedure B which has corresponding costs amounting to DM 13 000 and DM 0.055 (per unit). In this case it is a question of the customary comparison of procedures. For a quantity exceeding:

$$\frac{\text{DM } (20\,000 - 13\,000)}{\text{DM } (0.055 - 0.02)/\text{unit}} = \frac{7000}{0.035} \text{ units} = 200\,000 \text{ units}$$

procedure A is more cost effective.

In *Example 3*, a comparable door-handle is already manufactured. It could be produced henceforth, in the version made hitherto, without additional fixed costs and at a unit variable cost of DM 0.0184. A slightly changed version of the door-handle is now under consideration. This has a more modern form, another colour or a different material composition. This alternative would have fixed costs of DM 20 000 and unit variable costs of DM 0.02. It is clear from the numbers in the example that costs cannot be used here as the sole evaluation criterion. Even if the new version of the door-handle would yield savings in variable costs, costs would still not constitute a suitable evaluation criterion. The proposed alternative has advantages which lie outside the cost area. It may, for example, facilitate:

(a) the attaining of a higher sales volume,
(b) the (at least partial) arresting of a threatened decline in sales volume,
(c) the justifying of an increase in the price of the end-product,
(d) an improvement in the quality of the door-handle in order thereby to attain a better image, a reduction in complaints and liabilities arising under guarantees.

In cases (a) to (c), the desired effect is unlikely to be attained from a change in the door-handle of the products to which it is attached. The alternatives must be formulated more comprehensively in these cases in order more accurately to capture the actual decision-making situation. Thus, a new refrigerator design could differ with respect to surface, panel frame, front, interior fittings and door-handle. The question to be decided is whether the entire package of measures for changing the design is to be implemented or not. The total cost changes involved comprise additional fixed costs of DM 480 000 and additional variable costs of DM 7.2342 per refrigerator. These numbers already allow for the rise in the fixed costs and the unit variable costs of DM 0.0016 in respect of the change in the door-handle.

It must therefore be questioned whether the contemplated design change will have positive effects. It could, for example, be that, if the refrigerator is not modernised, it would be judged to be out of date and that its sales volume would be reduced to 90 000 units. The unit contribution would amount to DM 65. The comparative alternative is determined by these data. The break-even analysis must indicate the increase in sales volume Δx, the increase in selling price, and therefore the increase in contribution margin Δd, which must at least be attained in the existing cost situation in order to recover the costs of the change in design. If the data of the comparative alternative are denoted by x^{cp} and d^{cp}, the break-even approach is as follows:

$$K^f + k^v \cdot (x^{cp} + \Delta x) = \Delta x \cdot (d + \Delta d) + x^{cp} \cdot \Delta d. \qquad (4.66)$$

The left-hand side of (4.66) specifies the additional fixed costs of re-equipping and the additional variable costs for the new total output $x^{cp} + \Delta x$. The right-hand side indicates the additional contribution from the alternative that is contemplated. It comprises the contribution margin yielded by the sales volume increase and the increase in the contribution margin for the previous sales volume x^{cp}. Substituting the known data and rearranging:

$$480\,000 + 7.2342 \cdot (90\,000 + \Delta x) = \Delta x \cdot (65 + \Delta d) + 90\,000 \cdot \Delta d \qquad (4.67)$$

or

$$1\,131\,078 = 57.7658 \cdot \Delta x + 90\,000 \cdot \Delta d + \Delta x \cdot \Delta d.$$

This is the equation for the break-even line in this particular case. The set of break-even points M is therefore given by:

$$M = \{(\Delta x,\ \Delta d)\,|\,57.7658 \cdot \Delta x + 90\,000 \cdot \Delta d + \Delta x \cdot \Delta d = 1\,131\,078\}. \qquad (4.68)$$

Presented graphically this set forms a hyperbolic curve in the two-dimensional coordinate system $\Delta x / \Delta d$ (see Fig. 61). The corner points indicate the requisite isolated quantity and isolated price increases. The requisite values are: ($\Delta x = 19\,580$, $\Delta d = 0$) for an isolated sales volume increase and ($\Delta x = 0$, $\Delta d = 12.5675$) for an isolated increase in selling price. The break-even line in Fig. 61 is a non-linear connection between these two corner points. The break-even curve lies below the line connecting the two corner points because a synergetic effect, amounting to the products term $\Delta x \cdot \Delta d$, results from simultaneous increases in volume and price.

In case d, an improvement in the door-handle is intended to add to the product's image; and, to reduce the costs caused by complaints and liabilities arising under guarantees. The latter effect results in a corresponding cost saving which can be partially

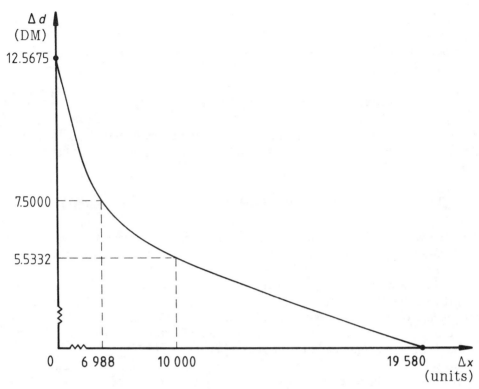

Figure 61 Break-even curve for the equalisation of a cost increase at intermediate production stages with quantity and price increases

fixed and partially variable. However, the quantification of the "image effect" is also a necessary part of the break-even analysis. To the extent that this effect manifests itself in the form of volume or price increases, the previous procedure can be applied. If no kind of quantification is possible, the computation of break-even values must be abandoned.

The positive effect with which Example 3 is concerned relates entirely to a single end-product. If the components for which the change in design is contemplated, are not only utilised in producing the refrigerator, but also for other end-products, the present analysis must be expanded into a multiproduct analysis in which case no new analytical problems arise.

In *Example 4* the motive for the contemplated change in the door-handle is similar to that in the case just discussed. It is concerned with the question of whether, in addition to the previously-manufactured door-handle, a second variant should be produced by way of product differentiation. The latter alternative is characterised as follows: no additional fixed costs; continuing production of an output x^{cp} at a unit variable cost of DM 0.0355; and, an end-product unit contribution amounting to $d^{cp} = $ DM 65. The contemplated alternative requires additional fixed costs of DM 20 000 and unit variable costs of DM 0.02. Using the previous facility only x_1 units $(x_1 < x^{cp})$ would still be produced in addition to x_2 units with the new facility $(x_1 + x_2 > x^{cp})$. The unit contribution of those end-products that are manufactured with the previous facility remains unchanged, whereas the selling price of those end-products that are manufactured with the new facility can be increased by an amount Δd.

Denoting the total increase in output with $\Delta x = x_1 + x_2 - x^{cp}$, the break-even equation is:

$$20\,000 + 0.0355 \cdot \Delta x - 0.0155 \cdot x_2 = 65 \cdot \Delta x + x_2 \cdot \Delta d. \qquad (4.69)$$

The left and right-hand sides of (4.69) specify the respective additional costs and additional contributions which arise. In total the break-even points can therefore be expressed as the following set:

$$M = \{(\Delta x,\, x_2,\, \Delta d) \geqslant 0 \,|\, 20\,000 = 64.9645 \cdot \Delta x + 0.0155 \cdot x_2 + x_2 \cdot \Delta d\}. \qquad (4.70)$$

The latter break-even set forms a concave surface in three-dimensional space with coordinates Δx, x_2, Δd. The axis intersection points denote isolated break-even points. Thus, for example, the additional costs of the contemplated alternative can only be equalised in the absence of a price increase for the new variant ($\Delta d = 0$), and without an increase in total output ($\Delta x = 0$), if the output x_2 of the end-product that is equipped with the new version of the door-handle is at least $x_2 = 20\,000/0.0155 = 1\,290\,323$ units. With a price increase Δd of only DM 5, the required output falls to $x_2 = 3988$ units. Further break-even combinations can be computed from (4.70).

The examples given indicate that the procedural principle is the same in all cases of production-related break-even analyses. Such analyses are strongly decision-related and are concerned with other stages in the multistage production relationship only to the extent that the decision has implications for two or more production stages. Problems concerning practical application can arise especially with respect to the definition of the existing alternative and the discovery and characterisation of an adequate comparable alternative. Furthermore, the operational quantification of particular objectives is frequently problematical. This is true, for example, of attempted quality improvements, higher advertising effectiveness, better image, smaller environmental burdens etc.

6. Dependence of the Design of a Multistage Break-even Analysis upon the Existing Cost Accounting System

The design of a multistage break-even analysis will, in most cases, necessarily be aligned with the existing cost accounting system. The more the structure of the break-even computation corresponds to that of the cost accounting system, the less problematical is the extraction and further usage of cost accounting data. For this reason the nature and number of manufacturing stages which are reproduced by the cost accounting system are therefore addressed on the one hand. Moreover, reference has already been made to the fact that above all *divergent* structures are explicitly and accurately depicted in multistage-structured accounting systems whilst the cases of convergence, which are accompanied by less complex allocation problems, are only implicitly discernible. However, on the other hand, in addition to the question of the scope and details of the stages to be depicted, the cost classification criteria on which the break-even analysis is to be based are also of fundamental importance. The presentation considered in this book always proceeds from a division of costs into their fixed and variable components in accordance with the criterion "cost behaviour with respect to activity (i.e. output) changes". However, for the purposes of break-even analysis, such a partitioning is frequently less important than a cost classification reflecting costs that would be incrementally *incurred or discontinued* as a consequence of the decision that is the subject of the analysis (cp. Riebel, 1982 [Einzelkostenrechnung] p. 67 et seq., p. 273 et seq.; Lüder and Streitferdt, 1978 [Erfolgsrechnung] p. 548 et seq.; Kaplan, 1982 [Management Accounting] p. 151; Morard, 1978 [Comptabilité] p. 62 et seq.). This idea corresponds to a classification into separately attributable and joint costs in accordance with Riebelian principles (cp. Riebel, 1982 [Einzelkostenrechnung] p. 36 et seq.), and, as an expressly decision-related cost classification, is especially suitable for break-even analysis. The formal implementation of the classification requires no modifications whatsoever to the forms of break-even analysis that have been described. However, apropos of the contents, at each stage *joint* and *separately attributable* costs replace fixed and variable costs respectively.

This application presupposes that the internal cost accounting system is based on *separately attributable costs* to a degree that also provides the necessary information for break-even analysis.

The system of accounting with separately attributable costs was developed by Paul Riebel (cp. Riebel, 1982 [Einzelkostenrechnung] p. 35 et seq., p. 204 et seq.; Schweitzer and Küpper, 1991 [Systeme] p. 386 et seq.). It is based on the principle that a determinant can be found for each category, or type, of cost which can thus be identified as that determinant's separately attributable costs. The determinants should be chosen in a manner which ensures that they are as low as possible in a hierarchy of managerial determinants, i.e. should be as concrete and specific as possible (cp. Riebel, 1982 [Einzelkostenrechnung] p. 150 et seq., p. 239). If, as proposed by Riebel, costs are defined as such payments as result from decisions concerning the determinant in question (cp. Riebel, 1982 [Einzelkostenrechnung] p. 81), it becomes clear that a cost accounting system based on separately attributable costs is closely aligned with decision-making situations. It therefore also constitutes the appropriate computational basis for break-even analyses. The number, type and meaning of the production stages that are represented in the accounting system are chosen here in accordance with a system of hierarchically-ordered determinants which define the respective separately attributable costs. Figure 62 illustrates a *determinant hierarchy* in the sense of Riebel (cp. Schweitzer and Küpper, 1991 [Systeme] p. 391).

In the case of a particular element in such a hierarchy, all costs which are the separately attributable costs of reference points above the element in question should be regarded as its joint costs. Hence, at each stage of a determinant hierarchy, the cost types that are needed for break-even analysis are specifiable. It is frequently advisable to draw on different versions of determinant hierarchies in dealing with different decision questions.

Each of the extensions of break-even analysis presented in this chapter can be implemented with cost information from an accounting system based on separately attributable costs. The method of analysis presented in Fig. 57 is particularly suitable for the break-even analysis of the individual stages of a determinant hierarchy.

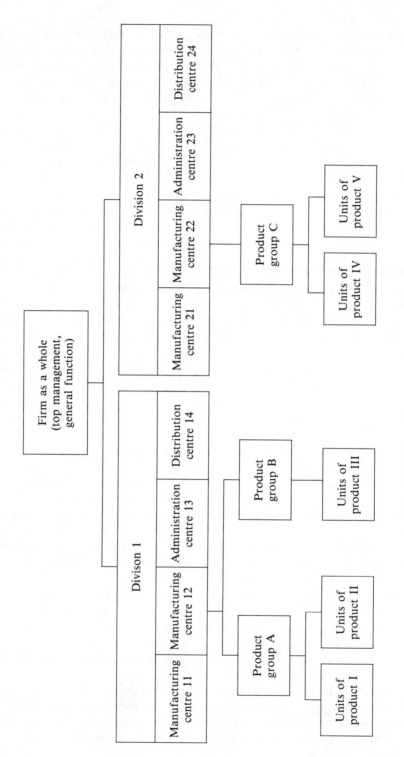

Figure 62 Example of a determinant hierarchy

IV. BREAK-EVEN ANALYSIS BASED ON MULTIDIMENSIONAL PRODUCTION FUNCTIONS

1. General Characterisation of Break-even Analysis in the Case of Multidimensional Production Functions

(a) Survey of Approaches which Allow for Specific Characteristics of the Production Procedure in the Production and Cost Functions Adopted

The previous extensions of break-even analysis dealt primarily with problems resulting from the structure of production. These include, in particular, problems of multiproduct manufacture in general, of multistage production processes and the features of convergence and divergence in the goods flow. Simple types of transformation function were adopted for the production–theoretic relationships between the individual production centres, namely, Leontief transformation functions of the form (cp. Schweitzer and Küpper, 1974 [Produktionstheorie] p. 51 et seq.):

$$r_{ij} = a_{ij} \cdot r_j. \tag{4.71}$$

Linear functions in the form of (4.71) depict a simple, though frequent, example of the input–output relations between two production centres. However, instead of a constant production coefficient, the general transformation relation may contain the function f_{ij} and be of the form (cp. Schweitzer and Küpper, 1974 [Produktionstheorie] p. 49; Kloock, 1969 [Input-Output-Modelle] p. 47 et seq.):

$$r_{ij} = f_{ij}(\ldots) \cdot r_j \tag{4.72}$$

The symbol $(\ldots)$ denotes that, at this centre, a multiplicity of specific determinants can be operative (cp. Schweitzer, 1979 [Funktionen] p. 11).

Of primary importance are those types of transformation function f_{ij} in which the characteristics of the technical production process constitute the determinants of the input–output relationships. For that reason they are also called *technical process functions or production functions*. Fundamental forms of transformation functions based on technical features of the production process are, first and foremost (cp. Zschocke, 1975 [Prozessfunktionen] col. 3258 et seq.):

—Gutenberg technical input functions,
—engineering production functions,
—throughput-functions.

The formulation of *technical input functions* in the sense of Gutenberg's (cp. 1983 [Produktion] p. 326 et seq.) concept can be regarded as being fundamental to the development of technically-oriented transformation functions. He considers a differentiated analysis of technical production features to be especially necessary in the case of the inputs of capacity centres. He starts with the intensity δ_j of machine j which he regards as a fundamental determinant of the consumption of particular input goods. In order to achieve the greatest accuracy in representing the input–output relationship, he suggests a two-stage approach to the formulation of transformation functions. First, work units should be defined as the work of an aggregate that is technically specified and measured in physical units (cp. Schweitzer and Küpper, 1974 [Produktionstheorie] p. 88). Next, the relationship between the consumption of input goods and work unit is analysed and expressed in so-called technical input functions $\tilde{f}_{ij}$. In the technical input functions, intensity appears first and foremost as the independent variable. The function presented in Fig. 11, which expresses gasoline consumption ρ_{ij} as a function of the number of revolutions (intensity) δ_j of an engine j, is an example of this type of technical input function. In general such a technical input function can be formulated as:

$$\rho_{ij} = \tilde{f}_{ij}(\delta_j)$$

where ρ_{ij} denotes input goods consumption per work unit. The link with economic performance, i.e. to the volume of productive output, is effected with hypotheses $\Phi_j(r_j)$ on the relationship between production volume and the requisite number of work units (cp. Schweitzer and Küpper, 1974 [Produktionstheorie] p. 91; Kilger, 1958 [Produktionstheorie] p. 65):

$$r_{ij} \quad = \quad f_{ij}(\delta_j) \quad \times \quad \Phi_j(r_j) \qquad (4.73)$$

input quantity of i for j	consumption of i per work unit of centre j	requisite number of work units at j for production volume r_j

In addition to the fuel consumption of an engine as a function of the number of revolutions, coke consumption per ton of pig-iron produced by a blast-furnace as a function of the speed of its productive output and the consumption of tools by a lathe per unit of cut metres as a function of its speed, represent further examples of typical technical input functions (cp. Gutenberg, 1983 [Produktion] p. 332 et seq.).

The development of *engineering production functions*, primarily by *Chenery* (cp. 1949, [Functions] p. 507 et seq.), is, in essence, also based on the idea of giving greater recognition to the technical aspect of production in input–output relationships. Taking the example of energy consumption as a function of different factors which are important influences on a pipeline's rate of throughput, Chenery (cp. 1949, [Functions] p. 514 et seq.) formulates engineering production functions in which a number of technical variables appear as determinants, e.g. the hardness of fixed components, the viscosity of fluids, the number of revolutions, engine velocity etc. In formulating transformation functions in general, he requires a return to the technological processes which behave in accordance with the natural scientific laws of physics, chemistry and biology.

Finally, the concept *"throughput-functions"* refers to technically-oriented transformation functions which, for example, are conspicuous in chemical processes. The origins of the concept can be traced to *Pichler* (cp., e.g. 1953 [Matrizenrechnung] p. 119 et seq. and 1953 [Erfassung] p. 157 et seq.). The features of the production process technology in particular are allowed for in the transformation functions. A characteristic of chemical processes is that it is frequently possible to relate the inputs and outputs of the goods involved to the transformed output, per unit of time, of one of the products concerned. Such reference products may be input goods, semi-(chemically) converted intermediate products or end-products. Their quantity per unit of time is designated *throughput*. Using a suitable reference product of this kind as a throughput, production technology can be purposefully included in the functions. They are described by Pichler as "production process-determined constraints" (Pichler, 1953 [Erfassung] p. 165). Examples of such constraints are temperature, pressure, available quantity of catalysts etc. They are thus magnitudes which have a significant influence on production but are not productive outputs themselves. A feature of Pichlerian throughput functions which distinguishes them from Gutenberg's technical input functions as well as from engineering production functions, is that they are linear in all components. Hence, in aggregating a number of such throughput-functions, matrix arithmetic can be used very advantageously.

All three of the basic types of technical process function just mentioned were developed in the 1950s and form the basis of an entire series of extensions, refinements and applications which, since then, have been developed and empirically tested in many ways (for an overview, cp. e.g. Schweitzer and Küpper, 1974 [Produktionstheorie] p. 87 et seq.; Schweitzer, 1979 [Produktionsfunktionen] p. 1504 et seq.; Trossmann, 1983 [Grundlagen] p. 18 et seq.). Among those that have become the best known are the "type C production function" of *Heinen* (cp. 1978 [Kostenlehre] p. 220 et seq.) and the approaches advocated by Pressmar (cp. 1971 [Leistungsanalyse] p. 116 et seq.) and Lassmann (cp. 1968 [Erlösrechnung]).

The above distinction between the individual forms of technically-oriented transformation functions is predominantly of an historical nature. The modern approach to micro-production theory first involves the sub-categorisation of a firm's total production process into individual constituent processes. These sub-processes constitute the supplier and recipient relationships subsisting between certain production centres. As far as possible, realistic transformation functions are formulated for these sub-processes. Such functions may contain, as independent variables, all determinants that are (possibly) of importance to the procurement level of the input relation analysed. In addition to production quantities, a range of other determinants is also involved. In general a transformation function for the input relationship between centres i and j can be formulated as follows:

$$r_{ij} = f_{ij}^* \text{ (for the input relationship relevant production} \qquad (4.74)$$
$$\text{quantities, other relevant determinants)}$$

where i and j represent supplier and recipient centres respectively, and each good is uniquely designated with the index of its production centre.

In individual cases, all magnitudes that are of importance in a transformation relationship can be included in that function as *other determinants*. In particular this will frequently be a question of some of the variables which characterise the production technique but also of other features, which affect the input quantity, of the input relationship in question. Thus, for example, organisational features of the production process, qualitative characteristics of input goods or external production factors, possibly climatic conditions, may play a part.

The origins of the micro-production theory outlined above are largely traceable to *Leontief* (cp. 1966 [Input-Output Economics]) and Kloock (cp. 1969 [Input-Output-Modelle] p. 44 et seq.) and can be regarded as the foundation of the present approach to all production–theoretic analyses (cp. Schweitzer and Küpper, 1974 [Produktionstheorie] p. 46 et seq.). In particular, by partitioning the production process into *sub-processes* it becomes possible to partition and analyse the total process to an extent, and in such detail, as are necessary, and advisable, for the attainment of a satisfactory degree of accuracy in depicting that process. By explicitly identifying *intermediate product quantities*, all goods flows that are of interest can be made visible. Furthermore, by adopting a suitable definition of *fictitious intermediate products*, the requisite partial analyses can also be undertaken for more complex transformation relationships using this production–theoretic approach. This means, in particular that the determinants of the input quantity of a particular supplier and recipient relationship, e.g. certain *work units* (as in *Gutenberg's* approach) or *throughput quantities* (as in Pichler's approach) can often be interpreted as intermediate products of a multistage production process.

The analysis of the specific features of the production process facilitates the formulation of precise transformation functions from which it is possible to derive a usable, well-based forecast of consumption quantities. If they are evaluated with adequate prices, transformation functions can be converted into constituent cost functions which, when added or aggregated, provide a precise cost function for the production process in question. A cost function that is built up in this way specifies how the level of costs depends upon the features of all such determinants as are of importance to the production process. A break-even analysis that is based upon such a *multidimensional production function* facilitates the derivation of more exact results than does a cost function containing constant unit variable costs alone. This kind of break-even analysis is naturally a somewhat more expensive procedure.

(b) Break-even Analysis Procedure in the Case of a Multidimensional Production Function

The following paragraphs contain a general outline of a break-even analysis procedure for dealing with the multidimensional production function. In that the technical determinants of production that are to be taken into account depend upon the concrete facts of the individual case, no more than an abstract symbolisation can be given here. For an input relationship (i, j), in which the input of good i for the production of good j is analysed, a transformation function of the following form is assumed:

$$r_{ij} = f_{ij}^{(1)}(e_{j1}, e_{j2}, \ldots, e_{jK}) + f_{ij}^{(2)}(e_{j1}, e_{j2}, e_{j3}, \ldots, e_{jK}) \cdot r_j. \qquad (4.75)$$

The variables $e_{j1}, e_{j2}, \ldots, e_{jK}$ denote the relevant significant determinants at centre j of the consumption of the individual input goods i. This formulation starts from the situation that is generally present so that the more general transformation function in the form of (4.74) can be split into two components (4.75): a component $f_{ij}^{(1)}$ that is *independent* of the volume of production and a component $f_{ij}^{(2)}$ which is a function of that volume. Substituting the determinant vector

$$\hat{e}_j = (e_{j1}, e_{j2}, \ldots, e_{jK})$$

the transformation function (4.75) can be written more compactly as:

$$r_{ij} = f_{ij}^{(1)}(\hat{e}_j) + f_{ij}^{(2)}(\hat{e}_j) \cdot r_j. \tag{4.76}$$

The total consumption r_i of the individual input goods $i = 1, 2, \ldots, n$ comprises all of their conceivable forms of usage. This can be represented by the goods flow system already represented by (4.48):

$$r_i = r_{i1} + r_{i2} + \cdots + r_{in} + x_i \qquad \text{for } i = 1, 2, \ldots, n. \tag{4.77}$$

The variables x_i $(i = 1, 2, \ldots, n)$ symbolise output levels that are determined by sales volumes. If the total consumption is divided into components that are respectively independent of, and dependent upon, production levels, the following totals are obtained:

$$r_i^{(1)} = \sum_{j=1}^{n} f_{ij}^{(1)}(\hat{e}_j) \tag{4.78}$$

$$r_i^{(2)} = \sum_{j=1}^{n} g_{ij}(\hat{e}_1, \hat{e}_2, \ldots, \hat{e}_n) \cdot x_j. \tag{4.79}$$

The first constituent total constitutes the sum of all amounts that are consumed independently of the level of production. They can now also be more precisely interpreted as consumption that is independent of the level of output. To obtain the second constituent sum it is necessary to solve the system of equations

$$r_i^{(2)} = \sum_{j=1}^{n} f_{ij}^{(2)}(\hat{e}_j) \cdot r_j^{(2)} + x_i \tag{4.80}$$

with respect to the production level variables $r_i^{(2)}$. The resultant total requirement functions are denoted in (4.79) by g_{ij} (cp. Schweitzer and Küpper, 1974 [Produktionstheorie] p. 50). The input levels depend on the variables $\hat{e}_1, \hat{e}_2, \ldots, \hat{e}_n$ which appear both in the technical input function, (4.78), that is independent of the level of output and in that, (4.79), which is dependent upon the level of output (production level dependent).

It is advisable to retain this partitioning to facilitate the construction of a corresponding cost function. If a unit of input good i is valued at DM c_i, the costs K^f that are independent of the level of output can be expressed as the function:

$$K^f = \sum_{i=1}^{n} c_i \cdot r_i^{(1)} = \sum_{i=1}^{n} \sum_{j=1}^{n} c_i \cdot f_{ij}^{(1)}(\hat{e}_j). \tag{4.81}$$

The analogous function for the costs K^v that are dependent upon the level of output is:

$$K^v = \sum_{i=1}^{n} c_i \cdot r_i^{(2)} = \sum_{i=1}^{n} \sum_{j=1}^{n} c_i \cdot g_{ij}(\hat{e}_1, \hat{e}_2, \ldots, \hat{e}_n) \cdot x_j. \tag{4.82}$$

The correspondence with the basic model becomes clear when the output-independent and output-dependent costs are described as (output) fixed and variable costs respectively. The fixed costs depend upon the determinants $\hat{e}_1, \hat{e}_2, \ldots, \hat{e}_n$ in accordance with (4.81):

$$K^f = H^f(\hat{e}_1, \hat{e}_2, \ldots, \hat{e}_n). \tag{4.83}$$

The following transformation shows that the variable costs k_j^v can be expressed as variable costs per unit of productive output and that they are also a function of the determinants $\hat{e}_1, \hat{e}_2, \ldots, \hat{e}_n$:

$$K^v = \sum_{j=1}^{n} \underbrace{\sum_{i=1}^{n} c_i \cdot g_{ij}(\hat{e}_1, \hat{e}_2, \ldots, \hat{e}_n)}_{=:k_j^v} \cdot x_j = \sum_{j=1}^{n} k_j^v \cdot x_j \qquad (4.84)$$

with $k_j^v = h_j^v(\hat{e}_1, \hat{e}_2, \ldots, \hat{e}_n)$.

Equations (4.83) and (4.84) constitute a general form of production-theoretic multidimensional cost function:

$$\begin{aligned}K = h(\hat{e}_1, \hat{e}_2, \ldots, \hat{e}_n) &= K^f + \sum_{j=1}^{n} k_j^v \cdot x_j \\ &= H^f(\hat{e}_1, \hat{e}_2, \ldots, \hat{e}_n) + \sum_{j=1}^{n} h_j^v(\hat{e}_1, \hat{e}_2, \ldots, \hat{e}_n) \cdot x_j.\end{aligned} \qquad (4.85)$$

The computation of break-even values when the cost function is of this form is carried out in the usual way. Unit sales revenue for product j is set at DM q_j. The equality of revenue and costs is described by the following situation:

$$\underbrace{\sum_{j=1}^{n} q_j \cdot x_j}_{\text{sales revenue}} = \underbrace{H^f(\hat{e}_1, \hat{e}_2, \ldots, \hat{e}_n) + \sum_{j=1}^{n} h_j^v(\hat{e}_1, \hat{e}_2, \ldots, \hat{e}_n) \cdot x_j}_{\text{costs}} \qquad (4.86)$$

A rearrangement results in the contribution and fixed costs equality requirement:

$$\underbrace{\sum_{j=1}^{n} \underbrace{(q_j - h_j^v(\hat{e}_1, \hat{e}_2, \ldots, \hat{e}_n)) \cdot x_j}_{\substack{\text{unit contribution} \\ \text{for product } j}}}_{\text{total contribution}} = \underbrace{H^f(\hat{e}_1, \hat{e}_2, \ldots, \hat{e}_n)}_{\text{fixed costs}}. \qquad (4.87)$$

All points $(x_1, x_2, \ldots, x_n)$, which satisfy this equation are break-even points. In this case, and in contrast to the simple break-even analysis in the multiproduct firm, fixed costs and unit contribution vary as a function of the production–theoretic determinants. Hence, in all cases, a *break-even (hyper) plane* results from (4.87). If there are two or more end-products (i.e. $x_j > 0$ for more than an individual j), (4.87) is the general expression for characterising the break-even points. If there is only a single end-product x (in which case the index j can therefore be dispensed with), the following further solution is possible (assuming the unit contribution is non-zero):

$$x = \frac{H^f(\hat{e}_1, \hat{e}_2, \ldots, \hat{e}_n)}{q - h^v(\hat{e}_1, \hat{e}_2, \ldots, \hat{e}_n)}. \qquad (4.88)$$

Equation (4.88) makes it clear that, even in the single-product case, a single break-even point does not emerge; and that there is a multidimensional break-even plane which depends upon the features of the production–theoretic determinants.

In order to elucidate the approach presented above, the next sub-section deals with a simple case of break-even analysis based on a multidimensional production function. In that this is primarily a question of the principle which underlies the approach, the example is restricted to the case of a single-product firm and, initially, also to one further (technical) determinant of the production process in addition to the quantity variables. In the second part of the example, a second such determinant is introduced. In the case of a sole determinant, all vectors $\hat{e}_1, \hat{e}_2, \ldots, \hat{e}_n$, are identical and comprise a single component. Denoting this sole determinant with ξ, the formula (4.88) for ascertaining the break-even set in this example is stated more generally as:

$$x = \frac{H^f(\xi)}{q - h^v(\xi)} .$$

(4.89)

The break-even set is therefore a function of the variable ξ and takes the form of a curve. The manner in which such a break-even curve is actually computed depends upon the individual case in which the analysis is applied. A typical application is described in the following section.

2. Multidimensional Break-even Analysis: An Example from the Plastics Industry

(a) Description of Polyurethane Soft Foam Material as an End-product

The production of a polyurethane foam material is analysed in the following case. Polyurethane foam materials (PUR foam materials) appear in many very diverse forms. Roughly speaking, they can be divided, in accordance with their main physical characteristic into hard foam material and soft foam material on the one hand; and, by reference to one of their main chemical inputs, into polyether-based and polyester-based foam material on the other. PUR hard foam materials have closed cells and a rigid cell-frame. They are therefore fairly resistant to pressure. Because of their enclosed air-cells, they have extremely effective thermal insulating properties and, in addition, a low gross density, i.e. have a very low weight. They are therefore frequently used as packing and insulating material (cp. [BASF-Kunststoffe] p. 107). The physical features and appearance of PUR hard foam material and its resilience to chemicals can be modified by resorting to appropriate admixture materials and treatments. Hard foam can therefore also be used for a multiplicity of other purposes. However, the physical and chemical characteristics of PUR soft foam material can be modified to a much greater extent via its formula and processing conditions than can the features of PUR hard foam material. Soft foam materials—they are colloquially described as "foam rubber"—are characterised by an open cell-structure. Their cell-frame is flexible and the soft foam material can be pressed together. The air that is thereby excluded is taken up again once the pressure is released and the foam material thus returns to its original form. This flexibility constitutes the distinctive feature of soft foams and explains their use for all forms of upholstery. The differences in composition affect various characteristics of the forms of foam material which are distinguished on a polyether or polyester basis by reference to one of their main chemical components. They can be distinguished externally in that polyester foams feel harder, more brittle and straw-like whilst polyether foams are softer and feel more pleasant (cp. Saunders and Frisch, 1962 [Polyurethanes I] p. 314 et seq.).

The following example refers to a polyether-based PUR-soft foam material. The firm in question produces the soft foam material in block form and offers it as raw material for further processing. It is used, among other things, in seating and upholstered furniture of all kinds, in mattresses, in camping equipment, in motor vehicle seats, as cushion fillings, for various packing and protective cushioning purposes, for cavity space and pipe-insulation, for particular floor-coverings, for the lining and insulating of textiles, for the lining of leather goods, and in a vast number of further applications as soft installation material in products of all kinds. Two different methods of chemistry can be used to produce polyurethane foam material (cp. [BASF-Kunststoffe] p. 105 et seq.; Oertel, 1983 [Polyurethane] p. 19; Stoeckhert, 1975 [Kunststoff-Lexikon] p. 443 et seq.). In the case of the *one-shot method*, the requisite amounts of all components and ancillary materials are, with no prior chemical reaction, put in adequate proportions into the foam equipment, mixed and removed for moulding. In the case of the *two-stage method*, a prior reaction is initiated in a first stage to produce a liquid intermediate "prepolymer" product. The actual foam material production takes place in a second stage, in which the intermediate product reacts with propellants and ancillary and other supplementary materials. Using this two-stage procedure, the resultant heat from the chemical reaction can be more effectively controlled, and particular features can thus be modified. The pure prepolymer procedure is nowadays largely obsolete. As a "semi-prepolymer procedure", the two-stage method is of course an important method of producing harder foam materials. In the first reaction stage of the latter procedure, the use of a disequilibrated mixture of input components results in an incomplete prior reaction. The resultant "semi-prepolymer" is only fully transformed in the second stage after the addition of the reaction components that were previously absent. The following pages are concerned with the single-stage procedure. In that all reaction components are simultaneously combined, the desired moulding must take place directly after the mixing. Injection or pouring techniques may be used for this purpose. The latter technique involves the pouring of the mixture into open or closed moulds which are completely filled by the foam reaction. The lining of hollow spaces in, for example, installation walls, the pouring of elastic parts like automobile and aircraft seats, the production of arm-rests, door-handles and armature-cladding are examples of such foam-moulding.

The injection technique involves the production of the foam mixture either directly with mobile foam-making machines at the place at which it is required, and its injection at the point of application; or, its production on a continuous conveyor belt. Examples of the first case are the spraying of insulation layers on to walls and roofs. The second case is represented by the block foam production technique that is the basis of the analysis which follows.

Figure 63 is a diagrammatic representation of the structure of such a plant. The main part of the plant is a small mixing-chamber, with a volume of approximately 1 cm^3, into which the individual components are injected under high pressure. Using reciprocally-arranged power jets, the required mixture is obtained in a matter of split seconds (cp. Stoeckhert, 1975 [Kunststoff-Lexikon] p. 445). Immediately after the mixing process, the mixture is placed on the conveyor belt where the actual chemical reaction takes place,

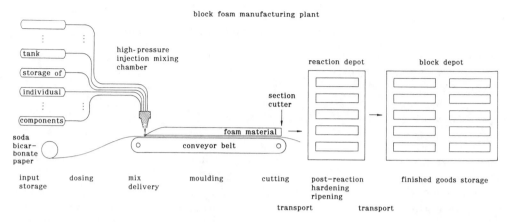

Figure 63 Sequence of processes in soft foam production using the block foam technique

i.e. where the foam material visibly swells up. Using a frame made of soda bicarbonate paper, a particularly strong type of paper which sticks only slightly to the foam material, a mould with a rectangular section is obtained. In order to achieve foam material of the desired quality, particular indicators of which are cell size and density (kg/m^3), the conveyor belt must, given the cross-sectional dimensions of that material, be run at a precisely calculated speed. It varies between 3 metres/minute and 10 metres/minute (cp.Oertel, 1983 [Polyurethane] p. 174). With continuous injection an endless sheet of block foam emerges which is cut into individual blocks at a certain distance from the mixing chamber. The distance must be such that it allows the basic reaction within the block to be entirely completed and the reaction temperature, which exceeds 100 °C, to fall sufficiently. 20-metre lengths of foam material block with a section measuring $2.10\,m \times 1.10\,m$ are produced in the present case. These blocks are sold either whole, or in parts, to customers who further divide them according to intended use, or cut them into particular shapes or, by cutting an initially-glued enormous foam material ring, produce continuous foam material strips. After being cut into 20-metre lengths, the foam material blocks go into a post-reaction depot for 1 or 2 days where the main part of a chemical "after-reaction" can take place. In this post-reaction, the foam material hardens under cooling and finally matures (cp. Oertel, 1983 [Polyurethane] p. 179). The detailed reactions which take place in this maturity phase are still largely unresearched. After this maturing period, the blocks go from the post-reaction depot to a block depot which should be regarded as a finished goods warehouse. The individual manufacturing stages of the soft foam production process are summarised in Fig. 63.

(b) Nature and Composition of Inputs in the Production of
    Polyurethane Soft Foam Material

Soft foam manufacture is of interest from the standpoint of break-even analysis because it involves *particular types of transformation* of individual input goods. To illustrate these special features, the real problem is simplified in respects that are, however, insignificant in relation to an overall analysis of the process. They facilitate a clear derivation of the procedural principle underlying a break-even analysis of this process.

The production in question is of a polyether-based PUR-soft foam with a density of 30 kg/m^3. To this end, the following (simplified) list of inputs is required:

(1) polyol
(2) toluylendiisocyanate (TDI)
(3) water
(4) activators
(5) stabilisers
(6) propellant gas.

The above inputs can be specified more accurately on an individual basis. Thus, polyol describes a whole class of components containing at least two hydroxyl groups per molecule but which are otherwise of a different chemical structure. In particular it may refer to polyester or polyether mixtures (but not, however, to polyester–polyether mixtures). In the present case it denotes a particular polyether mixture. The polyols that can be obtained as input materials are generally not homogeneous with respect to molecular size, but are mixtures of diverse lengths which have the same structure. They are described by the specification of their average molecular weights (cp. Oertel, 1983 [Polyurethane] p. 43). Like the description polyol, TDI does not describe a homogeneous substance. In fact, TDI is rather more accurately described by reference to isocyanate group content and the mixture level of two basic isomer forms of pure toluylendiisocyanate (= TDI = diisocyanato-toluol) and in accordance with further, more accurate designations (cp. Oertel, 1983 [Polyurethane] pp. 63, 69 et seq.; BASF [BASF-Kunststoffe] p. 104).

The polyhydroxyl compounds (polyols) and TDI (diisocyanate and polyisocyanate) are the two main reaction partners in the production of polyurethanes. The basic treatment, the polyaddition, was developed in 1937 by Otto Bayer, Leverkusen, Germany and is based on a multistage sequence of reactions in which the isocyanate components are intertwined with the polyhydroxyl compounds. Because carbon dioxide is also split-off in the process, it produces the foam effect which is of fundamental importance to foam production (cp. Oertel, 1983 [Polyurethane] p. 8). In addition to the two basic components, polyol and TDI, a small quantity of *water*, which is especially necessary for reactions which release carbon dioxide, is required. The other input components enumerated in the above list are not fundamentally necessary for the production of polyurethane. They can be used, however, as can several other additives that are not mentioned here, to affect the features, or appearance, and thereby maintain the desired quality, of the foam material that is to be produced (cp. Oertel, 1983 [Polyurethane] p. 92 et seq.). *Activators* serve as a means of accelerating and regulating the completion of the reaction. The controlling of the reaction speed is important because it determines the properties of the foam material; and also because the raw material input rate and the speed of the conveyor belt must be precisely synchronised with that reaction speed. *Stabilisers* are added in order to prevent undesired changes in the polyurethane product. In the absence of stabilisers, PUR-foam materials are subject to considerable changes that are caused by ageing and atmospheric conditions. Thus, with the effluxion of time, foam mateirals that were originally light-coloured take on a yellow to brown colouration primarily because of reactions with atmospheric oxygen, a process that is strongly influenced by light. Moreover, polyether foam materials decompose in air at high temperatures (those exceeding 100 °C) because polyether chains are then disrupted by oxidation. These and similar undesired changes in foam materials can be prevented by adding small quantities of adequate supplements (cp. Oertel, 1983 [Polyurethane] p. 104 et seq.). In the present context, stabiliser denotes an appropriate mixture of additives of this kind. The carbon dioxide which is generated in the partial reactions serves as a propellant in the basic polyurethane reaction. Frequently, however, the propellant effect is intentionally increased by the addition of further special *propellants* (e.g. frion). In the case of soft foam materials this is of particular importance vis-à-vis the maintaining of the requisite open cell structure. The cells need to be of a particular size to ensure the desired density (cp. Oertel, 1983 [Polyurethane] p. 103 et seq.).

A feature of polyurethane foam production is that the mixture of the individual input materials is not absolutely constant. Variations in the input mixture affect the quality of the end-product (cp. Oertel, 1983 [Polyurethane] p. 187). A weight–input ratio of 2 : 1 applies to polyol and TDI, the two main input materials, and the weight of the other materials amounts to no more than 10% of the polyol-input weight. A variation in a particular initial material input ratio primarily changes the physical properties of the polyurethane product albeit in varying degrees. This is not only of paramount importance in relation to the, quantitatively significant, polyol and TDI compounds but also in relation to the *water input quantity*. Pre-eminently the cell structure of the foam material depends upon the latter input and, in turn, the density and quality of the foam (cp. Saunders and Frisch, 1964 [Polyurethanes II] p. 59 et seq.). Controlling for the effects of the mix ratio is complicated by the additional effects of external factors which largely defy control. Thus, it might be discovered that, on two different days, different formulae must be used to obtain foam material of the same quality.

In the case in question, the desired polyether-foam material, having a gross weight of 30 kg/m^3, is produced, under particular production conditions, in accordance with the following formula:

polyol 100 : TDI 48.0 : water 4.1 : activators 0.5 : stabilisers 1.0 : propellant gas 5.8 (units of weight).

The same formula is used in producing the subsequent layer of the same product. However, it is ascertained that the resultant foam material has larger cells, a less resistant structure and a lower overall density. In extreme cases the previous mixture produces a foam material of a fundamentally different structure. If the cells are very large, the product may not be firm enough and it will tend to collapse under small burdens. If, on the other hand, the production conditions are such that they preclude an open porous structure and cause the cells to be virtually closed, an extremely rigid, hard foam-like product emerges. In the present relatively low density situation, an attempt is nevertheless made, by resorting to a careful reduction in the amount of water added, and corresponding addition of TDI and reductions in propellant gases, to attain the aspired density of 30 kg/m^3 under the existing conditions. After successive changes in the formula it emerges that, under current production conditions, the aspired foam material quality can be attained with the following input ratio (mixture):

polyol 100 : TDI 50.0 : water 3.92 : activators 0.5 : stabilisers 1.0 : propellant gas 5.59 (units of weight).

An exact calculation for this formula gives a density of 30.31 kg/m³ and a deviation of only 0.31 kg/m³. The individual conditions which, using the same formula, cause a different quality, and thus require a different formula for the same quality, are still unresearched in final detail (cp. Oertel, 1983 [Polyurethane] p. 101). Individual partial connections between molecular structure, reaction speed and reaction type as well as such external conditions as temperature, pressure and catalyst inputs have already been partially researched (cp. Saunders and Frisch, 1962 [Polyurethanes I] p. 316 et seq.; 1964 [Polyurethanes II] p. 61 et seq.). In an actual individual case, the particular composition of the chemical inputs and the prevailing conditions at the production location must of course be allowed for if usable input–output relationships for production analysis and production planning are to be ascertained.

In the present case it is presumed that the main external influence on the requisite formula for a 30 kg foam material quality results from the *temperature* and *atmospheric humidity* at which production takes place. Outside air which is subject to sharp fluctuations in atmospheric humidity is continuously conducted into the production hall. In that the quality of the PUR product is considerably influenced by the amount of water added, and because the possible effect of atmospheric humidity on the chemical reaction cannot be ruled out, it seems natural to assume such a connection (see also Oertel, 1983 [Polyurethane] pp. 176, 180). Accordingly, for a succession of production days the following magnitudes are recorded:

—temperature and relative atmospheric humidity as measures of the existing *production conditions*,
—the constituents of the formula that must be used to obtain foam material of the desired quality as *input*,
—percentage weight loss of the mixture, exact density of the foam material produced and the requisite preparation time for the formula as a basis for computing exact *output*.

Twenty-five observations of this kind are tabulated in Fig. 64. The number 25 should be regarded as a simplification. In practice there would be at least one value for each production day. For illustrative purposes, the coverage of Fig. 64 is probably sufficiently comprehensive. The formula is specified in the form of a *basic mixture* in which all input material quantities are determined by reference to 100 kg of polyol.

If the formula is changed, the yield also changes. The weight of the end-product cannot be ascertained simply by adding the weights of the input quantities. On the one hand a *loss of gas* due to the evaporation of gases during the chemical reaction must be taken into account; and, on the other, cutting losses at the margins of the finished foam material which result from the separation of the soda bicarbonate paper frame from the finished foam material. Depending upon the formula used, the overall weight loss varies between 4% and 7.5% of the total input weight. In converting inputs into end-product units that are measured in cubic metres it must also be noted that the aspired density of 30 kg/m³ is occasionally relaxed in favour of other properties when formula variations become necessary; and also because, in the absence of a more accurate control of the production technique, that density can only be approximated. The *density* of the foam material produced is therefore also recorded in Fig. 64. Finally, the *preparation time* for the chosen formula depends upon the extent to which the current production

Observation (order no.) (1)	External production conditions		Input magnitudes: formula (in kg)						Output magnitudes		
	Temperature (in °C) (2)	Relative atmospheric humidity (in %) (3)	Polyol $\bar{\rho}_{P,G}$ (4)	TDI $\bar{\rho}_{TDI,G}$ (5)	Water $\bar{\rho}_{W,G}$ (6)	Activators $\bar{\rho}_{A,G}$ (7)	Stabilisers $\bar{\rho}_{St,G}$ (8)	Propellant gas $\bar{\rho}_{Pr,G}$ (9)	Weight loss (in %) (10)	Density (in kg/m³) (11)	Preparation time for the formula (in min) (12)
1	21.3	64.2	100	48.0	4.10	0.5	1	5.80	5.0	30.01	3.8
2	22.7	75.5	100	50.0	3.92	0.5	1	5.59	5.6	30.31	4.1
3	23.0	77.6	100	50.2	3.90	0.5	1	5.57	5.6	30.34	4.2
4	25.0	76.2	100	51.5	3.68	0.5	1	5.45	6.0	30.51	4.7
5	22.5	68.9	100	49.3	3.99	0.5	1	5.66	5.4	30.21	4.0
6	23.4	78.7	100	51.0	3.82	0.5	1	5.50	5.9	30.44	4.4
7	20.8	65.5	100	47.6	4.13	0.5	1	5.85	4.9	29.97	4.0
8	19.5	61.8	100	47.3	4.16	0.5	1	5.88	4.9	29.88	4.1
9	18.7	60.5	100	46.7	4.18	0.5	1	5.95	4.8	29.75	4.3
10	20.4	64.8	100	47.4	4.15	0.5	1	5.87	4.9	29.89	4.1
11	21.5	69.5	100	48.3	4.07	0.5	1	5.77	5.1	30.04	4.0
12	21.4	71.8	100	48.7	4.04	0.5	1	5.73	5.2	30.12	3.9
13	24.1	78.8	100	51.7	3.75	0.5	1	5.43	6.1	30.54	4.7
14	27.0	69.0	100	52.5	3.70	0.5	1	5.33	6.4	30.61	5.0
15	32.0	78.5	100	58.0	3.00	0.5	1	4.88	8.7	31.10	10.4
16	28.8	68.4	100	53.0	3.60	0.5	1	5.31	6.5	30.71	5.4
17	26.7	83.1	100	53.5	3.54	0.5	1	5.26	6.7	30.76	6.0
18	27.5	88.9	100	55.4	3.28	0.5	1	5.10	7.5	30.93	7.7
19	19.2	63.5	100	47.3	4.17	0.5	1	5.88	4.9	29.88	4.1
20	18.6	63.3	100	46.4	4.22	0.5	1	5.98	4.7	29.71	4.4
21	16.3	55.0	100	45.9	4.25	0.5	1	6.05	4.6	29.62	4.8
22	17.1	59.6	100	46.1	4.24	0.5	1	6.02	4.6	29.67	4.6
23	15.9	47.9	100	45.0	4.30	0.5	1	6.16	4.5	29.43	5.3
24	10.5	36.0	100	43.5	4.36	0.5	1	6.38	4.3	29.14	6.9
25	12.5	43.6	100	44.0	4.36	0.5	1	6.31	4.3	29.26	6.2

Figure 64 Table of observations on determinants and consequences in the case of foam production

conditions deviate from the normal situation. The formula preparation time is the period that is necessary, in the case of a machine that is in operation, to make the necessary adjustments to the mixture by a process of trial and error. Additionally, other costs are incurred in respect of other preparations. These costs do not, however, depend upon the composition of the mixture, or upon the production conditions discussed here, and they are therefore not included in Fig. 64.

(c) Transformation Functions for the Production of the Fictitiously-constituted Intermediate Product "Basic Mixture" as a First Production Stage

Using the observations recorded in Fig. 64, the preconditions for a production–theoretic foundation of a break-even analysis of the production of the foam material described here can now be laid. To this end, transformation functions for the individual inputs must first be drawn up. As is apparent from the above considerations, these transformation functions contain, in addition to the production quantity, further determinants including the current production conditions. The following pages contain a description of the manner in which a production transformation function can be determined when the input–output transformation relationship is known in principle though—from particular observations—only indirectly in quantitative form. In the case of the transformation functions it is clearly known from the outset that, in relation to a variation in output (given other constant determinants), linear input–output relationships obtain. Were this not so, the input quantities could not be specified in relation to a 100-kg basic mixture of polyol. In order to examine the (possibly non-linear) effect of other determinants on the consumption of factor inputs, it is therefore advisable first to analyse the production of an individual unit of basic mixture. From a production–theoretic standpoint this means holding the level of output constant as a determinant. For the purposes of this computation it proves to be advantageous to interpret the actual single-stage process as a related two-stage procedure (cp. Fig. 65).

The composition of the basic mixture is considered in a first stage whereas the second stage contains an analysis of the relationship between the basic mixture and end-product. The principal advantage of this method of analysis is that it allows the respective input quantities to be related to the appropriate accounting units. In this way, inputs which are related to units of the basic mixture can be advantageously distinguished from those which are related to cubic metres of foam material.

Transformation functions for the production of the (fictitious) intermediate product "basic mixture" are sought in the first stage. As this is a question of a convergent process with five input goods, five transformation functions must be sought. The general transformation function $r_{P,\,G}$ for the polyol input is given by:

$$r_{P,\,G} = f_{P,\,G}(.\;.\;.) \cdot r_G \qquad (4.90)$$

where r_G denotes the number of basic mixtures; $f_{P,\,G}$ is the transformation function for the input of polyol per basic mixture; and, $r_{P,\,G}$ is the polyol input quantity.

Correspondingly, the other transformation functions can, using the symbolisation adopted in Fig. 65, be expressed as:

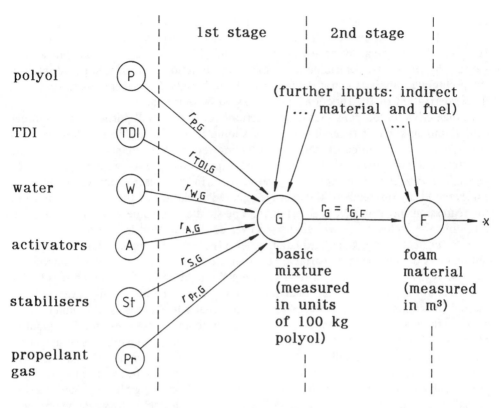

Figure 65 Two-stage analysis of the foam production process

input of TDI	$r_{TDI, G} = f_{TDI, G}(. . .)r_G$
input of water	$r_{W, G} = f_{W, G}(. . .)r_G$
input of activators	$r_{A, G} = f_{A, G}(. . .)r_G$
input of stabilisers	$r_{St, G} = f_{St, G}(. . .)r_G$
input of propellant gas	$r_{Pr, G} = f_{Pr, G}(. . .)r_G$

(4.91)

The dots included in the parentheses are intended to denote the influence of a range of determinants that is yet to be determined. If the basic mixture is measured in units, each of which contains 100 kg of polyol, some of the transformation functions can be directly specified (cp. Fig. 64), namely, the functions (which are constant)

$$f_{P, G} \equiv 100 \text{ for polyol,}$$
$$f_{A, G} \equiv 0.5 \text{ for activators,}$$
$$f_{St, G} \equiv 1.0 \text{ for stabilisers.}$$

The transformation functions for TDI, water and propellant gas are therefore still to be determined. They contain further determinants which appear as independent variables. The derivation of these functions is examined in detail hereafter. It can be assumed that the quantitative value of *absolute atmospheric humidity* has been ascertained in a preliminary analysis as the principal determinant and, therefore, that additional determinants are not included as functional variables. Thus, in particular, the actual measured values which were recorded as specified in Fig. 64 are not used directly. However, in that the absolute atmospheric humidity is computed from these measured values, they indirectly determine the value of the function. The procedure adopted in the preliminary analysis is not described in detail because it corresponds to that used in the derivation of the function that is now to be outlined.

In the derivation of transformation functions for operational purposes, the number of determinants that is taken into account should be minimised. In deciding between two systems of determinants, the system having fewer determinants should as a rule be preferred provided both have the same explanatory power with respect to the dependent variables. The explanatory power can, in the present context, be defined, for example, by reference to the average squared deviation of the observations from the regression function that is ascertained. The smaller the value which this deviation takes on, the higher is the explanatory power of the function in question.

In the present context a high explanatory level is obtained using absolute atmospheric humidity as the independent variable. The reason for examining the efficiency of this variable is the presumption that relative atmospheric humidity has a much smaller influence on the chemical reactions than does absolute atmospheric humidity measured, for example, in grams per cubic metre. It is assumed that absolute atmospheric humidity plays a part in the polyurethane chemical reaction—albeit to an unknown extent. The quantity of water which enters the raw mixture from the air consequently changes its composition and explains (at least partially) the need for variations in the formula. Deviations from a regression function in which absolute atmospheric humidity is the independent variable are traceable to other determinants which, because of their negligible effect and the cost of taking them into account, are ignored. Such remaining deviations between the observed values and the regression function are therefore interpreted as random influences.

The transformation function for *water usage* is ascertained in the first stage of the analysis. The conversion of relative to absolute atmospheric humidity is presented in Fig. 66.

The saturation humidities ξ^{max}, given in Table A.3 of Appendix II, of water as a function of temperature t are used as a basis for the conversion. Saturation humidity is the maximum absolute atmospheric humidity for a given temperature and is specified in grams per cubic metre (g/m^3). In converting relative humidity ξ^r into an absolute humidity ξ, the following general relation applies:

$$\xi = \underbrace{\xi^{max}(t)}_{\substack{\text{Value from}\\\text{Table A.3,}\\\text{Appendix II}}} \cdot \frac{\xi^r}{100}. \tag{4.92}$$

According to Table A.3, Appendix II, a maximum atmospheric humidity of $\xi^{max} = 18.696\,g/m^3$ results from a temperature of 21.3 °C—the first observation in Fig. 64. Thus, if the relative atmospheric humidity is 64.2%, there is an actual absolute atmospheric humidity of $\xi = 12.00\,g/m^3$. Values ranked in ascending order of atmospheric humidity are shown in Fig. 66, which also indicates water consumption per basic mixture (final column). It is now necessary to estimate an explicit regression function of the form

New order no.	Observation no. (from Fig. (64))	Temperature in °C	Relative atmospheric humidity (%)	Absolute atmospheric humidity (g/m³)	Water usage per basic mixture (kg)
i		t_i	$\tilde{\xi}_i^r$	$\tilde{\xi}_i$	$\bar{r}_{W, G, i}$
1	24	10.5	36.0	3.50	4.36
2	25	12.5	43.6	4.80	4.36
3	23	15.9	47.9	6.50	4.30
4	21	16.3	55.0	7.65	4.25
5	22	17.1	59.6	8.70	4.24
6	9	18.7	60.5	9.71	4.18
7	20	18.6	63.3	10.10	4.22
8	8	19.5	61.8	10.40	4.16
9	19	19.2	63.5	10.50	4.17
10	10	20.4	64.8	11.50	4.15
11	7	20.8	65.5	11.90	4.13
12	1	21.3	64.2	12.00	4.10
13	11	21.5	69.5	13.15	4.07
14	12	21.4	71.8	13.50	4.04
15	5	22.5	68.9	13.80	3.99
16	2	22.7	75.5	15.30	3.92
17	3	23.0	77.6	16.00	3.90
18	6	23.4	78.7	16.60	3.82
19	13	24.1	78.8	17.30	3.75
20	4	25.0	76.2	17.60	3.68
21	14	27.0	69.0	17.82	3.70
22	16	28.8	68.4	19.50	3.60
23	17	26.7	83.1	21.10	3.54
24	18	27.5	88.9	23.60	3.28
25	15	32.0	78.5	26.60	3.00

Figure 66   Comparison of observed values of absolute atmospheric humidity and usage of water classified by increasing absolute atmospheric humidity

$$f_{W, G}(\xi)$$

which expresses water consumption as a function of absolute atmospheric humidity ξ. In seeking an adequate type of function it is first advisable to plot the observations listed in Fig. 66 in $\xi/\rho_{W, G}$ two-dimensional space.

It can be inferred from Fig. 67, which shows the resultant scatter diagram, that the overall function is concave to the origin. A linear regression analysis is therefore precluded. A tentative computation using the function

$$f_{W, G}(\xi) = a_0 + a_1 \cdot \xi - a_2 \cdot \xi^2 \qquad \text{with } a_0, a_2 > 0 \qquad (4.93)$$

and the parameters a_0, a_1, and a_2, results, however, in a function which is excessively concave. From this it may be inferred that an adequate type of function must contain a term in which ξ appears with an exponent that takes on a value of between 1

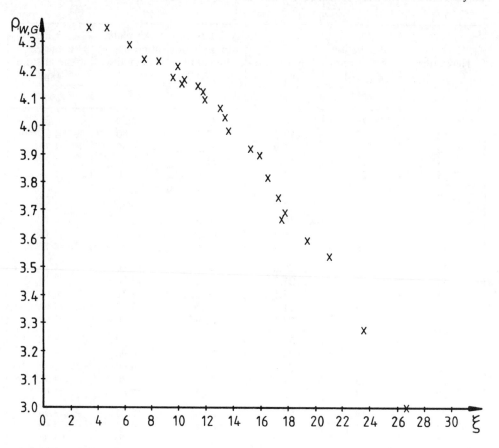

Figure 67 Scatter diagram for observations of water usage $\rho_{W, G}$ as a function of absolute atmospheric humidity ξ

and 2. The following basic model containing an (initially) undetermined exponent β is therefore chosen:

$$f_{W, G}(\xi) = -a \cdot \xi^{\beta} + c \qquad \text{with } a, c > 0. \qquad (4.94)$$

The parameters c, a and β are to be set in a manner such that the function best approximates, i.e. deviates as little as possible from, the (known) observed values (cp. Fig. 66).

A direct regression analysis using a function in the form of (4.94) is a matter of some complexity. The function can, however, be simplified if it is expressed in logarithmic form. Putting,

$$\rho_{W, G} = f_{W, G}(\xi) \qquad (4.95)$$

then,

$$\cdot c - \rho_{W, G} = a \cdot \xi^{\beta}.$$

In that, according to the definition of the parameters in (4.94), both sides of the latter equation are positive, it can be expressed in logarithmic form:

$$\ln(c - \rho_{W, G}) = \ln a + \beta \cdot \ln \xi \qquad (4.96)$$

This transformation shows that in the case of the (4.94) functional form, there is a linear relationship between the logarithmic value of atmospheric humidity ξ and the logarithmic value of water consumption $\rho_{W, G}$ after deducting an appropriate constant c from the latter. If the constant c is known, the remaining parameters can be ascertained, for example, in accordance with the standard procedure of simple linear regression analysis. This becomes evident if the following substitutions are made:

$$\begin{aligned} y &:= \ln (c - \rho_{W, G}) \\ \alpha &:= \ln a \\ x &:= \ln \xi. \end{aligned} \qquad (4.97)$$

The functional equation containing the required parameters α and β is then:

$$y = \alpha + \beta \cdot x. \qquad (4.98)$$

Thus, in the present case, the following successive procedures can be applied as a means of deriving a satisfactory regression function:

(1) determination of an appropriate constant c,
(2) determination of the parameters α and β in the case of a given constant c using the standard ordinary least squares method.

A suitable constant c can be determined heuristically in that, using a systematic trial and error method, the value of c is sought at which the pairs $(\bar{x}_i, \bar{y}_i)$ $(i = 1, 2, \ldots, 25)$ that are computed from the observed values $(\xi_i, \tilde{\rho}_{W, G, i})$ $(i = 1, 2, \ldots, 25)$ with

$$\begin{aligned} \bar{x}_i &= \ln \tilde{\rho}_i \\ \bar{y}_i &= \ln(c - \tilde{\rho}_{W, G, i}) \end{aligned} \qquad (4.99)$$

can most nearly be regarded as points on a straight line. This groping towards an adequate value for the parameter c can be based on graphical or arithmetic estimation. Adopting a graphical approach, the computed values $(\bar{x}_i, \bar{y}_i)$ $(i = 1, 2, \ldots, 25)$ for a given value of c are entered in an appropriate coordinate system. The constant c is then evaluated by reference to the curve indicated by the scatter points and changed as required. If, for example, a value of 5 is chosen for c, the outcome is that shown in Fig. 68(a). If the curve that is intended to approximate the individual points increases at an increasing rate, the indication is that the constant c should be reduced in order to obtain an approximate linear outcome. Figure 68(b) shows the scatter points when the constant c takes on a value of 4.5. In this case an increase at a slightly increasing rate can still be observed. After further trials, 4.40 is set as a suitable value for the constant c (cp. Fig. 68(c)).

Arithmetically the choice of an adequate constant c can be resolved by determining, for alternative values of c, the corresponding coefficients for the straight line and the sum of the squared deviations between the regression and observed values.

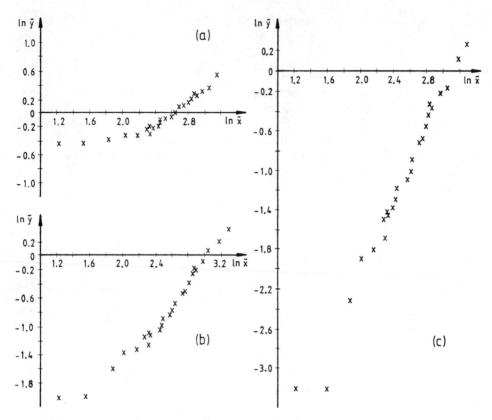

Figure 68 Scatter diagrams for the logarithmic values of water usage after subtracting constants
of 5.0 (a), 4.5 (b) and 4.4 (c) respectively

The chosen parameter value of c is that at which this latter measure of dispersion is
minimised.

It is now necessary to undertake a regression computation for the chosen parameter
value $c = 4.40$ as presented in Fig. 69. A detailed description of the ordinary least squares
method used in the latter case is presented in Fig. 7. The computation in Fig. 69 results
in the parameter values

$$\alpha = -5.91 \quad \text{and} \quad \beta = 1.9.$$

The function formulated in (4.98) is therefore:

$$y = -5.91 + 1.9x.$$

Conforming to the variables formulated in (4.97) with

$$a = e^{\alpha} = e^{-5.91} = 0.002\,712$$

the resultant functional equation (cp. (4.96)) is:

$$\ln(4.40 - \rho_{W,\,G}) = \ln 0.002\,712 + 1.9 \ln \xi$$

i	$\tilde{\xi}_i$	$\bar{x}_i = \ln \xi_i$	$4.40 - \bar{\rho}_{W,G,i}$	$\tilde{y}_i = \ln(4.40 - \bar{\rho}_{W,G,i})$	$(\bar{x}_i - \bar{x})$	$(\bar{x}_i - \bar{x})^2$	$(\tilde{y}_i - \bar{y})$	$(\bar{x}_i - \bar{x}) \cdot (\tilde{y}_i - \bar{y})$
1	3.50	1.252 76	0.04	−3.218 88	−1.257 17	1.580 48	−2.077 71	2.612 03
2	4.80	1.568 62	0.04	−3.218 88	−0.941 31	0.886 06	−2.077 71	1.955 77
3	6.50	1.871 80	0.10	−2.302 59	−0.638 13	0.407 21	−1.161 42	0.741 14
4	7.65	2.034 71	0.15	−1.897 12	−0.475 22	0.225 83	−0.755 95	0.359 24
5	8.70	2.163 32	0.16	−1.832 58	−0.346 61	0.120 14	−0.691 41	0.239 65
6	9.71	2.273 16	0.22	−1.514 13	−0.236 77	0.056 06	−0.372 96	0.088 31
7	10.10	2.312 54	0.18	−1.714 80	−0.197 39	0.038 96	−0.573 63	0.113 23
8	10.40	2.341 81	0.24	−1.427 12	−0.168 12	0.028 26	−0.285 95	0.048 07
9	10.50	2.351 38	0.23	−1.469 68	−0.158 55	0.025 14	−0.328 51	0.052 09
10	11.50	2.442 35	0.25	−1.386 29	−0.067 58	0.004 57	−0.245 12	0.016 57
11	11.90	2.476 54	0.27	−1.309 33	−0.033 39	0.001 11	−0.168 16	0.005 61
12	12.00	2.484 91	0.30	−1.203 97	−0.025 02	0.000 63	−0.062 80	0.001 57
13	13.15	2.576 42	0.33	−1.108 66	0.066 49	0.004 42	0.032 51	0.002 16
14	13.50	2.602 69	0.36	−1.021 65	0.092 76	0.008 60	0.119 52	0.011 09
15	13.80	2.624 67	0.41	−0.891 60	0.114 74	0.013 17	0.249 57	0.028 64
16	15.30	2.727 85	0.48	−0.733 97	0.217 92	0.047 49	0.407 20	0.088 74
17	16.00	2.772 59	0.50	−0.693 15	0.262 66	0.068 99	0.448 02	0.117 68
18	16.60	2.809 40	0.58	−0.544 73	0.299 47	0.089 68	0.596 44	0.178 62
19	17.30	2.850 71	0.65	−0.430 78	0.340 78	0.116 13	0.710 39	0.242 09
20	17.60	2.867 90	0.72	−0.328 50	0.357 97	0.128 14	0.812 67	0.290 91
21	17.82	2.880 32	0.70	−0.356 67	0.370 39	0.137 19	0.784 50	0.290 57
22	19.50	2.970 41	0.80	−0.223 14	0.460 48	0.212 04	0.918 03	0.422 73
23	21.10	3.049 27	0.86	−0.150 82	0.539 34	0.290 89	0.990 35	0.534 14
24	23.60	3.161 25	1.12	0.113 33	0.651 32	0.424 22	1.254 50	0.817 08
25	26.60	3.280 91	1.40	0.336 47	0.770 98	0.594 41	1.477 64	1.139 23
Σ	339.13	62.748 29	11.09	−28.529 24	0	5.509 82	0	10.396 96

Figure 69 Computation of the parameters α and β of the linear regression function of the transformed values of the observations $(\bar{x}_i, \tilde{y}_i)$ $(i = 1, 2, \ldots, 25)$

or

$$\rho_{W, G} = 4.40 - 0.002\,712\,\xi^{1.9}.$$

The overall transformation function for water consumption $\rho_{W, G}$ per basic mixture is ascertained accordingly. It is:

$$f_{W, G}(\xi) = 4.40 - 0.002\,712\,\xi^{1.9}. \tag{4.100}$$

These transformation functions and the original associated observed values are presented graphically in Fig. 70.

A comparison of the values of the function with observed values at corresponding atmospheric humidities shows that the function (4.100) represents a usable approximation to actual values in reality and that it can be adopted as a basis for dealing with all relevant planning questions.

The same approach is adopted in deriving the transformation functions for the TDI and propellant gas inputs per basic mixture. In the case of the *TDI-input* it is clear from

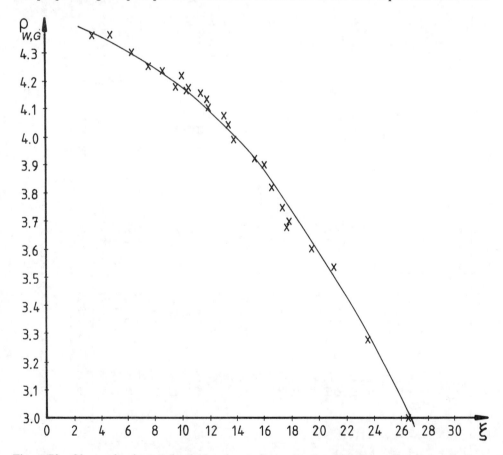

Figure 70 Observed values and calculated transformation function for water usage $\rho_{W, G}$ per basic mixture as a function of absolute atmospheric humidity ξ

the scatter diagram that this is a question of a function which increases at an increasing rate. To avoid negative numbers in the logarithmic transformation, the following type of function is preferred to (4.94):

$$\rho_{TDI, G} = f_{TDI, G}(\xi) = a \cdot \xi^\beta + c, \tag{4.101}$$

whereby the parameter a is positive. Expressed in logarithmic form (4.101) is:

$$\ln(\rho_{TDI, G} - c) = \ln a + \beta \ln \xi. \tag{4.102}$$

The parameter values of this function are computed, in the manner described above, as in the case of water consumption. After undertaking the individual computational steps, the following transformation for the input of TDI $\rho_{TDI, G}$ per basic mixture is obtained

$$f_{TDI, G}(\xi) = 42 + 0.3263 \cdot \xi^{1.175}. \tag{4.103}$$

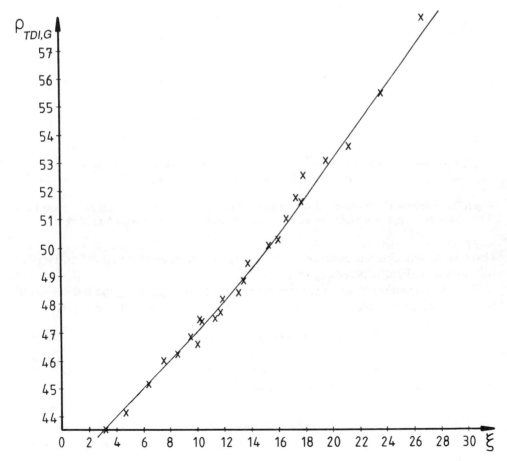

Figure 71 Observed values and calculated transformation function for the input of TDI $\rho_{TDI, G}$ per basic mixture as a function of absolute atmospheric humidity ξ

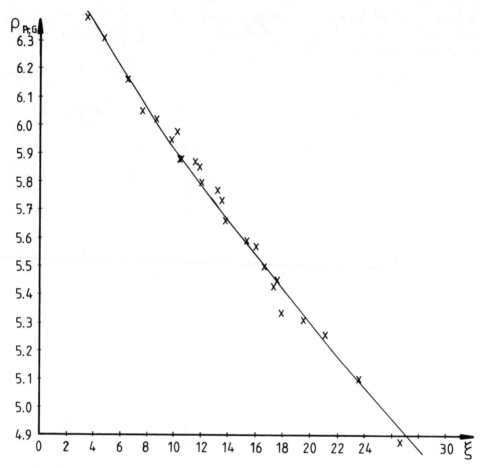

Figure 72 Observed values and calculated transformation function for the input of propellant gas $\rho_{Pr,\,G}$ per basic mixture as a function of absolute atmospheric humidity ξ

Given increasing absolute atmospheric humidity, the function in question (cp. Fig. 71) increases at a slightly increasing rate.

The transformation function for the input of propellant gas $\rho_{Pr,\,G}$ per basic mixture is ascertained in the same way as the water consumption function and is given by:

$$f_{Pr,\,G}(\xi) = 6.75 - 0.1275 \cdot \xi^{0.81}.\tag{4.104}$$

As indicated by the graphical presentation in Fig. 72, it turns out to be similar to the transformation function for the water input.

(d) Transformation Function for the Relationship between the Input of Basic Mixture and the Quantity of Foam Material Produced in the Second Production Stage

A consideration of the structure of foam material production sketched out in Fig. 65 indicates that all of the transformation functions so far analysed belong to the first production stage. The most important transformation in the second production stage concerns the input–output relation between the (fictitious) intermediate product "basic mixture" and the foam material product. In that foam material can be regarded as an end-product, its output level is symbolised with x. Precisely formulated, a transformation function $f_{G, F}$ is sought which specifies the number of *units of input of basic mixture per unit of foam material end-product*:

$$r_{G, F} = f_{G, F}(. . .) \cdot x \qquad (4.105)$$

or

$$\rho_{G, F} = f_{G, F}(. . .) \quad \text{and} \quad r_{G, F} = \rho_{G, F} \cdot x.$$

Following the same, previously-outlined prior considerations, it is clear that, as a constituent determinant of the desired transformation function $f_{G, F}$, only absolute atmospheric humidity needs to be taken into account. Before the derivation of a regression function for this transformation can start, the actual transformation coefficients $\bar{\rho}_{G, F}$ for the observed values must first be computed. This can be explicitly illustrated by reference to the first observation in Fig. 64.

Computation of the *actual transformation coefficients* $\bar{\rho}_{G, F}$ for the first observation (cp. Fig. 64, row 1, columns 4 to 9):

(1) Determination of the total gross weight of a basic mixture:

Polyol	100.00 kg
TDI	48.00 kg
Water	4.10 kg
Activators	0.50 kg
Stabilisers	1.00 kg
Propellant gas	5.80 kg
Total gross weight	159.40 kg

(2) Determination of the net weight of a basic mixture:

Weight loss (cp. Fig. 64, col. 10):	5%
Gross weight	159.400 kg
-5% weight loss	7.970 kg
Net weight	151.430 kg

(3) Computation of the yield of raw cubic metres of foam material per basic mixture:

Density of the foam material output (cp. Fig. 64, col. 11):
  30.01 kg/m^3
Yield per basic mixture:
  $151.430 \text{ kg} : 30.01 \text{ kg/m}^3 = 5.0460 \text{ m}^3$

(4) Conversion into a transformation coefficient: number of units of input of the basic mixture for a raw cubic metre of foam material:

$$\bar{\rho}_{G, F} = 1/5.0460 = 0.1982 \text{ basic mixture units per m}^3.$$

Order no. (from Fig. 66) i (1)	Absolute atmospheric humidity (from Fig. 66) ξ_i (2)	Gross weight of a unit of basic mixture (3)	Weight loss in % (from Fig. 64, col. 10) (4)	Net weight of a basic mixture (5)	Density of foam produced (from Fig. 64, col. 11) (6)	Foam yield per basic mixture ((5)/(6)) (7)	Transformation coefficient $\bar{\rho}_{G,F}$ ((6)/(5)) (8)
1	3.50	155.74	4.3	149.04	29.14	5.1146	0.1955
2	4.80	156.17	4.3	149.45	29.26	5.1077	0.1958
3	6.50	156.96	4.5	149.90	29.43	5.0934	0.1963
4	7.65	157.70	4.6	150.45	29.62	5.0793	0.1969
5	8.70	157.86	4.6	150.60	29.67	5.0758	0.1970
6	9.71	158.33	4.8	150.73	29.75	5.0666	0.1974
7	10.10	158.10	4.7	150.67	29.71	5.0714	0.1972
8	10.40	158.84	4.9	151.06	29.88	5.0556	0.1978
9	10.50	158.85	4.9	151.07	29.88	5.0559	0.1978
10	11.50	158.92	4.9	151.13	29.89	5.0562	0.1978
11	11.90	159.08	4.9	151.29	29.97	5.0480	0.1981
12	12.00	159.40	5.0	151.43	30.01	5.0460	0.1982
13	13.15	159.64	5.1	151.50	30.04	5.0433	0.1983
14	13.50	159.97	5.2	151.65	30.12	5.0349	0.1986
15	13.80	160.45	5.4	151.79	30.21	5.0245	0.1990
16	15.30	161.01	5.6	151.99	30.31	5.0145	0.1994
17	16.00	161.17	5.6	152.14	30.34	5.0145	0.1994
18	16.60	161.82	5.9	152.27	30.44	5.0023	0.1999
19	17.30	162.38	6.1	152.47	30.54	4.9925	0.2003
20	17.60	162.13	6.0	152.40	30.51	4.9951	0.2002
21	17.82	163.03	6.4	152.60	30.61	4.9853	0.2006
22	19.50	163.41	6.5	152.79	30.71	4.9753	0.2010
23	21.10	163.80	6.7	152.82	30.76	4.9681	0.2013
24	23.60	165.28	7.5	152.88	30.93	4.9428	0.2023
25	26.60	167.38	8.7	152.82	31.10	4.9138	0.2035

Figure 73 Calculation of the actual observed values for the transformation coefficient of $\rho_{G,F}$

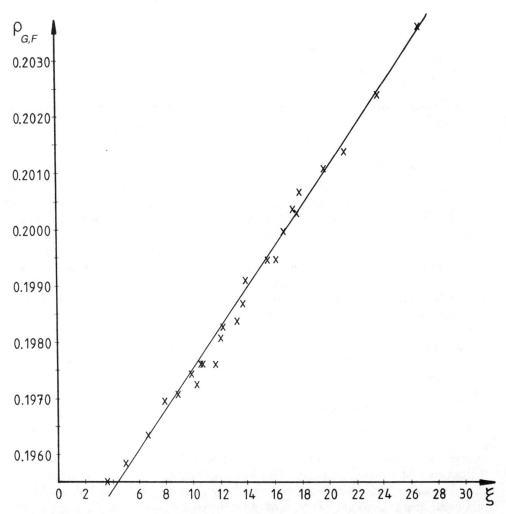

Figure 74 Observed values and calculated transformation coefficient function for the number of units of basic mixture $\rho_{G, F}$ per cubic metre of raw foam as a function of the absolute atmospheric humidity ξ

The value so ascertained specifies the number of units of basic mixture (measured in quantity units containing 100 kg of polyol (per unit)) required for the production of a raw cubic metre of finished foam material. For the first observation (Fig. 64, row 1) this amounts to 0.1982. The latter computation shows that two determinants which vary with atmospheric humidity enter the computation: the *weight loss* of the particular basic mixture in question and the *density* of the foam material output.

An analysis of the rows in Fig. 64 (table of observations) shows that both weight loss and density tend to increase with increasing atmospheric humidity.

The actual transformation coefficients are computed for all observations in Fig. 73. The example computed above is numbered $i = 12$ in Fig. 66. If, in conjunction with the related absolute atmospheric humidities, these values are plotted in two-dimensional space (cp. Fig. 74), they reveal a linear, gently increasing function.

The standard regression computation gives the function

$$\rho_{G, F} = f_{G, F}(\xi) \tag{4.106}$$

with $f(\xi) = 0.1940 + (3.52/10\,000) \cdot \xi$

for the transformation coefficients expressed as a function of absolute atmospheric humidity.

(e) Specifying a Function for the Costs which Vary with Respect to Output

The transformation functions so far analysed are concerned with the input of raw materials. When costed with appropriate unit prices these inputs provide raw material cost functions. The consumption of indirect materials and fuel has not been included hitherto. Here it is largely captured in the form of a lump sum. As in the case of raw materials, the two-stage analysis which was introduced in Fig. 65 also proves to be advantageous here. In the case of indirect materials and fuel, a distinction can be made between *time-related* and *end-product output-related* (i.e. cubic metre-related) consumption. It is advisable to attribute the costs which are traceable to cubic metres of output to the second stage and time-related costs to the first stage.

The time-related costs can be attributed to the (quantity) units of the basic mixture because the time taken for the basic mixture to settle is constant. In the case in point it is always the addition of 180 kg of polyol per minute. This corresponds to a first stage production intensity of:

$$\frac{180 \text{ kg polyol/min}}{100 \text{ kg polyol/basic mixture}} = 1.8 \text{ kg basic mixtures/min}$$

On the other hand, the speed of the conveyor belt must be varied in order to achieve the desired foam material quality. This ensures that, with varying weight loss and changing density, a foam material having the same section, and of similar quality, is produced. Energy costs and the costs of other fuels are time-related. The energy costs of plant and equipment are high principally because the pumping equipment which introduces the chemical inputs, the high pressure injection system together with the ventilators and other cooling installations are very energy intensive. The *energy costs* are specified at an hourly rate of DM 96. This corresponds to a cost rate per minute of DM 1.60. The energy costs incurred per unit of basic mixture (UBM) are therefore:

Energy costs per basic mixture:

$$\frac{\text{DM } 96/\text{h}}{60 \text{ min/h}} \cdot \frac{1}{1.8 \text{ UBM/min}} = \text{DM } 0.888\,89/\text{basic mixture.}$$

A similar calculation applies to the *other fuels*, the hourly costs of which amount to DM 30. Related to a basic mixture this represents cost amounting to:

$$\frac{\text{DM } 30/\text{h}}{60 \text{ min/h} \cdot 1.8 \text{ UBM/min}} = \text{DM } 0.277\,78/\text{basic mixture.}$$

The *cubic metre-related costs* comprise the soda bicarbonate paper for moulding the foam material and certain indirect materials. The length (0.4329 m) of a cubic metre of foam material can be determined from the foam material section (2.10 m × 1.10 m). Given information indicating how much the individual widths of paper overlap at the edges, and the extent of cutting spoilage, the paper requirement can be calculated in m² per cubic metre of foam material. It amounts to 3.38 m². The price of the special paper used is DM 2500 per ton. Allowing for the weight of that paper, the resultant cost rate is DM 0.20/m². The input of soda bicarbonate paper therefore costs DM 0.676 per cubic metre of foam material.

Other variable costs amount to DM 2.02 per cubic metre of foam material.

Of the other costs that are incurred in the production of foam material, only a part of interest costs is to be regarded as being variable with respect to the level of output. This is a question of such interest costs as are incurred in the maturing of the foam material output in the post-reaction depot. Overall, output-related interest costs for three working days are allowed for whereby interest is related to the provisional total (i.e. excluding interest) of variable costs. Assuming 250 working days a year, and an interest rate of 15%, this calculation results in an interest charge at the rate of 0.18% on the provisional total of variable costs.

The array of costs which varies with respect to the level of output can be computed in accordance with the following statement—assuming that the raw material prices are given and constant:

(1) Costs of the first production stage (per basic unit) k_G^v:

(a) *Raw material costs*

Input i	Quantity $\rho_{iG} = f_{iG}(\xi)$ (kg)	Unit price q_i (DM/kg)	Costs $q_i \cdot f_{iG}(\xi)$ (DM)
Polyol	100	2.91	291.00
TDI	$(42 + 0.3263\,\xi^{1.175})$	5.93	$(246.06 + 1.9350\,\xi^{1.175})$
Water	$(4.4 - 0.002712\,\xi^{1.9})$	0.0036	$(0.0158 - 0.0^59763\,\xi^{1.9})$
Activators	0.5	21.30	10.65
Stabilisers	1.0	12.40	12.40
Propellant gas	$(6.75 - 0.1275\,\xi^{0.81})$	2.36	$(15.93 - 0.3009\,\xi^{0.81})$

(b) *Fuel costs*	DM
Energy costs per unit of basic mixture	0.888 89
Other fuel costs per unit of basic mixture	0.277 78

Costs per unit of basic mixture
$$k_G^v = h_G^v(\xi) = DM\ \{580.2225 - 0.3009\,\xi^{0.81}$$
$$+ 1.9350\,\xi^{1.175} - 0.0^59763\,\xi^{1.9}\} \tag{4.107}$$

(2) Costs of the second production stage (per cubic metre of raw foam material):

(a) Conversion of the (basic mixture-related) costs of the first manufacturing stage:

costs per m^3 of foam material =

required number of units of basic mixture per $m^3 \cdot$ unit cost of basic mixture

$$= \rho_{G,\,F} \cdot k_G^v = f_{iG}(\xi) \cdot h_G^v(\xi)$$
$$= DM\ \{0.1940 + (3.52/10\,000)\ \xi\} \cdot \{580.2225 - 0.3009\ \xi^{0.81}$$
$$+ 1.9350\ \xi^{1.175} - 0.0^5 9763\ \xi^{1.9}\}$$

(b) Further costs which are attributable to cubic metres of raw foam material:

	DM
Costs of soda bicarbonate paper	0.6760
Other variable costs (indirect materials) per m^3 of foam material	2.0200

(Provisional) sum of costs per m^3 of foam material $\hat{k}^v = \hat{h}^v(\xi)$ (in DM rounded):

$$115.2592 - 0.05837\ \xi^{0.81} + 0.20424\ \xi$$
$$+ 0.37539\ \xi^{1.175} - 0.0001059\ \xi^{1.81}$$
$$- 0.0^5 1894\ \xi^{1.9} + 0.0^3 6811\ \xi^{2.175} \tag{4.108}$$

(3) $+0.18\%$ interest   (4.109)

Output-dependent costs in DM per m^3 of foam material

$$k^v = h^v(\xi)$$
$$= 1.0018 \cdot \hat{h}^v(\xi) = 115.4667 - 0.05848\ \xi^{0.81}$$
$$+ 0.20461\ \xi + 0.37607\ \xi^{1.175}$$
$$- 0.0001061\ \xi^{1.81}$$
$$- 0.0^5 1897\ \xi^{1.9} \tag{4.110}$$
$$+ 0.0^3 6823\ \xi^{2.175}$$

The computation of the provisional variable cost total reflects a degree of rounding because of the dropping of a term of the form $\alpha \xi^{2.9}$ which, even with large values of ξ only affects variable costs in the fifth decimal place. The function ultimately determined specifies the variable costs per cubic metre of foam material as a function of one determinant ξ, i.e. atmospheric humidity. This variable cost function constitutes the basic information for a break-even analysis of the production process in question.

A second piece of basic information is that on the level of fixed costs. In the present case it is necessary to distinguish more precisely as to whether this is a question of costs which are incurred once per layer or once a year. In the former case reference is made to the fixed costs of a layer—they are variable with respect to the *number* of layers, i.e. increase with the frequency of layers—whereas, in the latter case, it is a question of annual fixed costs. Under certain circumstances both "fixed" cost magnitudes are, in the present context, again dependent upon the additional determinant atmospheric humidity.

(f) Specifying a Function for the Costs which are Fixed with Respect to the Output of an Individual Layer

Costs which are fixed with respect to an individual layer result from consumption involving the following individual items:

(1) *General preparation costs*: particular indirect materials, e.g. cleaning agents, renewal of catalysts etc.: DM 780;

(2) *Raw material costs and other preparation time costs that are related to the basic mixture*: preparation period in minutes *times* the usage intensity of foam-making equipment in basic mixtures per minute *times* costs k_G per basic mixture;

(3) *Cubic metre-related further costs*: these are the costs of soda bicarbonate paper amounting to DM $0.676/m^3$ and other variable costs of DM $2.02/m^3$. Calculation: preparation period in minutes *times* usage intensity of the foam-making equipment in basic mixtures per minute *times* the number of cubic metres per basic mixture *times* DM $(2.02 + 0.676)$.

The number of cubic metres per basic mixture mentioned in this formula refers to that number of cubic metres which determines the (cubic metre-dependent) consumption of input material. Thus, the soda bicarbonate paper is also consumed during the preparation phase when indeed the foam material production does not meet expectations but when, however, loaded with soda bicarbonate paper, the frame of the conveyor belt runs at a particular speed. The consumption of indirect materials takes on a similar pattern. In that, in the preparatory phase, the speed of the conveyor belt is changed frequently and unpredictably, the use of an average is advisable here. It appears from past observations that 5 cubic metres per basic mixture is a reasonable approximation. This corresponds to a transformation coefficient for the second stage of 0.2. The overall cubic metre-related costs are therefore computed as follows:

Preparation period in minutes *times* usage intensity of foam-making equipment in basic mixtures per minute *times* 5 *times* DM 2.696.

(4) *Removal and recycling costs* of the production emerging in the preparation period. This is partly a question of units of basic mixture that are not fully converted and partly a matter of particular polyurethane products. Approximately 150 kg of the resultant chemical products can be expected from a basic mixture. The net costs (i.e. gross costs less revenue arising, if any) of this output are specified as DM 1.20/kg. The removal costs therefore can be computed as follows:

Preparation period in minutes *times* usage intensity of the foam-making equipment in basic mixtures per minute times 150 kg *times* DM 1.20 /kg.

The usage intensity of the foam-making equipment, which appears in cost components (2), (3) and (4), is held constant in the overall production process. As already calculated above, it is 1.8 basic mixtures/minute. Substituting the known values and adding the four cost components enumerated above, it turns out that the resultant cost total is a function of two parameters: preparation time and costs per basic mixture:

Costs per layer $k_A =$
780 + preparation time $\cdot 1.8 \cdot$ [costs per basic mixture + 13.48 + 180]   (4.111)

  (1)   (2)   (3)   (4)

The *costs per basic mixture* k_G^v are a function of atmospheric humidity ξ. This cost function has already been derived and is specified by (4.107). As indicated by Fig. 64,

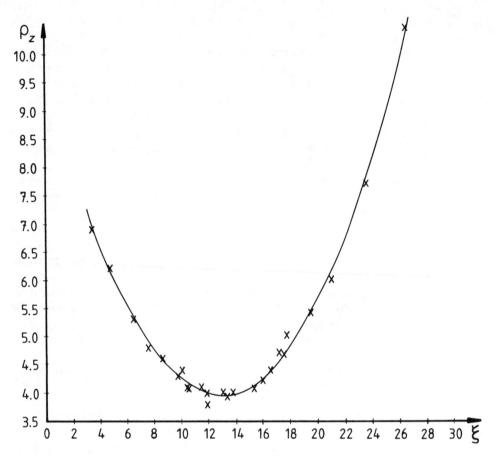

Figure 75 Observed values and calculated transformation function for the preparation time of the formula ρ_z as a function of the absolute atmospheric humidity ξ

the *preparation time*, for which an appropriate cost function still needs to be derived, also depends upon the climatic conditions which characterise the production process. This function can also be interpreted as a transformation function. This is namely a question of the time ρ_z that it takes to prepare the formula for the intermediate product "primed foam-making equipment". The procedure for determining a function

$$\rho_z = f_z(\xi)$$

corresponds to the procedure for determining the other transformation functions that was described above. A plot of the observed values $(\tilde{\xi}_i, \bar{\rho}_{zi})$ for $i = 1, 2, \ldots, 25$ in two-dimensional space (cp. Fig. 75) shows that a non-linear function needs to be assumed in this case too.

The approximately U-shaped disposition of the points, which is characterised by an obvious steep decline to the left of the assumed minimum and a gentle incline to the right suggests a function of the type

$$f_z(\xi) = a_0 - a_1 \cdot \xi + a_2 \cdot (\xi - c)^2 \tag{4.112}$$

as the basis of a regression analysis. Conforming to the observed values, trial-and-error calculations show that it is appropriate to set the minimum of the function at $\xi = 12$. The value of the parameter c is therefore set at $c = 12$. The computation of the further parameters a_0, a_1, a_2 is given in Fig. 76 from which, taking rounded solution values, the function

$$p_z = f_z(\xi) = 4.7 + 0.034 \cdot (\xi - 12)^2 - 0.061 \cdot \xi$$

can be inferred.

Multiplying out and collecting like terms gives:

$$f_Z(\xi) = 0.034 \cdot \xi^2 - 0.877 \cdot \xi + 9.596. \tag{4.113}$$

Substituting this preparation time function into the sum (4.111) and using the cost function (4.107), the resultant overall cost per layer k_A is given by:

$$k_A = h_A(\xi) = 780 + 1.8 \cdot \{0.034\,\xi^2 - 0.877\,\xi + 9.596\}$$
$$\cdot\, [580.2225 - 0.3009\,\xi^{0.81} + 1.9350\,\xi^{1.175}$$
$$- 0.0^5 9763\,\xi^{1.9} + 193.48\,]$$

Multiplying out gives:

$$k_A = h_A(\xi) = 14\,144.0085 - 5.1974\,\xi^{0.81} - 1221.3668\,\xi$$
$$+ 33.4229\,\xi^{1.175} + 0.47500\,\xi^{1.81}$$
$$- 0.0001686\,\xi^{1.9} + 47.3506\,\xi^2 - 3.0546\,\xi^{2.175}$$
$$- 0.01842\,\xi^{2.81} + 0.0^4 1541\,\xi^{2.9}$$
$$+ 0.118422\,\xi^{3.175} - 0.0^6 5975\,\xi^{3.9}.$$

The latter polynomial contains a few terms which contribute only negligible amounts to the total value. In such cases the values are rounded accordingly. For example, the term $0.0^4 1541\,\xi^{2.9}$ can be expressed as $0.0^4 1161\,\xi^{2.81} + 0.0^4 038\,\xi^{3.175}$. After making further similar rounding simplifications the following function for the costs which are fixed with respect to an individual layer is obtained.

$$h_A(\xi) = 14\,144.0085 - 5.1974\,\xi^{0.81} - 1221.3668\,\xi$$
$$+ 33.4229\,\xi^{1.175} + 0.47491\,\xi^{1.81} + 47.3505\,\xi^2 \tag{4.114}$$
$$- 3.0546\,\xi^{2.175} - 0.01841\,\xi^{2.81} + 0.11842\,\xi^{3.175}.$$

(g) Derivation of a Break-even Curve for an Individual Layer

A cost function for PUR-foam material production can be specified, in accordance with the previous analytical results, in which the costs of producing a layer are expressed as a function of productive output x (measured in cubic metres of foam material) and absolute atmospheric humidity ξ (measured in grams of water per cubic metre of air). It is of the general form

(1) Putting $x_1 := -\xi$; $x_2 := (\xi - 12)^2$; $y := \rho_z$, a function of the form:
$y = a_0 + a_1 \cdot x_1 + a_2 \cdot x_2$ is estimated.
There are $n = 25$ observed values $(\tilde{\xi}_i, \tilde{\rho}_z)$, which can be transformed into the values $(\tilde{x}_{1i}, \tilde{x}_{2i}, \tilde{y}_i)$.

(2) Normal equations derived in accordance with the ordinary least squared deviations principle (cp. e.g. Schneeweiss [Ökonometrie] 94 et seq.) are:

(a) $n \cdot a_0 + \left(\sum\limits_{i=1}^{n} \tilde{x}_{1i} \right) a_1 + \left(\sum\limits_{i=1}^{n} \tilde{x}_{2i} \right) a_2 = \left(\sum\limits_{i=1}^{n} \tilde{y}_i \right)$

(b) $\left(\sum\limits_{i=1}^{n} \tilde{x}_{1i} \right) a_0 + \left(\sum\limits_{i=1}^{n} \tilde{x}_{1i}^2 \right) a_1 + \left(\sum\limits_{i=1}^{n} \tilde{x}_{1i}\tilde{x}_{2i} \right) a_2 = \left(\sum\limits_{i=1}^{n} \tilde{x}_{1i}\tilde{y}_i \right)$

(c) $\left(\sum\limits_{i=1}^{n} \tilde{x}_{2i} \right) a_0 + \left(\sum\limits_{i=1}^{n} \tilde{x}_{1i}\tilde{x}_{2i} \right) a_1 + \left(\sum\limits_{i=1}^{n} \tilde{x}_{2i}^2 \right) a_2 = \left(\sum\limits_{i=1}^{n} \tilde{x}_{2i}\tilde{y}_i \right)$

(3) Table of calculated sigma values

i	$\tilde{x}_{1i} = -\xi_i$	$\tilde{x}_{2i} =$ $(\xi - 12)^2$	$\tilde{y}_i =$ $\tilde{\rho}_{zi}$	$\tilde{x}_{1i}^2$	$\tilde{x}_{2i}^2$	$\tilde{x}_{1i} \cdot \tilde{x}_{2i}$	$\tilde{x}_{1i} \cdot \tilde{y}_i$	$\tilde{x}_{2i} \cdot \tilde{y}_i$
1	−3.50	72.25	6.9	12.25	5220.06	−252.88	−24.15	498.53
2	−4.80	51.84	6.2	23.04	2687.39	−248.83	−29.76	321.41
3	−6.50	30.25	5.3	42.25	915.06	−196.63	−34.45	160.33
4	−7.65	18.92	4.8	58.52	357.97	−144.74	−36.72	90.82
5	−8.70	10.89	4.6	75.69	118.59	−94.74	−40.02	50.09
6	−9.71	5.24	4.3	94.28	27.46	−50.88	−41.75	22.53
7	−10.10	3.61	4.4	102.01	13.03	−36.46	−44.44	15.88
8	−10.40	2.56	4.1	108.16	6.55	−26.62	−42.64	10.50
9	−10.50	2.25	4.1	110.25	5.06	−23.63	−43.05	9.23
10	−11.50	0.25	4.1	132.25	0.06	−2.88	−47.15	1.03
11	−11.90	0.01	4.0	141.61	0.00	−0.12	−47.60	0.04
12	−12.00	0.00	3.8	144.00	0.00	0.00	−45.60	0.00
13	−13.15	1.32	4.0	172.92	1.74	−17.36	−52.60	5.28
14	−13.50	2.25	3.9	182.25	5.06	−30.38	−52.65	8.78
15	−13.80	3.24	4.0	190.44	10.50	−44.71	−55.20	12.96
16	−15.30	10.89	4.1	234.09	118.59	−166.62	−62.73	44.65
17	−16.00	16.00	4.2	256.00	256.00	−256.00	−67.20	67.20
18	−16.60	21.16	4.4	275.56	447.75	−351.26	−73.04	93.10
19	−17.30	28.09	4.7	299.29	789.05	−485.96	−81.31	132.02
20	−17.60	31.36	4.7	309.76	983.45	−551.94	−82.72	147.39
21	−17.82	33.87	5.0	317.55	1147.18	−603.56	−89.10	169.35
22	−19.50	56.25	5.4	380.25	3164.06	−1096.88	−105.30	303.75
23	−21.10	82.81	6.0	445.21	6857.50	−1747.29	−126.60	496.86
24	−23.60	134.56	7.7	556.96	18106.39	−3175.62	−181.72	1036.11
25	−26.60	213.16	10.4	707.56	45437.19	−5670.06	−276.64	2216.86
Σ	−339.13	833.03	125.1	5372.15	86675.69	−15276.05	−1784.14	5914.70

(4) The system of normal equations comprises:

(a) $25\, a_0 - 339.13\, a_1 + 833.03\, a_2 = 125.10$
(b) $-339.13\, a_0 + 5372.15\, a_1 - 15\,276.05\, a_2 = -1784.14$
(c) $833.03\, a_0 - 15\,276.05\, a_1 + 86\,675.69\, a_2 = 5914.70$

(5) The equation system has the solution values (rounded):

$a_0 = 4.7$; $a_1 = 0.061$; $a_2 = 0.034$.

Figure 76 Computation of the regression function for determining set-up time

$$
\begin{aligned}
K \quad &= k_A \qquad\qquad + k^v \cdot x \\
H(\xi, x) &= h_A(\xi) \qquad\quad + h^v(\xi) \cdot x.
\end{aligned}
\tag{4.115}
$$

total costs   fixed costs of   variable costs
per layer   a layer   of output
     (incurred once)

The substitution of the values for $h_A(\xi)$ from (4.114) and those for $h^v(\xi)$ from (4.110), results in a cost function in explicit numerical form. Presented graphically, it represents a surface in three-dimensional space as illustrated by Fig. 77.

In the present case, the sales revenue function which corresponds to the cost function has a simple structure. Sales revenue per cubic metre of raw foam material amounts to DM 250. Represented graphically sales revenue is therefore a plane that is constant with respect to variations in atmospheric humidity ξ and an increasing linear function of output x.

In Fig. 78 the cost and revenue surfaces are juxtaposed in the same system of coordinates. The curve constituting the locus of equal sales revenue and cost points is a section of both surfaces. The break-even points for varying atmospheric humidities are indicated by the projection of this curve on to the (ξ, x) plane. This line is called the *break-even curve* and it is also presented in two dimensions in Fig. 79.

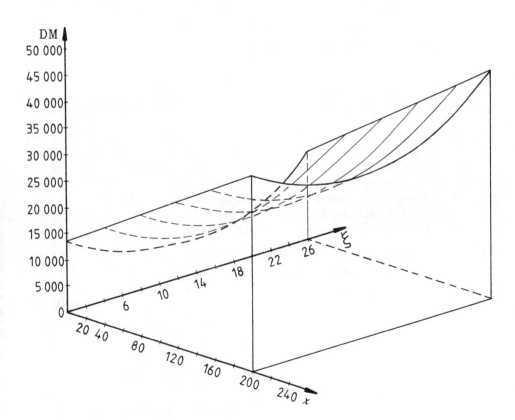

Figure 77 Presentation of the cost function of a layer of foam production as a non-linear cost surface

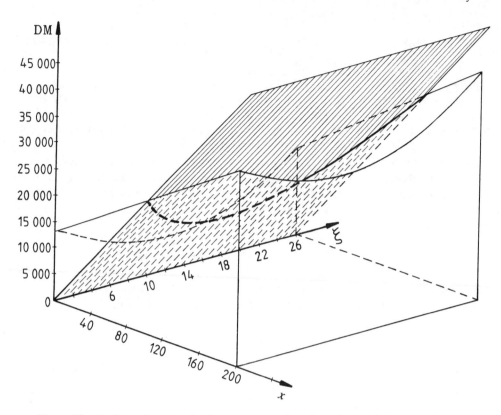

Figure 78 Section of cost and sales revenue surface for a layer of foam products

In conformance with the basic model, the break-even curve is ascertained arithmetically by dividing the layer-related fixed costs by the contribution margin per raw cubic metre of foam material. However, the latter magnitudes are, unlike the fixed costs and contribution margin in the basic model, both functions of absolute atmospheric humidity. Hence, in the present case, the break-even point, as a quotient, is also a function $g(\xi)$. In accordance with the functional equation (4.110) for k^v, the contribution margin per raw cubic metre of foam material is given by the following function:

$$d(\xi) = 134.53333 + 0.05848\ \xi^{0.81} - 0.20461\ \xi - 0.37607\ \xi^{1.175}$$
$$+ 0.0001061\ \xi^{1.81} + 0.0^51897\ \xi^{1.9} - 0.0^36823\ \xi^{2.175}.$$

The expression (4.114) for $k_A = h_A(\xi)$ gives the following functional equation for the break-even curve:

$$g(\xi) = \frac{h_A(\xi)}{d(\xi)} = \frac{\begin{aligned}&14\,144.0085 - 5.1974\ \xi^{0.81} - 1\,221.3668\ \xi \\ &+ 33.4229\ \xi^{1.175} + 0.47491\ \xi^{1.81} \\ &+ 47.3505\ \xi^2 - 3.0546\ \xi^{2.175} - 0.01841\ \xi^{2.81} \\ &+ 0.11842\ \xi^{3.175}\end{aligned}}{\begin{aligned}&134.53333 + 0.05848\ \xi^{0.81} - 0.20461\ \xi \\ &- 0.37607\ \xi^{1.175} + 0.0001061\ \xi^{1.81} \\ &+ 0.0^51897\ \xi^{1.9} - 0.0^36823\ \xi^{2.175}\end{aligned}} \qquad (4.116)$$

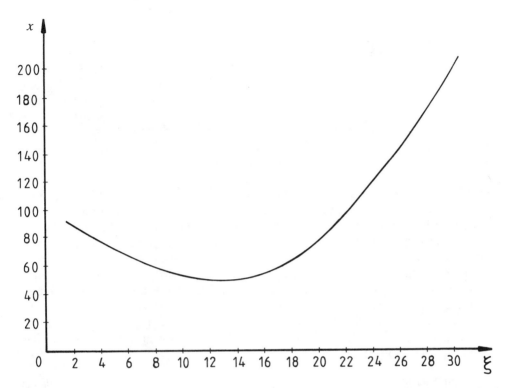

Figure 79 Break-even curve depicting the relationship between the determinant and break-even point

This function for the break-even curve specifies the level of the break-even point for a given atmospheric humidity. It can, therefore, be used to estimate the profitability of production of PUR-foam material on a particular day. It is necessary to check the production conditions, i.e. to ascertain the temperature and relative atmospheric humidity, determine the absolute atmospheric humidity and, using the latter in conjunction with the derived break-even function $g(\xi)$, to deduce the currently valid break-even point. A comparison with the possible or planned production level then indicates whether that production is worthwhile. The function specified by (4.116) can be simplified with the following approximation

$$\hat{g}(\xi) = 47.7109 + 0.4640 \cdot (\xi - 12)^2 + 0.1814\,\xi \qquad (4.117)$$

This approximation formula is of particular importance in the absence of "computational support" which can facilitate a simple evaluation of the function specified by (4.116). Figure 80 shows a comparison of exact and approximated values. An approximation formula of this kind can again be estimated by resorting to regression analysis.

(h) Derivation of a Break-even Surface for an Annual Revenue–cost Relationship

The corresponding magnitudes for a whole year can be analysed in the same way as the costs and sales revenue of an individual layer. Most importantly, annual fixed

Example	Atmospheric humidity ξ	Exact value $g(\xi)$ from (4.116)	Approximate value $\hat{g}(\xi)$ from (4.117)
1	5	71.25	71.35
2	10	54.04	51.38
3	15	55.43	54.61
4	20	78.74	81.03
5	25	128.34	130.66

Figure 80 Comparison of exact and approximated break-even points for different atmospheric humidity levels

costs can also be included in this analysis as can the variable costs (per cubic metre) of foam material. The number of layers in which the total annual productive output is divided is naturally a matter of importance. On the one hand this influences the cumulative sum of the layer-related (i.e. layer number-dependent) fixed costs incurred and, on the other, interest costs together with output-related storage costs (if any).

The costs that are here regarded as *annual fixed costs* are those which, in the forthcoming year, are incurred at a fixed level. They constitute costs the amount of which is uninfluenced by the level of output or by the number of layers into which that output is divided. Furthermore, they are also unaffected by such other significant production influences as the atmospheric humidity which is present in this case. They comprise the following items:

(1) Manufacturing wages   DM   1 053 600
(2) Costs of block foam-making equipment (interest, maintenance,
     insurance, depreciation, other)   DM   180 000
(3) Costs of storage equipment and warehousing equipment
     especially stacking and equipment for accessing
     the finished product, shelves, etc.   DM   127 500
(4) Input equipment costs especially of raw material tanks   DM   34 500
(5) Space costs re tanks, production facilities, post-
     reaction amenities and finished goods storage   DM   1 900 800
(6) Interest and other costs (insurances etc.) of capital
     deployed in inventories (it is assumed here that changes
     in output result in alterations in the storage
     throughput so that average inventories therefore
     remain constant)
     —for tank depots   DM   252 956
     —for finished goods warehousing   DM   224 032
(7) Costs of finished goods loading and transportation facilities   DM   1 452 867
(8) General (non-manufacturing) fixed costs of the firm   DM   6 430 872

Total annual fixed costs   DM 11 657 127

$$(4.118)$$

The *layer-related fixed costs (and the costs that are a function of the number of layers)* are also relevant components of the total annual cost computation. They are incurred once per layer. In the analysis of annual total costs the number of layers is therefore represented by the variable y. The layer-related fixed costs k_A can, in accordance with (4.114), only be specified as a function of atmospheric humidity. The annual layer-related fixed costs amount in total to

$$k_A \cdot y = h_A(\xi) \cdot y, \qquad (4.119)$$

where $h_A(\xi)$ stands for the polynomial (4.114).

In addition to the layer-related fixed costs, *further cost components* are also a function of the number of layers y. These are principally warehouse interest costs but may also include other, warehouse value-related storage costs. Output-dependent interest and storage costs are already included in the variable costs per cubic metre. They were computed (cp. (4.109)) on the assumption of daily production (and daily sales) and, consequently, only the minimum storage time that is necessary in each case for the maturing of the foam material was taken into account. This assessment of variable costs is pertinent to the previously-discussed category of questions relating to the break-even analysis of an individual order. In that this was a question of the output above which the acceptance of a given order is worthwhile, considerations of an alternative division into different lot sizes were not relevant. The situation is different in the case of a total analysis of a year's production. The division of the total level of production into lot sizes, i.e. the number of layers y per annum, must be added to the level of production and atmospheric humidity as a further cost determinant. Applying the concept described, the variable costs per raw cubic metre are aligned with working days. This implies 250 layers per annum (one year is fixed at approximately 250 working days). In the present application, the block foam-making equipment is actually run no more than once a day. On any one day, the pure productive time amounts, as a rule, to no more than 2–3 hours. The maximum number of layers can, in the present situation, thus be set at 250. However, a smaller number of layers can also be chosen. Assuming at least one series per working week, the minimum number of layers is 50.

In the simplest case of the analysis, the sales volume corresponding to a given annual output x is assumed to be equally distributed over the 250 working days. Any other distribution of sales volume would need to be explicitly allowed for by including at least one further determinant in the break-even analysis. Indeed, a sales volume that is subject to serial fluctuations can only be precisely analysed in a dynamic framework (cp. Section V).

In the case of an equal distribution, the accumulation of *interest costs* (and of *variable storage costs* (if any)) is easy to compute. If, for example, the number of layers is $y = 50 = 250/5$ then, for the 5 days over which the production is spread, the following further storage and interest costs are incurred in addition to those already taken into account:

> 1st day: additional storage of 4 days' production
> 2nd day: additional storage of 3 days' production
> 3rd day: additional storage of 2 days' production
> 4th day: additional storage of 1 day's production
> 5th day: no additional storage.

Thus, on average, inventories are always supplemented by $10/5 = 2$ days' production.

More generally, the additionally-stored daily production volume amounts to:

$$\left(\frac{250}{y} - 1\right) \cdot \frac{1}{2} \qquad (50 \leqslant y \leqslant 250),$$

where y denotes the number of layers produced.

In the case of a total annual production volume x, the average daily production volume is $x/250$. If, as above, interest costs (and storage costs (if any)) are assessed at 15% p.a., the following additional costs are incurred if the number of layers is less than 250:

$$\left(\frac{250}{y} - 1\right) \cdot \frac{1}{2} \cdot \frac{x}{250} \cdot 0.15 \cdot \hat{k}^{\text{v}}. \qquad (4.120)$$

The (provisionally-)derived variable costs $\hat{k}^{\text{v}}$ (before interest) from (4.108) which are a function of atmospheric humidity, should be taken as the basis of the interest computation. The *total costs of the foam material production* comprise the individually-derived components:

Annual fixed costs in accordance with (4.118)	DM 11 657 127.00
Layer-related fixed costs in accordance with (4.119)	$k_{\text{A}} \cdot y$
Storage interest costs in accordance with (4.120) which depend upon the number of layers	$\left(\dfrac{250}{y} - 1\right) \cdot \dfrac{1}{2} \cdot \dfrac{x}{250} \cdot 0.15 \, \hat{k}^{\text{v}}$
Annual variable costs of output in accordance with (4.110)	$k^{\text{v}} \cdot x = 1.0018 \cdot \hat{k}^{\text{v}} \cdot x$

Substituting the polynomials $h_{\text{A}}(\xi)$ from (4.114), $\hat{h}^{\text{v}}(\xi)$ from (4.108) and $h^{\text{v}}(\xi)$ from (4.110) for k_{A}, $\hat{k}^{\text{v}}$ and k^{v} respectively, and adding, the following total cost function $\tilde{H}(x, y, \xi)$ for K is obtained:

$$\tilde{K} = \tilde{H}(x, y, \xi) = 11\,657\,127 + \underbrace{[14\,144.0085 - 5.1974\,\xi^{0.81} - 1\,221.3668\,\xi}_{}$$
$$\underbrace{+ 33.4229\,\xi^{1.175} + 0.47491\,\xi^{1.81} + 47.3505\,\xi^2 - 3.054\,6\,\xi^{2.175}}_{}$$
$$\underbrace{- 0.018\,41\,\xi^{2.81} + 0.118\,42\,\xi^{3.175}] \cdot y}_{\text{fixed costs independent of the level of output}}$$

$$(4.121)$$

$$+ \underbrace{\left(\frac{3}{40y} + 1.0015\right) \cdot [115.2592 - 0.058\,37\,\xi^{0.81} + 0.204\,24\,\xi}_{}$$
$$\underbrace{+ 0.375\,39\,\xi^{1.175} - 0.000\,105\,9\,\xi^{1.81} - 0.0^518\,94\,\xi^{1.9}}_{}$$
$$\underbrace{+ 0.0^368\,11\,\xi^{2.175}] \cdot x.}_{\text{variable costs of output}}$$

For the *derivation of the break-even surface*, the previously assumed sales revenue function

$$E = 250 \cdot x$$

is used. A graphical representation of the sales revenue-cost situation as a function of the relevant production volume x, number of layers y and atmospheric humidity ξ is not possible because four dimensions would be necessary therefor. Nevertheless, in order to gain an impression of the cost behaviour, the partial behaviour of costs can be presented. In so doing, each of the determinants is held constant in turn. Figures 81(a) and 81(b) show the behaviour of costs when atmospheric humidity and number of layers respectively are held constant.

The break-even points are ascertained by equating sales revenue and costs as now illustrated arithmetically. The cost function (4.121) can be stated formally as:

$$\tilde{K} = \tilde{H}(x, y, \xi) = \tilde{a}(\xi, y) + \tilde{b}(\xi, y) \cdot x.$$

The sales revenue function is of the form:

$$E(x) = q \cdot x.$$

The break-even surface is therefore given by the values of x which satisfy the equation:

$$\tilde{a}(\xi, y) + \tilde{b}(\xi, y) \cdot x = q \cdot x,$$

whence,

$$x = \frac{\tilde{a}(\xi, y)}{q - \tilde{b}(\xi, y)}. \tag{4.122}$$

The numerator of (4.122) contains the costs which are fixed with respect to the level of output whereas its denominator can be interpreted as a modified unit contribution. The actual formula for the break-even surface in the present example is:

$$x = \frac{\begin{aligned}&11\,657\,127 + [\,14\,144.0085 - 5.1974\,\xi^{0.81} - 1221.3668\,\xi + 33.4229\,\xi^{1.175}\\&+ 0.474\,91\,\xi^{1.81} + 47.3505\,\xi^2 - 3.0546\,\xi^{2.175} - 0.018\,41\,\xi^{2.81}\\&+ 0.118\,42\,\xi^{3.175}\,]\cdot y\end{aligned}}{\begin{aligned}&250 - \left(\frac{3}{40y} + 1.001\,5\right)\cdot[\,115.259\,2 - 0.058\,37\,\xi^{0.81} + 0.204\,24\,\xi\\&+ 0.375\,39\,\xi^{1.175} - 0.000\,105\,9\,\xi^{1.81} - 0.0^518\,94\,\xi^{1.9} + 0.0^3681\,1\,\xi^{2.175}\,]\end{aligned}}. \tag{4.123}$$

In general, the break-even point is therefore a function of atmospheric humidity ξ and the number of layers y. That is to say, $x = \tilde{x}(\xi, y)$. The shape of the break-even surface as a function of these two determinants is sketched out in Fig. 82.

Apropos of *interpretation*, the leading question concerns the predictions that can be based upon the latter break-even computation—given its conceptual foundation and mode of derivation. The break-even surface described relates to a total analysis of an individual year and not to an analysis of the consequences for a year of measures taken in individual sub-periods within that year. This means that the implications of break-even relationships subsisting at particular points in time in the course of the year cannot be inferred from the present analysis; and, that interpretations must be restricted to

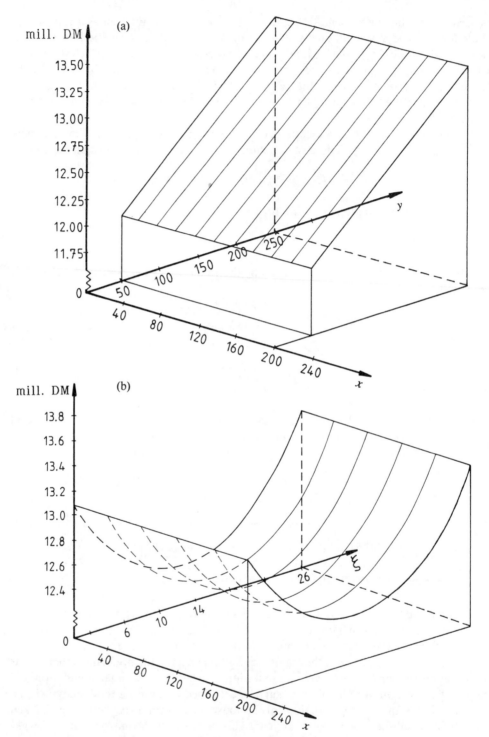

Figure 81 Illustration of an annual total cost function (a) when atmospheric humidity is constant, (b) when the number of layers is constant

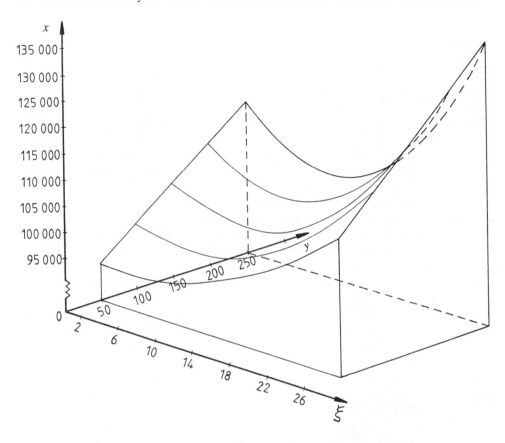

Figure 82 Development of the break-even surface for a year's foam production

annual total values. Thus, it may be inferred from Fig. 82, that, in the most propitious circumstances, i.e. low atmospheric humidity and a division of total production into cost-reducing layer sizes, the break-even point is still an output volume of at least $x_0^{min} \cong 92\,000\,\mathrm{m}^3$. On the other hand, in the most unpropitious circumstances the resultant break-even point is very high, namely, $x_0^{max} = 140\,000\,\mathrm{m}^3$ (cp. Fig. 82). It can thus be concluded that there are no circumstances in which a break-even point can be attained in the forthcoming year for any planned production volume which is less than x_0^{min}. Conversely, for any planned output exceeding x_0^{max}, costs are covered in all cases. This analysis is of paramount importance if the planned level of output lies somewhere between these two extremes. In that event, the attainment of a break-even output depends upon the values of the two determinants ξ and y. The number of layers y in the admissible interval $50 \leqslant y \leqslant 250$ is largely within the decision-maker's control, whereas atmospheric humidity ξ cannot be influenced at all. A cost surface of the kind shown in Fig. 82 therefore elucidates the extent to which break-even points are subject to such influences.

If it is intended to forecast the cost–sales revenue situation for a planning year using the break-even analysis presented above, a forecast of expected atmospheric humidity levels is first required. In that such a forecast can, from a firm's viewpoint, be regarded as a random variable, it is advisable to base such a forecast on a stochastic model.

The cost surface derived from (4.123) also provides in this case the basic information on the positions of the break-even values which, in turn, can be compared with the forecast values.

(i) Evaluation of the Production-theoretic Break-even Analysis in the Case Discussed

The two versions of the break-even analysis, which were presented for the case of PUR-foam material, show that the increased expense of deriving the components of the analysis culminates in detailed results. The approach is especially useful in the break-even analysis of an individual layer for actual analytical, planning and control purposes.

This type of break-even analysis is constructed in two stages: in the first stage by formulating transformation functions to capture the detailed physical characteristics of production, and, in the second stage, by converting the latter functions via a valuation process into cost relationships. In the present case it would also have been possible to analyse the cost dependences collectively, and directly, without explicitly referring back to the physical relationships. In that event, the expense of the analysis would have been somewhat lower. However, there are several reasons in favour of the procedure chosen here.

The derived transformation functions can be used pre-eminently for *cost analysis* purposes, but no less importantly, can also serve as a basis for the precise planning of *raw material quantities and mixture formulae*. Thus, in contrast to the trial-and-error procedure which is required for formula preparation in the absence of exact transformation functions, an approximately suitable (input) starting mixture can be suggested by reference to the interrelationships that have been found—provided that, at the time of the production, the prevailing absolute atmospheric humidity is known. This is a very important analytical result for the purposes of production planning.

A second advantage of a detailed analysis of individual constituent functions lies in the fact that it facilitates a simpler consideration of *changes* in the data, or changes in partial relationships, without necessitating a repetition of the entire analysis. Thus, in the case described, a new break-even point can readily be computed to allow for price changes as these do not affect the physical transformation functions; and, the latter need only be multiplied with new prices. Price change comparisons are also facilitated by a detailed analysis, as is an examination of the effects of price changes on break-even points.

However, changes are also conceivable within the individual transformation functions. Adopting the method outlined above, such changes can be substituted with newly-analysed functions without affecting the validity of the remaining (unchanged) transformation functions. In the present case it can, for example, be presumed that, after a while, the application of the transformation functions that have been deduced for the components of the basic mixture will lead to a reduction in preparation time, especially that for the setting of the formula. This particular function must then be re-analysed under the new conditions which obtain.

A break-even analysis based on a production-theoretic foundation can significantly increase the accuracy of the predictions derived from such analysis. In such cases, the additional effort necessarily incurred in recording and structuring the observations, in investigating possible functional relationships and in carrying out the requisite regression and interpretational computations, is defensible. The principal justification is the argument that, in addition to the level of output, other influences have such a considerable effect on the consumption of inputs, or generally on the level of costs, that to ignore these magnitudes would introduce significant inaccuracies into the cost computation.

V. MULTIPERIOD AND DYNAMIC BREAK-EVEN ANALYSIS

1. Multiperiod Break-even Analysis

(a) Multiyear Trend Computation as Multiperiod Break-even Analysis

By including the time dimension in break-even computations a switch is made from a single-period to a multiperiod approach. The simplest form of a time-related break-even analysis is one in which, instead of the level of output x, the time-parameter t is taken as the main determinant of costs and sales revenue. A simple, time-related break-even analysis of this kind has already been presented in Chapter 3, Section II.4—in a short-term framework.

Since 1952 (cp. Dean, 1952 [Break-Even-Analysis] p. 253), an approach has been suggested in the English-language literature whereby, as a basic form of longer-term analysis covering a number of years, a break-even analysis is based on a juxtaposition of costs and sales revenue for a succession of years. The results can be plotted in a *multiyear-cost–sales revenue diagram* ("P/V trend chart" cp. Wright, 1962 [Costs] p. 29). This is a simple extension of the single-period cost-sales revenue diagram presented in Section 4.II in which turnover is used as an index for measuring the (combined) output of two or more different product types. For each year there is an individual cost line which intersects the sales revenue diagonal thereby indicating that year's break-even level of turnover (cp. Fig. 83).

Trends of the relationship between costs and sales revenue, as well as for the break-even turnover, can be discerned from the comparative graphical analysis. A multiperiod cost-turnover function can be determined by subjecting the cost-turnover values to regression analysis, or to some other analytical procedure for ascertaining a two-dimensional relationship (cp. Chapter 2, Section I.4). It specifies how much (multiperiod average) profit can be expected at each level of turnover. Naturally such information, and any other which can be inferred from diagrams like Fig. 83 has little predictive power. Whilst it is possible to recognise a rough trend running through magnitudes that are depicted in such diagrams, concrete forecasts of the break-even point of the forthcoming year cannot be inferred from a break-even analysis that is conceived in this way. The necessary relationship with a time parameter, or other known magnitude, is absent. Hence, this version of a multiyear break-even analysis is predominantly backward-looking and therefore of little use for decision-making purposes.

A break-even model that is suitable for generating forecasts of relevant future periodic data must use known magnitudes as independent variables. In the simplest case this is the time parameter itself.

Figure 84 illustrates the principle underlying the procedure. Here the realised annual turnovers, and the respective break-even turnovers that were computed for those (past) years, are treated as being *time-dependent*. Functions are ascertained both for actual and break-even turnovers. A simple extrapolation of these functions provides a rough forecast of the development of these magnitudes in future years. Such a forecast is based

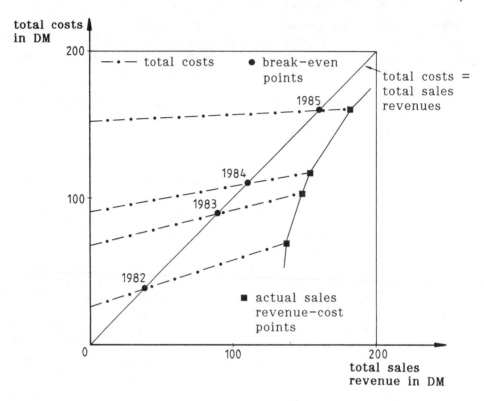

Figure 83 Sales revenue-related multiyear diagram of break-even points and actual values

on the hypothesis that the previous determinants of actual and break-even turnover remain fundamentally unchanged. In the situation illustrated by Fig. 84, computing the trend of previously-achieved turnovers and of the related break-even turnovers, could result in the prompt recognition of the danger of unfavourable developments in the years 1986 and 1987.

(b) Multiperiod Break-even Analysis in the Case of a Short Production Time and Long-term Capital Deployment

The simple multiyear break-even analysis just outlined gives a rough overall insight into a product's current and future break-even situations; or, into those of the complete product line of a business or business segment. It is necessary to resort to more precise computational approaches to obtain a more accurate multiperiod analysis of individual products. A multiperiod analysis is especially necessary in the case of *long-term processes* which also necessitate a recognition of the cost of capital. An especially common occurrence is a *short production time* combined with a *long period of capital deployment* in productive assets, start-up costs etc. The overall process can be regarded as an investment. Its duration is determined either by the useful service life of the productive assets involved, or by the period of time over which the product can be produced and sold. In analysing such a process on a break-even basis, the cost of capital must be

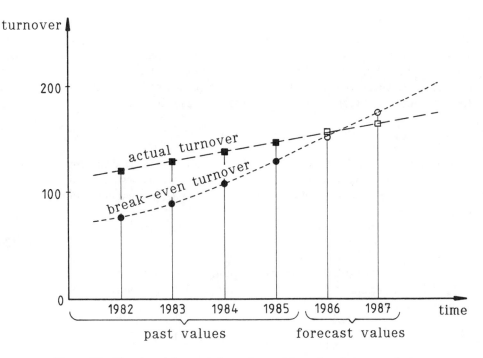

Figure 84   Trend and forecast data of a multiyear break-even analysis

allowed for up to the point in time at which the initial outlays necessitated by that process are recovered from its net cash flows.

   In undertaking a multiperiod analysis of this kind it is usually not appropriate to work with costs and contribution margins. In that the individual periods constituting the duration of the capital deployed are analysed explicitly, a periodic (accruals) basis of accounting can be dispensed with. In the case of the application described, a comparison of *initial outlays* with the stream of *net cash flows* expected therefrom is particularly appropriate; and the break-even question can be presented in two versions.

(1) What is the (annual) *sales volume* above which the project's initial outlays are recovered from its expected stream of net cash flows?
(2) How *long* does it take to recover the project's initial outlays from its expected stream of net cash flows?

The *second question* is concerned with the project's *pay-back period*. If the cash flow streams per unit of time are known, a *dynamic* time-related (point-in-time) *pay-back period* can be computed (cp. Lex, 1970 [Investitionsrechnung] p. 104 et seq., 144 et seq.). The first question is concerned with an output-related break-even point. Given the relationship between output and time, the two questions collapse into one. This is the case, for example, if the average daily, weekly, monthly or annual sales volume is known. This is assumed in what follows.

   To answer the *first question*, the following approach can be adopted (cp. Manes, 1966 [Dimension] p. 91 et seq.; Kaplan, 1982 [Management Accounting] p. 152 et seq.).

Let q denote sales receipts, $k^{v,a}$ the variable payments per unit of output, $K^{f,a}$ the additional annual fixed payments attributable to the production from the project (possibly salaries, rent, insurance, payments in respect of maintenance etc.) and $K_0^{f,a}$ the initial project outlays. For clarity of exposition q, $k^{v,a}$ and $K^{f,a}$ are assumed to be constant over time. However, the following analysis can readily accommodate different values for each individual year's data. The annual net cash flow amounts to:

$$(q - k^{v,a}) \cdot x - K^{f,a}.$$

The intra-period timing of cash flows is ignored and the multiperiod cost of capital is computed on an end-year basis. Assuming the investment in question has a useful service life of T years, the terminal value S_T of the compounded annual net cash flows at end-year T is given by:

$$S_T = [(q - k^{v,a})x - K^{f,a}] \cdot [z^{T-1} + z^{T-2} + z^{T-3} + \cdots + z + 1] - K_0^{f,a} \cdot z^T \qquad (4.124)$$

where $z = (1 + p/100)$ stands for a compounding factor at a cost of capital at $p\%$ p.a.

Applying the standard formula for summing a finite geometric progression (4.124) reduces to

$$S_T = [(q - k^{v,a}) \cdot x - K^{f,a}] \cdot \frac{z^T - 1}{z - 1} - K_0^{f,a} \cdot z^T. \qquad (4.125)$$

At the break-even sales volume x_0, the terminal value S_T takes on a value of zero. As can be deduced from (4.125), x_0 is given by:

$$x_0 = \frac{K^{f,a}}{(q - k^{v,a})} + \frac{K_0^{f,a} \cdot \dfrac{z^T \cdot (z - 1)}{z^T - 1}}{q - k^{v,a}} \qquad (4.126)$$

This break-even point thus indicates the minimum sales volume that must be achieved in each of the T years of the project's useful service life in order to recover all outlays resulting therefrom and making due allowance for the cost of capital. This result is therefore particularly suitable for an ex ante evaluation of an alternative method of production and the related investment project. The break-even analysis reduces the question of profitability measured on a compounded cash flow basis to the somewhat simpler question of whether, over the complete life of the project, a particular minimum annual level of sales volume can be attained or not. If an ongoing project is to be evaluated in such a break-even analytical framework, it is first necessary to ascertain how much capital is still deployed in that project, i.e. how much capital could be disinvested from the project were it to be terminated. This is measured by the project's salvage or disposal value, i.e. its market value, which then constitutes the basis of the break-even analysis.

A comparison of the formula, (4.126), for the multiperiod break-even point with that for the single-period version (cp. (2.14), p. 20), indicates that the latter corresponds formally to the first term in (4.126). There is of course a difference in content. The numerator $K^{f,a}$ in (4.126) captures the annual recurrent fixed *payments* only whilst, in the single-period version, fixed costs K^f also contain depreciation and notional interest charges in respect of initially-invested capital. Compared with (2.14), the single-period formula, the multiperiod version also contains an additional summation term in the form of a further quotient. Its denominator is the same as that of the first term and represents the unit contribution. In the numerator, the initial outlays are multiplied by the recovery factor which corresponds to a compounding factor z for a period of T years. This means that the numerator contains the initial outlays expressed as an *annuity* (re annuity cp. Blohm and Lüder, 1983 [Investition] p. 73 et seq.). *Kaplan* interprets these relationships as follows: the first term in (4.126) specifies the single-period break-even point whilst the second term represents the additional annual volume that is necessary to finance the initial investment outlays (cp. Kaplan, 1982 [Management Accounting] p. 154).

The single-period and multiperiod break-even computations can be compared and contrasted as in the following example:

Initial investment outlays:	$K_0^{f,a} = $ DM 100 000
Annual recurrent fixed payments:	$K^{f,a} = $ DM 12 000
Variable payments per unit:	$k^{v,a} = $ DM 8
Unit sales receipts:	$q = $ DM 18
Cost of capital (%):	$p = $ 10
Project life:	$T = $ 5 years
Realisable residual value of productive assets after five years:	$ = $ DM 5000

The unit cash flow contribution amounts to $q - k^{v,a} = $ DM 10. A five-year recovery factor calculated at 10% p.a. is

$$\frac{z^T(z-1)}{z^T-1} = \frac{1.1^5 \cdot (1.1-1)}{1.1^5-1} = 0.263\,797\,5.$$

The realisable residual value of DM 5000 arising at end-year 5 has a present value of

$$\text{DM } \frac{5000}{1.1^5} = \text{DM } 5000 \cdot 0.620\,92 = \text{DM } 3104.61.$$

The latter present value effectively reduces the initial capital outlay and the resultant annuity for the capital deployed is thus:

$$\text{DM } 96\,895.39 \cdot 0.263\,797\,5 = \text{DM } 25\,560.76.$$

The (4.126) break-even computation is therefore formulated as follows:

$$x_0^{mp} = \frac{\text{DM } 12\,000.00}{\text{DM } 10.00/\text{unit}} + \frac{\text{DM } 25\,560.76}{\text{DM } 10.00/\text{unit}}$$

$$= 1200 \text{ units} + 2556 \text{ units} = 3756 \text{ units}.$$

The multiperiod break-even point is 3756 units. The recurrent and initial outlays will be recovered if at least 3756 units of product are sold in each of the five years of the project's life.

By way of comparison, the single-period break-even computation for the same data is set out below. In order appropriately to allow for the high initial outlays in the single-period calculation, it is necessary to compute costs instead of payments. The fixed costs comprise (the basis of the calculation is discussed in Chapter 3, Section IV):

	DM
Annual recurrent fixed costs	12 000
Depreciation: DM $(100\,000 - 5000) \div 5 =$	19 000
Imputed cost of capital DM $(100\,000 + 5000) \cdot \frac{1}{2} \cdot 10\% =$	5 250
Total fixed costs	36 250

Assuming that the variable costs and variable operating payments coincide, the unit contribution is DM 10 in which case the single break-even point is:

$$x_0^{\text{stat}} = \text{DM } 36\,250/(\text{DM } 10/\text{unit}) = 3625 \text{ units}$$

which thus lies 131 units below the multiperiod break-even point.

This difference is entirely attributable to the simplified depreciation method used in the single-period break-even calculation. If, in the present case, the depreciation charge for the single-period break-even analysis is computed on an annuity basis, the single-period and multiperiod break-even points coincide.

The computation presented above provides an answer to the output-related multiperiod break-even question. To deal with the time-related question (point 2 on p. 199), it is necessary to have additional information about the development of turnover in the individual years. In some cases it is enough, for break-even purposes, to have information about expected sales volumes in the initial years of a project's life because, making due allowance for the cost of capital, the essential question is the point in time at which its cumulative cash inflows reach, and exceed its cumulative cash outflows. The following sales volume forecasts are assumed in the present example:

> 1st year: 5000 units
> 2nd year: 6000 units
> 3rd year: 7500 units.

Forecasts of sales volume are not available for the 4th and 5th years. All receipts and payments are discounted back to the beginning of the 1st year, i.e. end-year 0, to facilitate a comparison of the two streams. The different intra-period timing of cash flows is again ignored and an end-year discounting convention is adopted. The cash flow streams emerging in the first three years are as shown in Tables 17 and 18.

The stream of sales receipts net of variable operating payments constitutes the contribution stream from which the fixed payments are to be recovered. The annual net present values in Table 19 therefore represent the difference between the present value of the annual cash flow contributions and the present value of the corresponding annual fixed payments.

In these computations the values have been rounded to the nearest whole number after summation. The summary indicates that the cumulative fixed payments are first

Table 17   Cash inflows

		Cash flow contribution		
Year	Sales volume (units)	Actual value (DM)	Present value (DM)	Cumulative present value (DM)
1	5 000	50 000	45 455	45 455
2	6 000	60 000	49 587	95 041
3	7 500	75 000	56 349	151 390

Table 18   Cash outflows

	Fixed payments		
Year	Actual value (DM)	Present value (DM)	Cumulative present value (DM)
0	100 000	100 000	100 000
1	12 000	10 909	110 909
2	12 000	9 917	120 826
3	12 000	9 016	129 842

Table 19

	Net cash flows	
Year	Present value (DM)	Cumulative present value (DM)
0	− 100 000	− 100 000
1	34 545	− 65 455
2	39 669	− 25 785
3	47 333	21 548

recovered at some point during the course of the third year. At the start of that year there is still a cumulative deficit that amounts to a (present) value of DM 25 785 but which, by the end of the year, has been converted into a surplus with a present value of DM 21 548. To determine a somewhat more accurate break-even date, it can be assumed that the present value of the cash flow contributions is equally distributed across the year. Assuming 250 working days, the third year sales volume of 7500 units implies a daily sales volume of 30 units and a daily (cash flow) contribution of DM 300 which has a present value of approximately $300 \div 1.1^3 = DM\ 225.39$. Hence, the break-even point-in-time is reached after approximately

$$\frac{DM\ 25\ 785}{DM\ 225.39/\text{working day}} = 114 \text{ working days}$$

i.e. mid-June, in the third year. Figure 85 shows the course of the cash flow recovery in graphical form.

The break-even point-in-time relates to the recovery of the initial investment outlays. In that periodic fixed payments of DM 12 000 are made in each year, there are isolated break-even points for the subsequent years at which these periodic fixed payments are

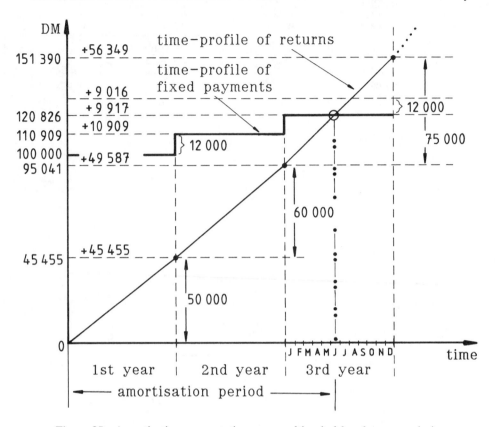

Figure 85 Amortisation computation as a multiperiod break-even analysis

recovered. The sales volume break-even point is always DM 12 000 ÷ DM 10/unit = 1200 units. Given a sales volume forecast for an individual year, a conversion to an isolated break-even point-in-time is possible.

The multiperiod break-even analysis undertaken here, using time as a reference magnitude, can be interpreted as a discounted *pay-back computation* (cp. for example, Blohm and Lüder, 1983 [Investition] p. 75 et seq.; Kruschwitz, 1985 [Investitionsrechnung] p. 40 et seq.) and is described as a *pay-off* or *pay-back calculation*. The pay-back method frequently employed in business practice corresponds to the procedure outlined above—assuming (erroneously) a cost of capital of 0% p.a.

A graphical presentation of the payments and receipts processes, as in Fig. 85, shows that the computation of the break-even point-in-time, and therefore the pay-back period, is related to an analysis of the behaviour of the cash flow generated by a project over time. The shape of this cash flow curve frequently provides additional valuable information for the evaluation of a project. It facilitates a complementary evaluation of different projects having approximately the same pay-back periods but which do not therefore provide a basis for decision-making. Furthermore, the cash flow curve is often judged to be of greater importance in evaluating alternative projects because it does not restrict the comparison to a single point in time but incorporates a project's entire receipts and payments profile into the analysis.

(c) Multiperiod Break-even Analysis when there are Long Production Times

The long-term character of a multiperiod break-even analysis may not only reflect the deployment of capital over a number of years, but may also result from the *duration of production* itself. Multiyear production processes which are a feature of large-scale asset construction, of shipyards, of underground and surface engineering projects, of particular forms of agriculture and forestry and of other processes, require a multiperiod analysis. In particular there are non-trivial simple, and compound, cost of capital effects which significantly affect sales revenue and cost relationships and therefore contribution margin relationships also.

The cultivation of Nordmann fir trees, which are sold as Christmas trees, is taken as an example. The complete plantation covers 40 hectares. It is divided into eight constituent areas, each of which measures 5 hectares. One of these constituent areas is harvested annually and is replanted with four-year-old saplings which are approximately 20–25 centimetres high when planted out. After a further eight years the saplings have grown to a height of between one and three metres at which time they are ready for harvesting. The entire constituent area is then cleared and its cultivation starts afresh. This production process therefore has an eight-year duration. The fixed and variable payments that are made during the production period have to be recovered from revenues earned from the sale of fir trees at the end of the period. Variable payments comprise two items only, namely, the purchase price of the four-year-old saplings costing DM 1.305 each, and, variable payments in respect of cutting and sale (dressing and wrapping) amounting to DM 0.1725 per tree. No other payments can be directly attributed to the individual tree. Non-attributable payments primarily include payments relating to planting, manuring, cultivation, protection from wild animals and parasites and thinning out. The payments can be specified per hectare of cultivated area. The (multiyear) sequence of fixed payments per planted hectare (expressed at end-year 0 prices) is:

Year	0	1	2	3	4	5	6	7	8
Fixed payments (DM)	1000	200	250	150	400	150	150	200	1400

The revenues earned on the sale of the Nordmann fir trees can be computed from the following data: 12 000 saplings are planted on each cultivated hectare and, after eight years, almost the same number of fir trees is cleared. However, the latter include a considerable number of deformed, asymmetrical and stunted trees and many with irregular branches. Such trees cannot be sold as Christmas trees and must be treated as waste. After being chopped up they are used in the subsequent planting as fertiliser. As regards the yield of saleable fir trees, experience suggests that 184 saplings are required in producing 100 marketable Christmas trees. Selling prices depend to a certain extent upon the growth of the firs. On average a unit revenue (expressed at end-year 0 prices) of DM 9.10 to the grower can, however, be assumed.

The production process just outlined can be regarded as a typical example of a multi-year production period. During this period a particular level of payments in respect of production is continuously incurred and is recovered from receipts which first arise when production is terminated. To facilitate a comparison of the individual cash flow items, all are discounted back to end-year 0 at a real cost of capital of 10% p.a. The present value of the cash flow contribution per fir tree is therefore calculated as shown in Table 20.

Table 20

Item	Actual value DM	End-year	Discounting factor	Present value DM	Present value DM
Sales revenue	9.10	8	0.466 507		4.245 21
Payments:					
Price per sapling	1.305	0	1.000 000		
Production coefficient (no. of saplings per saleable fir tree)	1.840				
Sapling payments per fir tree				2.401 20	
Variable payments for dressing and packing on sale	0.1725	8	0.466 507	0.080 47	
Total variable payments per fir tree					2.481 67
Present value of cash flow contribution per fir tree					1.763 54

Year	Actual value of fixed payments	Discount factors (at 10%)	Present value of fixed payments
0	DM 1 000.00	1.000 00	DM 1 000.00
1	DM 200.00	0.909 09	DM 181.82
2	DM 250.00	0.826 45	DM 206.61
3	DM 150.00	0.751 31	DM 112.70
4	DM 400.00	0.683 01	DM 273.21
5	DM 150.00	0.620 92	DM 93.14
6	DM 150.00	0.564 47	DM 84.67
7	DM 200.00	0.513 16	DM 102.63
8	DM 1 400.00	0.466 51	DM 653.11
Present value of all fixed payments			DM 2 707.88

Figure 86 Computation of the present values of fixed payments in the example of Nordmann fir tree cultivation

The present value of the fixed payments made in the individual years amounts to DM 2707.88 as computed in Fig. 86.

The resultant overall break-even point x_0 is given by:

$$x_0 = \frac{\text{DM } 2707.88}{\text{DM } 1.76354/\text{fir tree}} = 1535.48 \text{ fir trees} \simeq 1536 \text{ fir trees.}$$

The latter break-even point specifies the minimum number of fir trees that must be sold, after the eight-year cultivation of a hectare, in order to recover the payments that are incurred per hectare together with the relevant cost of capital. Assuming that the saleable specimens per hectare—the planting of 12 000 saplings results in $12\,000 \div 1.84 = 6522$ fir trees—are actually sold, the 1537th to 6522th fir trees generate a positive net present value (profit).

In order to derive a break-even proposition for the entire 40 hectares of cultivated land, it can be assumed that it is equally divided into sub-areas which correspond to the individual stages of fir tree maturity. There are therefore 5 hectares in each of the eight annual stages of maturity. Consequently, if the cash flow situation is the same for all constituent cultivated areas, at least

$$x_0^{tot.} = 5 \cdot 1535.48 \text{ fir trees} \approx 7678 \text{ fir trees}$$

must be sold annually if annual payments are to be covered.

The procedure outlined in the above fir tree example is generally applicable to multiyear production processes. The break-even point for the recovery of the fixed payments from the cumulative cash flow contribution is derived from the formula:

$$x_0 = \frac{\text{present value of fixed payments incurred in individual constituent periods}}{\substack{\text{present value of unit sales revenue} - \\ \text{present value of unit variable payments in the individual constituent periods}}}$$

$$(4.127)$$

(d) Multiperiod Break-even Analysis and Continuous Discounting

In the multiperiod version of break-even analysis so far considered, the timing differences between receipts and payments have been allowed for by discounting a project's annual cash flows. The cost of capital for *multiyear* processes can normally be adequately allowed for in this way. However, this form of discounting represents a simplification of the actual effect of the cost of capital in that it ignores *intra-year* timing-differences between payments and receipts and therefore compounding differences up to the year-end in question. In the case of processes having a useful service life extending over a number of years, the intra-year cost of capital effects are comparatively insignificant. In particular, the ignoring of these effects does not cause computational error because intra-year cash flows are frequently almost equally distributed, or because their behaviour in the individual years is to a large extent congruous.

In some cases these assumptions do not hold. Thus, the intra-period timing of cash flows may be so significant that the resultant intra-period (interest) costs of capital cannot be omitted from a break-even analysis. It is possible to allow for a more accurate timing of cash flows in the approaches hitherto outlined in a simple manner without changing the computation in principle. All cash flows must then be additionally compounded, from the points in time at which they arise to the following year-end, and enter the further computation compounded accordingly. If the number of annual cash flow items is relatively manageable, this is an appropriate extension of the basic version of multiperiod break-even analysis. However, if there are numerous individual cash flows and if, furthermore, some receipts and payments are characterised by a particular periodic time-profile, it is, in some circumstances, computationally cheaper to adopt a *continuous discounting* approach which captures time as a continuum. No point on this continuum is then of particular significance to the model. This also means that year-ends which are in reality important points in time in relation to the incidence of the cost of capital do not play a conspicuous role in the model. In fact the use of constant (continuous) discounting in the case of complex-structured receipts or payments functions allows the actual cost of capital to be captured in a computationally simple manner though nevertheless with greater precision.

A multiperiod break-even model based on continuous discounting can be clearly formulated. The relevant question is concerned with the minimum sales volume at which the resultant receipts cover the associated payments, taking account of the cost of capital. This general question covers the case of short-term production associated with long-term capital deployment and, in particular, that of long-term production with long-term capital deployment. This approach is especially suitable for depicting receipts and payments streams which flow continuously throughout a project's duration. The necessary prerequisite is information about a sales receipts function $E(x, t)$ and a payments function $A(x, t)$. These functions specify receipts and payments at point in time t, assuming the production of a constant volume x per unit of time. The difference $E(x, t) - A(x, t)$ is the net cash flow at point in time t. In the case of continuous discounting, the present value of this net cash flow at end-year 0 is arrived at by multiplying it by the *discount factor* applicable to point in time t:

$$e^{-\rho t} \tag{4.128}$$

where ρ is given by

$$\rho = \ln\left(1 + \frac{p}{100}\right) \tag{4.129}$$

which is ascertained from the cost of capital p. The cumulative *present value of net cash flows* up to point in time s is specified by the following integral:

$$R(x, s) = \int_0^s [E(x, t) - A(x, t)] \cdot e^{-\rho t} \, dt. \tag{4.130}$$

If the project in question has a complete life of T periods, the present value of the total cash flow contribution amounts to $R(x, T)$.

Break-even points are points (x, s) where the present value $R(x, s)$ takes on a value of zero:

$$R(x_0, s_0) \overset{!}{=} 0. \tag{4.131}$$

The general break-even condition in the case of continuous compounding is thus:

$$\int_0^{s_0} [E(x_0, t) - A(x_0, t)] \cdot e^{-\rho t} \, dt \overset{!}{=} 0. \tag{4.132}$$

The particular solution to this equation that is of interest depends upon the case in which it is to be applied. For example, in the case of a stable, constant level of output $x_0 = \bar{x}$ per unit of time, only the *break-even duration* (pay-back period) s_0, at which the net cash flows $R(x, s)$ are no longer negative but zero, can be ascertained. Multiplying this break-even period by the production rate x converts it into the total output-related break-even point $X = x \cdot s_0$. Conversely, if the production rate x per unit of time is variable, and the project has a fixed life ($s = T$), the lowest *production rate* x_0 which satisfies the equation can be ascertained. The total output at the break-even point is then $T \cdot x_0$. Depending upon the form of the receipts and payments functions, it may not always be possible to derive a solution for either of these two break-even variants.

The break-even analysis procedure which incorporates continuous discounting can be further elucidated with the following empirically-based application. It is concerned with the production of the Lockheed-Airbus "Tri Star L1011". This project caused a public sensation in the USA in the early 1970s when the producer proposed a US Federal guarantee for a $250 million loan to bridge an unforeseen financing shortfall. Reinhardt (cp. 1973 [Break-even Analysis] p. 821 et seq.) shows that, using a multiperiod break-even analysis based on data that were available at the start of the project, this liquidity shortfall could have been more accurately anticipated. He proceeds from the following assumptions: time is measured in months and the beginning of the analysis $t = 0$ is April 1968. The first research and development work in connection with the Tri Star production starts on this date. Having been planned for October 1971, the delivery of the first airbuses only commences in April 1972. In that the analysis must cover the period from the start of the project, a development phase lasting 3½ years, i.e. until $t = 42$ months, is assumed (cp. Reinhardt, 1973 [Break-even Analysis] p. 824). The outlays incurred during the development and production stages can be separately recorded. In the development stage, outlays are incurred in respect of research, on actual development and in respect of testing and checking procedures connected with plant and production installations for eventual mass production. Whilst these outlays are estimated at between $800 million and $1 billion before the start of the project, they are here put at US $900 million. In the absence of more accurate information, Reinhardt (cp. 1973 [Break-even Analysis] p. 823) further assumes that this amount is incurred in equal amounts over the 42-month period. Thus:

$$A(t) = \frac{900 \text{ mill.}}{42} \qquad \text{for } 0 < t \leqslant 42. \tag{4.133}$$

Reinhardt assumes that a *learning effect* (cp. Baur, 1967 [Planung] p. 46 et seq.; Baur, 1979 [Lerngesetz] p. 1115 et seq.; Ihde, 1970 [Lernprozesse] p. 457 et seq.) applies to outlays during the production phase. The variable payments $k^{a, v}$ in respect of a unit of output are a function of the overall volume X that is produced up to the date of that unit. The greater the number of units that has already been produced, the greater is the experience gained in that particular type of production and the lower is the cost rate per unit. In accordance with the general learning curve production principle, it is assumed that with each doubling of the overall volume of output, unit costs reduce at a constant rate. Letting $k^{a, v}(X)$ denote unit variable costs for a total output X, the latter relationship is of the form:

$$k^{a, v}(2 \cdot X) = \gamma \cdot k^{a, v}(X) \qquad \text{with } 0 < \gamma < 1. \tag{4.134}$$

The factor γ is described either as a learning coefficient or as an experience coefficient. Using equation (4.134), which expresses the cost relationship recursively, unit variable payments can be computed for each level of production if, for example, unit costs $k^{a, v}(1)$ for the first item and the *learning coefficient* γ are known. If so, the following relationship obtains (cp. Appendix III (A.9)):

$$k^{a, v}(X) = \frac{k^{a, v}(1)}{X^b} \qquad \text{with } b = -\frac{\ln \gamma}{\ln 2}. \tag{4.135}$$

Drawing on published estimates, *Reinhardt* (1973 [Break-even Analysis] p. 824) is able to assume the following two variable payments data (expressed in real terms)

—the production of the 150th Tri Star airbus will entail variable payments of US $15.5 million
—the production of the 300th Tri Star airbus will entail variable payments of US $12.0 million.

From these data an experience coefficient of $\gamma = 77.42\%$, implying a value for b of 0.3692, can be computed. Furthermore, variable costs for the first Airbus of approximately US $100 million can be reckoned with. If, up to point in time t, aircraft totalling $X(t)$ are produced, the unit variable payments up to this date therefore amount to:

$$k^{a, \, v}(X(t)) = \frac{100}{[X(t)]^{0.3692}} = \text{US } \$100 \text{ mill.} \cdot [X(t)]^{-0.3692}.$$

Multiplying the latter expression by output $X(t)$ gives total variable payments amounting to

$$X(t) \cdot k^{a, \, v}[X(t)] = 100 \cdot [X(t)]^{-0.3692} \cdot X(t)$$
$$= \text{US } \$100 \text{ mill.} \cdot [X(t)]^{(1-0.3692)}.$$

To derive the additional variable payments $A(t)$ incurred per unit of time (i.e. per month), it is necessary to differentiate the total payments function with respect to t. Thus, $A(t)$ is given by

$$A(t) = (1 - 0.3692) \cdot 100 \cdot [X(t)]^{-0.3692} \cdot \frac{dX}{dt}. \qquad (4.136)$$

These payments are made in the production phase, i.e. from the 42nd month. Equation (4.136) is thus valid for $t > 42$. The term dX/dt which appears in (4.136) specifies monthly changes in the total volume of production, i.e. monthly output. If, in the production phase, aircraft are produced at a constant monthly rate x, then

$$X(t) = (t - 42) \cdot x \quad \text{and} \quad (dX/dt) = x.$$

Equation (4.136) can therefore be simplified as follows:

$$A(t) = 63.08 [(t - 42) \cdot x]^{-0.3692} \cdot x$$
$$= \text{US } \$63.08 \text{ mill.} (t - 42)^{-0.3692} \cdot x^{0.6308} \text{ for } t > 42. \qquad (4.137)$$

Taken in conjunction, (4.133) and (4.137) fully specify the payments function.

A constant unit price of $q = \text{US } \$15.5$ million is assumed for the receipts function. In that, from month 42, x Tri Stars are sold each month, the sales receipts function is:

$$E(t) = \begin{cases} 0 & \text{for } t \leqslant 42 \\ \text{US } \$15.5 \text{ mill.} \cdot x & \text{for } t > 42. \end{cases} \qquad (4.138)$$

If the sales receipts and payments components (4.133), (4.137) and (4.138) are combined and substituted into the more general form represented by (4.130), the net present value of the Tri Star (cp. Reinhardt, 1973 [Break-even Analysis] p. 829) expressed in millions of dollars is obtained:

$$R(x, s) = \int_{42}^{s} 15.5 \cdot x \cdot e^{-\rho t} dt - \int_{0}^{42} \frac{900}{42} \cdot e^{-\rho t} dt \qquad (4.139)$$

$$- \int_{42}^{s} 63.08 \cdot (t-42)^{-0.3692} \cdot x^{0.6308} \cdot e^{-\rho t} dt$$

or, after rearranging:

$$R(x, s) = 15.5 x \cdot \int_{42}^{s} e^{-\rho t} dt - \frac{900}{42} \cdot \int_{0}^{42} e^{-\rho t} dt$$

$$- 63.08 x^{0.6308} \cdot \int_{42}^{s} (t-42)^{-0.3692} \cdot e^{-\rho t} dt.$$

Integrating in accordance with the formulae given in Appendix III.2 gives the following result (in US $million):

$$R(x, s) = 15.5 \cdot x \cdot \frac{1}{\rho} [e^{-\rho \cdot 42} - e^{-\rho \cdot s}] - \frac{900}{42} \cdot \frac{1}{\rho} [1 - e^{-\rho \cdot 42}]$$

$$- 63.08 \cdot x^{0.6308} \cdot e^{-\rho \cdot 42} \cdot \rho^{0.3692-1} \qquad (4.140)$$

$$\cdot \sum_{j=0}^{\infty} \frac{(-1)^j [\rho(s-42)]^{j+1-0.3692}}{j! \, (j+1-0.3692)}.$$

For greater realism, *Reinhardt* (1973 [Break-even Analysis] p. 829) also allows for tax effects. In that, in addition to the Tri Star project, the firm in question has numerous other ongoing projects, it can be assumed that loss-making projects lower the effective rate of profits tax. Hence, a proportional tax rate, which reduces losses and surpluses by the same factor can be applied. Here a 50% tax rate is used. The post-tax net present value $\tilde{R}(x, s)$ is therefore given by (in US $million):

$$\tilde{R}(x, s) = 7.75 \cdot \frac{1}{\rho} \cdot [e^{-42\rho} - e^{-\rho s}] \cdot x - 10.714 \cdot \frac{1}{\rho} \cdot [1 - e^{-42\rho}]$$

$$- 31.54 \cdot e^{-42\rho} \cdot \left(\frac{x}{\rho}\right)^{0.6308} \qquad (4.141)$$

$$\cdot \sum_{j=0}^{\infty} \frac{(-1)^j \cdot [(s-42)\rho]^{j+0.6308}}{j! \, (j+0.6308)}.$$

In order to compute a break-even point it is first assumed that the monthly production rate is $x = 3$ aircraft. The cost of capital is taken as 10% p.a., i.e. $\rho = 0.0953$ (cp. (4.129)).

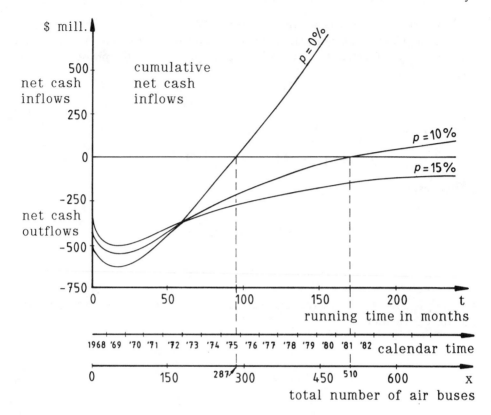

Figure 87 Time-profile of the present value of cash flow recovered from the Lockheed airbus project Tri Star L1011 at different discount rates

In conformity with break-even condition (4.132), the aim is to determine that period of time s for which (4.141) takes on a value of zero: $\bar{R}(3, s) = 0$. In practice a number of calculations would be made in groping towards the parameter values at which the net present value is zero. It turns out that in the production of the Tri Star L1011, the break-even point is at a value of $t = 170$. This means that the break-even point is reached after 170 months i.e. after approximately 14.2 years; by that date 510 airbuses will have been sold.

The behaviour of the net present value for the latter parameter values is plotted in Fig. 87. This presentation is the *continuous time variant* of the net present value graph of the familiar pay-back computation (cp. Fig. 85). The independent variable shown on the abscissa is time t measured in months. Because the monthly production rate $x = 3$ is constant, the cumulative total production at any point in time can be indicated directly. It is measured on the second abscissa in Fig. 87.

In this example of aircraft production the *cost of capital* constitutes a very significant determinant of the level of the break-even point. This is evidenced by the considerably lower (arithmetic) break-even point, namely 287 airbuses, at a zero ($p = 0\%$ p.a.) cost of capital. On the other hand, the break-even point rises above 1000 aircraft at a cost of capital of 15% (cp. Reinhardt, 1973 [Break-Even Analysis] p. 831). The behaviour of the net present value as a function of these two costs of capital is also shown in Fig. 87.

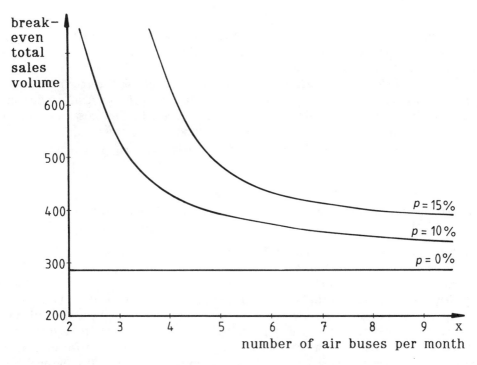

Figure 88   Break-even points representing the total number of Tri Star airbuses to be sold as a function of the monthly production rate at different discount rates

The foregoing analysis is based on the assumption of a constant monthly *production rate* of $x = 3$ aircraft and the results depend on this rate accordingly. The break-even point is reached sooner if the production rate is accelerated. This is not only because any given total volume of production (and therefore also the break-even volume) is attained earlier, but also because further savings in the (interest) cost of capital can be realised. Interpreted as a cumulative total production quantity X_0, and expressed as a function of the production rate x, the break-even point is illustrated graphically in Fig. 88 for $p = 0\%$, $p = 10\%$ and $p = 15\%$ (cp. Reinhardt, 1973 [Break-Even Analysis] p. 832).

It is noteworthy that if the cost of capital is ignored ($p = 0\%$), the monthly production rate is of no consequence. At a zero cost of capital, the break-even point is attained at a total production volume X_0 of 287 units at every monthly production rate. This is because no further savings in the (interest) cost of capital can be achieved by reaching the break-even point in a shorter period of time.

In his analysis of the Tri Star programme, *Reinhardt* demonstrates that, even on highly optimistic assumptions at the start of the project, sales exceeding 270 to 310 airbuses could not have been anticipated (cp. Reinhardt, 1973 [Break-even Analysis] p. 834). In the computations presented by the Lockheed Company, slightly higher sales volumes were actually assumed. But in all cases these were well below the break-even points that are indicated by a multiperiod analysis which allows for the cost of capital. The fact that the Tri Star project was nevertheless started and publicly promoted is, among other things, attributable to the use only of a single-period type of break-even analysis.

In that the undiscounted pay-back period is significantly lower than its discounted counterpart, a neglect of the cost of capital obscures the fact that the projected payments–volume–price relationship is not conducive to a recovery of those payments, or to the attainment of a net cash flow surplus.

The advantage of multiperiod (present value) break-even analysis over the undiscounted pay-back method is not always as obvious as in the above example of aircraft production. Nevertheless, it should generally be assumed that a neglect of the cost of capital in amortising initial expenditures, especially those of production processes with high initial development or investment outlays, is an analytical defect which may be either partially or wholly misleading.

2. Dynamic Break-even Analysis Based on a Dynamic Production Function

(a) Concept of Break-even Analysis in the Case of Dynamic Production Relations

The basic forms of multiperiod break-even analysis so far considered are based upon a simple production structure. However, no difficulties arise in applying the notion of discounting to cases of multistage multiproduct manufacture. Instead of the actual values of receipts and payments, the corresponding present values are used for evaluation purposes. However, no changes are involved in the method of analysis (for the methods, cp. Sections 4.II, 4.III). A different situation naturally arises if dynamic aspects are already to be included in the specification of the production structure. In that event the break-even analysis is based upon a *dynamic production function* which explicitly allows for the durations of the individual transformation processes. In the general case of multistage multiproduct manufacture this results in a different definition of the break-even analysis problem.

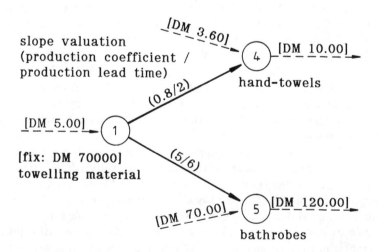

Figure 89 Section of the dynamic production structure of a textile factory

Break-even analysis based on a dynamic production function is described below by reference to a (greatly simplified) example from the textile industry. It involves a dynamic production function which assumes particular lead-times for all input processes that produce intermediate or end-products (cp. Küpper, 1980 [Interdependenzen] p. 83 et seq.; Schweitzer, 1979 [Produktionsfunktionen] col. 1507 et seq.; Trossmann, 1983 [Grundlagen] p. 53 et seq.). The basic features of this particular example are shown in Fig. 89.

Three products (1, 4, 5) appear in the relevant section of the firm's total goods flow system. Product 1 is towelling material. It is rolled in the form of a bale and is supplied as metres of product to other production centres for further processing. Products 4 and 5 are hand-towels and bathrobes respectively which are produced from the (product 1) towelling material. The *physical structure* of production is represented by the following Leontief coefficients: 0.80 metres of towelling material are required for each hand-towel and each bathrobe requires 5 metres of the same material. The *time-structure* is captured by the related *lead-times*. Here the length of a period is assumed to be one week. Thus, if a bathrobe is to be produced in period (week) t, the requisite towelling material needs to be completed 6 weeks earlier, i.e. in period $t-6$ and the lead-time for the towelling material input for bathrobe production is therefore 6 weeks. The corresponding lead-time for the hand-towel production is 2 weeks. In the Fig. 89 representation of the production relations, both the Leontief transformation coefficients and lead-times are indicated on the arrows in the form of a two-component vector. Its first component specifies the quantity coefficient whilst the second indicates the lead-time.

The cost and price structure data on the towelling material production process are as follows: the production of towelling material gives rise to total fixed costs of DM 70 000 in respect of design development, colour adjustment and other preparatory work. Variable costs per running metre of material amount to DM 5. In addition to material costs, unit variable costs of DM 3.60 and DM 70 are incurred in the production of hand-towels and bathrobes respectively. The respective selling prices of hand-towels and bathrobes are DM 10 and DM 120 as indicated in Fig. 89.

The break-even question is: what is the minimum number of hand-towels or bathrobes that needs to be produced in the individual weeks in order to recover the initial fixed costs from the contribution thereby earned? Because it relates to multiproduct manufacture, this question cannot be answered by calculating an unambiguous break-even point. Solely because of the physical structure of production, a set of break-even points emerges instead of a unique break-even point. However, the different transformation times raise a further consideration: some part of the contribution block can be recovered either two weeks later from a specific level of hand-towel production or six weeks later from a requisite number of bathrobes. The differences between the recovery periods can be equalised by allowing for the cost of capital in the respective two and six-week lead-time periods. The precise specification of the time-structure of production thus increases the size of the break-even set and thereby elucidates the production programme alternatives from which the fixed costs can be recovered.

To ensure comparability, all amounts are related to the beginning of the first week, i.e., to the end of period 0. The fixed costs of DM 70 000 are incurred at this point in time. In that hand-towels (product 4) have a towelling material lead-time of two periods, they can first be produced in period 3. Their output volume in week t is denoted with x_{4t} (for $t \geqslant 3$). Due to their 6-week towelling material lead-time, bathrobes (product 5)

Production of product 4 in week	3	4	5	6	7	8	9	10
Selling price (DM)	10.00	10.00	10.00	10.00	10.00	10.00	10.00	10.00
Discounting period in weeks	2	3	4	5	6	7	8	9
Discount rate	0.6%	0.9%	1.2%	1.5%	1.8%	2.1%	2.4%	2.7%
Interest deduction (DM)	0.0600	0.0900	0.1200	0.1500	0.1800	0.2100	0.2400	0.2700
Present value of sales revenue (DM)	9.9400	9.9100	9.8800	9.8500	9.8200	9.7900	9.7600	9.7300
Unit variable costs (DM)	7.6000	7.6000	7.6000	7.6000	7.6000	7.6000	7.6000	7.6000
Discounting period in weeks	0	1	2	3	4	5	6	7
Discount rate	0%	0.3%	0.6%	0.9%	1.2%	1.5%	1.8%	2.1%
Interest deduction (DM)	0.0000	0.0228	0.0456	0.0684	0.0912	0.1140	0.1368	0.1596
Present value of costs (DM)	7.6000	7.5772	7.5544	7.5316	7.5088	7.4860	7.4632	7.4404
Present value of unit contribution (DM)	2.3400	2.3328	2.3256	2.3184	2.3112	2.3040	2.2968	2.2896

Figure 90 Unit contributions of hand-towels for different production weeks in the example of towelling products manufacture

can first be produced in period 7. Their output volume in week t is symbolised with the variable x_{5t} (for $t \geqslant 7$). In order to compute the time-related contributions of the two products, the exact timing of costs and sales revenue must be estimated. Here it is assumed that sales revenue is realised in the week in which the products are manufactured; and that costs in respect of variable costs are made in full when the towelling material is inputted. Alternative timing assumptions merely affect interest charges reflecting the cost of capital and do not cause additional complications.

The unit contributions of products 4 and 5, discounted back to week 0, are computed in Figs 90 and 91 respectively. In both cases the outputs relate to the eight-week period to the end of the tenth week. The cost of capital is assumed to be 15% per annum which, for a 50-week working year, corresponds to 0.3% a week—ignoring the compounding effect because of the relatively short period of time involved.

The results tabulated in Fig. 90 show that the unit contribution from hand-towels falls from DM 2.34 in week 3 by DM 0.0072 a week. This weekly reduction represents the difference between the weekly discount on sales revenue of DM 10 and the weekly discount on variable costs of DM 7.60:

$$0.3\% \cdot DM\ 10.00 - 0.3\% \cdot DM\ 7.60 = DM\ 0.0072.$$

Production of product 5 in week	7		8		9		10	
Selling price (DM)	120.00		120.00		120.00		120.00	
Discounting period in weeks	6		7		8		9	
Discount rate	1.8%		2.1%		2.4%		2.7%	
Interest deduction (DM)		2.1600		2.5200		2.8800		3.2400
Present value of sales revenue (DM)		117.8400		117.4800		117.1200		116.7600
Unit variable costs (DM)		95.00		95.00		95.00		95.00
Discounting period in weeks	0		1		2		3	
Discount rate	0.0%		0.3%		0.6%		0.9%	
Interest deduction (DM)		0.0000		0.2850		0.5700		0.8550
Present value of costs (DM)		95.0000		94.7150		94.4300		94.1450
Present value of unit contribution (DM)		22.8400		22.7650		22.6900		22.6150

Figure 91 Unit contributions of bathrobes for different production weeks in the example of towelling products manufacture

The corresponding difference for bathrobes is:

$$0.3\% \cdot \text{DM } 120.00 - 0.3\% \cdot \text{DM } 95.00 = \text{DM } 0.075.$$

Hence, the unit contribution from hand-towels in week t can be expressed more generally as:

$$\text{DM } [2.34 - 0.0072 \cdot (t - 3)] \qquad \text{for } t \geqslant 3. \tag{4.142}$$

The unit contribution from bathrobes in week t is:

$$\text{DM } [22.84 - 0.075 \cdot (t - 7)] \qquad \text{for } t \geqslant 7. \tag{4.143}$$

For these data the break-even condition is:

$$\sum_{t=3}^{T} [2.34 - 0.0072 \cdot (t - 3)] \cdot x_{4t}$$
$$+ \sum_{t=7}^{T} [22.84 - 0.075 \cdot (t - 7)] \cdot x_{5t} \overset{!}{=} 70\,000. \tag{4.144}$$

Week T in (4.144) represents the latest period in which a contribution to the recovery of fixed costs can be made. For example, for $T = 10$, (4.144) is:

$$2.3400x_{43} + 2.3328x_{44} + 2.3256x_{45} + 2.3184x_{46} + 2.3112x_{47}$$
$$+ 2.3040x_{48} + 2.2968x_{49} + 2.2896x_{4,\,10} + 22.8400x_{57}$$
$$+ 22.7650x_{58} + 22.6900x_{59} + 22.6150x_{5,\,10} \overset{!}{=} 70\,000. \tag{4.145}$$

The remainder of the procedure corresponds to the analogous static approach in which the cost of capital is ignored. The resultant break-even hyperplane can again be specified by its corner points. Each break-even point is a convex linear combination of these corner points. The weighting parameters λ_{it} at the corner points of product i in period t thus specify the proportion contributed, by the output of product i in period t, to the recovery of the fixed cost block. Corner points and break-even points for the textile example are given in Fig. 92.

(b) Simultaneous Dynamic Break-even Analysis in the Case of Capacity Restrictions

The choice between alternative production programmes is generally constrained by existing *capacity*. The specification of capacity restrictions is especially important in the case of dynamic production models because such restrictions capture an additional indirect relationship between the outputs of different periods (cp. Trossmann, 1983 [Grundlagen] pp. 75, 117 et seq.). To facilitate a dynamic break-even analysis subject to capacity constraints, the previous example is extended by the inclusion of two other inputs, i.e., the hourly burdens resulting from cutting and sewing are now included in the analysis. These two inputs are included in the production model as goods 2 and 3. The resultant network representation is shown in Fig. 93 which also indicates the production coefficients and lead-times.

	Corner points		Break-even points
No.	Exclusive production of	With the quantity	set of all production programmes $(x_{43}, x_{44}, x_{45}, x_{46}, x_{47}, x_{48}, x_{49}, x_{4,10}, x_{57}, x_{58}, x_{59}, x_{5,10})$, where:
1	hand-towels in period 3	$\hat{x}_{43} = 29\,915$	$x_{43} = 29\,915 \cdot \lambda_{43}$
2	hand-towels in period 4	$\hat{x}_{44} = 30\,007$	$x_{44} = 30\,007 \cdot \lambda_{44}$
3	hand-towels in period 5	$\hat{x}_{45} = 30\,100$	$x_{45} = 30\,100 \cdot \lambda_{45}$
4	hand-towels in period 6	$\hat{x}_{46} = 30\,193$	$x_{46} = 30\,193 \cdot \lambda_{46}$
5	hand-towels in period 7	$\hat{x}_{47} = 30\,287$	$x_{47} = 30\,287 \cdot \lambda_{47}$
6	hand-towels in period 8	$\hat{x}_{48} = 30\,382$	$x_{48} = 30\,382 \cdot \lambda_{48}$
7	hand-towels in period 9	$\hat{x}_{49} = 30\,477$	$x_{49} = 30\,477 \cdot \lambda_{49}$
8	hand-towels in period 10	$\hat{x}_{4,10} = 30\,573$	$x_{4,10} = 30\,573 \cdot \lambda_{4,\,10}$
9	bathrobes in period 7	$\hat{x}_{57} = 3\,065$	$x_{57} = 3\,065 \cdot \lambda_{57}$
10	bathrobes in period 8	$\hat{x}_{58} = 3\,075$	$x_{58} = 3\,075 \cdot \lambda_{58}$
11	bathrobes in period 9	$\hat{x}_{59} = 3\,085$	$x_{59} = 3\,085 \cdot \lambda_{59}$
12	bathrobes in period 10	$\hat{x}_{5,10} = 3\,095$	$x_{5,10} = 3\,095 \cdot \lambda_{5,10}$

with $\lambda_{ij} \geqslant 0$ and $\Sigma\lambda_{ij} = 1$

Figure 92 Corner points and break-even points ignoring capacity restrictions in the example of towelling products manufacture

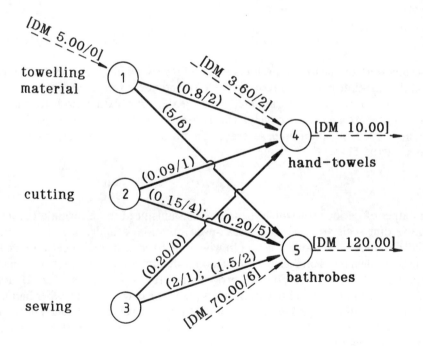

Figure 93 Section from the dynamic production structure of towelling products manufacture including the representation of limited capacities

A feature of the bathrobe production is that this product imposes a two-week burden on both cutting and sewing. The respective lead-times are 4 and 5 for cutting and 1 and 2 for sewing. This feature is indicated in Fig. 93 with the arrows that are inscribed with multiple values. The costs resulting from cutting and sewing are not separately indicated. They are already included in the (previously-used) variable costs of DM 3.60 and DM 70 respectively. The latter costs are incurred in addition to the main material costs and reflect lead-times of two and six periods respectively. The weekly cutting and sewing capacities are 360 and 1620 working-hours respectively.

To construct a break-even analysis, capacity restrictions for each period must first be precisely formulated. Because the lead-times are positive, the capacity of one period is constrained by the output of subsequent periods. Thus, in week t, the cutting department works $0.09x_{4, t+1}$ hours for the hand-towel output $x_{4, t+1}$ in week $t+1$, for $0.15x_{5, t+4}$ hours for the bathrobe production of week $t+4$ and $0.2x_{5, t+5}$ hours for that of week $t+5$. Consequently, the cutting department is subject to a capacity constraint in week t of:

$$0.09 \cdot x_{4, t+1} + 0.15 \cdot x_{5, t+4} + 0.20 \cdot x_{5, t+5} \leqslant 360. \qquad (4.146)$$

The capacity constraint on the sewing department in week t is ascertained in the same manner:

$$0.20 \cdot x_{4, t} + 2 \cdot x_{5, t+1} + 1.5 \cdot x_{5, t+2} \leqslant 1620. \qquad (4.147)$$

The sewing work on the hand-towels takes place in the week in which they are completed. Hence, the lead-time in the first term on the left-hand side is zero. The constraints (4.146) and (4.147) are first valid as formulated from the third and sixth periods for the cutting and sewing departments respectively. This is because in the earlier periods, for reasons concerned with production time, several of the production time variables must take on values of zero. Thus,

$$x_{41}, \; x_{42}, \; x_{51}, \; x_{52}, \; x_{53}, \; x_{54}, \; x_{55}, \; x_{56} = 0.$$

The number of periods for which the two constraints need to be formulated, depends upon the time-scale to which the break-even question is addressed. In general the stipulated number of periods T is that in which the fixed costs are to be recovered. The next question then turns on feasible production programmes which satisfy this condition. It is possible that there are no such programmes for small values of T. If not, the maximum attainable total contribution is less than DM 70 000. On the other hand, there may be many realisable break-even programmes for large values of T. Such programmes may differ not only with respect to the requisite outputs of the two products but principally in relation to their *time-profiles*.

As a practical method of ascertaining break-even points, it is advisable, for successive values of T, to solve the resultant linear programming model adopting the maximisation of the contribution as a formal objective function. So long as the maximum contribution amounts to less than DM 70 000, there are no break-even points within the first T periods. If the computed maximum is equal to, or greater than, the contribution block of DM 70 000, the calculation can be repeated with the break-even equation as an additional

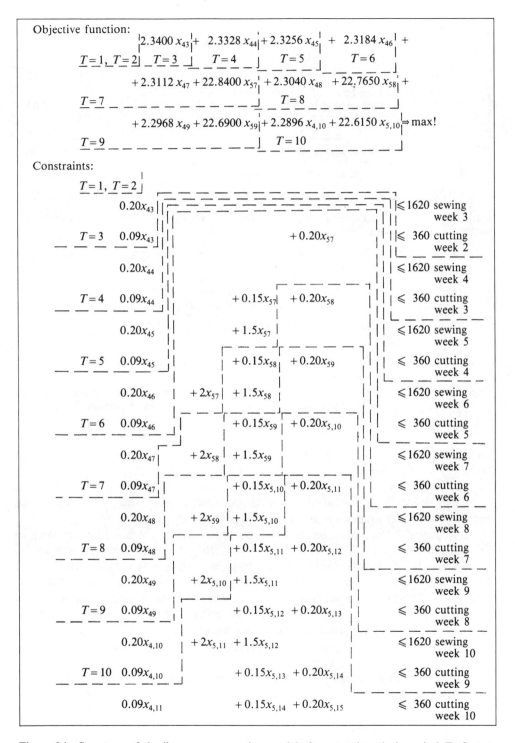

Figure 94 Structure of the linear programming models for a total analysis period T of up to 10 weeks in the example of towelling products manufacture

Planning period T in weeks	Contribution-maximising production programme subject to capacity restrictions	Total contribution (DM)
$T=1$	Prior to the 3rd week no products can be manufactured: even the faster of the two processes has a two-week production lead time	0.00
$T=2$		0.00
$T=3$	$x_{43}=4000$	9 360.00
$T=4$	$x_{43}=4000;\ x_{44}=4000$	18 691.20
$T=5$	$x_{43}=4000;\ x_{44}=4000;\ x_{45}=4000$	27 993.60
$T=6$	$x_{43}=4000;\ x_{44}=4000;\ x_{45}=4000;\ x_{46}=4000$	37 267.20
$T=7$	$x_{43}=4000;\ x_{44}=4000;\ x_{45}=4000;\ x_{46}=4000;\ x_{47}=4000;$ $x_{57}=0$	46 512.00
$T=8$	$x_{43}=4000;\ x_{44}=4000;\ x_{45}=4000;\ x_{46}=4000;\ x_{47}=4000;$ $x_{48}=4000;\ x_{57}=0;\ x_{58}=0$	55 728.00
$T=9$	$x_{43}=2200;\ x_{44}=2650;\ x_{45}=2025;\ x_{46}=0;\ x_{47}=2025;$ $x_{48}=0;\ x_{49}=4000;\ x_{57}=810;\ x_{58}=0\ x_{59}=810$	66 785.94
$T=10$	$x_{43}=2200;\ x_{44}=2650;\ x_{45}=2025;\ x_{46}=0;\ x_{47}=2025;$ $x_{48}=0;\ x_{49}=4000;\ x_{4,\,10}=4000;\ x_{57}=810;\ x_{58}=0;$ $x_{59}=810;\ x_{5,\,10}=0$	75 944.34

Figure 95 Optimal production programmes and related total contributions in the example of towelling products manufacture for alternative planning periods

constraint. The, now ambiguous, solution specifies the break-even points that are sought.

The linear programming models for successive analysis for $T=1, 2, 3, \ldots, 10$ weeks are shown in Fig. 94. The maximum contributions and related production programmes for (total analysis) time-scales of up to 10 weeks are listed in Fig. 95.

Up to period 9 the maximum contribution falls short of the contribution block of DM 70 000, which is first exceeded in period 10. The maximum contribution of approximately DM 76 000, that is reached in period 10, implies that over the first ten periods many different feasible production programmes will generate a contribution of exactly DM 70 000. In the towelling material case, there are no break-even points for production programmes which only extend over the first nine weeks. With existing capacity, the break-even period is at least ten weeks. From week 10 onwards there is a set of feasible break-even production programmes. They constitute a polyhedron and can be computed as the solution set for the corresponding linear programming model for production volume planning, with the break-even equation (4.145) as an additional constraint.

VI. NON-LINEAR BREAK-EVEN ANALYSIS

1. Survey of Non-linear Break-even Approaches

The vast majority of break-even models and break-even applications are based on linear cost and revenue functions. However, in some of these cases a closer analysis reveals that the behaviour of the curves is not linear. Nevertheless it frequently appears to be expedient to retain the linear analysis on the following grounds:

(1) The linear analysis is *computationally* much simpler and is therefore easier to implement. This implies that the additional expense of a non-linear analysis is only worthwhile in return for a corresponding increase in the accuracy of the results.

(2) Non-linearities in cost and revenue functions, or in contribution functions, are frequently so *weak* that they can be ignored at the cost of negligible loss in accuracy. The effect of larger divergences from linearity in the case of individual cost categories is frequently diminished when they are summed across all cost categories. It is also possible that summation equalises strong non-linearities in the behaviour of individual cost types (cp. Middleton, 1980 [Critical Look] p. 266).

(3) Even if the functions adopted are significantly non-linear, linear approaches can be used if it is known that the productive output in question is variable only within a (narrow) interval and that, within this *"relevant region"*, a linearity assumption provides sufficiently accurate results (Horngren, 1982 [Cost Accounting] pp. 48, 294).

Middleton (cp. 1980 [Critical Look] p. 265 et seq.) in particular has grave misgivings about argument (3). Figure 96 illustrates the form of the linearisation of non-linear cost and revenue behaviour in the region that is relevant at the time of the analysis.

The cost line approximating the non-linear original cost function exhibits no peculiarities from an interpretational and computational standpoint if the cost level at the zero output level and its slope coefficient are interpreted as the fixed cost block K^f and variable cost rate k^v respectively. The interpretation of the approximation function for sales revenue is more difficult. In this case also (cp. Fig. 96(b)), a particular basic revenue value is formally indicated at the zero output level. It can be described as *fixed sales revenue* or *fixed economic output* (cp. Chmielewicz, 1973 [Erfolgsrechnung] pp. 209, 217; Chmielewicz, 1972 [Qualitätsgestaltung] p. 598). However, it is only of interpretational significance to the extent that, in combination with the slope coefficient of the sales revenue line which has been inferred, it facilitates the computation of an approximately correct total sales revenue function. Hence *Middleton's* (cp. 1980 [Critical Look] p. 267) criticism of this approach (on the grounds that it results in a high sales revenue level at a zero level of output) is unjustified. The approximation in question is in no way valid for the zero output level which in fact lies outside the relevant region. An adequate interpretation of a linear approximation of a sales revenue function requires a recognition of the fact that this is a question of total sales revenue. For example, the original, non-linear sales revenue curve (Fig. 96(b)) could reflect a non-constant selling price function. Thus, it may perhaps be assumed that a reduction in selling price is necessary to achieve a higher sales volume. In the absence of a selling price reduction, an increase in sales volume may not be possible. In these circumstances the total revenue curve increases at a decreasing rate rather than at a constant rate and may eventually decline. A higher sales volume is then multiplied by a lower price and results in the concave total sales revenue curve shown in Fig. 96(b). The implication of a linear approximation is of course that the slope coefficient in a relevant region can in no way

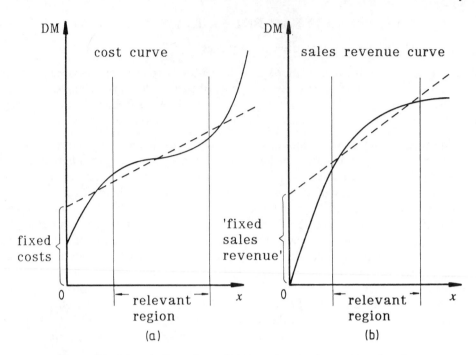

Figure 96   Linearisation of non-linear cost and sales revenue functions

be interpreted as an (average) unit selling price. For each value of the determinant x, i.e. for each level of output x, a different unit selling price applies. It can be ascertained by dividing the total sales revenue by the number of units of output. On the other hand, the slope of the total sales revenue line can be regarded as the marginal revenue of the output level in question.

No peculiarities are encountered in the formal implementation of the above approximation. Denoting the resultant (fixed) revenues and (fixed) costs at a zero output level with E^f and K^f respectively, the contribution block to be compensated is given by:

$$B = K^f - E^f. \tag{4.148}$$

Letting $\bar{e}$ and k^v be the slope coefficients of the respective linear functions, the break-even condition is formulated with the usual equation:

$$(\bar{e} - k^v) \cdot x \overset{!}{=} B. \tag{4.149}$$

The linearisation described above can in principle be applied to all extensions of break-even analysis—provided the linear deviation is not too large and given knowledge of the relevant region in the case in question.

2. Simplification of Non-linear Break-even Relationships by Stepwise Linearisation

In applications other than those that have so far been described, the necessary linearisation prerequisites are not fulfilled. It is not possible, especially in multiproduct situations or when end-product market conditions are uncertain, to restrict pertinent output ranges to sufficiently small relevant regions. If the non-linear features of the functions are then so pronounced that an analysis based on linearised values would be too imprecise, the non-linearities must be explicitly embodied in the computation. Two approaches can be followed:

(1) The non-linear functions can be analysed in each of the segments in which they are almost linear. The definitional regions for this purpose are the intervals in which the behaviour of the function in question is approximately linear. This is referred to as *stepwise linearisation* (cp. also Ijiri, 1965 [Goals] p. 15 et seq.).

(2) An attempt is made to express the non-linear functions in the *simplest possible form*. The intention is to capture the infinitesimal changes in the behaviour of the curves with a sufficient degree of accuracy whilst still facilitating a formal mathematical treatment.

Figure 97 exemplifies the stepwise linearisation method. In this case the cost function is divided into five "pieces". Particular cost parameters K_i^f, k_i^v ($i = 1, 2, \ldots, 5$) apply to each constituent interval $[x_{i-1}, x_i]$. The sales revenue function should, if necessary, be linearised in the same way. An individual break-even computation should then be undertaken for each constituent interval for which the contribution block (computed in accordance with (4.148)) and unit contribution are constant. Because of the linear relationships, this computation is of the standard form. The revenue and cost data which are valid for a constituent interval can result in a break-even point which lies outside that interval and is therefore inadmissible. Frequently the analysis of all constituent intervals finally results in a single break-even point. Such a break-even point is admissible provided it actually exists and takes on a unique value. Multiple solution values denote multiple break-even points.

The procedure described thus extends the analysis, using the standard technique, to cover cases of non-linearity. Stepwise increasing fixed costs, in particular, can be modelled in this way (cp. Shesai, Harwood and Hermanson, 1977/78 [Integer Goal Programming] p. 46; Horngren, 1982 [Cost Accounting] p. 295 et seq.). The analysis of unidimensional relationships i.e. of the single-stage, single-product case and of some special cases of multistage manufacture, is not expensive. Multidimensional break-even analysis, e.g. the multiproduct case, is a different matter. If a number of determinants, perhaps the outputs of different products, is partitioned into different intervals, the resultant combination gives rise to a multiplicative increase in the number of cases that needs to be separately analysed. Thus, if both the outputs of two products have five intervals, $5 \cdot 5 = 25$ individual fields need to be analysed. In such a situation, a separate analysis of each combination of intervals is therefore no longer expedient. Instead the partitioning into intervals can be effected by resorting to *indicator variables*. Indicator variables can only take on integer values of 0 or 1. They are intended to specify the interval of the definitional region for which an actual value of the variable x_1 is admissible. The different linear components of product 1's function whose output variable x_1 is partitioned into 5 intervals $(x_{1, i-1}, x_{1, i}]$ (where $i = 1, 2, \ldots, 5$), are summarised in an individual function. Using the symbols already introduced, the latter function is formulated as follows.

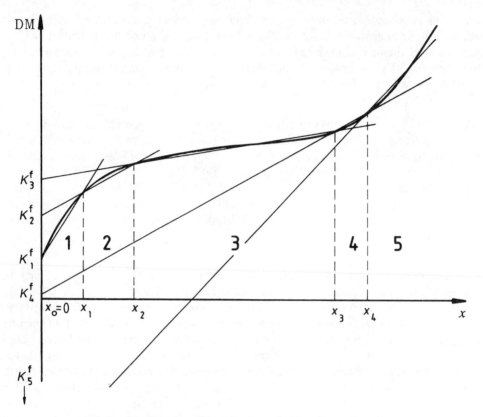

Figure 97 Piecemeal linearisation of a non-linear function

$$K_1(x) = [K_{1,1}^f + k_{1,1}^v \cdot x] \cdot \alpha_1 + [K_{1,2}^f + k_{1,2}^v \cdot x] \cdot \alpha_2 + [K_{1,3}^f + k_{1,3}^v \cdot x] \cdot \alpha_3$$
$$+ [K_{1,4}^f + k_{1,4}^v \cdot x] \cdot \alpha_4 + [K_{1,5}^f + k_{1,5}^v \cdot x] \cdot \alpha_5$$

(4.150)

with

$$\alpha_1 = \begin{cases} 1 \text{ if } x < x_{1,1} \\ 0 \text{ otherwise} \end{cases} \qquad \alpha_2 = \begin{cases} 1 \text{ if } x_{1,1} \leqslant x < x_{1,2} \\ 0 \text{ otherwise} \end{cases}$$

$$\alpha_3 = \begin{cases} 1 \text{ if } x_{1,2} \leqslant x < x_{1,3} \\ 0 \text{ otherwise} \end{cases} \qquad \alpha_4 = \begin{cases} 1 \text{ if } x_{1,3} \leqslant x < x_{1,4} \\ 0 \text{ otherwise} \end{cases}$$

$$\alpha_5 = \begin{cases} 1 \text{ if } x_{1,4} \leqslant x \\ 0 \text{ otherwise} \end{cases}$$

or

$$K_1(x) = \sum_{i=1}^{5} [K_{1,i}^f + k_{1,i}^v \cdot x] \cdot \alpha_i$$

$$\alpha_i = \begin{cases} 1 \text{ if } x_{1,i-1} \leqslant x < x_{1,i} \\ 0 \text{ otherwise} \end{cases}$$

$$(x_{1,0} = 0 \quad \text{and} \quad x_{1,5} = x_1^{\max}).$$

This formulation with indicator variables facilitates, principally in multiproduct approaches, the transfer of the previously-outlined procedure of break-even analysis with a linear programming model (cp. Section 4.II.2) to a situation that is specified with stepwise linearised functions. The corresponding extension lies in the introduction of indicator variables α_{ki} as integer variables into the linear programming approach. The value of one of the ith indicator variable of a product k can then be exactly attained, by imposing additional constraints, if the output variable x_k of this product lies in the ith interval (cp. Shesai, Harwood and Hermanson, 1977/78 [Integer Goal Programming] p. 46). The complete problem is one of mixed-integer-linear programming. The actual break-even analysis follows the form described in Section 4.II.2. The number of integer variables restricts the applicability of the mixed-integer approach with stepwise linearisation to a relatively small number of products and related intervals.

3. Possible Ways of Explicitly Allowing for Non-linearities in Break-even Analyses

The second alternative method of dealing with break-even components which behave non-linearly is their explicit inclusion in the most operational manner that can be achieved. Relevant detailed examples have already been considered in earlier sections of this book. Thus, particular *production–theoretic relationships* are the principal reason for non-linear cost functions. In the case of foam material production that was considered earlier, these production–theoretic relationships are such that their neglect would cause considerable deviations between the actual cost situation and that which is depicted in the break-even model. Relationships similar to those in foam material production are to be found in (technologically speaking) very disparate production processes. To facilitate an overview and operational applications, characteristic cost behaviour in these cases is represented and classified by reference to the simplest possible types of functional behaviour, i.e. particular forms of convexity or concavity. In the examples considered previously, particular non-homogeneous functions and quadratic functions were employed. Quadratic functions (for an example from the food industry, cp. Singh and Chapman, 1977/78 [Approximation] p. 53 et seq.) and higher polynomial functions (cp., for example, Goggans, 1965 [Curvilinear Functions] p. 868 et seq.) are frequently to be found in examples in the literature.

In addition to production–theoretic elements, *non-constant selling price functions* cause non-linear relationships (on the revenue side). Furthermore, non-constant functional behaviour can also be caused by discrete or continuous discounting. In each case it is necessary adequately to model the non-linear behaviour by including an operationally-quantifiable functional type in the break-even analysis.

The principle of break-even analysis is in no way affected by the inclusion of non-linear revenue functions $E(x)$ or non-linear cost functions $K^v(x)$. However, because of the non-constant unit contributions, it is in some circumstances interesting to analyse the total contribution. To this end, the *indifference curve* concept can be fruitfully employed in some cases (on this cp. Edwards and Johnson, 1974 [Indifference Approach] p. 580; Morrison and Kaczka, 1969 [Application] p. 331 et seq.). The aim is to determine the critical output levels at which the total contribution $D(x)$ is exactly equal to a contribution block B. These are given by solutions to the equation:

$$D(x) = E(x) - K^v(x) \overset{!}{=} B. \qquad (4.151)$$

Given linear relationships, the solution of the corresponding break-even condition causes no difficulty—at least not in the unidimensional case. Aside from a situation in which the slope coefficient of a linear sales revenue function is less than that of a linear cost function, there is always a (positive) break-even point. Moreover, such an exceptional case is not difficult to recognise. In the multidimensional case it is necessary to solve a linear system of equations. Here also there are comparatively simple possibilities for determining whether the problem is solvable and for identifying its solution (if any) (cp. 4.II.2). Such simple criteria are generally not to be found in the case of non-linearity. In a non-linear situation, and even in the case of univariable functions it is, in contrast to the linear approach, questionable,

—whether a solution *exists* at all, i.e. whether the equation is solvable,
—whether the solution is *unique*, i.e. whether perhaps multiple output levels x satisfy the equation (are critical);
—how the contribution function *behaves* before and after the break-even point, i.e. whether the unit contribution increases or decreases.

Four examples of possible features of a univariable, non-linear break-even analysis are sketched out in Fig. 98.

The problems are intensified by an increasing number of variables. To these problems must be added the additional computational difficulties which arise in solving a non-linear equation like (4.151). There are solution techniques for determining the zero point location only for special types of non-linear functions. In most cases it is necessary to fall back on trial and error procedures. Such heuristically-structured procedures must be carefully aligned with the particular application in question in order to provide usable results. Such a state of affairs explains why, in the vast majority of cases, it is first advisable to employ linear methods of analysis or at least methods which, in many respects, accord with linear approaches.

VII. STOCHASTIC BREAK-EVEN ANALYSIS

1. Survey of Stochastic Break-even Approaches

Numerous publications on break-even analysis are concerned with stochastic approaches. The following two categories of break-even models can be distinguished by reference to what are regarded as the stochastic components of break-even models:

(1) *Sales volume* alone is assumed to be stochastic and all of the model's other determinants are treated as deterministic variables.
(2) The *unit contribution of output*—or one or more of its individual constituents—or the *contribution block*, are assumed to be stochastic. Additionally the sales volume can here also be depicted as a stochastic variable.

A detailed analysis of assumption (1) does not result in an actual stochastic break-even analysis. In such a case, all components which are needed for the calculation of break-even points, namely, contribution block, price, variable costs and unit contribution are

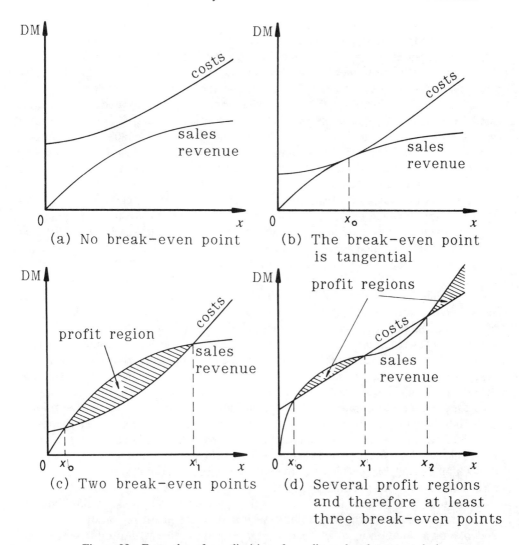

Figure 98 Examples of peculiarities of non-linear break-even analysis

deterministic. They can be used for calculating deterministic break-even points. The sole consequence of a stochastic sales volume is that it precludes an unambiguous sales volume forecast. That is to say, it is not possible to forecast with certainty whether the break-even point will be exceeded or not. Instead it is necessary to determine the probability that a computed break-even point will at least be attained, i.e. that a given contribution block will at least be recovered. The break-even analysis relates to the attainment of a zero loss–zero profit with fixed costs constituting the contribution block; or to the attainment of a profit minimum which is embodied in a correspondingly higher contribution block. The problems which arise in the case of the *first type* of stochastic analysis are not concerned with the calculation of the break-even point but rather with an adjunct analysis of sales volume risk. Relevant possibilities have already been discussed in Chapter 3, Section VI. In particular, the risk measure *probability of an erroneous decision* is a suitable means of providing the requisite probabilistic information. However, the latter description is hardly ever encountered in the literature on general stochastic break-even analysis. Computational forms and interpretations which are to be found in the literature nevertheless conform to the concept of the probability of an erroneous decision (cp. Colasse, 1971 [Variante statistique] p. 71 et seq.).

In individual publications, further considerations are incorporated into the basic method of computing probabilities of attaining particular sales volumes or turnover values. Thus, *Morse and Posey* (cp. 1979/80 [Income Taxes] p. 20 et seq.) combine a probability distribution for sales volume with the impact of taxes. From a probability distribution of taxable income they compute a distribution of post-tax income on which further results are then based.

An approach proposed by *Teller* (1975 [Modèle Bayésien] p. 37 et seq.) demonstrates the use of the Bayesian estimation principle in determining sales volume probabilities. Teller initially assumes that the decision-maker can, for example, specify three different sales volumes: that which appears to him to be the "most probable", a pessimistic and an optimistic. Probabilities are ascribed to these volumes, e.g. 0.2, 0.6 and 0.2, which thus constitute an *a priori distribution*. After the first sales period, e.g. after the first month, realised sales volumes are already known. Adopting the assumption that these sales volumes actually reflect, with a particular probability, the relationships which actually subsist during the year as a whole, Teller constructs a conditional sales volume distribution for realised sales. *A posteriori probabilities* are then computed as a basis for further derivations by combining the a priori and observed distributions (cp. Teller, 1975 [Modèle Bayésien] p. 45; for a general treatment of Bayesian estimation cp., e.g. Schaich et al., 1982 [Statistik II] p. 83 et seq.). The use of the Bayesian principle in the case of continuous sales volume estimation is advantageous in that additional information, gained in the meanwhile in the form of realised sales volume figures, is combined with the initial sales volume probabilities and thereby constitutes updated probabilistic sales volume data. Prior to the first realised sales volume, only the a priori distribution is available in which case the Bayesian procedure is not relevant to a decision on whether to produce or not (cp. 3.VI).

Dickinson (1974 [Uncertainty]) extends the approaches so far described to multiple products. He computes the probabilities of attaining the profit region of the firm as a whole for a situation in which there is an optional number of *n* products, the sales volumes of which are assumed to be normally distributed. He also allows for the non-negligible covariance values (cp. Dickinson, 1974 [Uncertainty] p. 183 et seq., 187).

All approaches categorised in the first group are based on a supplementation of a (deterministically) computed break-even point, which is expressed in terms of sales volumes or sales revenue, with information about its probability of occurrence. It is derived from prior stochastic information. The stochastic feature lies solely in the sales volume figures included in both the data and in the results that are derived whilst, on the other hand, the break-even point is deterministically established. It is therefore not correct to describe such cases as actual examples of stochastic break-even analysis.

In the *second category* of stochastic approaches, such components of the break-even model as directly enter the calculation of a break-even point as, for example, the contribution per unit of output or the contribution block (the fixed costs), are also treated stochastically. In these cases there is *not a unique break-even point*. On the contrary, a number of possible break-even points, each of which has a particular probability of occurrence can be specified; or, alternatively, an interval of possible break-even points with a related probability density. In addition to the issues that were considered by reference to the stochastic approaches discussed previously, it thus becomes possible to examine the probability distribution of the break-even point. The following three questions should be clearly distinguished:

(a) *What* is the *probability* of at least attaining a break-even point or a particular, predetermined level of profit?
(b) *What level of profit* can be attained with a particular, predetermined probability (e.g. 50%)?
(c) What is the *probability distribution* of a break-even point, i.e. what is the probability of a particular position of the break-even point?

Question (c) is only of significance in relation to the second category of stochastic break-even approaches and, as indicated, its resolution necessitates the determination of a probability distribution for the break-even point. Question (b) is the mirror-image question of (a). Both questions can be answered by an evaluation of the probability distribution of profit (cp. Kottas and Lau, 1978 [Simulation] p. 701). That is to say, they are in fact resolved if this distribution is known. Methods of ascertaining the distribution function for dealing with questions (a) and (b) are examined in Section 2 below whilst question (c) is the focus of Section 3.

These questions are concerned with probabilistic statements about break-even points. A further problem-area involves approaches for exploring the *optimal level of production in situations characterised by risk*. This question is related to the one examined here in that a situation characterised by risk can result from stochastic contribution blocks or stochastic contributions. However, the decision signalled in such situations does not constitute an actual break-even problem. Break-even questions are always related to the analysis of marginal points which separate "positive" and "negative" outcomes. The optimal output decision model neither directly allows for, nor computes such marginal points (cp. Adar, Barnea and Lev, 1977 [Uncertainty] p. 137 et seq. A special risk measure for such decision models is described in Magee, 1975 [Uncertainty] p. 257 et seq. A survey of optimising approaches in this category is to be found in Kaplan, 1982 [Management Accounting] p. 195 et seq.).

Finally, the previously-described methods cannot be used under *conditions of uncertainty*. Nevertheless, it may occasionally still be possible in such circumstances to estimate favourable, or unfavourable contribution tendencies in which case a region of possible break-even points may be ascertainable (cp. Lex, 1970 [Investitionsrechnung] p. 154). However, no probabilities can be specified for the individual potential break-even points. In the case of complete uncertainty, information on the level of future contribution margins is completely absent. *Henderson and Barnett* (cp. 1977/78 [Breakeven Present Value] p. 49 et seq.) propose a special procedure for dealing with this situation. Assuming a particular cost of capital and profit minima, they compute a minimum pay-back annuity for the project in question. This computation makes use of the annuity investment criterion (cp. Blohm and Lüder, 1983 [Investition] p. 73 et seq.) and, making due allowance for the cost of capital, allocates a project's acquisition cost over its expected life (cp. Henderson and Barnett, 1977/78 [Breakeven Present Value] p. 51). The annuity thus calculated is intended to serve as a yardstick for the requisite analysis of production: if the project evaluation is, for example, one in which unknown annual total contributions are, however, assumed to exceed the computed minimum annuity in any event, this is synonymous with the expectation that the (unknown) break-even point will be exceeded (cp. Henderson and Barnett, 1977/78 [Breakeven Present Value] p. 52). In the complete absence of contribution margin information it is, in some cases, possible to make a particular break-even statement in this way.

2. Probabilistic Statements on the Attainment of Break-even Points

(a) Break-even Probabilities in the Single-product Case

Of the three questions enumerated above, (a) has received the most intensive treatment in the literature on stochastic break-even analysis. Of fundamental importance is the publication entitled "Cost-Volume-Profit Analysis Under Conditions of Uncertainty" by *Jaedicke and Robichek* (cp. 1964 [Uncertainty] p. 917 et seq.) which adds a stochastic approach to break-even analysis. *Jaedicke and Robichek* first address themselves solely to probability distributions for sales volume but, in the second part of their paper, turn to probabilistic specifications of selling price, fixed costs and variable costs for the product in question (Jaedicke and Robichek, 1964 [Uncertainty] p. 924 et seq.). All stochastic variables are assumed to be *normally distributed*. Profit is thus regarded as the sum and product of normally distributed random variables:

$$G = (q - k^v) \cdot x - K^f \qquad (4.152)$$
$$\uparrow \quad \uparrow \qquad \uparrow$$
normally distributed variables

For simplicity, *Jaedicke and Robichek* assume that all the random variables on the right-hand side of this equation are mutually independent, i.e. uncorrelated. They therefore also assume that profit is also (at least approximately) a normally distributed random variable. Hence, the probabilities of attaining or exceeding the zero-profit line, or some specified minimum profit (or maximum loss) can be calculated with no particular computational or data-preparation difficulties (cp. Jaedicke and Robichek, 1964 [Uncertainty] p. 925 et seq.). The validity of the results is subject to the admissibility of the assumed probability distributions.

The latter assumptions lead to a complete series of extensions to the analysis proposed by *Jaedicke and Robichek*. For example, *Ferrara, Hayya and Nachman* (cp. 1972 [Normalcy] p. 299 et seq.) examine the normal distributions underlying the Jaedicke and Robichek model and, using a simulation analysis, demonstrate that if prices, costs and sales volumes are assumed to be normally distributed, the resultant profit defined by (4.152) can generally not be assumed to conform to a normal distribution. The crux of the argument is that the product of two normally distributed random variables, as in (4.152), does not give a further normally distributed random variable. If it is nevertheless assumed that the profit variable takes on a normal distribution, this can only be regarded as an approximation. Under certain conditions this is justified, i.e., if it does not cause significant deviations. The condition formulated by Ferrara, Hayya and Nachman is that the *sum of the coefficients of variation σ/μ of both factors may not exceed 0.12*. This means that the sum of the coefficients of variation of σ_d/μ_d and σ_x/μ_x of the unit contribution and sales volume respectively may at most amount to 0.12. This limit is inferred by *Ferrara, Hayya and Nachman* from their simulation results, which they also used in χ^2 tests in testing the hypothesis (at the 5% significance level) that the product in (4.152) is normally distributed (cp. Ferrara, Hayya and Nachman, 1972 [Normalcy] pp. 303, 307). If the sum of the coefficients of variation exceeds this upper value then according to the simulation results the normal distribution hypothesis should be rejected.

A limit of 0.12 is of course low. The *Ferrara, Hayya and Nachman* analysis therefore implies that, for most practical purposes, profit cannot be assumed to be normally distributed if reliable results are to be derived. Even if normal distributions can be justifiably assumed for all other parameters, the technical computational advantages of a normal distribution, which frequently outweigh the disadvantage of a somewhat inexact modelling of the actual probability structure, cannot be exploited in relation to profit estimates. Several procedures suggest a way out of this situation. An attempt can be made explicitly to formulate the *probability distribution for profit* retaining the assumption that prices, costs and sales volumes are normally distributed, but dropping the assumption that they are uncorrelated. This requires, among other things, a product distribution of two correlated, normally distributed random variables with non-zero mean values and unequal variances. Because there is no such distribution expressed in general form, the problem can only be resolved by resort to an approximation method. Expressions for the moments of the distribution which is sought are obtained in the construction of the characteristic function for the assumed multi-dimensional normal distribution of the parameters. In this way, *Starr and Tapiero* (1975 [Risk] p. 852 et seq.) derive general expressions for the expected value and variance of the profit distribution which is sought. It is only with difficulty that further exact probabilistic statements can be obtained using this method.

Hilliard and Leitch (cp. 1975 [Uncertainty] p. 69 et seq.) take the opposite approach. They consider the type of distribution that can be adopted for the factors in (4.152) which, while realistically modelling the relationships, also yields a probability distribution of mathematical form for the product of matched random variables. They therefore assume that the sales volume x and the contribution margin $d = q - k^v$ are *logarithmic normally distributed*. A random variable y is said to be logarithmic normally distributed when its logarithmic value $\ln y$ is normally distributed. The density function of a logarithmic normally distributed random variable (cp. e.g. Schaich et al., 1979 [Statistik I] p. 151) is given by:

$$\psi(y) = \frac{1}{y \cdot \sigma \cdot \sqrt{2\pi}} \cdot \exp\left\{ -\frac{(\ln y - \mu)^2}{2\sigma^2} \right\}. \tag{4.153}$$

A graphic presentation of this density function is shown in Fig. 99. From its mean value μ and variance σ^2, the corresponding values of the normally distributed variable $\ln y$ can be determined in accordance with the following relationships (cp. Hilliard and Leitch, 1975 [Uncertainty] p. 70; Chan and Laughland, 1976 [Break-even-Analysis] p. 46):

$$\mu_{\ln y} = \ln \frac{\mu^2}{\sqrt{(\sigma^2 + \mu^2)}} \tag{4.154}$$

$$\sigma_{\ln y}^2 = \ln\left\{ \left(\frac{\sigma}{\mu}\right)^2 + 1 \right\}. \tag{4.155}$$

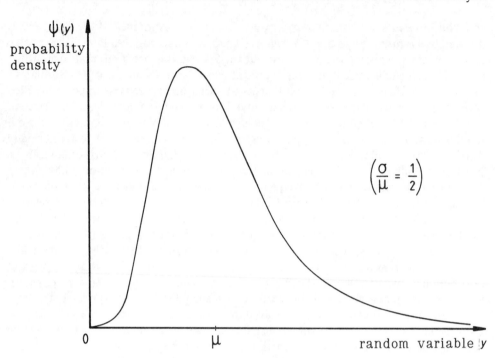

Figure 99 Density function of a logarithmic normally distributed random variable

Logarithmic normally distributed random variables have a positively-skewed probability distribution; the higher the value of its coefficient of variation σ/μ the higher is its degree of positive skewness. Moreover, the distribution function starts at the origin. This means that negative contributions and negative sales volumes have probabilities of zero. On the other hand, the normal distribution assumption implies that all negative values of random variables also have a particular non-zero probability of occurrence. This is occasionally cited as a criticism of such normal distribution assumptions cp. (cp. Hilliard and Leitch, 1975 [Uncertainty] p. 70 but see also the arguments adduced in Chapter 3, Section VI, p. 71 et seq.). The main advantage of the assumption of logarithmic normally distributed random variables in the present case is the property that the product of logarithmic normally distributed random variables is also logarithmic normally distributed. No further assumption, for example the mutual independence of the factors, is required. Thus, assuming that the unit contribution d and sales volume x are both logarithmic normally distributed, the total contribution $D = d \cdot x$ is also a logarithmic normal distribution. More precisely, it is necessary to determine the distribution of the product of the two components of an (assumed) two-dimensional logarithmic normal distribution. The parameters μ and σ of the probability distribution of the product are determined from the parameters of the two marginal distributions and, as the case may be, from the covariance values (the formulae are given in Hilliard and Leitch, 1975 [Uncertainty] p. 77 et seq.). Hence, a probability distribution for the total contribution is explicitly determined. There is therefore no difficulty in specifying the probability of attaining a particular total contribution. It is thus possible to compute, for example, the probability that the total contribution will at least equal a contribution block comprising the (constant) fixed costs. This specifies the probability of attaining the break-even point. The break-even point itself is unknown; and, because of the stochastic character of the unit contribution it is also ambiguous. The *Hilliard and Leitch* approach therefore facilitates more incisive, more exact predictions than the basic model of *Jaedicke and Robichek* with normal distribution assumptions. Its feasibility depends upon whether the special assumption, of logarithmic normally distributed contribution margins and sales volumes, models the true relationships in actual situations with sufficient accuracy.

The logarithmic normally distributed parameters which restrict the applicability of the model also exposed the Hilliard and Leitch approach to criticism. Kottas and Lau (cp. 1978 [Simulation] p. 705) contend that the assumption of logarithmic normal distributions is both unrealistic and restrictive; and, that very few cases can be captured by this model. But even if it turns out that the Hilliard and Leitch approach is applicable in particular cases, there will, in any event, be many situations for which an alternative procedure has to be found. The approaches to the problem of stochastic analysis so far described suggest that *only a few special cases* are amenable to a method which attempts to find an exact expression of the distribution functions in formal mathematical terms. On no account can this be regarded as a general way of gaining the probabilistic information that is sought.

The proposals of, for example, Liao (1975 [Sampling]) and Kottas and Lau (1978 [Simulation]) are intended to provide a general usable approach. Both approaches provide for optional types of probability distributions for all magnitudes which appear in the break-even model and no mutual independence assumptions about the variables are made. Liao (cp. 1975 [Sampling] p. 781 et seq.) takes the following individual steps:

(1) Using random numbers which must be distributed in accordance with the probability assumptions, a value for each parameter is first selected. The profit associated therewith can be derived from the relationship $G = (q - k^v) \cdot x - K^f$. This represents the first *sample value* of profit. A large number of further samples is constructed in the same way. These simulation results provide a sample of the probability distribution for profit.

(2) The possible values of profit are recorded in appropriately-constructed *class* intervals. A particular relative frequency is ascertained from the sample results recorded in each interval.

(3) The *frequency distribution* thus derived gives sample information which may deviate from the actual distribution. Hence, the frequency distribution is not used as a direct means of deriving the desired probability information but for the construction of an approximately appropriate density function. A second reason for this is the advantage of greater operationality in explicitly presenting the probability distribution in formal terms (cp. Liao, 1975 [Sampling] p. 788). In order to obtain a probability density function of this kind, the first *moments* of the frequency distribution are initially computed. They can then be used to choose an appropriate type of function from a set of possible basic forms. The exact parameter values that need to be determined to formulate the concrete function are also obtained from the moments of the frequency distribution. A number of special computational methods can be used to select, and determine, the parameters of a functional type. In principle they

are heuristically-based and are called *curve-fitting techniques*. Liao (cp. 1975 [Sampling] p. 783) uses the *Pearson* curve-fitting technique in his computations.
(4) Thus deduced, the approximation function for the probability density function of profit is then used in the normal way to compute the *probabilities of occurrence* of the specific profit levels. Of particular interest is the probability of achieving a zero-loss which is also the probability of attaining the break-even point.

Liao's procedure has the advantage that it can be used independently of particular assumptions about the probability distributions of the individual parameters. Step 3 has, however, been criticised. For example, *Kottas and Lau* (1978 [Simulation] p. 704) show that given four moments (the number assumed by Liao), an infinitesimally large number of individually very disparate functions can be found to be appropriate. Consequently, in the choice of such a function in the individual case, large *accuracy deviations* may occur between the values of the underlying frequency distribution and those values that are computed from the function. Furthermore, the overall accuracy of the function cannot be estimated. The crux of *Kottas and Lau's* proposal is therefore that the intermediate curve-fitting step should be dropped. If so, the frequency distribution should then be used directly as a hypothetical probability distribution of profit (cp. Kottas and Lau, 1978 [Simulation] p. 701). Specific additional assumptions, e.g. about the behaviour of the cumulative frequencies, within the intervals that are constructed in accordance with (2), are necessary in the case of large intervals only.

The *Kottas and Lau* procedure is not only technically simpler and requires less labour input from a computational standpoint, it is, as a rule, also more reliable. Probability values with an *accuracy deviation* of no more than one percentage point can be specified at the 95% confidence level for a sample size of 10 000 (cp. Kottas and Lau, 1978 [Simulation] p. 701).

(b) Break-even Probabilities in the Multiproduct Case

All of the approaches previously mentioned in this chapter relate only to a single product. Their application to the *multiproduct case* encounters no difficulty if the individual product probability density functions are uncorrelated. If so, then, making use of individual isolated analyses of the stochastic relationships, the corresponding multiproduct approach that is followed in the deterministic case can be applied (cp. Section 4.III).

The analysis becomes more complicated when it is necessary to assume mutual dependences in the probability structure of the parameters of different products. As yet, no more than isolated solutions to this problem have been proposed. An approach which can be relatively inexpensively implemented in practice and which nevertheless offers sufficient precision, is formulated by *Johnson and Simik* (1974 [Inequalities]). This approach does not presuppose a knowledge of the probability density functions of the stochastic parameters and confines itself to an analysis of three values: an "expected" value (which is interpreted as the expected value of the unknown distribution) and upper and lower limits for the stochastic parameter (cp. Johnson and Simik, 1974 [Inequalities] p. 71). This approach thus provides estimates of the probability that realised profit will deviate from its expected value by a particular minimum amount. To this end, *Johnson and Simik* draw on two different probability estimates and, in any given case, the one or the other will provide a better estimate (cp. Johnson and Simik, 1974 [Inequalities] p. 73). This is a question of the *Uspensky inequality*, which is a special case of the well-known Bienaymé–Tschebyscheff inequality, and of the *Hoeffding inequality* (cp. Johnson and Simik, 1974 [Inequalities] p. 73 et seq.; Hoeffding, 1963 [Inequalities] p. 16; Bennett, 1962 [Inequalities] p. 34).

In the present profit-estimation problem, these inequalities can, given the expected value of profit $E(G)$, the upper limit of $\bar{\sigma}^2$ of its variance and the deviation t, be expressed as follows:

The probability that realised profit exceeds its expected value by an amount t is
—in the case of the *Uspensky inequality* given by:

$$p\{G - E(G) \geqslant t\} \leqslant \frac{1}{1 + \dfrac{t^2}{\bar{\sigma}^2}} \quad \text{and,} \tag{4.156}$$

—in the case of the *Hoeffding inequality* given by:

$$p\{G - E(G) \geqslant t\} \leqslant \exp\left(-\frac{t^2}{2\bar{\sigma}^2}\right). \tag{4.157}$$

Moreover, it can be inferred from the derivation of these estimates that the same maximum probabilities also apply to a reversal of the sign of the required estimate of $G - E(G)$ (cp. Bennett, 1962 [Inequalities] p. 33):

$$p\{G - E(G) \leqslant -t\} \leqslant \frac{1}{1 + \dfrac{t^2}{\bar{\sigma}^2}} \tag{4.158}$$

$$p\{G - E(G) \leqslant -t\} \leqslant \exp\left(-\frac{t^2}{2\bar{\sigma}^2}\right). \tag{4.159}$$

The size of the deviation t is predetermined in accordance with the formulation of the question. The other two magnitudes, $E(G)$ and $\bar{\sigma}^2$, need to be computed from the specified data values (for each product there are three values). Any mutual (stochastic) dependence subsisting between the product parameters must also be taken into account. Thus, a total of n products is, as a first step, divided into K mutually independent *groups* of products; whereas within a group the products may be mutually dependent. Any group $k (k = 1, 2, \ldots, K)$ comprises n_k products:

$$\sum_{k=1}^{K} n_k = n.$$

To illustrate the procedure followed in the *Johnson and Simik* approach (cp. 1974 [Inequalities] p. 70 et seq.), a general case is assumed in which the total contribution $D_i = (q_i - k_i^v) \cdot x_i$ of a product i may contain two or more stochastic parameters so that this total contribution D_i is conceived as a single stochastic variable. The three known values of D_i are represented by D_i^u, D_i^e, and D_i^o, where the upper indices denote lower, expected and upper values respectively. To determine the required values of $E(G)$ and $\bar{\sigma}^2$, a product group-related stepwise approach is adopted. An *expected value of the total contribution* $\hat{D}_k^e$ and an *upper limit* $\hat{\sigma}_k^2$ *for the variance (k = 1, 2, . . ., K)* are first ascertained. The expected value of the group is given by the sum of the expected values of the individual products where the index i_{kj} denotes the *j*th product in group *k*:

$$\hat{D}_k^e = \sum_{j=1}^{n_k} D_{i_{kj}}^e.$$ (4.160)

Johnson and Simik (cp. 1974 [Inequalities] p. 71 et seq.) use the following estimate, which can be derived from basic mathematical-statistical relationships, for the *variance limit* $\hat{\sigma}_k^2$:

$$\hat{\sigma}_k^2 = \frac{1}{4}\left[\sum_{j=1}^{n_k} (D_{i_{kj}}^o - D_{i_{kj}}^u)\right]^2.$$ (4.161)

The required parameters for the totality of products can be ascertained from these product group-related values by simple addition because the groups are mutually independent. The upper limit for the total variance is therefore:

$$\bar{\sigma}^2 = \sum_{k=1}^{K} \hat{\sigma}_k^2$$ (4.162)

The *expected value of the total contributions* from all products is given by:

$$\sum_{k=1}^{K} \hat{D}_k^e$$ (4.163)

If the fixed costs K^f are constant, the expected value of profit is given by (cp. Johnson and Simik, 1974 [Inequalities] p. 75):

$$E(G) = \sum_{k=1}^{K} \hat{D}_k^e - K^f$$ (4.164)

If the values of $E(G)$ and $\bar{\sigma}^2$ thus computed are used in the estimates defined by (4.156) to (4.159), valuable probability information on the attainment of zero-profit or minimum profit break-even points can be obtained. Of the two maximum probabilities that can be derived from the respective inequalities (4.156) and (4.157) or (4.158) and (4.159), the smaller should be chosen because it provides a more accurate estimate.

The predictions that may be inferred can be illustrated with the example of television tube production that is presented in Section 4.II.1f (p. 98 et seq.). This is a question of six products. The lower and upper limits, and expected values of their respective total contributions are assumed to be known. These data are tabulated in Fig. 100.

Preliminary analyses suggest that the probabilities of the contribution levels of the first three products A, B and C are mutually dependent. The same applies to products D and E. However, products A, B and C are independent of the other products as, indeed, is product F. Thus, in this example, three groups can be constructed, namely, with products A, B and C in group 1, products D and E in group 2 and product F in group 3.

The break-even information that is of interest relates to:

(1) fixed costs amounting to DM 3 000 000 that are jointly attributable to the six products

Product group	Type i	Contribution margins D_i of product types			Range of deviation $(D_i^0 - D_i^u)$	Variance
		Lower value D_i^u	Upper value D_i^0	Expected value D_i		
1	A	580 000	740 000	660 000	160 000	
	B	1 000 000	1 355 000	1 177 500	355 000	
	C	550 000	830 000	690 000	280 000	
		$\hat{D}_1^e = \Sigma_{A, B, C} =$ 2 527 500			795 000	
				$\hat{\sigma}_1^2 = \frac{1}{4} [\Sigma_{A, B, C}(D_i^0 - D_i^u)]^2 = 158\ 006\ 250\ 000$		
2	D	150 000	162 000	156 250	12 500	
	E	195 000	225 000	210 000	30 000	
		$\hat{D}_2^e = \Sigma_{D, E} =$ 366 250			42 500	
				$\hat{\sigma}_2^2 = \frac{1}{4} [\Sigma_{D, E}(D_i^0 - D_i^u)]^2 = 451\ 562\ 500$		
3	F	1 200 000	1 440 000	1 320 000	240 000	
		$\hat{D}_3^e = \Sigma_F =$ 1 320 000			240 000	
				$\hat{\sigma}_3^2 = \frac{1}{4} (D_F^0 - D_F^u)^2 = 14\ 400\ 000\ 000$		
Σ		$\hat{D}^e = \hat{D}_1^e + \hat{D}_2^e + \hat{D}_3^e = 4\ 213\ 750$				$\bar{\sigma}^2 = \hat{\sigma}_1^2 + \hat{\sigma}_2^2 + \hat{\sigma}_3^2$ $= 172\ 857\ 812\ 500$
	$E(G) = \hat{D}^e - K^f = $ DM 4 213 750 $-$ DM 3 000 000 $=$ DM 1 213 750					$\bar{\sigma}^2 = 172\ 857\ 812\ 500$

Figure 100 Data and computations for an example of stochastic multiproduct analysis following *Johnson and Simik*

(2) a target minimum profit of $G_2 =$ DM 1 500 000 and
(3) the sustaining of a loss of $G_3 =$ DM $-$ 500 000.
   The contribution blocks for these three cases therefore amount to:
   $B_1 =$ DM 3 000 000 $(G_1 = 0)$,
   $B_2 =$ DM 4 500 000,
   $B_3 =$ DM 2 500 000.

The related deviations t_1, t_2, and t_3 of profit from its expected value are thus:

$t_1 = E(G) - G_1 = E(G) =$ DM 1 213 750
$t_2 = G_2 - E(G) =$ DM 286 250 and
$t_3 = E(G) - G_3 =$ DM 1 713 750.

Different applications of the probability estimates are of interest in the respective three cases. The value of the probability that a break-even point will at least be reached, or exceeded, can be specified in the first case.
   The calculations in Fig. 101 indicate that the probability of not reaching a break-even point amounts to no more than 1.41%. To obtain this result, the Hoeffding

	Required probability estimate		Relevant inequality	Upper probability limit following	
For the case	Transformation for the profit deviation			Uspensky	Hoeffding
(1)	$p\{D \leqslant B_1\} = p\{G \leqslant G_1\} = p\{G - E(G) \leqslant G_1 - E(G)\}$ $= p\{G - E(G) \leqslant -t_1\}$, $t_1 = 1\,213\,750$		(4.158), (4.159)	0.1050	0.0141
(2)	$p\{D \geqslant B_2\} = p\{G \geqslant G_2\} = p\{G - E(G) \geqslant G_2 - E(G)\}$ $= p\{G - E(G) \geqslant t_2\}$, $t_2 = 286\,250$		(4.156), (4.157)	0.6784	0.7890
(3)	$p\{D \leqslant B_3\} = p\{G \leqslant G_3\} = p\{G - E(G) \leqslant G_3 - E(G)\}$ $= p\{G - E(G) \leqslant -t_3\}$, $t_3 = 1\,713\,750$		(4.158), (4.159)	0.0556	0.0002

Figure 101 Probability estimates proposed by *Johnson and Simik* for the multiproduct situation illustrated in Fig. 100

inequality has been used. It provides the superior estimate. This means that the probability of attaining a break-even point is at least $1 - 0.0141 = 98.59\%$. Corresponding predictions can be inferred for the other cases. The probability that the profit exceeds DM 1.5 million is at most 67.84% (in this case the Uspensky inequality provides the more accurate estimate). Hence, the probability that profit will be no more than DM 1.5 million is at least 32.16%. In the third case, there is a maximum probability of 0.02% that a loss of at least DM 500 000 will occur. Thus, the probability that a loss not exceeding DM 500 000 will occur is at least 99.98%. Higher losses can therefore be virtually precluded.

3. Probabilistic Statements on the Locality of Break-even Points

(a) Approaches for Taking Account of the Stochastic Nature of Break-even Points

A genuine stochastic break-even analysis was initially described as an examination of the probability distribution of the locality of the break-even point. In the single-product case, the break-even point is the quotient of the fixed costs (or another contribution block) and the unit contribution:

$$x_0 = \frac{K^f}{d} \qquad (4.165)$$

If both of these magnitudes are stochastic, the probability distribution of the break-even point is generally difficult to ascertain. This distribution can be analysed at different levels of aggregation. *Liao* (1976 [Estimations]) chooses a global approach. Using regression analysis, he assumes that cost and revenue functions derived with regression techniques are estimates of the unknown "TRUE" functions. The past values from which the estimated functions are derived are therefore treated as sample information. An estimated function and a related confidence interval for a specified confidence level are derived from this information. The confidence interval captures a family of functions determined by the ranges of variation in their parameters. *Liao* recommends the computation of the break-even point for the lower and upper interval limits of the functions involved (cp. Liao, 1976 [Estimations] p. 924). The *region of variation* in the break-even point is determined in this way. This region can be interpreted in much the same way as a confidence interval. In particular it does not indicate probabilities of occurrence for the individual points within the break-even interval that has been derived.

The question of the probability distribution of the break-even point is answered in a more discriminating manner if *special types of distribution* are assumed for the contribution block (especially fixed costs K^f) and contribution margin d; and, the distribution of the break-even point is inferred accordingly. In the simplest case, a finite number of possibilities, each of which has an individual probability, is assumed for the numerator and denominator in (4.165). The (discrete) probabilities of the resultant very large (finite) number of possible break-even points can then be computed in the form of a probability tree (cp. Chan and Laughland, 1976 [Break-even Analysis] p. 45). This procedure is of course only practical in the case of a relatively small number of possible values of the numerator and denominator of the (4.165) break-even formula. Given a large number of possible values, this computational method is complex and the results have little predictive power. In sum, this means that a discrete method is probably unsuitable in the majority of cases. As a rule, therefore, it is more realistic to assume a continuous probability distribution for the numerator and denominator of (4.165). In most cases this of course involves the difficulty of expressing the probability distribution of the break-even point in operational form. For normally distributed values of the denominator and numerator in (4.165), a probability density function for the break-even point does exist and can be formally specified (cp. Starr and Tapiero, 1975 [Risk] p. 849). This is of course a complex problem which causes operational difficulties from a computational standpoint. The function can be simplified by additionally assuming independence or deterministic fixed costs, i.e. by restricting the stochastic features to the denominator (cp. Starr and Tapiero, 1975 [Risk] p. 850 et seq.).

The expression for the probability density function of the break-even point is computationally simpler and less complex if, again, *logarithmic normally distributed random variables* are assumed. If so, the quotient (4.165) is then also logarithmic normally distributed (cp. Chan and Laughland, 1976 [Break-even Analysis] p. 46). If K^f and d are logarithmic normally distributed, and have the respective parameters μ_k, σ_k and μ_d, σ_d, the following relations then apply (cp. Chan and Laughland, 1976 [Break-even Analysis] p. 46; Holt et al., 1960 [Planning] p. 285, cp. (4.153)): the mean and variance of the normally-distributed random variable $\ln K^f$ are:

$$\mu_{\ln K^f} = \ln \frac{\mu_K^2}{\sqrt{(\sigma_K^2 + \mu_K^2)}}; \qquad \sigma_{\ln K^f}^2 = \ln\left\{\left(\frac{\sigma_K}{\mu_k}\right)^2 + 1\right\}. \qquad (4.166)$$

The mean and variance of the normally distributed random variable $\ln d$ are:

$$\mu_{\ln d} = \ln \frac{\mu_d^2}{\sqrt{(\sigma_d^2 + \mu_d^2)}}; \qquad \sigma_{\ln d}^2 = \ln\left\{\left(\frac{\sigma_d}{\mu_d}\right)^2 + 1\right\}. \qquad (4.167)$$

The break-even point x_0 is logarithmic normally distributed; $\ln x_0$ is normally distributed. The random variables of the determinants are assumed to be independent. If so, the expected value $\mu_{\ln x_0}$ and variance $\sigma_{\ln x_0}^2$ of the logarithmic value of the break-even point are given by (cp. Hilliard and Leitch, 1975 [Uncertainty] p. 77; Chan and Laughland, 1976 [Break-even Analysis] p. 46):

$$\mu_{\ln x_0} = E(\ln x_0) = E(\ln K^f) - E(\ln d)$$
$$= \mu_{\ln K^f} - \mu_{\ln d} \tag{4.168}$$

$$\sigma^2_{\ln x_0} = \sigma^2_{\ln K^f} + \sigma^2_d. \tag{4.169}$$

The non-logarithmic values μ_{x_0} and $\sigma^2_{x_0}$ are given by:

$$\mu_{x_0} = E(x_0) = \exp\{ \tfrac{1}{2} \cdot \sigma^2_{\ln x_0} + E(\ln x_0)\}, \tag{4.170}$$

$$\sigma^2_{x_0} = \exp\{2 \cdot E(\ln x_0) + \sigma^2_{\ln x_0}\} \cdot [\exp(\sigma^2_{\ln x_0}) - 1]. \tag{4.171}$$

This specification fully defines the probability density function of the break-even point which can be purposefully evaluated accordingly. For example, it indicates the probability that the break-even point exceeds a particular output etc. The technique on which such computations are based wholly conforms to the procedure for the normal distribution that was outlined in Chapter 3, Section VI. Logarithmic values are used in the calculations; and the parameter values specified by (4.168) and (4.169) are employed in utilising the tabular values of the normal distribution.

Of the procedures for explicitly computing the probability distribution of a break-even point that have so far been described, only the *Chan and Laughland model* can be used for practical purposes. That it can only be used for dealing with the case of logarithmic normally distributed contribution blocks and contribution margins is however seen as a severe restriction. Proposals have therefore been made which allow normally distributed variables at least to be approximated. *Kim* (1973 [Analysis] p. 335 et seq.) analyses break-even probabilities of a *normally distributed* contribution block and *normally distributed* contribution margins assuming that these variables are *independent*. He gives the distribution function of the break-even point both in an exact functional formulation and in an approximate form (cp. Kim, 1973 [Analysis] pp. 336, 338). However, because of the complexity of the exact functions, only an approximation method of computation appears to be a practical proposition. An extension is provided by *Ekern* (1979 [Points] p. 271 et seq.) whose approach also allows for correlated variables. To capture the distribution function of a break-even point $x_0 = K^f/d$, *Ekern* (cp. 1979 [Points] p. 273) first defines the following supplementary variable in accordance with *Kim's* proposition (1973 [Analysis] p. 336):

$$z := \zeta(x_0) := \frac{x_0 \cdot \mu_d - \mu_k}{\sqrt{(\sigma^2_K - 2x_0 \hat{\rho} \sigma_K \sigma_d + x_0^2 \sigma^2_d)}} \tag{4.172}$$

The symbols μ_d, σ^2_d and μ_K, σ^2_K denote the respective means and variances of the contribution margin d and fixed costs K^f which are assumed to be normally distributed random variables. The value $\hat{\rho}$ specifies the correlation coefficient of the statistical connection between the two random variables. The transformation of the variable x_0 specified by (4.172) is known as a *Geary–Hinkley transformation*. It facilitates the specification of a simple approximation of the probability distribution of x_0: the transformed variable z is thus approximately normally distributed (cp. Geary, 1930 [Frequency Distribution] p. 442 et seq.). As shown by Hinkley, the deviation of the exact distribution function Ψ of x_0 from the normal distribution Φ of z is given by (cp. Ekern, 1979 [Points] p. 273):

$$|\Psi(x_0) - \Phi(\zeta(x_0))| < \Phi\left(-\frac{\mu_d}{\sigma_d}\right) = p\{d < 0\}. \tag{4.173}$$

It follows from this estimate of accuracy that an approximation of the probability distribution based on the Geary–Hinkley transformation function will be the more accurate, the smaller is the probability of negative unit contribution. In that, in many cases, negative contribution margins are highly improbable, the Geary–Hinkley transformation frequently offers a practical means of computing very accurate approximations.

(b) Analysis of an Example of Stochastic Break-even Analysis from the Glass-Fibre Industry

The following example is intended as an illustration of stochastic break-even analysis. It is concerned with the production of glass-fibre fabric which is used primarily as the basis of roofing-felt. Because this glass-fabric serves as the foundation for tar, sand and other layers it must provide an impervious surface. It is therefore also described as glass fleece. To attain the fleece-like properties, two different fibre-glass yarns are used in the weaving process: a thinner, endless fibre-glass yarn as a warp (i.e. the vertical thread in the weaving process) and a fleecy rayon yarn as the woof (i.e. the crosswise thread in the weaving process). The precise quality of the fibre-glass yarn is described by reference to a tex-number. It indicates the weight in grammes of 1000 metres of thread. In the present case, the vertical thread is a 68-tex yarn whereas the crosswise fleecy yarn is a 660-tex yarn. The feature of this input that is of interest in the present context is that its supplier cannot guarantee exact adherence to the agreed gramme weight. The manufacturing process for fibre-glass yarns is technically not completely controllable and large deviations in weight must therefore be reckoned with. In the case of the fibre-glass processor in question, a knowledge of such deviations is, among other things, of particular importance because the yarn is bought, and paid for, by weight, whereas the weaving process is planned in terms of running lengths. The sales volume index and the costing of the manufactured glass-fleece product are also not related to weight but to square metres. The product is sold in rolls of 2000 running metres of 1 metre width. The number of rolls of glass-fleece that is manufactured and sold is therefore the appropriate determinant for the purposes of break-even analysis.

The variations in the actual gramme weight of the input yarn make the *cost* per roll *uncertain*. Moreover, the sales volume per roll is also uncertain. A glass-fleece weighing 200 g/m² sells for DM 1.25/m². If the weight is lower, price reductions must be made to compensate for the lower quality; or, the products must be placed in a lower quality category which has a correspondingly lower selling price. Should the weight of the fibre-glass (end-product) fabric be higher, a correspondingly higher revenue can be realised. For example, the known selling prices of glass-fleece weighing 175 g/m² and 225 g/m² are DM $1.00/m^2$ and DM $1.50/m^2$ respectively. Going by experience, a linear relationship can be assumed between fabric weight v and selling price q_{m^2} in the region that is relevant for present purposes. Derived from the available data, q_{m^2} is given by:

$$q_{m^2} = \frac{1}{100} v - 0.75. \qquad (4.174)$$

In order precisely to allow for the uncertainty inherent in the costs and prices, the gramme weights of the input yarns are treated as random variables. The variable t_k denotes the gramme weight of an order of 68-tex quality warp; and, t_s stands for the gramme weight of an input of woof of 660-tex quality. Experience suggests that both can be assumed to be normally distributed. The warp has a mean $\mu_k = 68$ and a standard deviation of $\sigma_k = 6$. The dispersion is greater in the case of the fleecy woof because, in converting the fleece fibre into yarn, differences in lengths, within the stocks of glass-fleece fibre have a more significant effect on the yarn weight. In this case the mean and standard deviation are therefore $\mu_s = 660$ and $\sigma_s = 100$ respectively.

The *unit variable cost* of a roll of glass-fleece weighing approximately $200 \, g/m^2$ is calculated as follows:

(1) *Costs of warp yarn.*
   The glass fleece is produced with 1440 warp threads on weaving machines in double widths, i.e. in 2-m widths. A 2000-metre roll of 1-metre width therefore requires an input of $720 \cdot 2000 \, m = 1\,440\,000 \, m$ of warp thread. This gives a weight of:

$$1\,440\,000 \, m \cdot t_k \, g/1000 \, m = 1440 \cdot t_k \, g.$$

   As the price of the 68-tex fibre glass yarn input is DM 5.10/kg, the cost of the warp yarn per roll therefore amounts to:

$$1440 \cdot t_k \, g \cdot DM \, 5.10/1000 \, g = DM \, 7.344 \cdot t_k.$$

(2) *Costs of woof yarn.*
   The weaving machine is set at 19 woof threads per 10 cm of woven surface. A roll of 2000 running metres of fleece therefore contains 380 000 woof threads per 1-m width. This gives a weight of:

$$380\,000 \, m \cdot t_s \, g/1000 \, m = 380 \cdot t_s \, g.$$

   As the price of the 660-tex fibre glass fleece yarn input is DM 4.30/kg, the costs of the woof yarn per roll amount to:

$$380 \cdot t_s \, g \cdot DM \, 4.30/1000 \, g = DM \, 1.634 \cdot t_s.$$

(3) *Costs of chemical preparation.*
   The weaving of fibre glass requires a special chemical preparation. The structure of the fibre-glass yarn is characterised by a low degree of friction. Hence, without the application of additional fixing agents, it would be readily displaceable and therefore destructible. Only by means of chemical additives which are sprayed, or

introduced in particular layers, is it possible to attain the desired constancy and other necessary serviceability characteristics. A total of 25 g of chemical additives per m² need to be allowed for, that is, $2000 \, \text{m}^2 \cdot 25 \, \text{g/m}^2 = 50 \, \text{kg}$ additives per roll. At an average price of DM 1.70/kg, the cost of these additives therefore amounts to DM 85.

(4) *Variable machine-hour costs.*

The production of a double roll takes 30 hours. In addition to the above material costs, variable costs of DM 10 per machine hour are incurred. Hence, the resultant variable machine-hour costs per roll are:

$$\tfrac{1}{2} \cdot 30 \, \text{hrs} \cdot (\text{DM } 10/\text{hr}) = \text{DM } 150.$$

(5) *Other variable costs* amount to DM 100 per roll.

The production process in question comprises 16 identical weaving machines. The *fixed costs* of running this process amount in total to DM 800 000 a year.

The variable costs per roll of glass-fleece which emerge from the previous information and calculations add up to:

$$k^v = 335 + 7.344 \cdot t_k + 1.634 \cdot t_s. \tag{4.175}$$

To calculate the *sales revenue q* per roll, it is necessary to know the square metre weight v of the glass-fleece output. It can be ascertained from the above calculations as follows: warp yarn and woof yarn required per 2000 m² roll weigh $1440 \cdot t_k + 380 \cdot t_s$ grammes. This represents $(0.72 \cdot t_k + 0.19 \cdot t_s) \cdot \text{g/m}^2$. Allowing for the chemical agents, the total weight of the glass fabric is $v = (25 + 0.72 \cdot t_k + 0.19 \cdot t_s) \text{g/m}^2$. The selling price per m² derived from (4.174) is therefore:

$$q_{\text{m}^2} = \text{DM} \, (-0.50 + 0.0072 \cdot t_k + 0.0019 \cdot t_s). \tag{4.176}$$

The price per roll is thus:

$$q = \text{DM} \, (-1000 + 14.4 \cdot t_k + 3.8 \cdot t_s). \tag{4.177}$$

The contribution per roll is ascertained from (4.175) and (4.176):

$$d = q - k^v = \text{DM} \, (-1335 + 7.056 \cdot t_k + 2.166 \cdot t_s). \tag{4.178}$$

Consequently, the equation for the break-even point is:

$$x_0 = \frac{800 \, 000}{-1335 + 7.056 \cdot t_k + 2.166 \cdot t_s} \quad \text{rolls.} \tag{4.179}$$

Variable costs (4.175), selling price (4.177), unit contribution (4.178) and break-even point (4.179) are a function of the yarn input qualities, the random variables t_k and t_s. The values resulting from three different illustrative quality combinations are given in Fig. 102.

In the present context, useful predictions can only be of a stochastic nature. Deterministically-known fixed costs are to be juxtaposed with the unit contribution specified by (4.178).

Example	1	2	3
Tex-no. of warp yarn	$t_k = 68$	$t_k = 60$	$t_k = 74$
Tex-no. of woof yarn	$t_s = 660$	$t_s = 562.11$	$t_s = 772.2$
Variable cost per roll (DM)	$k^v = 1912.83$	$k^v = 1694.13$	$k^v = 2140.23$
Weight of glass-fleece per m² (g)	$v = 199.36$	$v = 175$	$v = 225$
Selling price per m² of glass fleece (DM)	$q_{m^2} = 1.2436$	$q_{m^2} = 1$	$q_{m^2} = 1.50$
Selling price per roll (DM)	$q = 2487.20$	$q = 2000.02$	$q = 2999.96$
Contribution per roll (DM)	$d = 574.37$	$d = 305.89$	$d = 859.73$
Break-even point in rolls	$x_0 = 1393$	$x_0 = 2615$	$x_0 = 931$

Figure 102   Consequences of different gramme weights of glass fibre input yarn in glass fleece production

The unit contribution can be expressed in a simpler form. As the sum of two stochastic normally distributed random variables, it is itself a normally distributed random variable d. It has a mean of:

$$\mu_d = -1335 + 7.056\,\mu_k + 2.166\,\mu_s$$
$$= -1335 + 7.056 \cdot 68 + 2.166 \cdot 660 = 574.368. \tag{4.180}$$

and a variance σ_d^2 of:

$$\sigma_d^2 = 7.056^2 \cdot \sigma_k^2 + 2.166^2 \cdot \sigma_s^2 = 7.056^2 \cdot 6^2 + 2.166^2 \cdot 100^2$$
$$= 48\,707.897. \tag{4.181}$$

The standard deviation is therefore $\sigma_d = 220.699$.

Using the above transformations, concrete *stochastic break-even information* can be ascertained. There is no probabilistic information on sales conditions. The probability of reaching a break-even point cannot therefore be specified. However, the region in which the break-even point is located can be accurately characterised by resorting to the Geary–Hinkley transformation (4.172). As the fixed costs K^f are known deterministically, $\mu_K = 800\,000$ and $\sigma_K = 0$ are put into (4.172). In accordance with (4.172), the supplementary variable z for the break-even point x_0 then has the following form:

$$z = \mathfrak{z}(x_0) = \frac{x_0 \cdot \mu_d - \mu_K}{x_0 \cdot \sigma_d} = \frac{574.368 \cdot x_0 - 800\,000}{220.699 \cdot x_0}. \tag{4.182}$$

In the present case, the probabilities of negative unit contributions are negligible. Therefore, in accordance with (4.173), it can be assumed that the Geary–Hinkley transformed z is a normally distributed usable approximation. The approximation of the distribution function of a possible break-even point x_0 is thus:

$$p\{x_0 \leqslant \bar{x}_0\} \cong \Phi\,[\,\mathfrak{z}(\bar{x}_0)\,] = \Phi\left(\frac{574.368 \cdot \bar{x}_0 - 800\,000}{220.699 \cdot \bar{x}_0}\right). \tag{4.183}$$

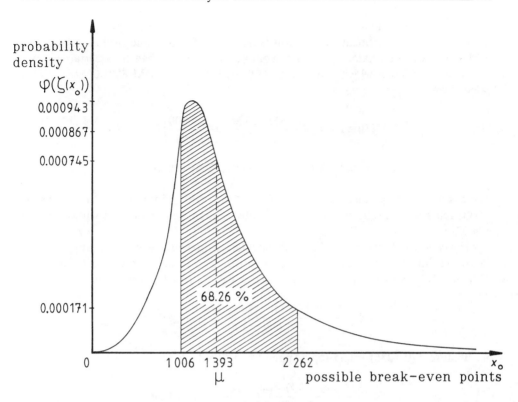

Figure 103 Probability density function for the break-even point in the example of glass fleece production

Hence, the approximation function for the probability density is:

$$p(x_0) \cong \frac{d\Phi}{d\zeta}[\zeta(x_0)] \cdot \frac{d\zeta}{dx}(x_0) = \varphi[\zeta(x_0)] \cdot \frac{800\,000}{220.699x_0^2}$$

(4.184)

$$= \varphi\left(\frac{574.368x_0 - 800\,000}{220.699x_0}\right) \cdot \frac{3\,624.847}{x_0^2}.$$

Fig. 103 is a graphical illustration of the probability distribution of the break-even point.

The results obtained can be used to calculate *break-even probabilities* for outputs that are of special interest. If, for example, it can be assumed with great certainty that an output of 1500 rolls can be sold in the year to be planned, the probability that the break-even point exceeds 1500 is of obvious interest. It amounts to (cp. Appendix II, Table A.1):

$$p\{x_0 > 1500\} \cong 1 - \Phi[\zeta(1500)] = 1 - \Phi(0.1859)$$
$$= 1 - 0.5737 = 0.4263 = 42.63\%.$$

There is thus a probability of 42.63% that, at a sales volume of 1500 rolls, the break-even point will not be attained. On the other hand, with a sales volume of 1500 rolls, there is a probability of 57.37% that the firm has already entered the profit region.

A second question concerns a *profit minimum*. If a satisfactory profit minimum for the production department in question is (say) DM 500 000, the probability that this profit level will be attained at a sales volume of 1500 rolls can be ascertained. With a contribution block which is now DM 1 300 000 instead of DM 800 000, the relevant calculation is:

$$p_2\{x_0 > 1500\} \cong 1 - \Phi\left(\frac{574.368 \cdot 1500 - 1\,300\,000}{220.699 \cdot 1500}\right)$$

$$= 1 - \Phi(-1.3244) = \Phi(1.3244) = 0.9073 = 90.73\%.$$

There is thus a probability exceeding 90% that the profit minimum of DM 500 000 will not be reached at a sales volume of 1500 rolls. The probability that it will be attained is 9.27%.

A *reversal* of the previous form of calculation provides ways of dealing with the following kind of question: what level of profit G will have a probability of at least 55% at a sales volume of 1500 rolls? In this case G satisfies the inequality:

$$\Phi\left(\frac{574.368 \cdot 1500 - (800\,000 + G)}{220.699 \cdot 1500}\right) \geqslant 0.55$$

or, because $\Phi(0.1256) = 0.55$ (cp. Appendix II, Table A.1):

$$\frac{574.368 \cdot 1500 - (800\,000 + G)}{220.699 \cdot 1500} \geqslant 0.1256.$$

Whence, $G \leqslant 19\,972$.

Consequently, the probability of attaining a minimum profit which exceeds DM 19 972 at a sales volume of 1500 rolls is less than 55%.

Finally, another type of question is concerned with the *level of output x* beyond which the break-even point can, for some specified probability, at least be attained. Assuming, for example, a minimum probability of 75%, then, since $\Phi(0.6744) = 0.75$, the required level of output is specified by:

$$\zeta(x) \geqslant 0.6744.$$

Using the transformation equation (4.182),

$$\frac{574.368 \cdot x - 800\,000}{220.699 \cdot x} \geqslant 0.6744$$

or,

$$x \geqslant \frac{800\,000}{574.368 - 220.699 \cdot 0.6744} = 1880.01.$$

At production levels exceeding approximately 1880 rolls, there is a probability of 75% that the break-even point will already have been attained or exceeded.

The above examples of probabilistic statements indicate that, by resorting to a *stochastic break-even analysis*, useful break-even predictions can also be gained in situations that are characterised by risk. In the example of glass-fleece production considered above, the risk in the situation is due to the uncertainty about the quality of the input material. This means, in turn, that variable costs, sales revenue and therefore unit contributions are not known deterministically and can only be defined on a probabilistic basis. The fixed costs are, however, unambiguous. The nature of the relevant considerations and computational procedure are also not affected by the need to treat fixed costs as a random variable or if, in addition to the material qualities, other additional determinants cause data ambiguities. If the resultant contribution block and unit contribution are both normally distributed, and the probability of negative contribution margins is comparatively slender, use can be made of the Geary–Hinkley transformation in the manner outlined above.

VIII. BREAK-EVEN ANALYSIS WITH DIFFERENT OBJECTIVES

1. Break-even Considerations in the Case of Non-Profit-making Objectives

In addition to the attaining of a predefined contribution block, other objectives may occupy an important place in a firm's goal system. Examples of other objectives include: a satisfactory liquidity level, a particular market share, an adequate sales revenue, some minimum level of costs, a prescribed level of capacity utilisation, high product quality and a desired degree of job satisfaction etc. More generally this can be a question of the formal, material, social or also ecological content of the goal system which is to be maximised, minimised, satisficed or driven to a predetermined point. An overview of the different possible forms of objectives has already been given in Chapter 3, Section II.4 (p. 30 et seq.).

The greater the importance that is attached to an objective in a firm's goal system, the greater is the apparent compulsion that it should be taken into account in break-even analyses. However, in many cases, non-profit-making objectives are not the exclusive individual goals of a firm. It is more frequently the case that they are simultaneously pursued in conjunction with other objectives. If so, it must then be decided whether a break-even analysis that is intended for use in the pursuit of a single objective still leads to usable results. This can be the case if the project which is the subject of the analysis (a) affects only a single goal in which case, the goal attainment levels of all other goals are effectively constant; or if, (b) in addition to its effect on a single goal, the project affects all other goals only to an insignificant extent. If this is not so, it is necessary to undertake a break-even analysis which simultaneously takes account of two or more prescribed goals. In this event, break-even analyses must be suitably modified. Appropriate modifications are discussed in sub-section 2 below.

On the other hand, if the intention is to pursue a single non-profit-making goal, the previously-described break-even methods can be applied without significant modification. Two examples have already been given in Chapter 2, Section II.4 which illustrate that, in the latter case, it is merely the interpretation of the contribution block and the contribution margins which changes. This is formally a question of applying the same instruments. A different interpretation is required as, and when, the "contribution block" and the "contribution margins" are perceived as positive and negative components respectively. As a related example, which also requires no modification in approach, the case of an insurance company, viewed from the perspective of the insurer was, among others, mentioned in Chapter 1. A further example in this category, but in which the effect on a social objective is to be evaluated, concerns the case of a firm in which, hitherto, a particular share of the profits was distributed annually to employees. It is now questioned whether this form of profit participation should not be replaced by another model. It is suggested that a greater number of employee shares should be issued but that, as a quid pro quo, no profit distributions in the form of cash should be made for a number of years. The paramount consideration is the effect on employee satisfaction. The issue of shares results in a considerable increase in employee satisfaction which, from a break-even standpoint, can be interpreted as a positive contribution block. On the other hand, each annual occasion on which, contrary to previous practice, the usual cash share of profit is not distributed will have a particular adverse effect on employee satisfaction. This negative factor can be regarded as a constituent contribution which slowly erodes the original contribution block. Using the usual terminology; it corresponds to the unit contribution. A break-even analysis of this problem would need to determine the number of years without profit distributions beyond which the initial increase in satisfaction is offset by the cumulative reduction in that initial increase. Apart from the fact that in cases of this kind, there are often particularly difficult problems of measurement, of data procurement, of data uncertainty and frequent difficulties stemming from the non-linearity in the behaviour of the relevant functions, this case nevertheless exemplifies the familiar definition of a break-even problem. Such a situation is amenable to a unidimensional basic form of break-even analysis and, in certain circumstances, also to a basic form of multiperiod analysis.

Break-even analysis based on *non-profit goals* is, at present, scarcely to be found in the literature. The few published cases of non-standard break-even applications have somewhat hesitatingly and cautiously detached themselves from the traditional profit orientation. It appears that instead of the usual magnitudes represented by output, revenues and costs, new components are apparently being introduced as determinants into break-even models rather than as goals. Examples of non-standard break-even applications which deserve special mention are the approaches of *Chmielewicz* (1972 [Qualitätsgestaltung]), *Larimore* (1974 [Education]) and *Nottingham* (1978 [Generators]). Chmielewicz continues to base his analysis on a profit goal but introduces *quality changes* as an independent variable in a new application of the break-even model (cp. Chmielewicz, 1972 [Qualitätsgestaltung] p. 601). In a break-even approach with which he analyses higher *education*, Larimore also takes account of qualitative influences and qualitative goals in addition to costs and revenues (cp. Larimore, 1974 [Education] p. 27). Nottingham's approach is concerned with the profitability of wind-powered *electricity generators*. As does Chmielewicz, he takes account of a physical determinant which cannot however be influenced, namely, average annual wind velocity. Using the basic break-even model he calculates, for alternative sizes of rotary blade, the break-even minimum wind velocity which must be guaranteed, at the location of the wind-driven generator, in order to render this method of electricity generation a profitable alternative (cp. Nottingham, 1978 [Generators] pp. 50, 52). Savings in outlays compared with those of the conventional method of electricity generation are used as a profitability criterion, i.e. an opportunity cost approach is used.

2. Break-even Analysis with Simultaneous Consideration of Multiple Goals

(a) General Presentation of Break-even Analysis with Multiple Goals

In each of the previously-described forms of break-even analysis, the break-even point was determined by a single break-even condition. In substance the break-even criterion is aligned with a goal, the minimum attainment of which is to be analysed. In the simplest case in which the break-even question is addressed to *multiple goals*, a multiplicity of formally identical calculations can be undertaken. The individual break-even point for each individual goal is then ascertained by reference to its contribution block and the related components (or individually relevant magnitudes). If each goal has a unique individual break-even point, it follows that the highest individual break-even point specifies the level of output (more generally the value of the determinant) above which the minimum level of all goals is simultaneously attained.

This simple approach is not possible if, rather than a single break-even point, one or more goals has a complete break-even line or break-even hyperplane. Furthermore, the simple route just described is closed off if the attainment levels are mutually dependent. In such cases, a simultaneous multi-goal break-even analysis is necessary. If the relationships are linear it is appropriate to use a *linear programming model*. The use of such approaches in the break-even context was first proposed by *Charnes, Cooper and Ijiri* (1963 [Break-even Budgeting] p. 19 et seq., p. 22 et seq.); *Ijiri* (1965 [Goals] p. 44 et seq.); and *Schweitzer and Trossmann* (1980 [Break-even-Analyse] p. 34 et seq.).

Simultaneous break-even analysis with multiple goals is illustrated in the remainder of this section by reference to the example of the multiproduct firm that was the subject of the multiproduct break-even analysis in Section 4.II.2 (cp. p. 119 et seq.). The firm's feasible output region is indicated by Fig. 46. In addition to the contributions given by the function

$$D = 8 \cdot x_1 + 5.5 \cdot x_2,$$

which is intended to cover fixed costs of DM 16 000, two further predetermined goals are to be taken into account. These are intended to indicate output levels at which a minimum level of *liquidity* or minimum level of *sales revenue* is guaranteed. In the case of product 1 it is assumed that, after covering (variable) payments per unit, liquidity amounting to DM 11 per unit remains. The corresponding unit liquidity contribution for product 2 is DM 3. The intention is to cover a block amounting to DM 15 000 with these liquidity contributions. The liquidity function is:

$$L = 11 \cdot x_1 + 3 \cdot x_2.$$

Additionally, a minimum target sales revenue of DM 80 000 is to be provided for. The unit sales revenue of products 1 and 2 are DM 20 and DM 50 respectively. The related sales revenue function is:

$$E = 20 \cdot x_1 + 50 \cdot x_2.$$

The three linear functions for the recovery of the minimum contribution, minimum liquidity and minimum sales revenue respectively are illustrated in two-dimensional space in Fig. 104.

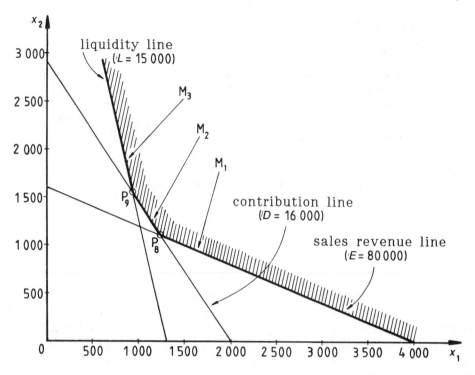

Figure 104   Break-even set in a three-goal situation

In extending the break-even analysis in the latter respects, the intention is to ascertain the output levels at which the contribution, liquidity and sales revenue requirements are satisfied in like manner. This means finding points in the admissible output region which simultaneously lie on each of the three linear functions that characterise the contribution, liquidity and sales revenue minima respectively. However, such a point only exists in an exceptional case, namely, one in which all three linear functions intersect at one point. The break-even analysis needs to be reformulated when applied to the general multi-goal case:

The output levels that are sought are those at which the satisficing level of at least one of the objective functions is *exactly* attained; and, at which the other objective functions are at *least* attained (or exceeded).

Figure 104 indicates that the break-even set M comprises three parts which are partitioned by the intersection points P_8 and P_9:

$$M = M_1 \cup M_2 \cup M_3$$
$$M_1 := \{(x_1, x_2) \in \mathbb{R}_+^2 \mid 20x_1 + 50x_2 = 80\,000$$
$$\text{and } 8x_1 + 5.5x_2 \geqslant 16\,000$$
$$\text{and } 11x_1 + 3x_2 \geqslant 15\,000\}$$
$$M_2 := \{(x_1, x_2) \in \mathbb{R}_+^2 \mid 8x_1 + 5.5x_2 = 16\,000$$
$$\text{and } 11x_1 + 3x_2 \geqslant 15\,000$$
$$\text{and } 20x_1 + 50x_2 \geqslant 80\,000\}$$
$$M_3 := \{(x_1, x_2) \in \mathbb{R}_+^2 \mid 11x_1 + 3x_2 = 15\,000$$
$$\text{and } 8x_1 + 5.5x_2 \geqslant 16\,000$$
$$\text{and } 20x_1 + 50x_2 \geqslant 80\,000\}. \qquad (4.185)$$

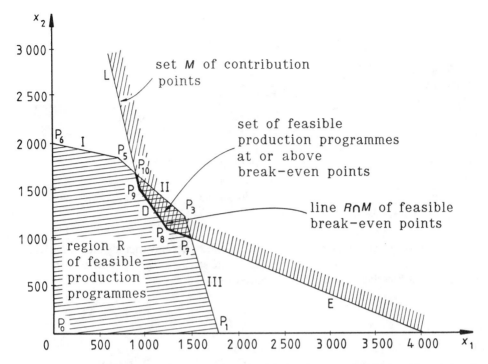

Figure 105 Graphical presentation of the set of feasible break-even points in a multi-goal situation

The sub-set M_1 denotes those output levels at which the minimum sales revenue is exactly attained, but at which the satisficing levels of the other two objectives are however exceeded. At P_8 both the minimum contribution and the minimum sales revenue are exactly attained but the minimum liquidity level is exceeded. The output levels in sub-set M_2 denote situations in which the minimum contribution is exactly attained whilst, in sub-set M_3, liquidity takes on its lower limit.

As yet no consideration has been given to the question of whether the outputs which correspond to the contribution points in set M are actually feasible. The set M must therefore be compared with the solution region R of admissible output levels (cp. Fig. 46) in order to obtain the feasible break-even points $R \cap M$. In Fig. 105 these feasible break-even points are denoted by the links between the points P_7, P_8, P_9 and P_{10}. In this case the break-even points form a combination of several (linear) frontier lines but in general they are depicted by a break-even hyperplane.

(b) Computation of the Break-even Hyperplane in the Case of Multiple Goals

As in the case of a single goal in a multiproduct situation, the feasible break-even points for multiple goals can also be computed with a linear programming model (cp. Schweitzer and Trossmann, 1980 [Break-even-Analyse] p. 37 et seq.). Different approaches to the latter problem are conceivable. If it is desirable to ascertain the break-even points on the frontier P_7 to P_{10} in Fig. 105 without discriminating further, a three-stage approach is possible. In the first stage the sales revenue is taken as the objective function whilst the contribution and liquidity goals enter the model as constraints. In other respects this model represents the same route that is taken when there is a single objective function. It runs as follows:

Minimise $x_{10} + x_{11}$
subject to

$$
\begin{array}{lll}
6x_1 + 27x_2 + x_3 & = 54\,000 & \\
6x_1 + 7x_2 + x_4 & = 16\,800 & \text{Constraints} \\
20x_1 + 6x_2 + x_5 & = 36\,000 &
\end{array}
$$

$$
\begin{array}{lll}
8x_1 + 5.5x_2 - x_7 & = 16\,000 \text{ (D)} & \\
11x_1 + 3x_2 - x_9 & = 15\,000 \text{ (L)} & \text{Objectives} \\
20x_1 + 50x_2 + x_{10} - x_{11} = 80\,000 \text{ (E)} & \leftarrow \text{Main objective}
\end{array}
$$

and: x_1 to x_5, x_7, x_9 to x_{11} non-negative. (4.186)

The solution to this model yields points P_7 and P_8, and thereby the complete link between them, as feasible break-even points. In the second stage the contribution is chosen as the main objective function. The procedure is:

Minimise $x_6 + x_7$
subject to

$$
\begin{array}{lll}
6x_1 + 27x_2 + x_3 & = 54\,000 & \\
6x_1 + 7x_2 + x_4 & = 16\,800 & \text{Constraints} \\
20x_1 + 6x_2 + x_5 & = 36\,000 &
\end{array}
$$

$$
\begin{array}{lll}
8x_1 + 5.5x_2 + x_6 - x_7 & = 16\,000 \text{ (D)} & \leftarrow \text{Main objective} \\
11x_1 + 3x_2 - x_9 & = 15\,000 \text{ (L)} & \text{Objectives} \\
20x_1 + 50x_2 - x_{11} & = 80\,000 \text{ (E)} &
\end{array}
$$

and: x_1 to x_7, x_9, x_{11} non-negative. (4.187)

The solution values of P_8 and P_9 are also obtained in this stage and so too, therefore, is the link between the two.

Finally, in the third stage, liquidity can be chosen as the main objective function. This stage, which corresponds to the procedure in (4.188), yields solution values for P_9 and P_{10}. The complete set $R \cap M$ of all feasible contribution points is ascertained in this way:

Minimise $x_8 + x_9$
subject to

$$
\begin{array}{lll}
6x_1 + 27x_2 + x_3 & = 54\,000 & \\
6x_1 + 7x_2 + x_4 & = 16\,800 & \text{Constraints} \\
20x_1 + 6x_2 + x_5 & = 36\,000 &
\end{array}
$$

$$
\begin{array}{lll}
8x_1 + 5.5x_2 - x_7 & = 16\,000 \text{ (D)} & \\
11x_1 + 3x_2 + x_8 - x_9 & = 15\,000 \text{ (L)} & \text{Objectives} \\
20x_1 + 50x_2 - x_{11} & = 80\,000 \text{ (E)} & \text{Main objective}
\end{array}
$$

and: x_1 to x_5, x_7 to x_9, x_{11} non-negative. (4.188)

Instead of computing the entire break-even set, the deviation of the values of all goals from their prescribed values can be minimised by using the following formulation:

Minimise $x_7 + x_9 + x_{11}$
subject to

$$
\begin{aligned}
6x_1 + 27x_2 + x_3 & = 54\,000 \\
6x_1 + 7x_2 \quad + x_4 & = 16\,800 \\
20x_1 + 6x_2 \qquad + x_5 & = 36\,000
\end{aligned}
\left.\right\} \text{Constraints}
$$

$$
\begin{aligned}
8x_1 + 5.5x_2 \qquad\quad - x_7 & = 16\,000 \text{ (D)} \\
11x_1 + 3x_2 \qquad\qquad - x_9 & = 15\,000 \text{ (L)} \\
20x_1 + 50x_2 \qquad\qquad - x_{11} & = 80\,000 \text{ (E)}
\end{aligned}
\left.\right\} \text{Objectives}
$$

and: x_1 to x_5, x_7, x_9, x_{11} non-negative. (4.189)

In contrast to the other linear programming models formulated above, the latter procedure generally provides only a single solution point. It lies on the kinked frontier line P_7 to P_{10}. This is due to the fact that, in the latter case, an objective function is adopted which comprises three goal-elements that have an implicit equal weighting. If, instead of (1, 1, 1), other weights are chosen as goal coefficients for the variables x_7, x_9, x_{11}, each of the points on the kinked frontier line P_7 to P_{10} can be obtained as a solution value.

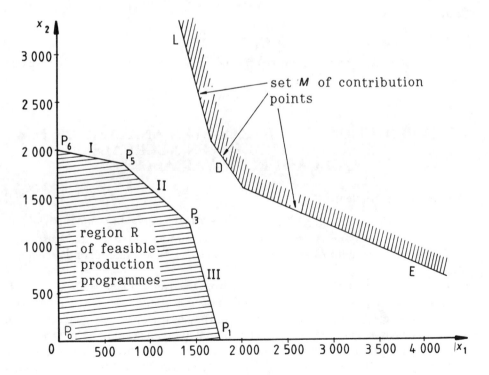

Figure 106 Set of contribution points in the multi-goal situation lying outside the solution region

This method breaks down if all the contribution points lie *outside* the region represented by the feasible output set R. For example, if the liquidity contribution block, contribution block and minimum sales revenue are DM 24 000, DM 25 000 and DM 120 000 respectively, the complete set M of contribution points lies outside the solution region R (cp. Fig. 106).

Consequently the set of feasible break-even points $R \cap M$ is empty. If, however, the question is which of the feasible output combinations most nearly approaches the prescribed objectives, a weighting of the sub-goals is again necessary—assuming the intention is to determine the goal deviations of the three goal components from a single objective function. In that event, a linear optimising method can be used to minimise the goal deviations. Using equal weights it is as follows:

Minimise $x_6 + x_7 + x_8 + x_9 + x_{10} + x_{11}$
subject to

$$
\begin{aligned}
6x_1 + 27x_2 + x_3 & = 54\,000 \\
6x_1 + 7x_2 + x_4 & = 16\,800 \\
20x_1 + 6x_2 + x_5 & = 36\,000 \\
\\
8x_1 + 5.5x_2 + x_6 - x_7 & = 25\,000 \text{ (D)} \\
11x_1 + 3x_2 + x_8 - x_9 & = 24\,000 \text{ (L)} \\
20x_1 + 50x_2 + x_{10} - x_{11} & = 120\,000 \text{ (E)}
\end{aligned}
$$

and: x_1 to x_{11} non-negative.   (4.190)

If the sub-goals are of greater or less significance in a firm's goal system, their weights can be varied accordingly.

IX. IMPLICATIONS FOR BREAK-EVEN ANALYSIS OF THE RELATIONSHIP BETWEEN ACCRUALS AND CASH FLOW VARIABLES

1. Nature of the Problem

As mentioned previously, empirical analyses of the single and multiperiod realtionships between conventionally-measured "accruals" accounting variables and cash flow variables have important implications for both single-period and multiperiod break-even analyses.

One of the main conclusions which emerges from the overall analysis of the accruals–cash flow relationship is that periodic accruals measures of historic cost profit generally *overstate* periodic earnings measured on a cash flow basis. The likely consequence of this overstatement is that break-even points computed on an accruals accounting basis will generally *understate* those that are derived from a cash flow break-even computation. Hence, the consistent attainment of a "conventionally-computed" break-even level of output will not ensure that a firm consistently attains a break-even level of cash flow, i.e. is self-financing. This and other related propositions are elaborated below.

2. Formal Analysis

(a) Structure of the Problem

Historic cost profit, G_j, measured on an entity basis, i.e. excluding interest expense, for any period j is given by:

$$G_j = E_j - (I_{j-1} + K_j - I_j) - W_j - T_{j+1} + (Y_j - X_j) \qquad (4.191)$$

where,

E_j denotes accrued sales in year j;

I_{j-1}, I_j denote inventory book values at the beginning and end of year j;

K_j is total revenue expenditure in year j;

W_j stands for depreciation based on historic cost in year j;

T_{j+1} denotes corporation tax charged in period j that is payable in period $j+1$; and,

$Y_j - X_j$ denotes the accounting profit on assets displaced (X_j represents their written down book value).

A firm's cash flow statement for any year j can be represented as:

$$(C_j - Z_j) - (J_j + Q_j - Y_j) - H_j - T_j \equiv (l_j - m_j) + (s_j - N_j - w_j) \qquad (4.192)$$

that is

entity cash flows $\equiv$ shareholder cash flows + lender cash flows

or, $\text{ENCF}_j \quad \equiv \quad \text{SHCF}_j \quad + \text{LCF}_j \quad$ where:

$C_j - Z_j$ denotes operating cash flow in year j represented by cash collected from customers, C_j, and operating payments, Z_j;

$J_j + Q_j - Y_j$ stands for replacement investment, J_j, growth investment, Q_j, and the proceeds from assets displaced, Y_j, in year j;

H_j denotes liquidity change in year j;

T_j stands for all taxes assessed on the corporation that are actually paid in year j;

l_j represents dividends paid to shareholders in year j;

m_j is equity capital raised or repaid in year j;

s_j represents period j interest payments;

N_j is medium and/or long-term debt raised or repaid in year j; and,

w_j is short-term debt raised or repaid in year j.

Whereas the variables contained in a firm's periodic cash flow statement can be specified in a wholly objective manner, its classification is intended to facilitate interpretation. A multiperiod version of the left-hand side of (4.192) discloses economic information on three separate decision areas, namely, trading and production, capital investment and liquidity. It can also reveal the effective incidence of taxation on corporate cash flows. The right-hand side provides information on dividend and debt/equity financing policies. In other words, the left-hand side of a multiperiod version of (4.192) is concerned with economic performance whereas the right-hand side has to do with matters of financial policy (over which management can perhaps exercise considerable discretion), namely, the levels of dividends and debt financing respectively.

Deducting the left-hand side of (4.192) from (4.191) (ignoring taxes) gives:

$$G_j - ENCF_j = (E_j - C_j) + (I_j - I_{j-1}) - (K_j - Z_j) + (J_j + Q_j - W_j - X_j) + H_j \qquad (4.193)$$

that is,

$G_j - ENCF_j =$ periodic change in periodic working capital investment (receivables, inventories and payables) + periodic depreciation shortfall + periodic liquidity change.

In an economy in which persistent inflation is characterised by a dispersion of (mainly) positive price changes (expressed in money terms), and, as a rule, real growth in gross domestic product, all five terms in the previous expression will normally take on positive values so that, in general: $G_j > ENCF_j$. This contention is elucidated in the following paragraphs.

(b) Periodic Working Capital Investment

If outstanding receivables usually constitute the proportion Φ of the previous year's sales, sales receipts, C_j, are given by

$$C_j = \Phi E_{j-1} + (1 - \Phi)E_j. \qquad (4.194)$$

But if,

$$E_j = E_{j-1}(1 + v_j)(1 + sp_j) \qquad (4.195)$$

where, v_j and sp_j denote the respective rates of change in sales volume and selling prices in year j,

then,

$$C_j = \Phi E_{j-1} + (1 - \Phi)E_{j-1}(1 + v_j)(1 + sp_j) \qquad (4.196)$$

and,

$$E_j - C_j = \Phi E_{j-1}[(1 + v_j)(1 + sp_j) - 1] \qquad (4.197)$$

If Φ, v_j, and sp_j are positive so too is the periodic change, $E_j - C_j$, in receivables. Since Φ is virtually always at least equal to zero, the sufficient condition for $E_j - C_j > 0$ is, for all practical purposes, $(1 + v_j) \cdot (1 + sp_j) - 1 > 0$. The latter condition is obviously satisfied for many pairs of values of v_j and sp_j with opposite signs, e.g. increasing volume and decreasing selling prices and vice versa. Thus, if $v_j = 0.05$, $(1 + v_j)(1 + sp_j) - 1 > 0$, provided $sp_j > 1.05^{-1} - 1 (= -0.04762)$.

Turning to the periodic change, $I_j - I_{j-1}$, in inventory value; let $I_{j-1} = IV_{j-1} \cdot UC_{j-1}$ and $I_j = IV_j \cdot UC_j$, where, IV_{j-1}, IV_j denote inventory volumes at the beginning and end of year j respectively; and, UC_{j-1}, UC_j represent *unit* inventory book values at the beginning and end of year j respectively.

If $v_j > 0$, IV_j will normally exceed IV_{j-1}, and, given rising prices, UC_j is normally greater than UC_{j-1}. Hence, generally under inflation and conditions of economic growth, $IV_j \cdot UC_j > IV_{j-1} \cdot UC_{j-1}$ that is $I_j - I_{j-1} > 0$. But more generally $I_j - I_{j-1} > 0$ when $(UC_j / UC_{j-1}) \cdot (IV_j / IV_{j-1}) - 1 > 0$. This condition is satisfied for many pairs of values of the periodic rate of inventory volume change, $(UC_j / UC_{j-1}) - 1$, and the periodic rate of unit inventory value change, $(IV_j / IV_{j-1}) - 1$, with opposite signs.

The periodic change, $K_j - Z_j$, in payables *countervails* the periodic changes in receivables and inventories to a greater or lesser degree, and may be analysed as follows.

Total accrued revenue expenditure, K_j, is a cost function of the form

$$K_j = K^f_{j-1}(1 + p^f_j) + K^v_{j-1}(1 + v_j)(1 + p^v_j) \tag{4.198}$$

where,

K^f_{j-1} denotes fixed operating costs incurred in year $j - 1$;
K^v_{j-1} stands for total variable costs incurred in year $j - 1$;
p^f_j represents the rate of change in fixed costs in year j (compared with year $j - 1$); and,
p^v_j is the rate of change in unit variable costs in year j (compared with year $j - 1$).

Thus, if outstanding payables usually constitute the proportion γ of the previous year's accrued revenue expenditure, operating payments, Z_j, are given by:

$$Z_j = \gamma K_{j-1} + (1 - \gamma) K_j \tag{4.199}$$

But if, $\qquad\qquad p^f_j, p^v_j \qquad$ and $\qquad v_j > 0,$

then, $\qquad\qquad K_j > K_{j-1}$

and, $\qquad\qquad Z_j < K_j \quad$ or $\quad K_j - Z_j > 0.$

(c) Periodic Depreciation Shortfall (Excess of Periodic Capital Expenditure over Periodic Depreciation)

Although embodied technological progress reduces the real cost of successive generations of assets, unit capital expenditure generally increases in money terms over time, i.e. at a rate g'_j which is less than the rate of inflation g_j. Thus, even if a firm's scale of operating capacity remains constant over time, historic cost depreciation policy will usually generate a sequence of periodic depreciation charges each of which falls short of the corresponding periodic capital expenditure. If capital expenditure increases in real terms over time, the depreciation shortfall will be commensurately higher.

The foregoing contentions can be illustrated as follows:

Let the capital expenditure incurred at end-years 0, 1, 2, . . . , n by a firm commencing business at end-year 0 be:

$$CE_0, \; CE_0(1+g'), \; CE_0(1+g')^2, \; . \; . \; ., \; CE_0(1+g')^n,$$

where g' is the annual rate of increase in fixed asset prices expressed in money terms. Assume that each of these expenditures is written off over n years.

In period n a fixed installment depreciation policy will result in a depreciation charge W_n, given by:

$$W_n = \frac{CE_0}{n} + \frac{CE_0(1+g')}{n} + \frac{CE_0(1+g')^2}{n} + \cdots$$

$$+ \frac{CE_0(1+g')^{n-1}}{n} = \frac{CE_0}{n}\left[\frac{(1+g')^n - 1}{g'}\right] \tag{4.200}$$

compared with capital expenditure of $CE_0(1+g')^n$ in that period. A comparison of the latter two expressions, the second factor of each of which is a standard mathematical function for which there are readily accessible published tabular values, reveals that for positive values of g',

$$CE_0(1+g')^n > \frac{CE_0}{n}\left[\frac{(1+g')^n - 1}{g'}\right].$$

If capital expenditure increases in some real or physical sense by an annual scale factor u, the depreciation shortfall will obviously be proportionately higher than in the previous case since it reflects the relationship:

$$CE_0(1+g'')^n > \frac{CE_0}{n}\left[\frac{(1+g'')^n - 1}{g''}\right] \tag{4.201}$$

where $g'' = (1+u)(1+g') - 1$.

(d) Periodic Change in Liquidity

Apropos of the periodic change in liquidity, H_j; it can be stated that on the general assumption that firms maintain liquidity for transactions, precautionary and speculative motives, H_j can, for example, reasonably be assumed to be a direct function of real sales volume growth. If the latter condition constitutes the general case, real liquidity will increase by an annual increment $-H_j(1+g_j)$, where g_j denotes the rate of inflation in year j.

(e) Summary: Periodic Differences between Accruals and Cash Flows

The characteristic excess of G_j over $ENCF_j$ is a function of at least ten variables. These are:

(1) the value of Φ (which reflects the period of credit allowed to customers),
(2) the periodic rate of sales volume change v_j,
(3) the periodic rate of selling price change sp_j,
(4) the periodic rate of inventory volume change $(IV_j/IV_{j-1})-1$,
(5) the periodic rate of unit inventory value change $(UC_j/UC_{j-1})-1$,
(6) the value of γ (which reflects the period of credit allowed by suppliers),
(7) the periodic rates of change, p_j^f, p_j^v, in fixed and variable costs respectively,
(8) the periodic liquidity change H_j (which is a function of anticipated transactions and inflation),
(9) the periodic rate of change, g_j', in asset prices,
(10) the periodic rate of change, u_j, in the scale of capital expenditure.

In short,

$$G_j - ENCF_j = f\,[\Phi,\ v_j,\ sp_j,\ (IV_j/IV_{j-1}),\ (UC_j/UC_{j-1}),\ \gamma,\ p_j^f,\ p_j^v,\ H_j,\ g_j',\ u_j].$$
(4.202)

Empirical analysis generally confirms that, in a world of economic growth and rising prices, γ, p_j^f and p_j^v are usually more than offset by the seven other variables so that $G_j > ENCF_j$. As can also be corroborated empirically, $G_j/ENCF_j$ is neither equal across firms nor constant over time in the case of the individual firm.

(f) Cumulative G_j and Cumulative $ENCF_j$ over the Full Lifetime of a Firm

It follows from the foregoing analysis that, if a firm has a finite life of n years, its total profit (before interest), $\Sigma_{j=1}^{n} G_j$, is given by:

$$\sum_{j=1}^{n} G_j = \sum_{j=1}^{n} [E_j - (I_{j-1} + K_j - I_j) - W_j - T_j + (Y_j - X_j)]$$
(4.203a)

$$= \sum_{j=1}^{n} [(C_j - Z_j) - (J_j + Q_j - Y_j) - T_j - H_j]$$

$$+ \sum_{j=1}^{n} (E_j - C_j) + I_j - \sum_{j=1}^{n} (K_j - Z_j)$$

$$+ \sum_{j=1}^{n} (J_j + Q_j - W_j - X_j) + \sum_{j=1}^{n} H_j$$
(4.203b)

The last five terms denote the end-year n balance sheet values of: receivables, inventory, payables, written down book values and liquidity respectively. Hence, whatever values these items actually realise, total historic cost profit $\Sigma_{j=1}^{n} G_j$ will equal total entity cash flows, $\Sigma_{j=1}^{n} ENCF_j$, since any difference between recorded and realised end-year n net asset values requires both (4.203a) and (4.203b) to be adjusted accordingly.

If recorded end-year n net asset values are exactly realised, the terminal year profit, G_n, and terminal year entity cash flows, $ENCF_j$, are respectively given by:

$$G_n = E_n - (I_{n-1} + K_n - I_n) - W_n - T_n - (Y_n - X_n)$$
(4.204)

and

$$ENCF_n = E_n - (I_{n-1} + K_n - I_n) - W_n - T_n - (Y_n - X_n) + \sum_{j=1}^{n-1} (E_j - C_j) + I_{j-1}$$

$$+ \sum_{j=1}^{n-1} (K_j - Z_j) + \sum_{j=1}^{n-1} (I_j + K_j - L_j - X_j) + \sum_{j=1}^{n-1} H_j \qquad (4.205)$$

The algebraic sum of the last five terms on the right-hand side of (4.205) constitute the cumulative excess, $\sum_{j=1}^{n-1} G_j - \sum_{j=1}^{n-1} ENCF_j$, of historic cost profit over entity cash flows during the first $n-1$ years of the firm's life. That is to say, the equality of $\sum_{j=1}^{n} G_j$ and $\sum_{j=1}^{n} ENCF_j$ will generally require a significant excess of the terminal year entity cash flow $ENCF_n$ over the terminal year profit G_n.

3. Empirical Analysis

Notes for Figures 107(a)–109(c).

(1) *Accruals measures*

Pre-depreciation profit	$= E_j - (I_{j-1} + K_j - I_j) + Y_j$
Pre-tax entity profit	$= E_j - (I_{j-1} + K_j - I_j) - W_j + (Y_j - X_j)$
Post-tax profit (before interest)	$= E_j - (I_{j-1} + K_j - I_j) - W_j + (Y_j - X_j)$ $\quad - T_{j+1}$
Interest expense	$= s_j$
Post-tax profit	$= E_j - (I_{j-1} + K_j - I_j) - W_j - T_{j+1} - s_j$ $\quad + (Y_j - X_j)$
Retained earnings	$= E_j - (I_{j-1} + K_j - I_j) - W_j - T_{j+1} - s_j$ $\quad + (Y_j - X_j) - l_j$

(2) *Cash flow measures*

Operating cash flow	$= C_j - Z_j$
Capital expenditure	$= J_j + Q_j - Y_j$
Liquidity change	$= H_j$
Pre-tax entity cash flow	$= (C_j - Z_j) - (J_j + Q_j - Y_j) - H_j$
Post-tax entity cash flow	$= (C_j - Z_j) - (J_j + Q_j - Y_j) - H_j - T_j$
Real interest	$= s_j - gMV_{j-1}^{(\text{debt})}$
Earned for equity	$= (C_j - Z_j) - (J_j + Q_j - Y_j) - H_j - T_j$ $\quad - [s_j - gMV_{j-1}^{(\text{debt})}]$
Dividends (net of new equity)	$= l_j - m_j$
Real debt reduction (deficit)	$= (C_j - Z_j) - (J_j + Q_j - Y_j) - H_j - T_j$ $\quad - [s_j - gMV_{j-1}^{(\text{debt})}] - (l_j - m_j)$

[$MV_j^{(\text{debt})}$ denotes market value of debt at end-year j]

(3) *Original sources of data.* Figures 107(a) and 107(b): Department of Trade and Industry, Cardiff, UK, 1986. Figures 108(a), 108(b) and 109(c): *Flow of Funds Accounts*, Board of Governors of the Federal Reserve System, Washington DC, 1986. Figure 109(a): Data Bank, University of Augsburg, Federal Republic of Germany, 1982. Figure 109(b): *Annual Abstract of Statistics* (various editions) UK.

(4) *Profits and Cash Flows of Federal German, UK and US Companies.*

Pre-depreciation profit	1000	911	Operating cash flow
Depreciation	291	538	Capital expenditure
		65	Liquidity change
Pre-tax entity profit	709	308	Pre-tax entity cash flow
Tax charged at 29%	204	186	Tax paid at 60%
Post-tax profit (before interest)	505	122	Post-tax entity cash flow
Interest expense	192	64	Real interest
Post-tax profit	313	58	Earned for equity
Dividends (51%)	160	29	Dividends (net of new equity) (50%)
Retained earnings	153	29	Real debt reduction

Figure 107(a) DTI: large listed manufacturing companies 1978–84 accruals and cash flows expressed at June 1984 prices

Pre-depreciation profit	1000	907	Operating cash flow
Depreciation	222	547	Capital expenditure
		125	Liquidity change
Pre-tax entity profit	778	235	Pre-tax entity cash flow
Tax charged at 28%	214	142	Tax paid at 60%
Post-tax profit (before interest)	564	93	Post-tax entity cash flow
Interest expense	174	49	Real interest
Post-tax profit	390	44	Earned for equity
Dividends (44%)	170	42	Dividends (net of new equity) (95%)
Retained earnings	220	2	Real debt reduction

Figure 107(b) DTI: large listed non-manufacturing companies 1978–84 accruals and cash flows expressed at June 1984 prices

Pre-depreciation profit	1000	892	Operating cash flow
Depreciation	338	510	Capital expenditure
		38	Liquidity change
Pre-tax entity profit	662	344	Pre-tax entity cash flow
Tax charged at 28%†	185	189	Tax paid at 55%†
Post-tax profit (before interest)	477	155	Post-tax entity cash flow
Interest expense	226	110	Real interest
Post-tax profit	251	45	Earned for equity
Dividends (36%*)	90	88	Dividends* (net of new equity) (200%)
Retained earnings	161	(43)	Real debt-financed deficit

*Net of dividend tax at the rate of 30% to afford comparisons with the UK data.
†Including dividend tax.

Figure 108(a) US non-financial corporate business 1977–82 accruals and cash flows expressed at June 1984 prices

Pre-depreciation profit	1000	904	Operating cash flow
Depreciation	373	498	Capital expenditure
		48	Liquidity change
Pre-tax entity profit	627	358	Pre-tax entity cash flow
Tax charged at 30%†	188	171	Tax paid at 48%†
Post-tax profit (before interest)	439	187	Post-tax entity cash flow
Interest expense	240	140	Real interest
Post-tax profit	199	47	Earned for equity
Dividends (46%*)	92	102	Dividends* (net of new equity) (217%)
Retained earnings	107	(55)	Real debt-financed deficit

*Net of dividend tax at the rate of 30% to afford comparisons with the UK data.
†Including dividend tax.

Figure 108(b) US non-financial corporate business 1978–84 accruals and cash flows expressed at June 1984 prices

Pre-depreciation profit	1000	981	Operating cash flow
Depreciation	404	558	Capital expenditure
		29	Liquidity change
Pre-tax entity profit	596	394	Pre-tax entity cash flow
Tax charged at 50%†	297	297	Tax paid at 76%
Post-tax profit (before interest)	299	97	Post-tax entity cash flow
Interest expense	126	60	Real interest
Post-tax profit	173	37	Earned for equity
Dividends (76%*)	132	56	Dividends (net of new equity) (151%)
Retained earnings	41	(19)	Real debt-financed deficit

Figure 109(a) Profits and cash flows of the 100 largest German AG companies (excluding banks and insurance companies): averages of values for 1967–77 which were first expressed at 1977 prices

Pre-depreciation profit	1000	839	Operating cash flow
Depreciation	235	444	Capital expenditure
		27	Liquidity change
Pre-tax entity profit	765	368	Pre-tax entity cash flow
Tax charged at 33%†	250	250	Tax paid at 68%
Post-tax profit (before interest)	515	118	Post-tax entity cash flow
Interest expense	97	17	Real interest
Post-tax profit	418	101	Earned for equity
Dividends (34%*)	141	128	Dividends (net of new equity) (127%)
Retained earnings	277	(27)	Real debt-financed deficit

Figure 109(b) Profits and cash flows of UK quoted manufacturing companies: averages of values for 1954–77 which were first expressed at 1974 prices

Pre-depreciation profit	1000	883	Operating cash flow
Depreciation	338	530	Capital expenditure
		32	Liquidity change
Pre-tax entity profit	662	321	Pre-tax entity cash flow
Tax charged at 42%†	281	281	Tax paid at 88%†
Post-tax profit			
(before interest)	381	40	Post-tax entity cash flow
Interest expense	112	25	Real interest
Post-tax profit	269	15	Earned for equity
Dividends (38%*)	101	75	Dividends* (net of new equity) (500%)
Retained earnings	168	(60)	Real debt-financed deficit

*Net of dividend tax at the rate of 30% to afford comparisons with the UK data.
†Including dividend tax.

Figure 109(c)   Profits and cash flows of US non-financial corporate business averages of values for 1949–80 which were first expressed at 1980 prices

The results of a number of empirical studies on the relationship between accruals variables and cash flow variables have been reported in the literature (cp. Lawson, 1982 [Woolworth]; Lawson and Stark, 1981 [Inflation]; and Lawson, Möller and Sherer, 1982 [Verwendung]). Relevant data for the USA, UK and FRG covering different periods and at varying levels of aggregation are summarised in Figs 107(a), 107(b), 108(a), 108(b), 109(a), 109(b) and 109(c) which contain multiperiod averages.

In deriving the latter averages the data of each individual year were first restated at a base-year price level using indexation factors which measure changes in the purchasing power of money. It should be emphasised that such a transformation is wholly intended to reveal the multiperiod relative orders of magnitude of the accruals–cash flow relationship and is not an exercise in inflation-adjusted accounting. It is, indeed, questionable whether historic cost profits have a significant economic content and therefore equally dubious whether the restatement of a time-series of historic profits at a base-year price level is economically meaningful other than for the purpose that the restatement is used in the present context.

A second feature of the data summarised in Figs 107(a), 107(b), 108(a), 108(b), 109(a), 109(b) and 109(c) which should be clarified is the partitioning of the accrued interest expense (left-hand column) into real interest and the repayment of lenders' principal (cp. Modigliani and Cohn, 1978 [Financial Analysts Journal]). The average (annual) amount of the latter (expressed at a base-year level) is included in the last line of the right-hand column.

The lenders' principal element of interest expense, RLP_j, is initially computed, i.e. before being restated at a base-year price level, as follows:

$$RLP_j = (\text{annual inflation rate in year } j) \cdot (\text{market value of debt at the beginning of year } j)$$

In the context of break-even analysis the significance of the accruals–cash flow relationship also depends upon the definition of the contribution block from which the break-even point is to be derived. Comparisons of the corresponding accruals and cash flow sub-categories shown in Figs 107(a), 107(b), 108(a), 108(b), 109(a), 109(b) and 109(c) strongly suggest that, regardless of the level at which it is defined, a contribution block specified on an accruals basis will generally constitute a lower break-even target than will that of its cash flow counterpart. This conclusion is corroborated with the analysis that appears in the section which follows.

4. Break-even Implications of the Accruals–Cash flow Relationship from a Managerial Standpoint: Detailed Illustration

This section extends the analysis contained in the previous two sections by means of numerical examples and a more detailed algebraic specification of the pre-depreciation profit-operating cash flow relationship.

Figures 110, 111, 112 and 113 illustrate a four-period situation which starts at end-year 0. Figure 110 is a base-case in which costs, selling price, output and sales volume are constant following the initial build-up of an inventory of 270 units in period 1. The periods of credit given to customers and taken from suppliers are also assumed to be constant. In all four cases the effects of the initial inventory build-up, including its effect on credit taken, work themselves out by the end of period 2.

It can readily be inferred from Figure 110 that it is only under the very restrictive assumptions, i.e. everything constant, on which that illustration is based that (after period 2) the accruals and cash flow variables take on identical values.

The assumptions underlying Fig. 111 differ from those which underlie Fig. 110 in one respect. In Fig. 111 costs increase at an annual rate of 15%, whilst the profit mark-up remains at 6%. The consequence of these cost and price increases (again, ignoring the first two periods) is that the pre-depreciation profit exceeds operating cash flow. This relationship will continue as long as the cost and selling price increase (and the other) assumptions continue to hold.

The Fig. 112 assumptions differ from those which underlie Fig. 110 in three respects. In Fig. 112 the sales and inventory volumes are, following the initial inventory build-up, assumed to increase at annual rates of 10% and 5% respectively. The periodic level of output is derived from these two rates of increase accordingly. The consequence (after period 2) of the sales volume, inventory volume and output increases in Fig. 112 is that pre-depreciation profit exceeds operating cash flow. Again it can be stated that this relationship will continue to hold in future periods so long as the underlying assumptions are maintained.

The Fig. 113(a) assumptions differ from those which underlie Fig. 110 (the base-case) in five respects. That is to say, the Fig. 113(a) assumptions combine the Fig. 111 rates of increase in costs and prices with the Fig. 112 rates of increase in sales volume, inventory volume and output. The predictable consequence (ignoring periods 1 and 2) is that, as in Figs 111 and 112, the Fig. 113(a) pre-depreciation profit exceeds its operating cash flow. Once more it can be said that this relationship will continue as long as the underlying assumptions hold.

Figures 110, 111, 112 and 113(a) raise the presumption that a break-even level of output computed on an accruals accounting basis will generally be lower than its cash flow counterpart. Hence, at a break-even point computed on an accruals basis, negative operating cash flows will generally be sustained. Conversely, at a cash flow break-even point positive accruals-based profits will generally emerge.

Period	1		2		3		4	
	Units	DM	Units	DM	Units	DM	Units	DM
I_{j-1} opening inventory	—	—	270	203	270	203	270	203
K_j { variable costs	1270	953	1000	750	1000	750	1000	750
{ fixed costs		250		250		250		250
	1270	1203	1270	1203	1270	1203	1270	1203
I_j closing inventory	270	203	270	203	270	203	270	203
$I_{j-1}+K_j-I_j=$ cost of sales	1000	1000	1000	1000	1000	1000	1000	1000
E_j sales invoiced		1060		1060		1060		1060
$E_j-(I_{j-1}+K_j-I_j)$ $\;\;= $ profit*	1000	60	1000	60	1000	60	1000	60
$I_j-I_{j-1}=$ periodic inventory investment	270	203	—		—		—	
$I_j=$ total inventory investment	270	203	270	203	270	203	270	203
$Z_j=$ cash paid out		1002		1034		1000		1000
$K_j-Z_j=$ periodic credit taken		201		-34		—		—
$\Sigma(K_j-Z_j)=$ total credit taken		201		167		167		167
$C_j=$ cash collected		848		1060		1060		1060
$E_j-C_j=$ periodic credit given		212		—		—		—
$\Sigma(E_j-C_j)=$ total credit given		212		212		212		212
$C_j-Z_j=$ operating cash flow		-154		26		60		60
$(E_j-C_j)+(I_j-I_{j-1})$ $\;\;-(K_j-Z_j)=$ periodic working capital investment		214		34		—		—
$I_j+\Sigma\{(E_j-C_j)-(K_j-Z_j)\}$ $\;\;=$ total working capital investment		214		248		248		248

Assumptions
(1) The company in question commences business at the beginning of period 1.
(2) Excluding period 1 when it builds up a permanent inventory of 270 units, the company's periodic production remains at a constant level of 1000 units.
(3) Costs and selling prices are constant in money terms. (Profit mark-up is 6%.)
(4) Inventories are valued at variable cost on a FIFO basis.
(5) Credit taken constitutes 1/6 of periodic costs, i.e. $\Sigma(K_j-Z_j)=1/6K_j$.
(6) Credit given constitutes 20% of periodic sales invoiced, i.e. $\Sigma(E_j-C_j)=0.2E_j$.
*Before depreciation.

Figure 110 Inventory investment, credit given and taken (constant costs, prices, inventories and sales volume)

Period	1		2		3		4	
	Units	DM	Units	DM	Units	DM	Units	DM
I_{j-1} opening inventory	—	—	270	203	270	233	270	268
K_j { variable costs	1270	953	1000	863	1000	992	1000	1141
fixed costs		250		287		331		380
	1270	1203	1270	1353	1270	1556	1270	1789
I_j closing inventory	270	203	270	233	270	268	270	308
$I_{j-1}+K_j-I_j=$ cost of sales	1000	1000	1000	1120	1000	1288	1000	1481
E_j sales invoiced	1000	1060	1000	1187	1000	1365	1000	1570
$E_j-(I_{j-1}+K_j-I_j)$ $=$ profit*	1000	60	1000	67	1000	77	1000	89
$I_j-I_{j-1}=$ periodic inventory investment	270	203	—	30	—	35	—	40
$I_j=$ total inventory investment	270	203	270	233	270	268	270	308
$Z_j=$ cash paid out		1002		1159		1294		1488
$K_j-Z_j=$ periodic credit taken		201		-9		29		33
$\Sigma(K_j-Z_j)=$ total credit taken		201		192		221		254
$C_j=$ cash collected		848		1162		1329		1529
$E_j-C_j=$ periodic credit given		212		25		36		41
$\Sigma(E_j-C_j)=$ total credit given		212		237		273		314
$C_j-Z_j=$ operating cash flow		-154		3		35		41
$(E_j-C_j)+(I_j-I_{j-1})$ $-(K_j-Z_j)=$ periodic working capital investment		214		64		42		48
$I_j+\Sigma\{(E_j-C_j)-(K_j-Z_j)\}$ $=$ total working capital investment		214		278		320		368

Assumptions
(1) The company in question commences business at the beginning of period 1.
(2) Excluding period 1 when it builds up a permanent inventory of 270 units, the company's periodic production remains at a constant level of 1000 units.
(3) Costs increase at an annual rate of 15%. (Profit mark-up is 6%.)
(4) Inventories are valued at variable cost on a FIFO basis.
(5) Credit taken constitutes 1/6 of periodic costs, i.e. $\Sigma(K_j-Z_j)=1/6K_j$.
(6) Credit given constitutes 20% of periodic sales invoiced, i.e. $\Sigma(E_j-C_j)=0.2E_j$.
*Before depreciation.

Figure 111 Inventory investment, credit given and taken, cost and selling price increases (constant sales and inventory volumes)

Period	1		2		3		4	
	Units	DM	Units	DM	Units	DM	Units	DM
I_{j-1} opening inventory	—	—	270	203	284	213	298	224
K_j { variable costs	1270	953	1114	836	1224	918	1346	1010
$\quad$ { fixed costs		250		250		250		250
	1270	1203	1384	1289	1508	1381	1644	1484
I_j closing inventory	270	203	284	213	298	224	313	235
$I_{j-1}+K_j-I_j=$ cost of sales	1000	1000	1100	1076	1210	1157	1331	1249
E_j sales invoiced	1000	1060	1100	1166	1210	1283	1331	1411
$E_j-(I_{j-1}+K_j-I_j)$ $\quad=$ profit*	1000	60	1100	90	1210	126	1331	162
$I_j-I_{j-1}=$ periodic $\quad$ inventory investment	270	203	14	10	14	11	15	11
$I_j=$ total $\quad$ inventory investment	270	203	284	213	298	224	313	235
$Z_j=$ cash paid out		1002		1106		1154		1245
$K_j-Z_j=$ periodic $\quad$ credit taken		201		-20		14		15
$\Sigma(K_j-Z_j)=$ total $\quad$ credit taken		201		181		195		210
$C_j=$ cash collected		848		1145		1259		1386
$E_j-C_j=$ periodic $\quad$ credit given		212		21		24		25
$\Sigma(E_j-C_j)=$ total $\quad$ credit given		212		233		257		282
$C_j-Z_j=$ operating $\quad$ cash flow		-154		39		105		141
$(E_j-C_j)+(I_j-I_{j-1})$ $\quad-(K_j-Z_j)=$ periodic $\quad$ working capital $\quad$ investment		214		51		21		21
$I_j+\Sigma\{(E_j-C_j)-(K_j-Z_j)\}$ $\quad=$ total working $\quad$ capital investment		214		265		286		307

Assumptions
(1) The company in question commences business at the beginning of period 1.
(2) Sales and inventory volumes increase annually at 10% and 5% respectively following the inventory build-up to 270 units in period 1.
(3) Costs and selling prices are constant in money terms.
(4) Inventories are valued at variable cost on a FIFO basis.
(5) Credit taken constitutes 1/6 of periodic costs, i.e. $\Sigma(K_j-Z_j)=1/6K_j$.
(6) Credit given constitutes 20% of periodic sales invoiced, i.e. $\Sigma(E_j-C_j)=0.2E_j$.
*Before depreciation.

Figure 112   Credit given and taken, inventory and sales volume growth (constant costs and prices)

Period	1		2		3		4	
	Units	DM	Units	DM	Units	DM	Units	DM
I_{j-1} opening inventory	—	—	270	203	284	245	298	296
K_j { variable costs	1270	953	1114	961	1224	1214	1346	1535
{ fixed costs		250		288		331		381
	1270	1203	1384	1452	1508	1790	1644	2212
I_j closing inventory	270	203	284	245	298	296	313	357
$I_{j-1}+K_j-I_j=$ cost of sales	1000	1000	1100	1207	1210	1494	1331	1855
E_j sales invoiced	1000	1060	1100	1306	1210	1652	1331	2090
$E_j-(I_{j-1}+K_j-I_j)$ $=$ profit*	1000	60	1100	99	1210	158	1331	235
$I_j-I_{j-1}=$ periodic inventory investment	270	203	14	42	14	51	15	61
$I_j=$ total inventory investment	270	203	284	245	298	296	313	357
$Z_j=$ cash paid out		1002		1242		1495		1855
$K_j-Z_j=$ periodic credit taken		201		7		50		61
$\Sigma(K_j-Z_j)=$ total credit taken		201		208		258		319
$C_j=$ cash collected		848		1257		1583		2002
$E_j-C_j=$ periodic credit given		212		49		69		88
$\Sigma(E_j-C_j)=$ total credit given		212		261		330		418
$C_j-Z_j=$ operating cash flow		−154		15		88		147
$(E_j-C_j)+(I_j-I_{j-1})$ $-(K_j-Z_j)=$ periodic working capital investment		214		84		70		88
$I_j+\Sigma\{(E_j-C_j)-(K_j-Z_j)\}$ $=$ total working capital investment		214		298		368		456

Assumptions
(1) The company in question commences business at the beginning of period 1.
(2) Sales and inventory volumes increase annually at 10% and 5% respectively following the inventory build-up to 270 units in period 1.
(3) Costs increase at an annual rate of 15%. Selling prices are as in Fig. 111.
(4) Inventories are valued at variable cost on a FIFO basis.
(5) Credit taken constitutes 1/6 of periodic costs, i.e. $\Sigma(K_j-Z_j)=1/6K_j$.
(6) Credit given constitutes 20% of periodic sales invoiced, i.e. $\Sigma(E_j-C_j)=0.2E_j$.
*Before depreciation.

Figure 113(a) Credit given and taken: cost and selling price increases combined with output, inventory, and sales volume growth

Break-even selling price (DM)	1.319		1.237		1.188		1.155	
	Units	DM	Units	DM	Units	DM	Units	DM
I_{j-1} opening inventory	284	245	284	245	284	245	284	245
K_j { variable costs	914	907	1214	1204	1514	1502	1814	1799
fixed costs		331		331		331		331
	1198	1483	1498	1780	1798	2078	2098	2375
I_j closing inventory	298	296	298	296	298	296	298	296
$I_{j-1} + K_j - I_j =$ cost of sales	900	1187	1200	1484	1500	1782	1800	2079
E_j sales invoiced	900	1187	1200	1484	1500	1782	1800	2079
$E_j - (I_{j-1} + K_j - I_j)$ $= $ profit*		0		0		0		0
$I_j - I_{j-1} =$ periodic inventory investment	14	51	14	51	14	51	14	51
$I_j =$ total inventory investment	298	296	298	296	298	296	298	296
$Z_j =$ cash paid out		1239		1487		1735		1982
$K_j - Z_j =$ periodic credit taken		-2		48		98		147
$\Sigma(K_j - Z_j) =$ total credit taken		206		256		306		355
$C_j =$ cash collected		1211		1448		1687		1924
$E_j - C_j =$ periodic credit given		-24		36		95		155
$\Sigma(E_j - C_j) =$ total credit given		237		297		356		416
$C_j - Z_j =$ operating cash flow		-28		-39		-48		-58
$(E_j - C_j) + (I_j - I_{j-1})$ $- (K_j - Z_j) =$ periodic working capital investment		29		39		48		59
$I_j + \Sigma\{(E_j - C_j) - (K_j - Z_j)\}$ $= $ total working capital investment		327		337		346		357

Assumptions
(1) Cash paid out $= 208 + (0.833)$ (variable costs + fixed costs).
(2) Cash collected $= 261 + (0.8)$ (sales).
(3) Total credit taken is $1/6$ of periodic cost, K_j.
(4) Total credit given is 20% of periodic sales, E_j.
*Before depreciation

Figure 113(b) Break-even price–volume relationships (accruals basis) (extension of Fig. 113, period 3)

Break-even selling price (DM)	1.358		1.277		1.228		1.195	
	Units	DM	Units	DM	Units	DM	Units	DM
I_{j-1} opening inventory	284	245	284	245	284	245	284	245
K_j { variable costs	914	907	1214	1204	1514	1502	1814	1799
{ fixed costs		331		331		331		331
	1198	1483	1498	1780	1798	2078	2098	2375
I_j closing inventory	298	296	298	296	298	296	298	296
$I_{j-1}+K_j-I_j=$ cost of sales	900	1187	1200	1484	1500	1782	1800	2079
E_j sales invoiced	900	1222	1200	1532	1500	1842	1800	2151
$E_j-(I_{j-1}+K_j-I_j)$ $=$ profit*		35		48		60		72
$I_j-I_{j-1}=$ periodic inventory investment	14	51	14	51	14	51	14	51
$I_j=$ total inventory investment	298	296	298	296	298	296	298	296
$Z_j=$ cash paid out		1239		1487		1735		1982
$K_j-Z_j=$ periodic credit taken		−2		48		98		147
$\Sigma(K_j-Z_j)=$ total credit taken		206		256		306		355
$C_j=$ cash collected		1239		1487		1735		1982
$E_j-C_j=$ periodic credit given		−17		45		107		169
$\Sigma(E_j-C_j)=$ total credit given		244		306		368		430
$C_j-Z_j=$ operating cash flow		0		0		0		0
$(E_j-C_j)+(I_j-I_{j-1})$ $-(K_j-Z_j)=$ periodic working capital investment		36		48		60		73
$I_j+\Sigma\{(E_j-C_j)-(K_j-Z_j)\}$ $=$ total working capital investment		334		346		358		371

Assumptions
(1) Cash paid out $= 208 + (0.833)$ (variable costs + fixed costs).
(2) Cash collected $= 261 + (0.8)$ (sales).
(3) Total credit taken is 1/6 of periodic cost, K_j.
(4) Total credit given is 20% of periodic sales, E_j.
*Before depreciation

Figure 113(c) Break-even price–volume relationships (cash flow basis) (extension of Fig. 113, period 3)

The latter conclusions are unlikely to be altered by the inclusion of depreciation and capital expenditure in the accruals and cash flow conputations respectively since, as illustrated by Figs 107(a), 107(b), 108(a), 108(b), 109(a), 109(b) and 109(c) a firm's periodic capital expenditure characteristically exceeds its periodic depreciation charge. Indeed, as already indicated, each of the alternative contributions defined on an accruals basis will usually exceed its cash flow counterpart.

5. Algebraic Analysis of Break-even Price-output Decisions and Further Illustrations

Figure 113 can be used as a starting point in deriving both arithmetic and algebraic analyses of the accruals–cash flow break-even relations mentioned at the end of the penultimate paragraph.

(a) Analysis of Conventionally Calculated Pre-depreciation Profit

Making the distinction between fixed, K_j^f, and variable costs, K_j^v, conventional pre-depreciation profit for any period j can be illustrated symbolically and numerically (using the numbers in Fig. 113(a), period 3) as follows:

$$\begin{aligned} \text{Profit} &= E_j - [\, I_{j-1} + K_j^v + K_j^f - I_j \,] \\ &= 1652 - (245 + 1214 + 331 - 296) \\ &= \text{DM } 158 \end{aligned} \tag{4.206}$$

Equation (4.206) can be written more comprehensively as:

$$\begin{aligned} \text{Profit} &= x_j \cdot p_j - [\, IV_{j-1} \cdot k_{vj-1} + K_j^f + k_{vj}(x_j + IV_j - IV_{j-1}) - IV_j \cdot k_{vj} \,] \\ &= x_j \cdot (p_j - k_{vj}) - IV_{j-1}(k_{vj-1} - k_{vj}) - K_j^f \end{aligned} \tag{4.207}$$

where,

$$\begin{aligned} x &= \text{sales volume;} \\ p &= \text{selling price;} \\ IV &= \text{inventory volume;} \\ k_v &= \text{unit variable cost.} \end{aligned}$$

(b) Break-even Conditions (Conventional "Accruals" Basis)

Break-even price-output policies are specified by the price–sales volume relationships, i.e., the values of x_j and p_j, which satisfy the equation:

$$0 = x_j(p_j - k_{vj}) - IV_{j-1}(k_{vj-1} - k_{vj}) - K_j^f \tag{4.208}$$

It may be noted that the second term on the right-hand side of (4.208) is absent from the familiar textbook treatment of break-even analysis.

(1) Equation (4.208) can be used to derive either a break-even selling price p_j' for any given sales volume or a break-even sales volume x_j' for any given selling price. Thus, p_j' is given by:

$$p_j' = \frac{x_j \cdot k_{vj} + IV_{j-1}(k_{vj-1} - k_{vj}) + K_j^f}{x_j} \tag{4.209}$$

Using the numbers in Fig. 113(a), period 3 (other than the selling price of DM 1.365);

$$p_j' = \frac{1210\ (0.991875) + 284\ (0.8625 - 0.991878) + 331}{1210}$$

$$= \text{DM } 1.235.$$

(2) Similarly, the break-even sales volume x_j' for any assumed selling price p_j is given by:

$$x_j' = \frac{IV_{j-1}(k_{vj-1} - k_{vj}) + K_j^f}{p_j - k_{vj}} \qquad (4.210)$$

Putting $p_j = 1.235$ and, as in Fig. 113(a), period 3, $IV_{j-1} = 284$, $k_{vj-1} = 0.8625$, $k_{vj} = 0.991875$ and $K_j^f = 331$;

$$x_j' = \frac{284\ (0.8625 - 0.991875) + 331}{1.235 - 0.991875}$$

$$= 1210 \text{ units.}$$

(c) Cash Flow Analysis

Operating cash flow for any period j (sales receipts minus *operating* payments) is given by:

$$c_j - z_j = [\,\Phi E_{j-1} + (1 - \Phi)E_j\,] - [\,\gamma K_{j-1} + (1 - \gamma)K_j\,] \qquad (4.211)$$

In the latter equation, Φ and γ denote the periods of credit given to and taken from trade debtors and trade creditors respectively. Therefore, ΦE_{j-1} and γK_{j-1} denote outstanding trade debtors and trade creditors respectively at the beginning of period j and are perhaps more conveniently represented by using initials TRD_{j-1} and TRC_{j-1} respectively. Substituting, as in equation (4.207), for (the remaining) E_j and K_j in equation (4.211), periodic cash flow can be written as:

$$TRD_{j-1} + (1 - \Phi)x_j \cdot p_j - \{TRC_{j-1} + (1 - \gamma)[\,K_j^f + k_{vj}(x_j + IV_j - IV_{j-1})\,]\} \qquad (4.212)$$

Using the numbers in Fig. 113(a), period 3;

$$= 261 + (1 - 0.2)(1210)(1.365) - \{208 + (1 - 0.167)\,[\,331 + 0.991875\ (1210 + 298 - 284)\,]\}$$
$$= \text{DM } 88.$$

(d) Break-even Conditions (Cash Flow Basis)

The cash flow break-even selling price p_j^* is, for any given sales volume x_j, derived by setting the right-hand side of equation (4.212) equal to zero and is given by:

$$p_j^* = \frac{TRC_{j-1} - TRD_{j-1} + (1 - \gamma)[\,K_j^f + k_{vj}(x_j + IV_j - IV_{j-1})\,]}{x_j(1 - \Phi)} \qquad (4.213)$$

Using the numbers in Fig. 113(a), period 3 (other than the selling price of DM 1.365);

$$p_j^* = \frac{208 - 261 + (1 - 0.167)[331 + 0.991875\ (1210 + 298 - 284)]}{1210\ (1 - 0.2)}$$

$$= \text{DM } 1.27483 \text{ (compared with the "conventional"}$$
break-even selling price p_j' of DM 1.235).

Similarly, the (cash flow) break-even sales volume x_j^* for any given selling price p_j is given by:

$$x_j^* = \frac{TRC_{j-1} - TRD_{j-1} + (1 - \gamma)[K_j^f + k_{vj}(IV_j - IV_{j-1})]}{p_j(1 - \Phi) - (1 - \gamma)k_{vj}} \tag{4.214}$$

Using the previously computed selling price $p_j^* = 1.27483$ and other numbers as in Fig. 113, period 3;

$$x_j^* = \frac{208 - 261 + (1 - 0.167)[331 + 0.991875\ (298 - 284)]}{1.27483\ (1 - 0.2) - (1 - 0.167)(0.991875)}$$

$$= 1210 \text{ units.}$$

(e) Selling Price—Sales Volume Relationship for Attaining a Target Cash Flow

The selling price p_j'' which, for any given sales volume x_j, will generate a target cash flow TCF_j is given by:

$$TCF_j = TRD_{j-1} + (1 - \Phi)x_j \cdot p_j'' - \{TRC_{j-1} + (1 - \gamma)[K_j^f + k_{vj}(x_j + IV_j - IV_{j-1})]\} \tag{4.215}$$

whence,

$$p_j'' = \frac{TCF_j - TRD_{j-1} + TRC_{j-1} + (1 - \gamma)[K_j^f + k_{vj}(x_j + IV_j - IV_{j-1})]}{x_j(1 - \Phi)} \tag{4.216}$$

(Except for the inclusion of TCF_j in its numerator, equation (4.216) is the same as equation (4.213).) Using the numbers in Fig. 113(a), period 3 (other than the unit selling price of DM 1.235);

$$p_j'' = \frac{TCF_j - 261 + 208 - (1 - 0.167)[331 + 0.991875\ (1210 + 298 - 284)]}{1210\ (0.8)}$$

$$= \frac{TCF_j + 1234}{968}$$

Substituting $TCF_j = 100$, $p_j'' = \text{DM } 1.378$; and substituting $TCF_j = 200$, $p_j'' = \text{DM } 1.481$.

The sales volume x_j'' which, for any given selling price p_j, will generate a target cash flow TCF_j is derived by including the latter term in the numerator of equation (4.214) and solving for x_j'' accordingly, i.e.,

$$x_j'' = \frac{TCF_j + TRC_{j-1} - TRD_{j-1} + (1 - \gamma)\,[\,K_j^f + k_{vj}(IV_j - IV_{j-1})\,]}{p_j(1 - \Phi) - (1 - \gamma)k_{vj}} \tag{4.217}$$

Using the numbers in Fig. 113(a), period 3 (other than the sales volume of 1210 units);

$$x_j'' = \frac{TCF_j + 208 - 261 - (1 - 0.167)\,[\,331 + 0.991875\ (298 - 284)\,]}{1.27483\ (1 - 0.2) - (1 - 0.167)(0.991875)}$$

$$= \frac{TCF_j + 234.3}{0.19363}$$

Substituting $TCF_j = 100$, $x_j'' = 1726$ units; and substituting $TCF_j = 200$, $x_j'' = 2243$ units.

(f) Break-even Volumes and Break-even Selling Prices

The "accruals-based" break-even relationship between selling price and sales volume (alternative price-output combinations) for period 3 of Fig. 113(a) is:

Transferred to Fig. 113(b)

x_j	300	600	900	1200	1500	1800
p_j' (DM)	1.973	1.482	1.319	1.237	1.188	1.155

The last four pairs of break-even values are embodied in Fig. 113(b) which also shows the related cash flow position.

The corresponding "cash flow based" break-even relationship between selling price and sales volume for period 3 of Fig. 113(a) is:

Transferred to Fig. 113(c)

x_j	300	600	900	1200	1500	1800
p_j^* (DM)	2.009	1.521	1.358	1.277	1.228	1.195

The price–output relationship illustrated by the last four columns is incorporated in Fig. 113(c) which also shows the resultant "accruals-based" earnings.

6. Summary

This appendix serves to elucidate possible economic consequences of conventional "accruals-based" break-even analysis. Such possibilities usually stem from the characteristic excess of "accruals earnings" over "cash flow earnings". However, any deviation between the former and the latter will cause deviations between their respective break-even relationships (combination of selling price and sales volume).

For any given (periodic) selling price, conventional break-even analysis will usually signal a lower break-even sales volume than does cash flow analysis. The conventional analysis does not therefore preclude the possibility that, whilst a firm's periodic operating activity may be at or above the conventionally-computed break-even point, it may simultaneously require periodic external finance on a continuous basis (cp. Fig. 113(b)). In other words, a break-even position in the conventional accounting sense does not ensure that a firm can operate as a self-financing entity.

Similarly, given the level of output, the accruals-based break-even selling price will usually be lower than its cash flow counterpart. If so, the consequence will again be a cash flow deficit. Thus, in most cases, break-even price–volume conditions computed on an accruals basis will understate the price and/or volume at which a firm attains a break-even cash flow position. In any event the differences between equations (4.207) and (4.212) clearly imply that the respective break-even conditions derived therefrom will usually deviate.

Chapter 5

The Significance of Break-even Analyses in the Planning, Management and Control of the Business Process

Break-even analyses are an important technique for the planning, management and control of business processes. In *planning* they facilitate an overview of the individual effects of alternative courses of action on a firm's goals. In particular they provide a means of judging and comparing alternatives by reference to satisficing goals or critical goal minima. Break-even analyses also furnish decision criteria in that they indicate the minimum output volumes below which satisficing levels cannot be attained.

Break-even analyses are of importance in the day-to-day *management* of a business process when immediate decisions are to be based on simple criteria. In such cases, break-even points indicate which decision is profitable within the ranges of variation of the individual determinants. The addition of a time-dimension to break-even analyses is also useful in some cases from the standpoint of managerial intervention. Milestones can then be set as a basis for measuring the profitability of previous activities. When separate break-even analyses are undertaken for each product or product group, weaknesses, and therefore the points at which managerial intervention should begin, become evident.

In the *control* of the business process the importance of break-even analysis lies in the fact that it uncovers the strengths and weaknesses of products, product groups or procedures, or of measures in general. Achieved profit can then be judged by reference to the extent to which actual output deviates from the projected break-even point. The consequential analyses of such a deviation provide information for future planning.

Break-even points are the *marginal points of the profitability evaluation* of managerial action. They therefore provide important information in the search for optimal alternatives when decisions are analysed on a break-even basis and in relation to such satisficing goals as are specified in break-even-analyses by sales levels as contribution blocks. It is therefore not surprising that break-even notions are also used as important basic information in many areas of *optimisation*. The planning, management and control of output levels and sales volumes, and of the costs and contribution margins of output levels, constitute the traditional and best-known applications. In addition, break-even results also enter optimisation considerations in the planning, management and control of many of the other constituent activities of a firm. In this way, break-even analyses simplify, or support, optimisation calculations. Break-even analyses do not, however, give effect to maximisation or minimisation objectives. They are primarily concerned with the attainment of a *satisficing level*. Consequently, the direct use of break-even results in exact optimising models, which are often deliberately intended to determine maxima or minima, is less frequent. In heuristic approaches however, break-even analyses, which are simpler to implement, often replace more thorough-going optimisation calculations. For example, break-even points constitute a basis for simple *heuristic optimisation rules*. This is illustrated below by reference to some practical applications.

In the case of *dynamic order quantity optimisation* with deterministically known, though variable, order levels, the problem is to determine the sub-periods, within a year, in which procurement orders should be placed. If negative orders are inadmissible, the sub-period in which each order should be placed, and the related order quantity, are simultaneously determined. The objective of the optimisation is the minimisation of the relevant costs. These comprise fixed order costs on the one hand and, on the other, the interest and storage costs of procurements up to the time they are used. In that case, an exact optimisation calculation for minimising the relevant costs does not always appear to be worthwhile in view of the expense involved. For this reason *DeMatteis and Mendoza* (cp. DeMatteis, 1968 [Algorithm] p. 30 et seq.; Mendoza, 1968 [Analysis] p. 39 et seq.) have devised a heuristic approach to the problem. They start from the basic idea that, in the case of a cost-efficient order quantity, the fixed order costs that are independent upon that quantity must correspond to some minimum order size. The heuristic principle of their optimisation calculation is the requirement that fixed order costs and the sum of interest and storage costs, which are a function of order quantity, are approximately equal. Interest and storage costs depend upon the quantity stored and the storage period. This means that the aspired level of fixed costs is attained, for example, via smaller quantities in the case of a long storage period or via larger quantities in the case of a short storage period. *DeMatteis and Mendoza* therefore introduce the notion of *part periods*. A part period is defined as the storing of one unit for exactly one period. The aspired equality of fixed costs and the sum of storage and interest costs can be converted into the requirement of a specific number of part periods. This number may be interpreted as a *break-even point* which relates a contribution block comprising fixed order costs to the costs of a part period in the form of a "unit contribution". The computed break-even point is used as a heuristic optimisation principle in the following manner: the possible alternative quantities of an individual order—i.e. the required quantities for the current period and alternatively for many subsequent periods—are converted into part periods. In this conversion, the number of part periods of a unit of a later period's requirements is given by the number of periods which represent the time-lag between these requirements and the order point, i.e. the actual period in question. A summation of the number of part periods of the constituent requirements for each order alternative gives the total number of part periods of the related orders. The alternative that is selected as the optimal order is that which has the number of part periods most closely approximating the initially-computed break-even point (cp. DeMatteis, 1968 [Algorithm] p. 31). To avoid adverse effects on the order sequence, this solution should be slightly amended in some cases in accordance with the proposal of *DeMatteis and Mendoza*. However, in principle, the search for an optimal solution is based on a break-even point.

The same principle is followed in a series of further optimisation approaches in different areas of application. In choosing an *optimal organisational form* for a growing organisation, break-even points can be calculated at which, subject to particular objectives, an organisational change is propitious. Here the break-even points are, for instance, measures of firm size (an optimisation approach to this problem is described in *Schweitzer*, 1973 [Reorganisationsstrategien] p. 292 et seq.). Break-even analyses are also helpful in the compilation of an optimal assortment of *precautionary inventory levels* of different forms of goods which, within limits, can be substituted for each other in case of need. In this case, the break-even points specify the additional precautionary inventory level for a substitute good up to which it is advantageous to substitute a specific precautionary inventory of the substituted good (cp. Trossmann, 1979 [Optimierung] p. 170). In *cutting optimisation* it is important to know, in respect of identical cut parts, the minimum number thereof that necessitates the drawing up of a cutting pattern. When this minimum is exceeded, the savings in cutting costs outweigh additional set-up costs (cp. Trossman, 1983 [Verschnittoptimierung] p. 112). This kind of number is also a break-even point.

In the same way, the computation of break-even points in many other optimisation problems can provide at least heuristic magnitudes which may be used in simple form for decision-making purposes. In addition to the cases mentioned above, there are also the following further typical applications:

—in all variants of the *make or buy decision* (cp. Tucker, 1980 [Break-Even System] p. 165 et seq.; Tucker, 1973 [Einführung] p. 264 et seq.),

—in the decision on whether to engage a *travelling salesman* (at a fixed salary) or a *commercial agent* (on a pure commission basis) (cp. Tucker, 1980 [Break-Even System] p. 177 et seq.; Tucker, 1973 [Einführung] p. 275 et seq.),

—in further decisions on the *choice* of various categories of *employees* (cp. Kossbiel, 1976 [Personalbereitstellung] p. 1055),

—in individual *financial decisions*, for example, in the choice between the collection of receivables and factoring,

—in the decision on alternative *training programmes for employees* which differ with respect to costs, duration and results.

It is evidently the case that the various forms of break-even analysis constitute an important instrument for business planning, management and control. However, they not only fulfil the main purpose for which they are prepared and implemented. On the contrary, simply because they are prepared, and pre-eminently because they involve the capturing and processing of the requisite data, break-even analyses have various *side-effects* which of themselves frequently justify the implementation of the analysis. In the standard application, break-even analyses presuppose a decomposition of costs. This requires an intensive *cost analysis* to elucidate the structure and composition of costs. Frequently this results in the uncovering of hitherto unrecognised *functional relationships*, perhaps between particular production determinants, and their cost consequences. Moreover, a correct break-even analysis requires costs and sales revenue—or in non-standard applications of break-even analyses the corresponding relevant magnitudes—to be analysed by reference to their dependence on *determinants*. Such an analysis elucidates those components that are irreversibly committed and such other components as are actually manageable, and thereby clarifies the decision situation. In some cases this can also result in a more exact co-ordination of *responsibilities*. This effect is reinforced by the fact that quantitative formulation forces exactness and precision. The importance of preparation in break-even analyses is ultimately reinforced by the fact that the same data can be used for *other planning, management and control purposes*, for example, budgeting.

The applicability of the results of break-even analysis depends to a large extent upon the reliability and completeness of the input *information*. If the results of break-even analysis are to be adequately interpreted and used, the following matters in particular must be clearly understood: the implicitly assumed structure of the goods flow; the nature and features of the goals that are to be pursued; the structure of cost, outlay and sales revenue functions; and, the other conditions in which a break-even analysis may be implemented. Precisely because break-even applications are severely constrained in the latter respects, the traditional basic model has proved itself to be viable to only a very limited extent. As early as 1951 this caused *Dean* (1952 [Break-Even Analysis] p. 250) to caution, "Break-even analysis is only one of many instruments in modern management". In the light of the extensions of break-even analysis that are presented in this book, the applications of which are less constrained, one is tempted to add, "*Break-even analysis is only one of many instruments in modern management but, when appropriately applied, proves to be an extremely valuable technique.*"

Rearrangement of the Formula for the Expected Value of Normally Distributed Uncertainty Costs to Facilitate the Use of Tabular Values

1. Computation of the Partial Expected Value of a Standard Normally Distributed Random Variable within the Limits $-\infty$ to z_0

φ is the density function of the standard normal distribution:

$$\varphi(z) = \frac{1}{\sqrt{2\pi}} \exp(-\tfrac{1}{2} z^2);$$

and

$$\exp(x) = \sum_{\nu=0}^{\infty} \frac{x^\nu}{\nu!};$$

Φ is the distribution function of the standard normal distribution:

$$\Phi(z_0) = \int_{-\infty}^{z_0} \varphi(z)\, dz. \tag{A.1}$$

The partial expected value within the limits $-\infty$ to z_0 is computed as follows:

$$\int_{-\infty}^{z_0} z \cdot \varphi(z)\, dz = \int_{-\infty}^{z_0} z \cdot \frac{1}{\sqrt{2\pi}} \sum_{\nu=0}^{\infty} \frac{(-\tfrac{1}{2} z^2)^\nu}{\nu!}\, dz$$

$$= \frac{1}{\sqrt{2\pi}} \sum_{\nu=0}^{\infty} \frac{(-\tfrac{1}{2})^\nu}{\nu!} \int_{-\infty}^{z_0} z^{2\nu+1}\, dz$$

$$= \left[\frac{1}{\sqrt{2\pi}} \sum_{\nu=0}^{\infty} \frac{(-\tfrac{1}{2})^\nu \cdot z^{2\nu+2}}{\nu!\,(2\nu+2)} \right]_{-\infty}^{z_0}$$

$$= \left[\frac{1}{\sqrt{2\pi}} \sum_{\mu=1}^{\infty} \frac{(-\tfrac{1}{2})^{\mu-1} z^{2\mu}}{(\mu-1)! \cdot 2\mu} \right]_{-\infty}^{z_0} \tag{A.2}$$

$$= -\left\{\left[\frac{1}{\sqrt{2\pi}} \sum_{\mu=1}^{\infty} \frac{(-\frac{1}{2} z^2)^\mu}{\mu!}\right]_{-\infty}^{z_0}\right\}$$

$$= -\left\{\left[\frac{1}{\sqrt{2\pi}} \sum_{\mu=0}^{\infty} \frac{(-\frac{1}{2} z^2)^\mu}{\mu!} - \frac{(-\frac{1}{2} z^2)^0}{0!}\right]_{-\infty}^{z_0}\right\}$$

$$= -\{[- \quad \varphi(z) \quad\quad 1 \quad]_{-\infty}^{z_0}\}$$

$$= -\{[\varphi(z_0) - 1] - \underbrace{[\varphi(-\infty) - 1]}_{= 0}\}$$

$$= -\varphi(z_0).$$

2. Computation of the Expected Value of Uncertainty Costs

(a) Expected Value of Uncertainty Costs if Production is Undertaken

In accordance with (3.33):

$$E(U_{\substack{\text{undertaking} \\ \text{production}}}) = \int_{-\infty}^{x_0} d \cdot (x_0 - x) \cdot \varphi_{\mu, \sigma}(x) \, dx.$$

Rearranging:

$$z_0 := \frac{x_0 - \mu}{\sigma}$$

$$E(U_{\substack{\text{undertaking} \\ \text{production}}}) = d \cdot (z_0 \sigma + \mu) \cdot \int_{-\infty}^{z_0} \varphi(z) \, dz - d \cdot \int_{-\infty}^{z_0} (z\sigma + \mu) \cdot \varphi(z) \, dz$$

$$= d \cdot \sigma \cdot [z_0 \cdot \int_{-\infty}^{z_0} \varphi(z) \, dz - \int_{-\infty}^{z_0} z \cdot \varphi(z) \, dz] \tag{A.3}$$

$$\leftarrow \text{result from 1.}$$

$$= d \cdot \sigma \cdot [z_0 \cdot \Phi(z_0) + \varphi(z_0)].$$

Because there are no tabular values for the formulation within the square brackets a rearrangement is expedient. Moreover, in the case of a decision in favour of production, z_0 is generally negative (because $x_0 < \mu = x^{\text{exp}}$).
    Putting

$$\hat{z}_0 := -z_0 \text{ (positive in the general case).}$$

Because the density function of a normal distribution is symmetrical:

$$\varphi(\hat{z}_0) = \varphi(z_0)$$

$$\Phi(\hat{z}_0) = 1 - \Phi(z_0). \tag{A.4}$$

Hence,

$$E(U_{\substack{\text{undertaking} \\ \text{production}}}) = d \cdot \sigma \cdot [\varphi(\hat{z}_0) - \hat{z}_0 \cdot (1 - \Phi(\hat{z}_0))]$$

$$= d \cdot \sigma \cdot \Omega(\hat{z}_0) = d \cdot \sigma \cdot \Omega(-z_0). \tag{A.5}$$

The values of $\Omega(\hat{z}_0) := \varphi(\hat{z}_0) - \hat{z}_0 \cdot (1 - \Phi(\hat{z}_0))$ are listed in Table A.2 of Appendix II for positive values of $\hat{z}_0$. If, exceptionally, $\hat{z}_0$ is negative, $\Omega(\hat{z}_0)$ cannot be taken directly from Table A.2 in which case the following relation can be utilised:

$$
\begin{aligned}
\Omega(-z) &= \varphi(-z) + z \cdot (1 - \Phi(-z)) \\
&= \varphi(z) + z \cdot \Phi(z) \\
&= \varphi(z) - z \cdot (1 - \Phi(z)) + z \\
&= \Omega(z) + z.
\end{aligned}
\tag{A.6}
$$

(b) Expected Value of Uncertainty Costs if Production is not Undertaken

In accordance with (3.35):

$$
E(U_{\substack{\text{not undertaking} \\ \text{production}}}) = \int_{x_0}^{\infty} d \cdot (x - x_0) \cdot \varphi(x) \, dx
$$

Rearranging:

$$
z_0 := \frac{x_0 - \mu}{\sigma}
$$

$$
E(U_{\substack{\text{not undertaking} \\ \text{production}}}) = d \cdot \int_{z_0}^{\infty} (z\sigma + \mu) \cdot \varphi(z) \, dz - d \cdot (z_0 \sigma + \mu) \cdot \int_{z_0}^{\infty} \varphi(z) \, dz
$$

$$
= d \cdot \sigma \cdot \left[\int_{z_0}^{\infty} z \cdot \varphi(z) \, dz - z_0 \cdot \int_{z_0}^{\infty} \varphi(z) \, dz \right]
$$

$\leftarrow \varphi$ is symmetrical

$$
= d \cdot \sigma \cdot \left[-\int_{-\infty}^{-z_0} z \cdot \varphi(z) \, dz - z_0 \cdot (1 - \Phi(z_0)) \right]
$$

$\leftarrow$ result from 1. (A.7)

$$
= d \cdot \sigma \cdot [\, \varphi(-z_0) - z_0 \cdot (1 - \Phi(z_0)) \,]
$$

$\leftarrow \varphi$ is symmetrical

$$
= d \cdot \sigma \cdot [\, \varphi(z_0) - z_0 \cdot (1 - \Phi(z_0)) \,]
$$

$$
= d \cdot \sigma \cdot \Omega(z_0).
$$

If production is not undertaken z_0 is generally positive because $\mu < x_0$.

Extracts from Tables

Table A.1 Selected values of the distribution function $\Phi(z^*) = \int_{-\infty}^{z^*} \varphi(z)\,dz$ of the standard normal distribution

z	00	01	02	03	04	05	06	07	08	09
0.0	0.500 0	0.504 0	0.508 0	0.512 0	0.516 0	0.519 9	0.523 9	0.527 9	0.531 9	0.535 9
0.1	0.539 8	0.543 8	0.547 8	0.551 7	0.555 8	0.559 7	0.563 6	0.567 5	0.571 4	0.575 3
0.2	0.579 3	0.583 2	0.587 1	0.591 0	0.594 8	0.598 7	0.602 6	0.606 4	0.610 3	0.614 1
0.3	0.617 9	0.621 7	0.625 5	0.629 3	0.633 1	0.636 8	0.640 6	0.644 3	0.648 0	0.651 7
0.4	0.655 4	0.659 1	0.662 8	0.666 4	0.670 0	0.673 6	0.677 2	0.680 8	0.684 4	0.687 9
0.5	0.691 5	0.695 0	0.698 5	0.701 9	0.705 4	0.708 8	0.712 3	0.715 7	0.719 0	0.722 4
0.6	0.725 7	0.729 1	0.732 4	0.735 7	0.738 9	0.742 2	0.745 4	0.748 6	0.751 8	0.754 9
0.7	0.758 0	0.761 2	0.764 2	0.767 3	0.770 4	0.773 6	0.776 4	0.779 4	0.782 3	0.785 2
0.8	0.788 1	0.791 0	0.793 9	0.796 7	0.799 6	0.802 3	0.805 1	0.807 9	0.810 6	0.813 3
0.9	0.815 9	0.818 6	0.821 2	0.823 8	0.826 4	0.828 9	0.831 5	0.834 0	0.836 5	0.838 9
1.0	0.841 3	0.843 8	0.846 1	0.848 5	0.850 8	0.853 1	0.855 4	0.857 7	0.859 9	0.862 1
1.1	0.864 3	0.866 5	0.868 6	0.870 8	0.872 9	0.874 9	0.877 0	0.879 0	0.881 0	0.883 0
1.2	0.884 9	0.886 9	0.888 8	0.890 7	0.892 5	0.894 4	0.896 2	0.898 0	0.899 7	0.901 47
1.3	0.903 20	0.904 90	0.906 58	0.908 24	0.909 88	0.911 49	0.913 09	0.914 66	0.916 21	0.917 74
1.4	0.919 24	0.920 73	0.922 20	0.923 64	0.925 07	0.926 47	0.927 85	0.929 22	0.930 56	0.931 89
1.5	0.933 19	0.934 48	0.935 74	0.936 99	0.938 22	0.939 43	0.940 62	0.941 79	0.942 95	0.944 08
1.6	0.945 20	0.946 30	0.947 38	0.948 45	0.949 50	0.950 53	0.951 54	0.952 54	0.953 52	0.954 49
1.7	0.955 43	0.956 37	0.957 28	0.958 18	0.959 07	0.959 94	0.960 80	0.961 64	0.962 46	0.963 27
1.8	0.964 07	0.964 85	0.965 62	0.966 38	0.967 12	0.967 84	0.968 56	0.969 26	0.969 95	0.970 62
1.9	0.971 28	0.971 93	0.972 57	0.973 20	0.973 81	0.974 41	0.975 00	0.975 58	0.976 15	0.976 70
2.0	0.977 25	0.977 78	0.978 31	0.978 82	0.979 32	0.979 82	0.980 30	0.980 77	0.981 24	0.981 69
2.1	0.982 14	0.982 52	0.983 00	0.983 41	0.983 82	0.984 22	0.984 61	0.985 00	0.985 37	0.985 74
2.2	0.986 10	0.986 45	0.986 79	0.987 13	0.987 45	0.987 78	0.988 09	0.988 40	0.988 70	0.988 99
2.3	0.989 28	0.989 56	0.989 83	0.990 10	0.990 36	0.990 61	0.990 86	0.991 11	0.991 34	0.991 58
2.4	0.991 80	0.992 02	0.992 24	0.992 45	0.992 66	0.992 86	0.993 05	0.993 24	0.993 43	0.993 61
2.5	0.993 79	0.993 96	0.994 13	0.994 30	0.994 46	0.994 61	0.994 77	0.994 92	0.995 06	0.995 20
2.6	0.995 34	0.995 47	0.995 60	0.995 73	0.995 85	0.995 98	0.996 09	0.996 21	0.996 32	0.996 43
2.7	0.996 53	0.996 64	0.996 74	0.996 83	0.996 93	0.997 02	0.997 11	0.997 20	0.997 28	0.997 36
2.8	0.997 44	0.997 52	0.997 60	0.997 67	0.997 74	0.997 81	0.997 88	0.997 95	0.998 01	0.998 07
2.9	0.998 13	0.998 19	0.998 25	0.998 31	0.998 36	0.998 41	0.998 46	0.998 51	0.998 56	0.998 61

(The above table is compiled from values contained in a more comprehensive table in Wetzel, Jöhnk and Naeve, 1967 [Tabellen] pp. 99–102.)

Table A.2 Selected values of the function $\Omega(z) = \varphi(z) - z \cdot (1 - \Phi(z))$, ($\varphi$ and Φ respectively denote the density function and distribution function of the standard normal distribution)

z	00	01	02	03	04	05	06	07	08	09
0.0	0.398 9	0.394 0	0.389 0	0.384 1	0.379 3	0.374 4	0.369 7	0.364 9	0.360 2	0.355 6
0.1	0.350 9	0.346 4	0.341 8	0.337 3	0.332 8	0.328 4	0.324 0	0.319 7	0.315 4	0.311 1
0.2	0.306 9	0.302 7	0.298 6	0.294 4	0.290 4	0.286 3	0.282 4	0.278 4	0.274 5	0.270 6
0.3	0.266 8	0.263 0	0.259 2	0.255 5	0.251 8	0.248 1	0.244 5	0.240 9	0.237 4	0.233 9
0.4	0.230 4	0.227 0	0.223 6	0.220 3	0.216 9	0.213 7	0.210 4	0.207 2	0.204 0	0.200 9
0.5	0.197 8	0.194 7	0.191 7	0.188 7	0.185 7	0.182 8	0.179 9	0.177 1	0.174 2	0.171 4
0.6	0.168 7	0.165 9	0.163 3	0.160 6	0.158 0	0.155 4	0.152 8	0.150 3	0.147 8	0.145 3
0.7	0.142 9	0.140 5	0.138 1	0.135 8	0.133 4	0.131 2	0.128 9	0.126 7	0.124 5	0.122 3
0.8	0.120 2	0.118 1	0.116 0	0.114 0	0.112 0	0.110 0	0.108 0	0.106 1	0.104 2	0.102 3
0.9	0.100 4	0.098 60	0.096 80	0.095 03	0.093 28	0.091 56	0.089 86	0.088 19	0.086 54	0.084 91
1.0	0.083 32	0.081 74	0.080 19	0.078 66	0.077 16	0.075 68	0.074 22	0.072 79	0.071 38	0.069 99
1.1	0.068 62	0.067 27	0.065 95	0.064 65	0.063 36	0.062 10	0.060 86	0.059 64	0.058 44	0.057 26
1.2	0.056 10	0.054 96	0.053 84	0.052 74	0.051 65	0.050 59	0.049 54	0.048 51	0.047 50	0.046 50
1.3	0.045 53	0.044 57	0.043 63	0.042 70	0.041 79	0.040 90	0.040 02	0.039 16	0.038 31	0.037 48
1.4	0.036 67	0.035 87	0.035 08	0.034 31	0.033 56	0.032 81	0.032 08	0.031 37	0.030 67	0.029 98
1.5	0.029 31	0.028 65	0.028 00	0.027 36	0.026 74	0.026 12	0.025 52	0.024 94	0.024 36	0.023 80
1.6	0.023 24	0.022 70	0.022 17	0.021 65	0.021 14	0.020 64	0.020 15	0.019 67	0.019 20	0.018 74
1.7	0.018 29	0.017 85	0.017 42	0.016 99	0.016 58	0.016 17	0.015 78	0.015 39	0.015 01	0.014 64
1.8	0.014 28	0.013 92	0.013 57	0.013 23	0.012 90	0.012 57	0.012 26	0.011 95	0.011 64	0.011 34
1.9	0.011 05	0.010 77	0.010 49	0.010 22	0.0^29957	0.0^29698	0.0^29445	0.0^29198	0.0^28957	0.0^28721
2.0	0.0^28491	0.0^28266	0.0^28046	0.0^27832	0.0^27623	0.0^27418	0.0^27219	0.0^27024	0.0^26835	0.0^26649
2.1	0.0^26468	0.0^26292	0.0^26120	0.0^25952	0.0^25788	0.0^25628	0.0^25472	0.0^25320	0.0^25172	0.0^25028
2.2	0.0^24887	0.0^24750	0.0^24616	0.0^24486	0.0^24358	0.0^24235	0.0^24114	0.0^23996	0.0^23882	0.0^23770
2.3	0.0^23662	0.0^23556	0.0^23453	0.0^23352	0.0^23255	0.0^23159	0.0^23067	0.0^22977	0.0^22889	0.0^22804
2.4	0.0^22720	0.0^22640	0.0^22561	0.0^22484	0.0^22410	0.0^22337	0.0^22267	0.0^22199	0.0^22132	0.0^22067
2.5	0.0^22004	0.0^21943	0.0^21883	0.0^21826	0.0^21769	0.0^21715	0.0^21662	0.0^21610	0.0^21560	0.0^21511
2.6	0.0^21464	0.0^21418	0.0^21373	0.0^21330	0.0^21288	0.0^21247	0.0^21207	0.0^21169	0.0^21132	0.0^21095
2.7	0.0^21060	0.0^21026	0.0^39928	0.0^39607	0.0^39295	0.0^38992	0.0^38699	0.0^38414	0.0^38138	0.0^37870
2.8	0.0^37611	0.0^37359	0.0^37115	0.0^36879	0.0^36650	0.0^36428	0.0^36213	0.0^36004	0.0^35802	0.0^35606
2.9	0.0^35417	0.0^35233	0.0^35055	0.0^34883	0.0^34716	0.0^34555	0.0^34398	0.0^34247	0.0^34101	0.0^33959

(The above table is taken from Schlaifer, 1959 [Probability] p. 706 et seq.)

Table A.3 Selected values of absolute atmospheric humidity ξ in g/m^3 in the case of steam saturation over water (saturation humidity) as a function of temperature t in °C

t	0.0	0.1	0.2	0.3	0.4	0.5	0.6	0.7	0.8	0.9
0	4.847	4.881	4.915	4.949	4.983	5.018	5.053	5.088	5.123	5.158
1	5.194	5.229	5.265	5.302	5.338	5.375	5.412	5.449	5.486	5.524
2	5.561	5.599	5.637	5.676	5.715	5.753	5.793	5.832	5.872	5.911
3	5.951	5.992	6.032	6.073	6.114	6.155	6.197	6.239	6.281	6.323
4	6.365	6.408	6.451	6.494	6.538	6.581	6.625	6.670	6.714	6.759
5	6.804	6.849	6.895	6.941	6.987	7.033	7.080	7.126	7.174	7.221
6	7.269	7.317	7.365	7.413	7.462	7.511	7.561	7.610	7.660	7.710
7	7.761	7.812	7.863	7.914	7.966	8.018	8.070	8.122	8.175	8.228
8	8.282	8.335	8.389	8.444	8.498	8.553	8.608	8.664	8.720	8.776
9	8.833	8.889	8.946	9.004	9.062	9.120	9.178	9.237	9.296	9.355
10	9.415	9.475	9.535	9.596	9.657	9.719	9.780	9.842	9.905	9.968
11	10.031	10.094	10.158	10.222	10.286	10.351	10.416	10.482	10.548	10.614
12	10.681	10.748	10.815	10.883	10.951	11.019	11.088	11.157	11.227	11.297
13	11.367	11.438	11.509	11.580	11.652	11.724	11.797	11.870	11.943	12.017
14	12.091	12.166	12.241	12.316	12.392	12.468	12.545	12.622	12.699	12.777
15	12.855	12.934	13.013	13.092	13.172	13.252	13.333	13.414	13.496	13.578
16	13.660	13.743	13.826	13.910	13.994	14.079	14.164	14.250	14.335	14.422
17	14.509	14.596	14.684	14.772	14.861	14.950	15.039	15.129	15.220	15.311
18	15.402	15.494	15.587	15.679	15.773	15.867	15.961	16.056	16.151	16.247
19	16.343	16.440	16.537	16.635	16.733	16.832	16.931	17.030	17.131	17.231
20	17.333	17.434	17.537	17.639	17.743	17.847	17.951	18.056	18.161	18.267
21	18.374	18.481	18.588	18.696	18.805	18.914	19.024	19.134	19.245	19.356
22	19.468	19.581	19.694	19.807	19.921	20.036	20.151	20.267	20.384	20.501
23	20.618	20.736	20.855	20.974	21.094	21.215	21.336	21.458	21.580	21.703
24	21.826	21.950	22.075	22.200	22.326	22.453	22.580	22.708	22.836	22.965
25	23.095	23.225	23.356	23.487	23.619	23.752	23.886	24.020	24.154	24.290
26	24.426	24.563	24.700	24.838	24.977	25.116	25.256	25.396	25.538	25.680
27	25.822	25.966	26.110	26.255	26.400	26.546	26.693	26.840	26.988	27.137
28	27.287	27.437	27.588	27.740	27.892	28.046	28.199	28.354	28.509	28.665
29	28.822	28.980	29.138	29.297	29.457	29.617	29.778	29.940	30.103	30.266
30	30.431	30.596	30.761	30.928	31.095	31.263	31.432	31.602	31.772	31.943
31	32.115	32.288	32.462	32.636	32.811	32.987	33.164	33.342	33.520	33.699
32	33.879	34.060	34.242	34.424	34.608	34.792	34.977	35.163	35.350	35.537
33	35.726	35.915	36.105	36.296	36.488	36.680	36.874	37.068	37.264	37.460
34	37.657	37.855	38.054	38.253	38.454	38.656	38.858	39.061	39.266	39.471
35	39.677	39.884	40.092	40.301	40.510	40.721	40.933	41.145	41.359	41.573
36	41.788	42.005	42.222	42.440	42.660	42.880	43.101	43.323	43.546	43.770
37	43.995	44.221	44.448	44.676	44.905	45.135	45.366	45.598	45.831	46.065
38	46.300	46.536	46.774	47.012	47.251	47.491	47.732	47.974	48.218	48.462
39	48.708	48.954	49.202	49.450	49.700	49.951	50.202	50.455	50.709	50.964
40	51.221	51.478	51.736	51.996	52.256	52.518	52.781	53.044	53.310	53.576

(This table is extracted from [Aspirations-Psychrometer-Tafeln], 1979, p. 6 et seq.)

General Mathematical Formulation of the Industrial Learning Curve

1. Proof of the Relationship Between the Recursive and Non-Recursive Formulation of the Learning Curve

The non-recursive formulation of the industrial learning curve runs (cp. e.g. Baur, 1967 [Planung] p. 56; Baur, 1979 [Lerngesetz] col. 1119; Ihde, 1970 [Lernprozesse] p. 457):

$$k^{a,\,v}(X) = \frac{k^{a,\,v}(1)}{X^b}. \qquad (A.8)$$

This formulation can be used to compute the following unit cost rate for a total production volume $2 \cdot X$:

$$k^{a,\,v}(2 \cdot X) = \frac{k^{a,\,v}(1)}{(2 \cdot X)^b} = \frac{k^{a,\,v}(1)}{2^b \cdot X^b}.$$

Substituting equation (A.8) for $k^{a,\,v}(X)$ gives:

$$k^{a,\,v}(2 \cdot X) = \frac{1}{2^b} \cdot k^{a,\,v}(X).$$

The recursive formulation of the learning curve runs (see (4.134)):

$$k^{a,\,v}(2 \cdot X) = \gamma \cdot k^{a,\,v}(X).$$

When $\gamma = 1/2^b$ the formulations coincide. Hence,

$$\ln \gamma = \ln\left(\frac{1}{2^b}\right) = -(\ln 2) \cdot b$$

or (cp. Baur, 1967 [Planung] p. 64):

$$b = -\frac{\ln \gamma}{\ln 2}. \qquad (A.9)$$

2. Integral of the Discount Factor

For $t_1 = 0$ and because of $e^0 = 1$:

$$I_1 = \int_{t_1}^{t_2} e^{-\rho t} \, dt = \left[-\frac{1}{\rho} \cdot e^{-\rho t} \right]_{t_1}^{t_2} = -\frac{1}{\rho} e^{-\rho t_2} + \frac{1}{\rho} e^{-\rho t_1}$$

$$= \frac{1}{\rho} [e^{-\rho t_1} - e^{-\rho t_2}].$$

$$I_1 = \int_0^{t_2} e^{-\rho t} = \frac{1}{\rho} \cdot (1 - e^{-\rho t_2}).$$

3. Integral of the Terms of the Variable Payment Per Unit

(cp. Reinhardt, 1973 [Break-Even Analysis] p. 837)

$$I_2 = \int_{t_0}^{t_2} (t - t_0)^{-b} \cdot e^{-\rho t} \, dt.$$

Substituting the integration variable with $t - t_0$ yields:

$$I_2 = e^{-\rho t_0} \cdot \int_0^{t_2 - t_0} t^{-b} \cdot e^{-\rho t} \, dt = e^{-\rho t_0} \cdot \rho^b \cdot \int_0^{t_2 - t_0} (\rho t)^{-b} \cdot e^{-\rho t} \, dt.$$

Substituting the integration variable with $v = \rho t$ gives:

$$I_2 = e^{-\rho t_0} \cdot \rho^b \cdot \frac{1}{\rho} \cdot \underbrace{\int_0^{\rho(t_2 - t_0)} v^{-b} \cdot e^{-v} \, dv}_{=: I_3}$$

Putting $\alpha := (1 - b)$ and $z := \rho(t_2 - t_0)$, the integral I_3 can be written:

$$I_3 = \int_0^z v^{\alpha - 1} \cdot e^{-v} \, dv,$$

which is a special value of the gamma function. The latter function and its integral are:

$$\Gamma(\alpha, z) = \int_0^z v^{\alpha - 1} \cdot e^{-v} \, dv = \sum_{j=0}^{\infty} \frac{(-1)^j z^{j+\alpha}}{j! \, (j+\alpha)} .$$

Hence, I_2 is given by:

$$I_2 = e^{-\rho t_0} \cdot \rho^{b-1} \sum_{j=0}^{\infty} \frac{(-1)^j \cdot [\rho(t_2 - t_0)]^{j+1-b}}{j! (j+1-b)} .$$

Bibliography

Adar, Z., Barnea, A. and Lev, B. (1977) [Uncertainty] A Comprehensive Cost-Volume-Profit Analysis Under Uncertainty. *The Accounting Review*, **52**, 137–149.

Anderson, L. K. (1975) [Expanded Breakeven Analysis] Expanded Breakeven Analysis for a Multi-Product Company. *Management Accounting*, **57**, 30–32.

BASF (ed.) [BASF-Kunststoffe] *BASF-Kunststoff*. 4th edn, published by the BASF Aktiengesellschaft (no publisher, place of publication or year).

Baur, W. (1979) [Lerngesetz] Lerngesetz der industriellen Produktion, in W. Kern (ed.) *Handwörterbuch der Produktionswirtschaft*. Stuttgart: Poeschel, col. 1115–1125.

Baur, W. (1967) [Planung] *Neue Wege der betrieblichen Planung*. Berlin, Heidelberg, New York: Springer.

Bennett, G. (1962) [Inequalities] Probability Inequalities for the Sum of Independent Random Variables. *Journal of the American Statistical Association*, **57**, 33–45.

Bierman, H. Jr., Bonini, C. P. and Hausman, W. H. (1981) [Analysis] *Quantitative Analysis for Business Decisions*. 6th edn. Homewood, Illinois: Irwin.

Blohm, H. and Lüder, K. (1983) [Investition] *Investition. Schwachstellen im Investitionsbereich des Industriebetriebs und Wege zu ihrer Beseitigung*. 5th edn. Munich: Vahlen.

Brown, D. (1975) [Advertising Costs] Break-even analysis and advertising costs. *Accountancy*, **86** (January), 42–45.

Bücher, K. (1910) [Massenproduktion] Das Gesetz der Massenproduktion. *Zeitschrift für die gesamte Staatswissenschaft*, **66**, 429–444.

Chan, K. H. and Laughland, A. R. (1976) [Break-even Analysis] Towards Probabilistic Break-even Analysis. *Cost and Management*, **50** (4), 44–47.

Charnes, A., Cooper, W. W. and Ijiri, Y. (1963) [Break-even Budgeting] Break-even Budgeting and Programming to Goals. *Journal of Accounting Research*, **1**, 16–43.

Chenery, H. B. (1949) [Functions] Engineering Production Functions. *The Quarterly Journal of Economics*, **63**, 507–531.

Chmielewicz, K. (1972) [Qualitätsgestaltung] Qualitätsgestaltung und Break-Even-Analyse. *Betriebswirtschaftliche Forschung und Praxis*, **24**, 595–621.

Chmielewicz, K. (1973) [Erfolgsrechnung] *Betriebliches Rechnungswesen. Vol. 2: Erfolgsrechnung*. Reinbek: Rowohlt.

Chmielewicz, K. (1974) [Gewinnschwellenanalyse] Gewinnschwellenanalyse (Break-Even-Analyse). *Wirtschaftswissenschaftliches Studium*, **3**, 49–54.

Coenenberg, A. G. (1967) [Absatzrisiko] Die Berücksichtigung des Absatzrisikos im Break-even-Modell. *Betriebswirtschaftliche Forschung und Praxis*, **19**, 343–355.

Coenenberg, A. G. (1969) [Entscheidungskriterien] Entscheidungskritierien im Gewinnschwellen-Kalkül, in W. B. von Colbe and G. Sieben (eds) *Betriebswirtschaftliche Information, Enscheidung und Kontrolle*. Wiesbaden: Gabler, pp. 171–194.

Colasse B. (1971) [Variante statistique] Variante statistique de la méthode du point mort. *Techniques Economiques*, **37**, 69–73.

Dean, J. (1952) [Break-Even Analysis] Methods and Potentialities of Break-Even Analysis, in D. Solomons (ed.) *Studies in Costing*. London: Sweet & Maxwell, pp. 227–266.

Deutscher Wetterdienst (ed.) (1979) [Aspirations-Psychrometer-Tafeln] *Aspirations-Psychrometer-Tafeln*. 6th edn. Braunschweig, Wiesbaden: Vieweg.

Dickinson, J. P. (1974) [Uncertainty] Cost-Volume-Profit Analysis Under Uncertainty. *Journal of Accounting Research*, **12**, 182–187.

Dinkelbach, W. (1975) [Programmierung] Programmierung, stochastische, in E. Grochla and W. Wittmann (eds) *Handwörterbuch der Betriebswirtschaft*, 4th edn. Stuttgart: Poeschel, col. 3329–3250.

Dorn, G. (1977) [Besteuerung] Die Auswirkungen der Besteuerung auf die Kostenrechnung. *Kostenrechnungspraxis*, 127–138.

Edwards, E. O. and Johnson L. T. (1974) [Indifference Approach] An Indifference Approach to Profit-Volume Analysis. *The Accounting Review*, 49, 579–583.

Ekern, S. (1979) [Points] Stochastic Breakeven Points. *The Journal of the Operational Research Society*, 30, 271–275.

Ferrara, W. L., Hayya, J. C. and Nachman, D. A. (1972) [Normalcy] Normalcy of Profit in the Jaedicke-Robichek Model. *The Accounting Review*, 47, 299–307.

Frisch, R. (1935/36) [Notion] On the Notion of Equilibrium and Disequilibrium. *Review of Economic Studies*, 3, 100–105.

Gardner, F. V. (1955) [Profit Management] *Profit Management and Control*. New York, Toronto, London: McGraw-Hill.

Geary, R. C. (1930) [Frequency Distribution] The Frequency Distribution of the Quotient of Two Normal Variates. *Journal of the Royal Statistical Society*, 93, 442–446.

Gibson, C. J. (1972) [Strategies] Selecting Pricing Strategies with Break-Even Analysis. *Cost and Management*, 46, (November/December), 8–11.

Goggans, T. P. (1965) [Curvilinear Functions] Break-even Analysis with Curvilinear Functions. *The Accounting Review*, 40, 867–871.

Gutenberg, E. (1983) [Produktion] *Grundlagen der Betriebswirtschaftslehre*. Volume 1. *Die Produktion*. 24th edn. Berlin, Heidelberg, New York: Springer.

Haberstock, L. (1982) [Grundzüge] *Grundzüge der Kosen- und Erfolgsrechnung*. 3rd edn. Munich: Vahlen.

Haidacher, O. B. (1969) [Break-even-Punkt] Der Break-even-Punkt als Instrument unternehmerischer Führung. Dissertation. Munich.

Heinen, E. (1971) [Zielsystem] *Grundlagen betriebswirtschaftlicher Entscheidungen. Das Zielsystem der Unternehmung*. 2nd edn. Wiesbaden: Gabler.

Heinen, E. (1978) [Kostenlehre] *Betriebswirtschaftliche Kostenlehre. Kostentheorie und Kostenentscheidungen*. 5th edn. Wiesbaden: Gabler.

Heinen, E. (1982) [Einführung] *Einführung in die Betriebswirtschaftslehre*. 8th edn. Wiesbaden: Gabler.

Henderson, G. V. Jr. and Barnett, A. H. (1977/78) [Breakeven Present Value] Breakeven Present Value: a Pragmatic Approach to Capital Budgeting Under Risk and Uncertainty. *Management Accounting*, 59, (January), 49–52.

Hildebrandt, R. (1925) [Rentabilitätsverhältnisse] *Mathematisch-graphische Untersuchungen über die Rentabilitätsverhältnisse des Fabrikbetriebs*. Berlin: Julius Springer.

Hilliard, J. E. and Leitch, R. A. (1975) [Uncertainty] Cost-Volume-Profit Analysis Under Uncertainty: A Log Normal Approach. *The Accounting Review*, 50, 69–80.

Hoeffding, W. (1963) [Inequalities] Probability Inequalities for Sums of Bounded Random Variables. *Journal of the American Statistical Association*, 58, 13–30.

Holt, C. C., Modigliani, F., Muth, J. F. and Simon, H. A. (1960) [Planning] *Planning Production, Inventories and Work Force*. Englewood Cliffs, NJ: Prentice-Hall.

Horngren, C. T. (1982) [Cost Accounting] *Cost Accounting. A Managerial Emphasis*. 5th edn. Englewood Cliffs, NJ: Prentice-Hall.

Horngren, C. T. (1984) [Management Accounting] *Introduction to Management Accounting*. 6th edn. Englewood Cliffs, NJ: Prentice-Hall.

Ihde, G.-B. (1970) [Lernprozesse] Lernprozesse in der betriebswirtschaftlichen Produktionstheorie. *Zeitschrift für Betriebswirtschaft*, 40, 451–468.

Ijiri, Y. (1965) [Goals] *Management Goals and Accounting for Control*. Amsterdam, Chicago: Elsevier, North Holland.

Jaedicke, R. K. (1961) [Analysis] Improving B-E Analysis by Linear Programming Technique, in National Association of Accountants (ed.), *N.N.A.-Bulletin*. New York, vol. 42, (March), pp. 5–12.

Jaedicke, R. K. and Robichek, A. A. (1964) [Uncertainty] Cost-Volume-Profit Analysis under Conditions of Uncertainty. *The Accounting Review*, 39, 917–926. Reprinted in:

T. H. Williams and C. H. Griffin (eds) (1967) *Management Information. A Quantitative Accent.* Homewood, Illinois: R. D. Irwin, pp. 331–343; also in A. Rappaport (ed.) (1970) *Information for Decision Making. Quantitative and Behavioral Dimensions.* Englewood Cliffs, NJ: Prentice Hall, pp. 238–248.

Jenny, H. (1922) [Charakteristik] *Die wirtschaftliche Charakteristik industrieller Unternehmen.* Zürich: Rascher & Cie.

Johnson, G. L. and Simik, II, S. S. (1974) [Inequalities] The Use of Probability Inequalities in Multiproduct C-V-P Analysis Under Uncertainty. *Journal of Accounting Research*, **12**, 67–79.

Kaplan R. S. (1982) [Management Accounting] *Advanced Management Accounting.* Englewood Cliffs, NJ: Prentice-Hall.

Kelvie, W. E. and Sinclair, J. M. (1968) [New Technique] New Technique for Breakeven Charts. *Financial Executive*, **36**, 31–43.

Kern, W. (1974) [Break-even-Analysis] Break-Even-Analysis, in E. Grochla and W. Wittmann (eds) *Handwörterbuch der Betriebswirtschaft.* Stuttgart: Poeschel, col. 992–998.

Kilger, W. (1958) [Produktionstheorie] *Produktions- und Kostentheorie.* Wiesbaden: Gabler.

Kilger, W. (1981) [Plankostenrechnung] *Flexible Plankostenrechnung und Deckungsbeitragsrechnung.* 8th edn. Wiesbaden: Gabler.

Kim, C. (1973) [Analysis] A Stochastic Cost Volume Profit Analysis. *Decision Sciences*, **4**, 329–342.

Kleinebeckel, H. (1976) [Break-even-Analysen] Break-even-Analysen. *Zeitschrift für betriebswirtschaftliche Forschung*, **28** (ZfbF-Kontaktstudium), 51–58.

Kleinebeckel, H. (1976) [Planung] Break-even-Analysen für Planung and Plan-Berichterstattung. *Zeitschrift für betriebswirtschaftliche Forschung*, **28**, (ZfbF-Kontaktstudium), 117–124.

Kleinebeckel, H. (1983) [Break-even-Analyse] Die Break-even-Analyse als Steuerungs- und Überwachungsinstrument, in R. Mann and E. Mayer (eds) *Der Controlling-Berater (CB).* Freiburg/Brsg.: Haufe, pp. 4/35–4/60.

Klipper, H. (1977/78) [Breakeven Analysis] Breakeven Analysis with Variable Product Mix. *Management Accounting*, **59** (April), 51–54.

Kloock, J. (1969) [Input-Output-Modelle] *Betriebswirtschaftliche Input-Output-Modelle.* Wiesbaden: Gabler.

Knoeppel, C. E. (1933) [Engineering] *Profit Engineering. Applied Economics in Making Business Profitable.* New York, London: McGraw-Hill.

Koch, H. (1966) [Kostenrechnung] *Grundprobleme der Kostenrechnung.* Cologne, Opladen: Westdeutscher Verlag.

Kolbe, K. (1967) [Theorie] *Theorie und Praxis des Gesamtwertes und Geschäftswertes der Unternehmung.* 3rd edn. Düsseldorf: Institut der Wirtschaftsprüfer.

Kosiol, E. (1972) [Aktionszentrum] *Die Unternehmung als wirtschaftliches Aktionszentrum. Einführung in die Betriebswirtschaftslehre.* Reinbek: Rowohlt.

Kosiol, E. (1930) [Betriebsgrösse] Die Beziehungen zwischen Kostengestaltung und Betriebsgrösse (im Warenhandel). *Die Betriebswirtschaft*, **23**, 331–336. Published again in E. Kosiol (1973) *Bausteine der Betriebswirtschaftslehre.* 2nd Vol. Berlin: Duncker & Humblot, pp. 1084–1094.

Kossbiel, H. (1976) [Personalbereitstellung] *Personalbereitstellung und Personalführung.* Wiesbaden: Gabler.

Kottas, J. F. and Lau, H.-S. (1978) [Simulation] Direct Simulation in Stochastic CVP Analysis. *The Accounting Review*, **53**, 698–707.

Kruschwitz, L. (1985) [Investitionsrechnung] *Investitionsrechnung.* 2nd edn. Berlin, New York: de Gruyter.

Küpper, H.-U. (1979) [Produktionstypen] Produktionstypen, in W. Kern (ed.) *Handwörterbuch der Produktionswirtschaft.* Stuttgart: Poeschel, col. 1636–1647.

Küpper, H.-U. (1980) [Interdependenzen] *Interdependenzen zwischen Produktionstheorie und der Organisation des Produktionsprozesses.* Berlin: Duncker & Humblot.

Lägel, R. (1980) [Nutzschwellen] Nutzschwellen-Rechnungen. *Kostenrechnungspraxis*, pp. 121–126.

Lardner, D. (1850) [Railway Economy] *Railway Economy: A Treatise on the New Art of Transport, its Management, Prospects, and Relations, Commercial, Financial and Social.* London, New York: Taylor, Walton and Maberly/Harper & brothers. (quoted from O. B. Haidacher (1969) [Break-even-Punkt] VII).

Larimore, L. K. (1974) [Education] Break-even Analysis for Higher Education. *Management Accounting*, **56** (September), pp. 25–29.

Lassman, G. (1968) [Erlösrechnung] *Die Kosten- und Erlösrechnung als Instrument der Planung und Kontrolle in Industriebetrieben*. Düsseldorf: Stahleisen.

Lassmann, G. (1981) [Einflussgrössenrechnung] Einflussgrössenrechnung, in E. Kosiol, K. Chmielewicz and M. Schweitzer (eds) *Handwörterbuch des Rechnungswesens*. 2nd edn. Stuttgart: Poeschel, col. 427–438.

Lawson, G. H. (1982) [Woolworth] Was Woolworth Ailing? *Accountant*, November.

Lawson, G. H., Möller, P. and Sherer, M. (1982) [Verwendung] Zur Verwendung anschaffungswertorientierter Aufwand-Ertrag-Rechnungen als Grundlage für die Bemessung von Zinsen, Steuern und Dividenden, in W. Lück and V. Tromsdorff (eds) *Internationalisierung der Unternehmung*. Berlin: Schmidt, pp. 643–662.

Lawson, G. H. and Stark, A. W. (1981) [Inflation] Equity Values and Inflation, Dividends and Debt Financing. *Lloyds Bank Review*, January, 40–54.

Leontief, W. (1966) [Input-Output Economics] *Input-Output Economics*. New York: Oxford University Press.

Lex, H. (1970) [Investitionsrechnung] Investitionsrechnung auf der Basis kumulierter Wertflüsse. Dissertation. Cologne.

Liao, M. (1975) [Sampling] Model Sampling: A Stochastic Cost-Volume-Profit Analysis. *The Accounting Review*, **50**, 780–790.

Liao, M. (1976) [Estimations] The Effect of Chance Variation on Revenue and Cost Estimations for Breakeven Analysis. *The Accounting Review*, **51**, 922–926.

Lücke, W. (1962) [Massenproduktion] Das "Gesetz der Massenproduktion" in betriebswirtschaftlicher Sicht, in H. Koch (ed.) *Zur Theorie der Unternehmung. Commemorative publication for the 65th birthday of Erich Gutenberg*. Wiesbaden: Gabler, pp. 313–365.

Lüder, K. and Streitferdt, L. (1978) [Erfolgsrechnung] Kurzfristige Erfolgsrechnung als Kontrollinstrument der Unternehmensführung. *Betriebswirtschaftliche Forschung und Praxis*, **30**, 545–564.

Magee, R. P. (1975) [Uncertainty] Cost-Volume-Profit Analysis, Uncertainty and Capital Market Equilibrium. *Journal of Accounting Research*, **13**, 257–266.

Manes, R. (1966) [Dimension] A New Dimension of Break-even Analysis. *Journal of Accounting Research*, **4**, 87–100.

Mann, J. (1904) [Oncost] Oncost, in G. Lisle (ed.) *Encyclopaedia of Accounting*. Vol. V. Edinburgh, London, pp. 199–225.

DeMatteis, J. J. (1968) [Algorithm] An economic lot-sizing technique I. The part-period algorithm. *IBM System Journal*, **7**, 30–38.

Matz, A. (1964) [Planung] *Planung und Kontrolle von Kosten und Gewinn, Handbuch der Planungsrechnung*. Wiesbaden: Gabler.

Matz, A. and Usry, M. F. (1980) [Cost Accounting] *Cost Accounting. Planning and Control*. 7th edn. Cincinnati, Ohio: South Western Publishing Co.

Mellerowicz, K. (1970) [Kalkulationsverfahren] *Neuzeitliche Kalkulationsverfahren*. 3rd edn. Freiburg/Brsg: Haufe.

Mendoza G. A. (1968) [Analysis] An economic lot-sizing technique II. Mathematical analysis of the part-period algorithm. *IBM System Journal*, **7**, 39–42.

Meredith, G. G. (1969) [Decisions] *Profit-Volume Decisions. A Manual for Managerial Planning and Control*. New York, London, Tokyo, St. Lucia: University of Queensland Press.

Middleton, K. A. (1980) [Critical Look] A Critical Look at Break-Even Analysis. *Australian Accountant*, **50**, 264–268.

Modigliani, F. and Cohn, R. (1978) [Financial Analysts Journal] *Financial Analysts Journal*.

Moore, B. L. and Talbott, J. C. (1978) [Application] An Application of Cost-Volume-Profit Analysis. *Cost and Management*, (March/April), 31–38.

Morard, B. (1978) [Comptabilité] Direct costing et comptabilité. *Économie et comptabilité*, **32**, (124), 59–67.

Morimoto, M. (1980) [Analysis] A Study on C-V-P Analysis under Uncertainty: especially with emphasis to examination of Jaedicke & Robichek model and Hilliard & Leitch model. *Osaka Economic Papers*, **30** (1), (June).

Morimoto, M. (1983) [Breakeven] Breakeven Analysis under Inflation by D. G. Dhavale & H. G. Wilson. *Matsuyama University Review*, **34** (4), (October).

Morrison, T. A. and Kaczka, E. (1969) [Application] A New Application of Calculus and Risk Analysis to Cost-Volume-Profit Changes. *The Accounting Review*, **44**, 330–343.

Morse, W. J. and Posey, I. A. (1979/80) [Income Taxes] Income Taxes Do Make a Difference in C-V-P Analysis. *Management Accounting*, **61** (December), 20–24.

Müller-Merbach, H. (1973) [Operations Research] *Operations Research, Methoden und Modelle der Optimalplanung*. 3rd edn. Munich: Vahlen.

Nebelung, C. (1950) [Ermittlung] Statistische Ermittlung der fixen und variablen Kosten in Betrieben der Grosserienfertigung. *Zeitschrift für Betriebswirtschaft*, **20**, 416–421.

Nottingham, C. (1978) [Generators] A cost benefit analysis of wind powered generators. *Accountancy*, **89** (June), 48–52.

Oertel, G. (ed.) (1983) [Polyurethane] *Kunststoff-Handbuch. Volume 7: Polyurethane*. 2nd edn. Munich, Vienna: Hanser.

Pichler, O. (1953) [Erfassung] Anwendung der Matrizenrechnung zur Erfassung von Betriebsabläufen. *Ingenieur-Archiv*, **21**, 157–175.

Pichler, O. (1953) [Matrizenrechnung] Anwendung der Matrizenrechnung auf betriebswirtschaftliche Aufgaben. *Ingenieur-Archiv*, **21**, 119–140.

Poensgen, O. H. (1981) [Break-Even-Analysis] Break-Even-Analysis, in E. Kosiol, K. Chmielewicz and M. Schweitzer (eds) *Handwörterbuch des Rechnungswesens*. 2nd edn. Stuttgart: Poeschel, col. 303–313.

Pressmar, D. B. (1971) [Leistungsanalyse] *Kosten- und Leistungsanalyse im Industriebetrieb*. Wiesbaden: Gabler.

Pressmar, D. B. (1974) [Losgrössenanalyse] Stationäre Planung und Losgrössenanalyse. *Zeitschrift für Betriebwirtschaft*, **44**, 729–748.

Raun, D. L. (1964) [Limitations] Limitations of Profit Graphs, Breakeven Analysis, and Budgets. *The Accounting Review*, **39**, 927–945.

Rautenstrauch, W. (1930) [Profits] *The Successful Control of Profits*. New York: B. C. Forbes.

Reinhardt, U. E. (1973) [Break-Even Analysis] Break-Even Analysis for Lockheed's Tri Star: An Application of Financial Theory. *Journal of Finance*, **28**, 821–838.

Riebel, P. (1963) [Erzeugungsverfahren] *Industrielle Erzeugungsverfahren in betriebswirtschaftlicher Sicht*. Wiesbaden: Gabler.

Riebel, P. (1982) [Einzelkostenrechnung] *Einzelkosten- und Deckungsbeitragsrechnung. Grundfragen einer markt- und entscheidungsorientierten Unternehmensrechnung*. 4th edn. Wiesbaden: Gabler

Saunders, J. H. and Frisch, K. C. (1962) [Polyurethanes I] *Polyurethanes. Chemistry and Technology. Part I: Chemistry*. New York, London, Sydney: Interscience Publishers.

Saunders, J. H. and Frisch, K. C. (1964) [Polyurethanes II] *Polyurethanes. Chemistry and Technology. Part II: Technology*. New York, London, Sydney: Interscience Publishers.

Schaich, E., Köhle, D., Schweitzer, W. and Wegner, F. (1979) [Statistik I] *Statistik I für Volkswirte, Betriebswirte und Soziologen*. 2nd edn. Munich: Vahlen.

Schaich, E., Köhle, D., Schweitzer, W. and Wegner, F. (1982) [Statistik II] *Statistik II für Volkswirte, Betriebswirte und Soziologen*. 2nd edn. Munich: Vahlen.

Schär, J. F. (1911) [Handelsbetriebslehre] *Allgemeine Handelsbetriebslehre*. Vol. I. Leipzig: Gloeckner.

Scherrer, G. (1983) [Kostenrechnung] *Kostenrechnung*. Stuttgart, New York: Fischer.

Schlaifer, R. (1959) [Probability] *Probability and Statistics for Business Decisions. An Introduction to Managerial Economics under Uncertainty*. New York, Toronto, London: McGraw-Hill.

Schmalenbach, E. (1919) [Selbstkostenrechnung] Selbstkostenrechnung. *Zeitschrift für handelswissenschaftliche Forschung*, **13**, 257–299, 321–356.

Schneeweiss, H. (1978) [Ökonometrie] *Ökonometrie*. 3rd edn. Würzburg, Vienna: Physika.

Schweitzer, M. (1973) [Reorganisationsstrategien] Zur Bestimmung optimaler Reorganisationsstrategien wachsender Unternehmungen, in E. Grochla and N. Szyperski (eds) *Modell-und computergestützte Unternehmungsplanung*. Wiesbaden: Gabler, pp. 281–306.

Schweitzer, M. (1979) [Funktionen] Betriebswirtschaftliche Produktionsfunktionen, M. Schweitzer (ed.) *Performance Report no. 12* of the Research Institute for Industrial Management, University of Tübingen. Tübingen.

Schweitzer, M. (1979) [Produktionsfunktionen] Produktionsfunktionen, in W. Kern (ed.) *Handwörterbuch der Produktionswirtschaft*. Stuttgart: Poeschel, col. 1494–1512.

Schweitzer, M. (1990) [Gegenstand] Gegenstand der Betriebswirtschaftslehre, in F. X. Bea, D. Dichtl and M. Schweitzer (eds) *Allgemeine Betriebswirtschaftslehre. 1st volume: Grundfragen*. 5th edn. Stuttgart: Fischer, pp. 15–55.

Schweitzer, M. and Küpper, H.-U. (1974) [Produktionstheorie] *Produktions- und Kostentheorie der Unternehmung*. Reinbek: Rowohlt.

Schweitzer, M. and Küpper, H.-U. (1991) [Systeme] *Systeme der Kostenrechnung*. 5th edn. Landsberg: Moderne Industrie.

Schweitzer, M. and Trossmann, E. (1980) [Break-even-Analyse] Break-even-Analyse, in G. Haberland (ed.) *Der kaufmännische Geschäftsführer*. 5th Nachlieferung. Munich: Moderne Industrie, Beitrag 7.8, pp. 1–41.

Schweitzer, M. and Trossmann, E. (1986) [Break-even-Analysen] *Break-even-Analysen. Grundmodell, Varianten, Erweiterungen*. Stuttgart: Poeschel.

Shesai, K. M. El., Harwood, G. B. and Hermanson, R. H. (1977/78) [Integer Goal Programming] Cost Volume Profit Analysis with Integer Goal Programming. *Management Accounting*, **59** (October), 43–47.

Singh, P. S. and Chapman, G. L. (1977/78) [Approximation] Is Linear Approximation Good Enough? *Management Accounting*, **59** (January), 53–55.

Starr, M. K. and Tapiero, C. S. (1975) [Risk] Linear Breakeven Analysis Under Risk. *Operational Research Quarterly*, **26**, 847–856.

Stoeckhert, K. (ed.) (1975) [Kunststoff-Lexikon] *Kunststoff-Lexikon*. 6th edn. Munich: Hanser.

Teller, R. (1975) [Modèle Bayésien] Un Modèle Bayésien de Gestion. Le Point-Mort Probabilisé. *Economie et Comptabilité*, **29**, (109), 37–49.

Trossmann, E. (1979) [Optimierung] Simultane Optimierung von Papierbeständen eines Verlages unter Ausnutzung von Substitutionsbeziehungen. *Angewandte Planung*, **3**, 162–173.

Trossmann, E. (1983) [Grundlagen] *Grundlagen einer dynamischen Theorie und Politik der betrieblichen Produktion*. Berlin: Duncker & Humblot.

Trossmann, E. (1983) [Verschnittoptimierung] *Verschnittoptimierung, dargestellt an Beispielen aus der Textilindustrie*. Berlin: Duncker & Humblot.

Tschernikow, S. N. (1971) [Ungleichungen] *Lineare Ungleichungen*. Revised by H. Hollatz after a translation by H. Weinert, Berlin.

Tucker, S. A. (1963) [Tool] *The Break-Even System: A Tool for Profit Planning*. Englewood Cliffs, NJ.

Tucker, S. A. (1966) [Break-even-Analyse] *Break-even-Analyse. Die praktische Methode der Gewinnplanung*. German edn. of S. Tucker, *The Break-even System: A Tool for Profit Planning*. Translated and revised by A. Deyhle. Munich: Moderne Industrie.

Tucker, S. A. (1973) [Einführung] *Einführung in die Break-even Analyse*. German edition by S. Tucker, *The Break-Even System*. Translated and revised by A. Deyhle (contents identical to those of Tucker [Break-even-Analyse]). Munich: Moderne Industrie.

Tucker, S. A. (1980) [Break-Even-System] *Profit Planning Decisions with the Break-Even System*. (Contents nearly identical to those of Tucker [Tool]). New York, NJ: Thomond Press.

Vickers, D. (1966) [Economics] On the Economics of Break-Even, in H. R. Anton and P. A. Firmin (eds) *Contemporary Issues in Cost Accounting. A Discipline in Transition*. Boston: Houghton Mifflin, pp. 250–260.

Wagner, F. W. and Heyd, R. (1981) [Steuern] Ertrags- und Substanzsteuern in der entscheidungsbezogenen Kostenrechnung. *Zeitschrift für betriebswirtschaftliche Forschung*, **33**, 922–935.

Weinwurm, E. H. (1970) [Break-Even Analysis] Break-Even Analysis, in E. Kosiol (ed.) *Handwörterbuch des Rechnungswesens*. 1st edn. Stuttgart: Poeschel, col. 302–307.

Welsch, G. A. (1976) [Planning] *Budgeting: Profit Planning and Control*. 4th edn. Englewood Cliffs, NJ: Prentice-Hall.

Wetzel, W., Jöhnk, M.-D. and Naeve, P. (1967) [Tabellen] *Statistische Tabellen*. Berlin: de Gruyter.

Wild, J. (1982) [Planung] *Grundlagen der Unternehmungsplanung*. 4th edn. Opladen: Westdeutscher Verlag.

Williams, J. H. (1922) [Technique] A Technique for the Chief Executive—A definite responsibility—a definite procedure—a definite measure of results. *Bulletin of the Taylor Society*, New York, 47–68.

Wright, W. (1962) [Costs] *Direct Standard Costs for Decision Making and Control*. New York, Toronto, London: McGraw-Hill.

Zschocke, D. (1975) [Prozessfunktion] Prozessfunktion, technische, in E. Grochla and W. Wittmann (eds) *Handwörterbuch der Betriebswirtschaft*. 4th edn, Volume 1/2. Stuttgart: Poeschel, col. 3256–3268.

Author Index

Subject Index